PATERNOSTER THEOLOGICAL MONOGRAPHS

The Omnipresence of Jesus Christ

A Neglected Aspect of Evangelical Christology

PATERNOSTER THEOLOGICAL MONOGRAPHS

The Omnipresence of Jesus Christ

A Neglected Aspect of Evangelical Christology

Theodore Zachariades

Foreword by Michael A.G. Haykin

Copyright © Theodore Zachariades 2015

First published by Paternoster 2015

Paternoster is an imprint of Authentic Media
52 Presley Way, Crownhill, Milton Keynes, Bucks, MK8 0ES, UK

www.authenticmedia.co.uk
Authentic Media is a division of Koorong UK, a company limited by guarantee

09 08 07 06 05 04 03   8 7 6 5 4 3 2 1

The right of Theodore Zachariades to be identified as the Author of this Work has been asserted by him in accordance with the Copyright, Designs and Patents Act 1988.

All rights reserved. No part of this publication may be reproduced, stored in a retrieval system, or transmitted, in any form or by any means, electronic, mechanical, photocopying, recording or otherwise, without the prior permission of the publisher or a license permitting restricted copying. In the UK such licenses are issued by the Copyright Licensing Agency, 90 Tottenham Court Road, London W1P 9HE.

British Library Cataloguing in Publication Data
A catalogue record for this book is available from the British Library

ISBN 978–1–84227–849-9

Printed and bound in Great Britain
for Paternoster
by Lightning Source, Milton Keynes

Series Preface

In the West the churches may be declining, but theology—serious, academic (mostly doctoral level) and mainstream orthodox in evaluative commitment—shows no sign of withering on the vine. This series of *Paternoster Theological Monographs* extends the expertise of the Press especially to first-time authors whose work stands broadly within the parameters created by fidelity to Scripture and has satisfied the critical scrutiny of respected assessors in the academy. Such theology may come in several distinct intellectual disciplines—historical, dogmatic, pastoral, apologetic, missional, aesthetic and no doubt others also. The series will be particularly hospitable to promising constructive theology within an evangelical frame, for it is of this that the church's need seems to be greatest. Quality writing will be published across the confessions—Anabaptist, Episcopalian, Reformed, Arminian and Orthodox—across the ages—patristic, medieval, reformation, modern and counter-modern—and across the continents. The aim of the series is theology written in the twofold conviction that the church needs theology and theology needs the church—which in reality means theology done for the glory of God.

Series Editors

Trevor A. Hart, Head of School and Principal of St Mary's College School of Divinity, University of St Andrews, Scotland, UK

Anthony N.S. Lane, Professor of Historical Theology and Director of Research, London School of Theology, UK

Anthony C. Thiselton, Emeritus Professor of Christian Theology, University of Nottingham; Research Professor in Christian Theology, University College Chester; and Canon Theologian of Leicester Cathedral and Southwell Minster, UK

Kevin J. Vanhoozer, Research Professor of Systematic Theology, Trinity Evangelical Divinity School, Deerfield, Illinois, USA

For Chrisa:
wife, lover, and friend,
who shows me each day
that Jesus Christ is near;

and, to honor the memory of my father,
George "Giorgis" Zachariades
1933-2015;

and,
for Jesus Christ, Who is and ever shall be:
ὁ Πανταχοῦ Παρὼν καὶ τὰ Πάντα Πληρῶν

Contents

Acknowledgements	xiii
Foreword by Michael A.G. Haykin	xvi
Abbreviations	xvii

Introduction		**1**
Chapter 1	**Christology: An Introduction**	**3**
	A. Incarnation	3
	B. Presuppositions	5
	B.1. Faith	5
	B.2. Trinity	6
	B.3. Theology Proper	8
	B.4. Christological Method	13
	B.5. Purpose	14
	B.6 Conclusion	15
	C. Thesis	15
	D. Outline of the Book	17
	E. Conclusion	18
Chapter 2	**Christology: Current Status of Scholarly Research**	**19**
	A. Introduction	19
	B. The Modern Era	22
	B.1. Introduction	24
	B.2. From Revelation to Reason	24
	B.3. Modern Christologies	26
	B.4. From Doctrine to Experience &	
	Modern Critical Methods	29
	B.5. Reactions to the Modern	31
	B.6. Christology: A Myth?	33
	C. Conclusion	35
Chapter 3	**Contemporary Christology and Kenosis**	
	A. Introduction	36
	B. History	36
	C. Theology	39
	D. Kenotic Theology	39

	D.1. Ronald Feenstra	40
	D.2. C. Stephen Evans	43
E.	Sub-Kenotic Theology	44
	E.1 Millard J. Erickson	45
	E.2. Loring Prest	46
	E.3. Gerald F. Hawthorne	47

Chapter 4	Contemporary Evangelical Christology and Chalcedon	
	A. Introduction	50
	B. Anthony Lane	51
	B.1. Introduction	51
	B.2. Objections to Chalcedon	51
	B.3. Omniscient or not?	53
	B.4. Enhypostatic Christology	54
	B.5. Abiding Value of Chalcedon	54
	B.6. Christological Method	55
	B.7. Conclusion	56
	C. Ronald Leigh	57
	C.1. Introduction	57
	C.2. Nature . . . What is it?	57
	C.3. Antinomy–Not Sufficient	58
	C.4. One Nature Not Two	59
	C.5. Method and Hermeneutics	59
	C.6. Conclusion	60
	D. Conclusion on Contemporary Thinkers	60

Chapter 5	Patristic Christology: A Survey of the Early Church	
	A. Introduction	61
	B. Ante-Nicene Theology	61
	B.1. Irenaeus (ca. 115-ca. 202)	62
	B.2. Tertullian (ca. 160-ca. 220)	64
	B.3. Origen (ca. 185-ca.251)	68
	C. Nicene Theology	71
	C.1. The Search for the Christian God	72
	C.2. Athanasius of Alexandra's Christology	74
	D. Post-Nicene Theology	80
	D.1. Augustine of Hippo (344-430)	81
	D.2. Nestorius of Constantinople (ca. 381-451)	85
	E. Chalcedonian Christology	91

	E.1. The Chalcedonian Definition	92
	E.2. The Value of Chalcedon	94
	F. Leontius of Byzantium (c. 475-543)	95
	F.1. Origenist or Cyrillian?	96
	F.2. The Christology of Leontius	98
	G. John of Damascus (ca. 650-749)	100
	G.1. John Damascene's Christology	101
	H. Conclusion	104
Chapter 6	**Reformation Christology: Calvin's *Extra Calvinisticum***	**105**
	A. Introduction	106
	B. Extra Calvinisticum	107
	C. Calvin's Extra Calvinisticum	109
	D. Calvin's Trinitarianism	112
	E. Calvin on God's Majesty	116
	F. Calvin on *Communicatio Idiomatum*	118
	G. Calvin's Christology: Nestorian or Not?	123
	H. Calvin's Doctrine of Knowledge of God the Redeemer: Through *Logos ensarkos* or *Logos asarkos*?	126
	I. Conclusion	129
Chapter 7	**Biblical and Theological Evidence for Jesus Christ's Omnipresence**	**131**
	A. Introduction	131
	B. Biblical Evidence for God's Omnipresence	131
	B.1. Psalm 139	131
	B.2. Jeremiah 23	133
	C. Omnipresence as Doctrine	135
	C.1. Essential Presence	138
	C.2. Moral Presence	140
	C.3. Heavenly Presence	143
	C.4. Christological Presence	143
	D. The Omnipresence of Jesus Christ	145
	D.1. Biblical Evidence for Jesus' Omnipresence	145
	D.2. Theological Evidence for Jesus Christ's Omnipresence	159
	E. Conclusion	179

Chapter 8	**An Exegetical and Theological Look at Philippians 2:5-8**		**181**
	A. Introduction		181
	B. The Passage		181
		B.1. Philippians 2:5-8	181
		B.2. The Traditional Framework	183
		B.3. Traditional Interpretation	184
		B.4. Alternate Framework	190
		B.5. Alternative Interpretation	192
	C. Kenotic Theologians		195
		C.1. Millard Erickson	195
		C.2. Ronald Feenstra	198
	D. Conclusion		199
Chapter 9	**Conclusion**		**202**
Bibliography			**208**
	Books		208
	Articles		227
	Theses and Dissertations		235
Indexes			**237**
	Author Index		237
	Scripture Index		245
	Subject Index		250

Acknowledgements

Writing a book, like raising a child, as the maxim goes, takes a village. The analogy may be more apropos than one would imagine. Others have spoken of books being birthed with the obvious allusions to 'labor pain.' That would probably well describe my initial forays into doctoral work at the Southern Baptist Theological Seminary Louisville, Kentucky, and the dissertation from which this book has grown. And grown it has, just like the child who year by year increases in stature and also wisdom. I hope this is a better book now. And if it is, that is solely because of the villagers' direct or indirect involvement. My youngest son, Nathan was born the year (2004) I submitted, defended, and received my bound copy of the thesis. In 2015 Nathan has reached his 11th year. So this dearly loved child has accompanied the expansion and development of my initial research. May the book, and my son[s], bring glory to Christ, who is its grand subject. All errors shall be laid at my hut's doorstep.

Beyond those that are included in the notes and bibliography, special thanks are due to several individuals. The thesis was written under the guidance of Dr. Steve Wellum, astute Christologian himself. Many conversations and directives came forth from his office. Also, on my doctoral committee or in my seminars I had the privileged services of Drs. Marvin Anderson, Bruce Ware, Craig A. Blaising, David L. Puckett, Mark A. Seifrid, and especially Michael A. G. Haykin, who agreed to serve on my doctoral committee at very late notice. Dr. Haykin was the first to encourage me to seek publication and was responsible for initiating contact with Paternoster. Michael also wrote a forward for the work that initially went into print as an Amazon Kindle book.

Also, Dr. Robin Parry (now with Wipf and Stock) and, in succession Dr. Mike Parsons of Paternoster have been gracious to receive the volume for their Theological Monograph series. Mike has been extremely patient and gracious with me. Thanks so much!

Dr. Gerald L. Bray, who served as my external reader for the dissertation was also kind to include a recommendation for the volume. It has been many years since Dr. Bray instructed me on my initial trek along theological lanes, and his scholarship over the years has been immensely helpful.

Finally, the villagers closest to home. First, my wife, Chrisa, to whom the initial dissertation was dedicated, and it is fitting that she be honored again. Her love and support in our past twenty-four years of marriage are a miracle. And many thanks are due to our four boys Luke, Thomas, Jonah and the aforementioned Nathan, who continue to bring unmatched joys to our lives. These all live in my hut, and are to be recognized for numerous sacrifices along the way. But the Supreme One lives in my heart. He is the Village Chief, Christ almighty, the *summum bonum*. Thank you, Lord for saving this sinner with the greatest sacrifice ever. And Lord, please forgive me, for as your servant, G.

Campbell Morgan once quipped: "Oh, the ugliness of human words when we try to speak about Jesus." Take these ugly words and derive glory from them now and forever more.

Theodore "Doros" Zachariades

Manchester, TN
April, 2015

Foreword

Possession of the attribute of omnipresence has been central to Western theological and philosophical thinking about God. The idea that God could be limited in regard to his presence throughout space has been rightly regarded as part and parcel of ancient polytheism that thought in terms of local gods confined to set geographical regions.

Thus, when divines in this tradition have confessed that the person of Jesus Christ is marked by this attribute of omnipresence, they have been making an explicit affirmation of his deity. As Doros Zachariades skillfully shows in this book, such a confession is warranted by the biblical evidence, was developed in the patristic era as part of the Fathers' campaign against various Christological errors, and received a classical statement at the hands of the French Reformer John Calvin in what has been called the *extra Calvinisticum*. I have long felt that Calvin's theologizing in this regard is one of the most important aspects of his theological heritage and Zachariades does an excellent job in laying out its details and Calvin's reasoning.

Given the turmoil of the past two centuries in Christian thought caused both by the emergence of the Enlightenment project of modernity and now its post-modern rejection—or as some would have it, its post-modern extension—it should occasion no surprise to find that the omnipresence of Christ and his deity in general have been the subject of critical investigation. This investigation has led far too many New Testament scholars and systematic theologians to reject the thinking of classical theology on this subject. Even certain self-professing evangelical scholars have sometimes shown the influence of this rejection of the classical approach by their adoption of a kenotic Christology.

But as Zachariades demonstrates, such evangelical authors are not only failing to pass on the contours and content of classical Christology, they are also out of touch with the Scriptures. He thus grounds what is essentially a classical Chalcedonian view of Christ in the Word of God, especially as it relates to Christ's omnipresence. As such, this is a valuable study and this writer hopes it gets a wide reading.

Michael A.G Haykin
Professor of Church History and Biblical Spirituality
Director of The Andrew Fuller Center for Baptist Studies
The Southern Baptist Theological Seminary, USA

Abbreviations

ABR	*Australian Biblical Review*
ACCSNT	Ancient Christian Commentary on Scripture New Testament
ANF	Ante-Nicene Fathers
AthR	*Anglican Theological Review*
AUS	American University Studies
BECNT	Baker Exegetical Commentary on the New Testament
BNTC	Black's New Testament Commentary
Bsac	*Bibliotheca Sacra*
BV	*Biblical Viewpoint*
CBQ	*Catholic Biblical Quarterly*
CCCS	*Concordia Classic Commentary Series*
CCR	*Coptic Church Review*
CCT	Contours of Christian Theology
ConJ	*Concordia Journal*
CSR	*Christian Scholar's Review*
CTJ	*Calvin Theological Journal*
Di	*Dialog*
Dio	*Dionysius*
Drev	*Downside Review*
EGGNT	*Exegetical Guide to the Greek New Testament*
EvJ	*Evangelical Journal*
EvQ	*Evangelical Quarterly*
EvT	*Evangelische Theologie*
EBC	*The Expositor's Bible Commentary*
EGT	*The Expositor's Greek Testament*
GOTR	*Greek Orthodox Theological Review*
GJ	*Grace Journal*
HisPQ	*History of Philosophy Quarterly*
HNTC	Harper's New Testament Commentary
HQ	*Hartford Quarterly*
HTR	*Harvard Theological Review*
Institutes	*Institutes of the Christian Religion*
JBL	*Journal of Biblical Literature*
JBTM	*Journal for Baptist Theology and Ministry*
JianDao	*Jian Dao*
JECS	*Journal of Early Christian Studies*
JEH	*Journal of Ecclesiastical History*
JETS	*Journal of the Evangelical Theological Society*
JTS	*Journal of Theological Studies*

ModRef	*Modern Reformation*
ModTheol	*Modern Theology*
MS	*Mediaeval Studies*
NCT	New Century Theology
NIBC	The New International Biblical Commentary
NICNT	The New International Commentary on the New Testament
NICOT	The New International Commentary on the Old Testament
NIDNTT	The New International Dictionary of New Testament Theology
NIGTC	The New International Greek Testament Commentary
NovT	*Novum Testamentum*
NPNF	A Select Library of the Nicene and Post-Nicene Fathers of the Christian Church
NPNF 2	A Select Library of the Nicene and Post-Nicene Fathers of the Christian Church, Second Series
OPASRR	*Occasional Papers of the American Society for Reformation Research*
PatByzR	*Patristic and Byzantine Review*
PG	Patrologia Graeca
ProEccl	*Pro Ecclesia*
RB	*Revue Biblique*
RelS	*Religious Studies*
SBJT	*Southern Baptist Journal of Theology*
SJT	*Scottish Journal of Theology*
StPatr	*Studia Patristica*
ThTo	*Theology Today*
ThSt	*Theologische Studiën*
TNTC	Tyndale New Testament Commentary
Trinj	*Trinity Journal*
TS	*Theological Studies*
VC	*Vigiliae christianae*
VT	*Vetus Testamentum*
WBC	Word Biblical Commentary
WTJ	*Westminster Theological Journal*

INTRODUCTION

In his book, which surveys philosophical thinking through the centuries, Anthony Gottlieb cites a definition made famous by William James. "The psychologist William James once described philosophy," notes the writer, "as 'a peculiarly stubborn effort to think clearly.'" To this Gottlieb adds, "This is a rather dry definition, but is more nearly right than any other I know."[1] At the outset of this book I believe that Christology should be defined in brief along similar lines to that of philosophy. Christology is a stubborn effort to think rightly about Jesus of Nazareth, the Messiah. The topic of the incarnation, the subject directly engaged in this work, falls in the broader topical area of Christology.[2] The doctrine of Christ, as Christology is often referred to, is sometimes

---

[1] Anthony Gottlieb, *The Dream of Reason: A History of Philosophy from the Greeks to the Renaissance* (New York: W.W. Norton, 2000), ix.

[2] Incarnation has to do with God's becoming man while remaining God. In assessing this matter, it is significant that one maintains an appreciation of the distinctive Christian doctrine of the Trinity. Christian Link says, "Theology's confession of the Triune God is not a proposition that can be intellectually accounted for. It is the frame in which all understanding of Christian faith and living moves" ("Incarnation and Creation: Interpreting the World through the Theology of the Trinity," trans. Christoph Stenschke, *GOTR* 43 [1998]: 327). I must agree, however, with Peter van Inwagen, "Three Persons in One Being," in Michael Rea, ed., *Oxford Readings in Philosophical Theology Volume 1: Trinity, Incarnation, Atonement* (Oxford: Oxford University Press, 2009), 61-74, that Christian theology must be logical, and this is so especially with the church's teaching on the Trinity. The incarnation presupposes the Trinity, as it is one of the persons of the triune Godhead and not the entire Godhead, which becomes incarnate in the historical figure of Jesus Christ. This concept of the "order of being" is significant to make sense of the incarnation as a truth revealed about God by God himself. However, some theologians emphasize the so-called "order of knowing," which begins with the facts of the incarnate life of Jesus, then they deduce the Trinity from what is revealed by Jesus. A good advocate of this approach is Christopher B. Kaiser, "The Incarnation and the Trinity: Two Doctrines Rooted in the Offices of Christ," *GOTR* 43 (1998): 221-55. Whichever starting point one prefers, the same result ensues: Jesus Christ is the Word made flesh (John 1:14), God manifested in the flesh (1 Tim 3:16), the Son of God who was born under the law and sent at the appropriate time (Gal 4:4), the perfect revelation of God (Heb 1:2), God's equal (Phil 2:6), One with the Father (John 10:30), Creator of all (Col 1:16), and the fullness of Deity in bodily form (Col 2:9). Classical Christology, which summarized and synthesized the Scriptural data, is exemplified in the doctrinal affirmations of the Council of Chalcedon in A.D. 451. See J. Stevenson, ed., *Creeds, Councils and Controversies: Documents Illustrating the History of the Church, AD 337-461*, new ed., rev. W.H.C. Frend (London: SPCK, 1989), 350-54. The crucial expression in the

classified into two main sections: (1) The person of Christ, and (2) The work of Christ.[3] Without slighting the significance of Christ's life and death, by which his people obtain eternal redemption, the focus of our attention will primarily be the identity[4] of Jesus Christ, and particularly the concept of the hypostatic union as perceived in evangelical Christology.[5] The purpose is to narrow the investigation to the "how" of the incarnation, rather than to look upon the "why." As such, this Christological endeavor must take a long hard look at the primary materials, in this case the New Testament documents. In addition, one must engage with reflections by interpreters who have stubbornly thought about the person of Jesus. This task will be necessary to show the reasons for advocating the omnipresence of Jesus Christ.

---

definition of faith is as follows: "We all with one voice confess our Lord Jesus Christ one and the same Son, the same perfect in Godhead, the same perfect in manhood, truly God and truly man . . . one and the same Christ, Son, Lord, Only-begotten, to be acknowledged in two natures, without confusion, without change, without division, without separation . . ." (352).

[3] For example, see Millard J. Erickson, *Christian Theology*, 2nd ed. (Grand Rapids: Baker, 1998). Part 7 of Erickson's text is entitled "The Person of the Mediator," where he deals with issues such as the deity of Christ, the humanity of Christ, the unity of the person of Christ, etc. Part 8 of the book is called "The Work of Christ," where Erickson discusses the central aspects of the atonement. Also from an earlier generation, see Benjamin Breckinridge Warfield, *The Person and Work of Christ* (Phillipsburg, NJ: P & R, 1950). The volume shows how Warfield has thought about the various aspects of Christology throughout his career. The essays in this anthology fall into the categories "Person" and "Work" fairly well.

[4] A very helpful introduction to this specific task is found in Carl F.H. Henry, *The Identity of Jesus of Nazareth* (Nashville: Broadman, 1992). Henry is hopeful that a reappraisal and appreciation of the tradition of Augustine, Anselm, and the Reformers will lead to renewed vigor in Christological development. For a different perspective, see Hans W. Frei, *The Identity of Jesus Christ: The Hermeneutical Bases of Dogmatic Theology* (Philadelphia: Fortress, 1975).

[5] *Hypostatic union* is a term which refers to the two natures of the God-man existing in one person. The union is hypostatic, i.e. personal. The eternal Son of God assumed a human nature and therefore became a man in time. A significant contribution to Christological formulation is found in the idea of an *enhypostatic* Christology, where the human nature is said to find its existence not in itself but only in union with the person of the Word who was made flesh. This matter will be discussed in more detail in a subsequent chapter. Suffice for now to mention that this ingenious development safeguards both the integrity of the human Jesus and his deity and alerts one to the fact that although Jesus Christ is both God and Man, he is only one person; the human nature has no independent existence.

CHAPTER 1

CHRISTOLOGY: AN INTRODUCTION

A. Incarnation

The incarnation of Jesus Christ is a crucial doctrine. To understand properly the revelation concerning the person of Christ is a goal toward which each generation of Christians should aspire. The question of the ages remains: "Who do you [the disciples] say that I am?" (Matt 16:15). The goal of theology, beyond that of establishing doctrine in contemporary idiom as an apologetic and engagement with the culture at large, needs to be primarily a service for the church. Theology should strive to help both clergy and laity to come to ever increasing clarity concerning God and his plan, especially as it centers on Jesus.[1] As such, theology must be conducted by the church and for the church. The question posed by Jesus in Matthew 16 was really twofold. First, the Lord

---

[1] Much attention has been focused on the incarnation in the twentieth century. Released near the end of the nineteenth century, Robert Ottley's *The Doctrine of the Incarnation* (London: Methuen, 1896) went into at least eight editions, my copy dating from 1946. The classic work by H.R. Mackintosh, *The Doctrine of the Person of Jesus Christ* (New York: Charles Scribner's Sons, 1912) added important considerations. Sydney Cave, *The Doctrine of the Person of Christ* (London: Duckworth, 1952) was issued originally in 1925. Lionel Spencer Thornton, *The Incarnate Lord: An Essay Concerning the Doctrine of the Incarnation in Its Relation to Organic Conceptions* (London: Longmans, Green, 1928) was heavily influenced by Alfred North Whitehead. A helpful volume discussing various proposals was issued in John Stewart Lawton, *Conflict in Christology: A Study of British and American Christology From 1889-1914* (London: SPCK, 1947). See also D.M. Baillie, *God Was in Christ: An Essay on Incarnation and Atonement* (New York: Charles Scribner's Sons, 1948); G.C. Berkouwer, *Studies in Dogmatics: The Person of Christ,* trans. John Vriend (Grand Rapids: Eerdmans, 1954); John McIntyre, *The Shape of Christology: Studies in the Doctrine of the Person of Christ* (London: SCM, 1966), reprinted, (Edinburgh: T & T Clark, 1998); Wolfhart Pannenberg, *Jesus—God and Man,* trans. Lewis L. Wilkins & Duane A. Priebe (Philadelphia: Westminster, 1968); John Hick, ed., *The Myth of God Incarnate* (London: SCM, 1977); Michael Green, ed., *The Truth of God Incarnate* (Grand Rapids: Eerdmans, 1977); Michael Goulder, ed., *Incarnation and Myth: The Debate Continued* (London: SCM, 1979); Bernard L. Ramm, *An Evangelical Christology: Ecumenic and Historic* (Nashville: Thomas Nelson, 1985); Douglas F. Webster, *A Passion for Christ: An Evangelical Christology* (Grand Rapids: Zondervan, 1987); Jean Galot, *Who Is Christ? A Theology of the Incarnation,* trans. M. Angeline Bouchard (Chicago: Franciscan Herald, 1981) and Elizabeth A. Johnson, *Consider Jesus: Waves of Renewal in Christology* (New York: Crossroad, 1990); Millard J. Erickson, *The Word Became Flesh* (Grand Rapids: Baker, 1991). Near the end of the century an important symposium was held in April 2000 on this perennially curious topic and resulted in the following volume: Stephen T. Davis, Daniel Kendall, and Gerald O' Collins, eds., *The Incarnation: An Interdisciplinary Symposium on the Incarnation of the Son of God* (Oxford: Oxford University Press, 2002). In the early part of the twenty-first century this pre-occupation with Christological themes continues.

asks: "Who do men say that I, the Son of Man, am?" (Matt 16:13). Back then, many had different notions concerning the identity of Jesus of Nazareth. Today, many speculate about the person of Christ.[2] The general public will, no doubt, continue to reflect on Jesus as a result of influence from mainline scholarship. In recent years popular thinking about Jesus grew exponentially with the publication of Dan Brown's novel, *The Da Vinci Code*. Furthermore, people will view Jesus as the "Mediterranean Jewish peasant,"[3] or the "non-eschatological prophet,"[4] or the "cynical social misfit,"[5] or the "would-be Messiah."[6] Yet Jesus

---

[2] For an evangelical engagement with contemporary views of Jesus, see Gregory A. Boyd, *Cynic Sage or Son of God: Recovering the Real Jesus in an Age of Revisionist Replies* (Wheaton, IL: BridgePoint, 1995); Craig A. Evans, *Fabricating Jesus: How Modern Scholars Distort the Gospels* (Downers Grove, IL: InterVarsity, 2006); J. Ed Komoszewski, M. James Sawyer, & Daniel B. Wallace, *Reinventing Jesus: How Contemporary Skeptics Miss the Real Jesus and Mislead Popular Culture* (Grand Rapids: Kregel, 2006); Ben Witherington III, *What Have They Done With Jesus? Beyond Strange Theories and Bad History – Why We Can Trust the Bible* (San Francisco: Harper, 2006); and Darrell L. Bock & Daniel B. Wallace, *Dethroning Jesus: Exposing Popular Culture's Quest to Unseat the Biblical Christ* (Nashville: Thomas Nelson, 2007). Important works on the biblical materials include, Seyoon Kim, *The Son of Man as The Son of God* (Grand Rapids: Eerdmans, 1985); Richard Bauckham, *Jesus and the Eyewitnesses: The Gospels as Eyewitness Testimony* (Grand Rapids: Eerdmans, 2006) and Simon J. Gathercole, *The Pre-existent Son: Recovering the Christologies of Matthew, Mark, and Luke* (Grand Rapids: Eerdmans, 2006).

[3] John Dominic Crossan, *The Historical Jesus: The Life of a Mediterranean Jewish Peasant* (San Francisco: Harper, 1991); idem, *Jesus: A Revolutionary Biography* (San Francisco: Harper, 1994). See the debate between Crossan, perhaps the most vocal of the Jesus Seminar fellows, and the evangelical apologist William Lane Craig in Paul Copan, ed., *Will the Real Jesus Please Stand Up? A Debate between William Lane Craig and John Dominic Crossan* (Grand Rapids: Baker, 1998). For a rebuttal of the Jesus Seminar from a cross section of evangelical scholars, see Michael J. Wilkins and J.P. Moreland, eds., *Jesus under Fire: Modern Scholarship Reinvents the Historical Jesus* (Grand Rapids: Zondervan, 1995). Also very helpful in assessing the Jesus Seminar is Luke Timothy Johnson, *The Real Jesus: The Misguided Quest for the Historical Jesus and the Truth of the Traditional Gospels* (San Francisco: Harper, 1996). For a refutation of the thesis found in the *Da Vinci Code*, see Richard Abanes, *The Truth Behind the Da Vinci Code: A Challenge to the Bestselling Novel* (Eugene: Harvest House, 2004); Darrell L. Bock, *Breaking the Da Vinci Cod: Answers to the Questions Everyone's Asking* (Nashville: Thomas Nelson, 2004); James L. Garlow & Peter Jones, *Cracking Da Vinci's Code: You've Read the Fiction, Now Read the Facts* (Colorado Springs: Victor, 2004); Hank Hanegraaff & Paul L. Maier, *The Da Vinci Code: Fact or Fiction?* (Carol Stream: Tyndale, 2004); Stephen Clark, *The Da Vinci Code On Trial: Filtering Fact From Fiction* (Bryntirion, Wales: Bryntirion, 2005); and James Garlow, *The Da Vinci Code Breaker* (Grand Rapids: Bethany, 2006).

[4] Marcus J. Borg, *Jesus: A New Vision: Spirit, Culture and the Life of Discipleship* (San Francisco: Harper, 1987); idem. *Jesus in Contemporary Scholarship* (Valley Forge: Trinity, 1994). Also noteworthy is the dialog between Borg and N.T. Wright in Marcus J. Borg and N.T. Wright, *The Meaning of Jesus: Two Visions* (San Francisco: Harper, 1999).

[5] See Boyd, *Cynic Sage*, 71-109, for a helpful presentation of Crossan's and Burton L. Mack's views along these lines.

[6] A most significant publication that draws many scholars together discussing the topic of "Messiah" is James H. Charlesworth, ed., *The Messiah: Developments in Earliest Judaism and Christianity* (Minneapolis: Fortress, 1992). More recently, Kornel Zathureczky has written the following study: *The Messianic Disruption of Trinitarian Theology* (Lanham, MD: Lexington, 2009) interacting with Walter Benjamin and Jürgen

narrowed the focus by emphatically asking an immediate follow up question. He asks, "But who do you say that I am?" The Greek word ὑμεῖς ("you") is a plural. The question is directed to the disciples as the nucleus that would become the New Testament church. This interrogative enquiry must be heard anew by each generation in the church.[7] The church's answer, unlike the conjecture of the masses, is based on divine revelation. Peter was blessed because it was the Father who revealed to Peter that the one asking the question is the "Son of the Living God." This confession is normative; it is God's declaration of the identity of Jesus. We in the church today must conform to this confessional norm. Only then can we claim true solidarity with the church that Christ established. Jesus of Nazareth, a Jewish man of the first century who stood among other Jewish men in his day, was and still is God's only Son.

The perennial central matter of Christology is the explication of this revealed truth that Jesus is both man and God. An exposition must grapple with the obvious problems of such a confession, yet it is surely grounded in faith. All Christians believe and hence confess *that* Jesus is God's Son. Nevertheless, Christians may differ in their musings over *how* this is so.[8] It is perhaps needless to mention that however one explains the revealed majestic truth of the incarnation, human persons do not have the capacity to understand all that is involved in this teaching. Nevertheless, it is revealed so that people can grasp it in truth, if not in totality.

B. Presuppositions

It is important to note my presuppositions as this book progresses. These convictions bear on how the project will unfold, and relate to the value of the study for the perspective of faith.

B.1. Faith

In this book the perspective of faith is an *a priori* given. I write as one who believes that Jesus is the Christ, God the Son, as expressed in the historic

---

Moltmann. From an evangelical persuasion, see Michael F. Bird, *Jesus the Christ: The Messianic Testimony of the Gospels* (Downers Grove, IL: InterVarsity, 2012).

[7] For a survey of current thinking about the identity and message of Jesus of Nazareth, see Ben Witherington III, *The Jesus Quest: The Third Search for the Jew of Nazareth*, 2nd ed. (Downers Grove, IL: InterVarsity, 1997); and A. Roy Eckardt, *Reclaiming the Jesus of History: Christology Today* (Minneapolis: Fortress, 1992), which is a thoroughly postmodernist study highly emphasizing the Jewishness of Jesus. And for a wonderful textbook-like volume with a survey of biblical, theological, historical, and contemporary thought concerning Jesus, see Richard A. Burridge and Graham Gould, *Jesus: Now and Then* (Grand Rapids: Eerdmans, 2004).

[8] Two very different perceptions of the incarnation are found in the following evangelical writers. Robert L. Reymond, *A New Systematic Theology of the Christian Faith* (Nashville: Thomas Nelson, 1998), 253-70, 545-52; and Gerald F. Hawthorne, *The Presence and the Power: The Significance of the Holy Spirit in the Life and Ministry of Jesus* (Dallas: Word, 1991), 199-225. Reymond is in line with the classic ideals. He believes Chalcedon has had the final say about Christ. Hawthorne, on the other hand, believes what Chalcedon affirms yet insists that we must explicate the incarnation along kenotic lines. Both of these scholars unequivocally affirm the deity of Jesus Christ. Reymond's classic books on the biblical witness to the person of Christ have been reissued in one volume. See Robert L. Reymond, *Jesus Divine Messiah: The New and Old Testament Witness* (Fearn: Christian Focus, 2003).

creeds of the church. Moreover, I write as an evangelical Christian. I take seriously that the Bible is the inspired, infallible, and inerrant Word of God. As a Christian, who seeks to follow Christ, my scholarly pursuits are not divorced from my discipleship experience. I follow David Wells, who said, "In Christology . . . we can only philosophize from faith, not to faith."[9] I desire the knowledge of Christ and pursue academic investigation only to strengthen what I embrace by faith. In the tradition of Augustine of Hippo and Anselm of Canterbury, I do not understand in order to believe, but I believe and seek out of the context of that belief to know and understand more fully that which is "graspable" about Jesus Christ.[10]

B.2. Trinity

My commitments also include belief in the Trinitarian doctrine of God. Along with countless evangelical thinkers, I have "stumbled over" the contention that God is a Trinity or Tri-unity. In short, the Bible presents the truth that there is only one God (Deut 6:4, 32:39; Isa 44:6,8; 45:5-6; 1 Cor 8:6; Eph 4:6; and 1 Tim 2:5). Also, the Scriptures teach that there is a plurality in the Godhead (Gen 19:24; Isa 48:12-16, 61:1, 63:8-10; Ps 45:6-7 [cf. Heb 1:8]; Matt 3:13-17, 28:19; Luke 1:35; Acts 2:33; Rom 8:15-17; 2 Cor 13:14; 1 Pet 1:2; and Rev 1:4-5). Finally, there are three, and no more than three distinct "persons" which are spoken of as God in the Bible without identifying the one with the other (cf. John 1:1-18 with 7:39 and 20:19-23). So the result or conclusion is that the *Father* is God but is not the Son or the Spirit; the *Son* is God but is not the Father or the Spirit; and the *Spirit* is God but is not the Son or the Father.[11] The

---

[9] David F. Wells, *The Person of Christ: A Biblical and Historical Analysis of the Incarnation* (Alliance, OH: Bible Scholar Press, 1984), 175.

[10] For Augustine, see Allan D. Fitzgerald, ed., *Augustine through the Ages: An Encyclopedia* (Grand Rapids: Eerdmans, 1999), s.v. "Faith."; Robert Meagher, *Augustine: An Introduction* (New York: Harper & Row, 1978; Rebecca West, *St. Augustine* (New York: D. Appleton, 1933); Gary Wills, *Saint Augustine* (New York: Penguin, 1999); and Serge Lancel, *St. Augustine*, trans. Antonia Nevill (London: SCM, 2002). For Anselm, see Eugene R. Fairweather, ed., *A Scholastic Miscellany: Anselm to Ockham*, LCC 10, ed. John Baillie, John T. McNeill, and Henry P. van Dusen (Philadelphia: Westminster/John Knox, 1956), 70-73; and Anselm of Canterbury, *The Major Works*, ed., and intro. Brian Davies & G.R. Evans (New York: Oxford University Press, 1998).

[11] The biblical data is dealt with most competently by Robert Morey, *The Trinity: Evidence and Issues* (Grand Rapids: World Publishing, 1996), *passim*; and John S. Feinberg, *No One Like Him: The Doctrine of God* (Wheaton, IL: Crossway, 2001), 443-71. Theologically, the doctrine of the Trinity is best expounded by Millard J. Erickson, *God in Three Persons: A Contemporary Interpretation of the Trinity* (Grand Rapids: Baker, 1995), 264-310; idem, *Who's Tampering with the Trinity: An Assessment of the Subordination Debate* (Grand Rapids: Kregel, 2009); Gerald Bray, *The Doctrine of God* (Downers Grove, IL: InterVarsity, 1993), 110-224, esp., 197-212; and more recently Kevin Giles, *The Trinity and Subordinationism: The Doctrine of God and the Contemporary Gender Debate* (Downers Grove, IL: InterVarsity, 2002), 21-117; and idem., *Jesus and the Father: Modern Evangelicals Reinvent the Doctrine of the Trinity* (Grand Rapids: Zondervan, 2006). Theological proposals are found in both popular works such as Walter Russell Bowie, *Jesus and the Trinity* (New York: Abingdon, 1960); Robert M. Bowman, Jr., *Why You Should Believe in the Trinity: An Answer to Jehovah's Witnesses* (Grand Rapids: Baker, 1989); and in more rigorous academic works as Gordon H. Clark, *The Trinity* (Jefferson, MD: The Trinity Foundation, 1985); Αδαμαντιου Δ. Αποστολοπουλου, *Το Τριαδικο Δογμα* (Αθηνα" Νεκταριος Παναγιοπουλος); Alan J. Tor-

biblical testimony, in my opinion, is best explained and summarized by the Athanasian Creed.[12] My present sympathies lie with a model of Trinitarian thought as expressed by Millard Erickson who maintains that subordination language is strictly functional and temporary.[13] A commitment to a Trinitarian view of God allows that the doctrine of "incarnation" is the correct approach vis à vis adoptionism in explaining the person of Christ.[14] What this means is

---

rance, *Persons in Communion: Trinitarian Description and Human Participation* (Edinburgh: T & T Clark, 1996; Stephen T. Davis, Daniel Kendall, & Gerald O'Collins, eds., *The Trinity: An Interdisciplinary Symposium on the Trinity* (Oxford: Oxford University Press, 1999); and Paul Molnar, *Divine Freedom and the Doctrine of the Immanent Trinity* (Edinburgh: T & T Clark, 2002).

[12] See Gerald Bray, *Creeds, Councils and Christ: Did the Early Christians Misrepresent Jesus?* (Fearn: Mentor, 1984, 1997), Appendix A, for a modern translation of the major creeds.

[13] See Erickson, *God in Three Persons*, 306-10. Particularly noteworthy is Henri Blocher, "Immanence and Transcendence in Trinitarian Theology," in *The Trinity in a Pluralistic Age: Theological Essays on Culture and Religion*, ed. Kevin J. Vanhoozer (Grand Rapids: Eerdmans, 1997), 104-23. Also helpful in dealing with the "subordination" issue is Kevin Giles, *The Trinity and Subordinationism*, 1-121. I agree with Giles in his explanation of the Trinity, yet I remain convinced of the accuracy of the Danvers Statement on gender roles within the family and the Church, and so disagree with his view of gender roles, (see John Piper and Wayne Grudem, eds., *Recovering Biblical Manhood and Womanhood: A Response to Evangelical Feminism* [Wheaton, IL: Crossway, 1991], 469-71). One need not embrace a position of eternal functional subordination of the Son and the Spirit to the Father within the ontological/essential Trinity in order to hold to different roles of men and women based on the created order. In my opinion, those in the traditionalist/complementarian camp have the direct teaching of Scripture in their favor, and as such I am a traditionalist on this issue of gender roles. For a defense of *eternal* functional subordination within the eternal Trinity, see Bruce A. Ware, "How Shall We Think about the Trinity," in *God Under Fire: Modern Scholarship Reinvents God*, ed. Douglas S. Huffman and Eric L. Johnson (Grand Rapids: Zondervan, 2002), 254-77; and idem, *Father, Son, and Holy Spirit: Relations, Roles, and Relevance* (Wheaton, IL: Crossway, 2005). However, the warning of Thomas F. Torrance should be heeded to avoid confusion on the nature of the Triune God we strive to serve and worship aright. Torrance charges, "The subjection of Christ to the Father in his incarnate economy as the suffering and obedient servant cannot be read back into the eternal hypostatic relations and distinctions subsisting in the Holy Trinity" (*The Christian Doctrine of God: One Being Three Persons* [Edinburgh: T. & T. Clark, 1996], 180). Also, see the important article by Gerald Bray, "The Double Procession of the Spirit in Evangelical Theology Today: Do We Still Need It?" *JETS* 41 (1998): 415-26. Bray speaks of matters that are of utmost importance for Trinitarianism. In discussing the common notion in Eastern Orthodox Christianity concerning the Father as the fount of divinity, which is embraced by some evangelicals, Bray cautions that this "is inevitably to raise the possibility that the Son and the Holy Spirit are inferior to him in this vitally important respect" (Bray, "Double Procession," 422). Bray is correct as he continues with the following claim: "However we interpret the concepts of [eternal] generation and procession, we cannot say that any of the three persons of the trinity derives his divinity from the Father since all three are coequal and coeternal" (Bray, "Double Procession," 424). Furthermore, see the similar reservations about subordinationism in Thomas H. McCall, *Which Trinity? Whose Monotheism? Philosophical and Systematic Theologians on the Metaphysics of Trinitarian Theology* (Grand Rapids: Eerdmans, 2010), 175-188. Now the definitive study is Dennis W. Jowers & H. Wayne House, eds, *The New Evangelical Subordinationism? Perspectives on the Equality of God the Father and God the Son* (Eugene: Pickwick, 2012).

[14] Adoptionism is the view that Jesus was a mere man, and was chosen by God to fulfill the functions of Messiah, and thus became the "Son of God" in time. See Walter A.

the very notion of a preexisting Son of God who becomes man, rather than an ordinary man taken up into divine status, is the correct way of thinking about Jesus Christ. Out of this matrix of belief my Christology will be explored. However, on this matter, Gerald O'Collins makes a distinction between two interpretations of the term "incarnation." For O'Collins, one type is an interpretation much like what is described in the preceding sentences, God descends, so to speak, from above. Another interpretative type is a milder form of the concept of "incarnation," which could be true in an adoptionist sense, whereby a man is given a status of divinity. I believe the first type, or stronger form of interpreting the idea of incarnation is the correct one in relation to Jesus Christ.[15] "The central figure of the Gospels is to be understood, not only as the revealer of God," Hebblethwaite claims, "but as himself the content of that revelation, God the Son made man for our salvation, and the doctrine of God implied by that revelation is to be expressed in trinitarian terms."[16]

B.3. Theology Proper

Contributions by evangelicals to the doctrine of God have set a high standard.[17] Some of this production is in part a response to current trends in the "openness of God" movement, where even evangelicals have challenged the traditional concepts of God.[18] Many contemporary theologians are advocating a mutable and passible understanding of God.[19] My concerns on this very important ques-

---

Elwell, ed., *Evangelical Dictionary of Theology* (Grand Rapids: Baker, 1984), s.v. "Adoptionism," and Harold O. J. Brown, *Heresies: Heresy and Orthodoxy in the History of the Church* (Peabody, MA: Hendrickson, 1998), 96-99.

[15] Gerald O' Collins, *Incarnation* (New York: Continuum, 2002), 1-12.

[16] Brian Hebblethwaite, "The Propriety of the Doctrine of the Incarnation as a Way of Interpreting Christ," *SJT* 33 (1980): 201. This article is reproduced in Brian Hebblethwaite, *The Incarnation: Collected Essays in Christology* (Cambridge: Cambridge University Press, 1987), 53-76.

[17] Most notable are John S. Feinberg, *No One Like Him: The Doctrine of God* (Wheaton, IL: Crossway, 2001); John M. Frame, *The Doctrine of God* (Phillipsburg, NJ: P & R, 2002); and K. Scott Oliphint, *God With Us: Divine Condescension and the Attributes of God* (Wheaton, Il: Crossway, 2012), though I have some reservations about the model espoused by Oliphint. A valuable work that treats the doctrine in its classic manner fully cognizant of the Patristic and Reformation traditions is Gerald Bray, *The Doctrine of God* (Downers Grove, IL: InterVarsity, 1993). I cannot recommend this book too highly. For discussion of the "God" question in a broader setting, see James M. Byrne, ed., *The Christian Understanding of God Today: Theological Colloquium on the Occasion of the 400TH Anniversary of the Foundation of Trinity College, Dublin* (Dublin: Columba, 1993).

[18] The Evangelical "openness of God" manifesto emerged with Clark Pinnock et al., eds., *The Openness of God: A Biblical Challenge to the Traditional Understanding of God* (Downers Grove, IL: InterVarsity, 1994). A fully developed apologetic for an "openness" view is found in John Sanders, *The God Who Risks: A Theology of Providence* (Downers Grove, IL: InterVarsity, 1998). For a thorough critique of Openness theology, see Gerald Bray, *The Personal God: Is the Classical Understanding of God Tenable?* (Carlisle: Paternoster, 1998); John M. Frame, *No Other God: A Response to Open Theism* (Phillipsburg, NJ: P & R, 2001); and Bruce A. Ware, *God's Lesser Glory: The Diminished God of Open Theism* (Wheaton, IL: Crossway, 2000); idem, *God's Greater Glory: The Exalted God of Scripture and the Christian Faith* (Wheaton, IL: Crossway, 2004).

[19] As an example, see Jürgen Moltmann, *The Trinity and the Kingdom: The Doctrine of God*, trans. Margaret Kohl (New York: Harper and Row, 1981), 21-60.

tion are noted here for the matter directly relates to the way of God becoming man. I believe that theologians who insist that God is mutable and passible have a worthy goal of attempting to establish that God is active and loving. With this desire, as an evangelical committed to the active and gracious God who initiates his covenant with his own, one must be in full sympathy. There is a misunderstanding, however, that those theologians expounding immutability in reality deny the relationality and passion of God, as if they conceived the deity as an unmoved mover. It is true that in classical theology-proper change in God was sorely resisted. Process theologian, Charles Hartshorne pointed this out in relation to Anselm's view of impassibility.[20] Yet, Anselm himself has given a spirited defense of the incarnation in his famous *Cur Deus Homo*.[21] Despite his lofty claims for the divine nature, which I find necessary to sound theology, Anselm's theology affirms that Jesus "is true God and true man, one person in two natures and two natures in one person."[22] This is very different from a concept that removes God completely from any relationality with the created order. Hence, the notion of an absolutely unmoved mover must be contested and a re-conceptualization of God's immutability in general and impassibility in particular must be affirmed anew.[23] Ironically, I find this kind of approach in Anselm.

---

[20] Charles Hartshorne, *The Divine Relativity: A Social Conception of God* (New Haven, CT: Yale University Press, 1948, 1964), 54-55. Dealing with several difficulties in Process thought, see Royce Gordon Gruenler, *The Inexhaustible God: Biblical Faith and the Challenge of Process Theism* (Grand Rapids: Baker, 1983) and Ronald H. Nash, *The Concept of God: An Exploration of Contemporary Difficulties with the Attributes of God* (Grand Rapids: Zondervan, 1983). However, I do not affirm all of Nash's solutions!

[21] Fairweather, *A Scholastic Miscellany*, 100-83.

[22] Fairweather, *A Scholastic Miscellany*, 110.

[23] It is not the place or purpose of this discussion to enter the debate the matter of whether God is impassible or not. However, given the prominence of recent proposals which have challenged this "classic" view of God, it should be noted that I am in substantial agreement with authors who have affirmed that impassibility is essential to a correct understanding of God. For recent defenses of impassibility, one may consult the following: Rob Lister, *God is Impassible and Impassioned: Toward a Theology of Divine Emotion* (Wheaton: Crossway, 2013); Richard E. Creel, *Divine Impassibility: An Essay in Philosophical Theology* (Cambridge: Cambridge University Press, 1986); Millard Erickson, *God the Father Almighty: A Contemporary Exploration of the Divine Attributes* (Grand Rapids: Baker, 1998), 141-64. Thomas G. Weinandy, *Does God Suffer?* (Notre Dame, IN: University of Notre Dame Press; Edinburgh: T. & T. Clark, 2000) in my opinion a terrific title that warrants widespread exposure; Gerald Bray, "Suffering Servant, Sovereign Lord: Can God Suffer?" *Modern Reformation* [on-line publication], I originally accessed this good article on: 23 March 2001; available from http://www.alliancenet.org/pub/mr/mr99/1999.02.MarApr/mr9902.gb.sovreignlord.html, Internet; Norman L. Geisler and H. Wayne House, with Max Herrera, *The Battle for God: Responding to the Challenge of Neotheism* (Grand Rapids: Kregel, 2001), 170-91; Paul Gravrilyk, *The Suffering of the Impassible God: The Dialectics of Patristic Thought* (Oxford: Oxford University Press, 2004); Daniel Castelo, *The Apathetic God: Exploring the Contemporary Relevance of Divine Impassibility* (Eugene: Wipf and Stock, 2009); David Bentley Hart, "Impassibility as Transcendence: On the Infinite Innocence of God" in James F. Keating & Thomas Joseph White, eds., *Divine Impassibility and the Mystery of Human Suffering* (Grand Rapids: Eerdmans, 2009), 299-323; and D. Stephen Long, "Aquinas and God's Sovereignty" in D. Stephen Long & George Kalantzis, eds., *The Sovereignty of God Debate* (Eugene: Cascade, 2009). Those challenging the classical view include Wayne Grudem, *Systematic Theology: An Introduction to Biblical Doc-*

On the matter of immutability Dorner's monumental essay sought to reestablish the doctrine in line with the vitality of God and his involvement with the world.[24] This essay was written in the middle of the nineteenth century while the kenotic controversy was very much alive and it prompted Dorner's contribution. He sought a middle ground between the extremes of classic doctrine, which viewed any change in God as necessarily involving an imperfection, and on the other hand the kenotic teaching, which placed such a premium on God's self divestment and involvement that it had no place for any notion of immutability. Dorner replaces the old view of God's simplicity with a conception of God's complexity. This draws on a bi-polar view of God that affirms insights from both theism and pantheism, and he finally asserts that "the whole historical life of God in the world takes place, not at the expense of the eternal perfection of God himself, but by virtue of this permanent perfection."[25] Although writing in a subsequent era, and from a very different theological tradition, Thomas Weinandy says some things which come very close to the model presented by Dorner. The positions or arguments of the two men are not the same, but their conclusions concerning the way of God's involvement in the world that does not jeopardize his "Otherness" or "Immutability," but is rather the *basis* for it, are very similar indeed. Weinandy draws on Thomistic and Patristic thought, but is especially grounding his conclusions concerning impassibility on biblical statements. Weinandy notes,

> Within the Hebrew scriptures, to say that Yahweh is One, Savior, Creator and All Holy is to say, at once and the same time, within the same concepts, that he is present and active as the one who is wholly other, and that he is present and active in time and history, as the Wholly Other without jeopardizing his total otherness in so doing.[26]

---

trine (Grand Rapids: Zondervan; Leicester: InterVarsity, 1994), 165-66; Marcel Sarot, *God, Passibility and Corporeality* (Kampen: Kok Pharos, 1992); Paul S. Fiddes, *The Creative Suffering of God* (Oxford: Clarendon, 1988); Jürgen Moltmann, *The Crucified God*, trans. R.A. Wilson and John Bowden (Minneapolis: Fortress, 1993), 200-90. For a particularly creative proposal within the sphere of Christological thinking, see Alan Torrance, "Does God Suffer? Incarnation and Impassibility," in *Christ in Our Place: The Humanity of God in Christ for the Reconciliation of the World, Essays Presented to Professor James Torrance*, eds. Trevor A. Hart and Daniel P. Thimell (Exeter: Paternoster; Allison Park, PA: Pickwick, 1989), 345-68.

[24] See "The Reconstruction of the Immutability Doctrine," in Isaak August Dorner, *Divine Immutability: A Critical Reconsideration*, trans. Robert R. Williams and Claude Welch (Minneapolis: Fortress, 1994), 131-95. The other two essays in this volume are "The Kenotic Attack on Immutability" and "The History of the Doctrine of the Immutability of God."

[25] Dorner, "The Reconstruction of the Immutability Doctrine," 160.

[26] Weinandy, *Does God Suffer?*, 53. Weinandy offers also the best conception of how God can be immutable and nonetheless become incarnate in Jesus Christ. See his *Does God Change? The Word's Becoming in the Incarnation* (Still River, MA: St. Bede's, 1985). For an evangelical approach with similar conclusions, see Dennis Edward Johnson, "Immutability and Incarnation: An Historical and Theological Study of the Concepts of Christ's Divine Unchangeability and His Human Development" (Ph.D. diss., Fuller Theological Seminary, 1984). This is an important study on the notion of Incarnation.

Weinandy is a sure guide here. He takes seriously the biblical testimony concerning God's involvement in the world, and at the same time conceives of God as remaining absolutely transcendent to the created order. Both aspects must be affirmed. This goal of maintaining both truths is accomplished admirably by Bruce Ware. In his important article on this topic, Ware succinctly presents the findings and conclusions from his dissertation research, tackling head-on the need to re-express the doctrine of immutability.[27] God is unchangeable, according to Ware, in two ways. First, God is ontologically immutable. This means that his inner divine nature is not subject to change. Second, Ware expresses the changelessness of God's ethical will. This has to do with God's promises to act in conformity to his nature, given the changing circumstances of the world, in which God relates with people. According to Ware this is a "second-order" immutability, which stresses God's faithfulness.

On the matter of impassibility, as Erickson warns, it is important to realize that "the concept of impassibility is quite complex, and several different meanings are intended by those who use the term."[28] So it is significant to establish precisely what is and what is not meant by impassibility. First, impassibility does not mean that God does not have emotions. The Bible is replete with passages affirming God's emotions.[29] Second, what is key in the discussion is expressing that God cannot experience suffering in his divine nature, and that no outside influence can subject God to anything for God is the most powerful being.[30] Yet God as God knows what it is for *humans* to suffer. Moreover, suffering was mainly thought about in the early centuries of Christianity as bodily suffering. As such, God is surely impassible as he is Spirit, without a body. Recent discussions about the pain and suffering which have plagued humanity have noted that it is more than merely bodily suffering, but suffering that involves acute emotional and psychological disturbance. It is this type of suffering that has been projected onto God. One would never rejoice to worship a

---

[27] Bruce A. Ware, "An Evangelical Reformulation of the Doctrine of the Immutability of God," *JETS* 29 (1986): 431-46. Also see my brief article "Immutability: God Unchangeable and Unchanging," *The Gospel Witness* (September 2009): 3-6, where I discuss God's immutability in his counsel and his character. Other defenses of Immutability include: Ron Highfield, *Great is the Lord: Theology for the Praise of God* (Grand Rapids: Eerdmans, 2009), 358-74; Paul Helm, *Eternal God: A Study of God Without Time* 2d. ed. (New York: Oxford, 2011 [1988]), 85-94, Norman L. Geisler, H. Wayne House, with Max Herrera, *The Battle for God: Responding to the Challenge of Neotheism* (Grand Rapids: Kregel, 2001), 100-41; and Herman Bavinck, *The Doctrine of God*, trans. William Hendricksen (Grand Rapids: Baker, 1977 [1951]), 145-52.

[28] Erickson, *God the Father Almighty*, 141.

[29] Even Norman Geisler in his model of classical theism affirms this. Geisler asserts, "A view that God expresses no emotional states would be clearly contrary to the teachings of the Old and New Testaments" (Geisler, House, and Herrera, *The Battle for God*, 171).

[30] I am in full agreement with Erickson's comment: "If it is the case that God has planned from eternity all that occurs, and that this includes the various events in the lives of all persons, then although God may experience certain emotions, make certain choices, and take certain actions in connection with those events, they really are not the cause of these events in God's life" (Erickson, *God the Father Almighty*, 161). Also see idem, "God and Change," *SBJT* 1 (Summer 1997): 38-51, for a succinct and very helpful defense of immutability where Erickson distinguishes between the notions of God's being static and God's being stable. Erickson denies the former but affirms the latter.

God who could not feel our plight, so the argument goes. Yet the familiar analogy of a doctor and his patient serves as a helpful solution to this seeming dilemma. Bray poignantly illustrates,

> Someone lying in a hospital bed does not want to be solely treated by a machine, which functions regardless of the pain it might inflict. Rather, the patient wants to be treated by someone who understands what he or she is going through, and who will sensitively adjust his approach. . . . But having said that, what patient wants the doctor to climb into bed next to him or her and start making groaning noises, as if to indicate that the doctor, too, is experiencing the same pain? This is not the kind of "empathy" desired, because the fundamental reason the patient wants the doctor is not to receive sympathy from him or her; the patient can get that just as easily from any medically unskilled visitor. What the patient wants is to be cured. *Understanding* pain is all very well, but *overcoming* it is what all sufferers really want.[31]

It appears that the only way to safeguard the divine transcendence is to affirm anew both the doctrines of immutability and impassibility. The transcendence of God is rooted in the truth of God as Creator.[32] Patrick Lee argues that this entails certain concomitant doctrinal affirmations. "The proposition that God is the Creator," asserts Lee, "implies at least three other points: (1) God creates freely; (2) God possesses his complete perfection within himself; and (3) God is immutable and is not in time."[33] God's transcendence therefore leads via immutability to impassibility. Lee's approach focuses heavily on the unknowability of God's essential being. As he states, "We do not grasp what God is in Himself." If this is conceded, which I am inclined to agree with, then it follows that relationality is essential to any knowledge we do in fact have of God, which itself presupposes divine revelation. This is what we find in Scripture: God has revealed to us, not his essence as God, but that we can relate to him as creatures made in his image, and in thus relating to him as God, we discover he is wholly other or transcendent but knowable, and that he is dynamic, not static, but unchanging and therefore dependable. A part of this revelation includes the truth that even as we ponder intensely his revelation God is greater than what we think about him. "God's being or nature is incomprehensible and ineffable," says Lee,[34] and this is a feature revealed to us. Those aspects of God's constancy of character, purpose, and will are not threatened by relationality, nor for that matter, by the incarnation itself. God can remain essentially God and entail no change in his divine nature, while assuming human nature.[35] This means that

---

[31] Bray, "Suffering Servant, Sovereign Lord," 4. Erickson also utilizes the medical analogy in his "synthetic solution." By distinguishing between empathy and sympathy, God is seen like a professional who can understand a client's feelings without actually experiencing them himself. Thus, Erickson argues, "The closest analogy for understanding God is an emotionally mature person, one who experiences emotions but does not let them control him or her" (*God the Father Almighty*, 163).

[32] Patrick Lee, "Does God Have Emotions?," in *God under Fire*, 214-18.

[33] Lee, "Does God Have Emotions?," 215.

[34] Lee, Does God Have Emotions?," 224.

[35] Helpful on this is Richard A. Muller, "Incarnation, Immutability, and the Case for Classical Theism," *WTJ* 45 (1983): 32-36.

Chapter 1. Christology: An Introduction

God the Son remains essentially unchanged in the divine nature though becoming incarnate.

B.4. Christological Method

The very concept of an incarnation requires that one should begin Christological exposition "from above."[36] This does not mean that we can discard the details of the historical Jesus when articulating our theology of Christ. Indeed, much of our Christology will be a direct reflection and interpretation of the Gospel texts.[37] It does, however, suggest the legitimacy of discussing the issue much as it was pursued in the early centuries of the Christian church age.[38] God became man, or "the Word was made flesh" (John 1:14) is the basic axiom of any Bible-centered Christology.[39]

---

[36] See Wells, *The Person of Christ: A Biblical and Historical Analysis of the Incarnation* (Alliance, OH: Bible Scholar, 1992), 172-73, who argues that the christs [lower case intended] which emerge from a methodology of Christology from below may be admired but never worshiped. Also, Reymond echoes these concerns: "Every humanist Christology 'from below' while it may stress the genuine humaness of Jesus, must still face this problem: does it say enough to justify the church calling him, in its worship and in its confessions, 'true God and true man'?" (*Jesus Divine Messiah*, 19). Moreover, Donald Macleod while discussing the adherents of the "Christology from below" school of thought, unequivocally declares: "The fact itself is clear: the New Testament starts from above" (*The Person of Christ* [Downers Grove, IL: InterVarsity, 1998], 22). Hence, the best evangelical Christological scholarship advocates "Christology from above."

[37] See Darrell L. Bock, *Jesus According to Scripture: Restoring the Portrait from the Gospels* (Grand Rapids: Baker, 2002); Jakob van Bruggen, *Christ on Earth: The Gospel Narratives as History*, trans. Nancy Forest-Flier (Grand Rapids: Baker, 1998); and idem, *Jesus the Son of God: The Gospel Narratives as Message*, trans. Nancy Forest-Flier (Grand Rapids: Baker, 1999) as superior examples of this type of literature. Furthermore, one cannot praise too highly the work of both exegetical and theological exposition in Murray J. Harris, *Jesus as God: The New Testament Use of* Theos *in Reference to Jesus* (Grand Rapids: Baker, 1992). For theologians who have implemented serious Bible scholarship into their Christology, see Jean Galot, *Who Is Christ? A Theology of the Incarnation*, trans. M. Angeline Bouchard (Chicago: Franciscan Herald, 1981), who argues that the notion of incarnation is broad and thus stretches back to the Old Testament within the covenantal arrangement initiated by God. See also Reymond, *A New Systematic Theology of the Christian Faith*; idem, *Jesus Divine Messiah*; J. Oliver Buswell, *A Systematic Theology of the Christian Religion*, vol. 2, *Soteriology and Eschatology* (Grand Rapids: Zondervan, 1963); Wayne Grudem, *Systematic Theology*; Hawthorne, *The Presence and the Power*; and John Stott, *The Incomparable Christ* (Downers Grove, IL: InterVarsity, 2001).

[38] Crisp offers his approach as a safe course. He says, "In my view Christology should begin with divine revelation and the catholic creeds. This should yield a 'high' Christology. It should also yield an orthodox Christology – attention to the tradition will certainly help in this regard" (Oliver Crisp, *God Incarnate: Explorations in Christology* [London: T and T Clark, 2009], 32-33).

[39] I am well aware of attempts to coalesce the (possibly) divergent approaches. For example, Thomas F. Torrance argues, "The proper theological procedure we adopt in Christology [is that], in which we do not seek to understand the Person of and work of Jesus Christ by approaching him either from below or from above, but from below and from above at the same time, for it is in the light of what we learn from below that we appreciate what derives from above, and in light of what derives from above that we really understand what we learn from below" (*The Christian Doctrine of God: One Being Three Persons* [Edinburgh: T. & T. Clark, 1996], 114). Gerald O'Collins also notes, "Christologies from below and from above complement each other. . . . In Christology

B.5. Purpose

I undertake the study of Christology not as a problem to be solved, which would preclude further reflection once the solution has been pronounced, but rather as a mystery to be delved into at deeper and deeper levels.[40] Of course, our cognitive understanding may find some satisfaction with the "solutions" such as *enhypostasia* and *communicatio idiomatum*,[41] both of which will appear useful in this book. As a never-ending endeavor, however, theologizing about the person of Christ will and must continue as "Jesus will never find a theologian worthy of him."[42] Hence, someone will always be found to add insight to the mystery of Christ.

---

we need both approaches, 'from above' and 'from below' " (*Christology: A Biblical, and Systematic Study of Jesus* [New York: Oxford University Press, 1995], 17). Of course, when dealing with Jesus of Nazareth, we are still dealing with the eternal Son of God, the second person of the Trinity, so aspects of his person which are particularly true of one specific nature must help in our overall understanding of the person. The disciples who first encountered Jesus no doubt saw him as a man among men, yet very early in their experience of Jesus the man, they encountered Jesus the God. Christ himself stated that he was not from below, but from above (see John 1:1-18; 1:27, 30; 3:13, 16-17; 3:31, 34 [John the Baptist's testimony]; 4:34; 5:37; 6:33, 38, 41-42, 51; 7:28-29; 8:23, 26, 42, 58; 9:39; 10:36; 12:44-50; 16:28; 17:5, 8, 24). Jesus' "order of being," helps us evaluate his person correctly when our knowing conforms to this order of being, namely, to the descent of God the Son. Only by starting like this may we even speak of an incarnation. For a helpful treatment of this matter, see Colin E. Gunton, *Yesterday and Today: A Study of Continuities in Christology* (London: Darton, Longman and Todd, 1983), 10-57.

[40] Thomas G. Weinandy has been particularly influential in this regard. "The true goal of theological inquiry," he asserts, "is not the resolution of theological *problems*, but the discernment of what the mystery of the faith is. Because God, who can never be fully comprehended, lies at the heart of all theological enquiry, theology by its nature is not a problem solving enterprise, but rather a mystery discerning enterprise" (*Does God Suffer?* [Notre Dame, IN: University of Notre Dame Press, 2000], 32).

[41] *Communicatio idiomatum* or communion of properties is an expression of significance in Christology. Richard A. Muller defines it as "a term used in Christology to describe the way in which the properties, or *idiomata*, of each nature are communicated to or interchanged in the unity of the person" (*Dictionary of Latin and Greek Theological Terms: Drawn Principally from Protestant Scholastic Theology* [Grand Rapids: Baker; Carlisle: Paternoster, 1985], 72-74). Muller conveniently distinguishes different uses of this concept and alerts the reader to the distinctions maintained by Lutheran and Reformed theologians in their debates about the person of Christ. Briefly, Lutherans asserted the *communicatio idiomatum in abstracto*; this refers to the abstractive consideration of the relation of the two natures. This method allowed Lutherans to affirm an actual exchange of properties between the natures such that they could claim that the body of Jesus was omnipresent. The Reformed theologians tended to utilize the *communicatio idiomatum in concreto*. This particular nuance refers to the concretion of the person. Attributes are therefore seen as true of the person in the incarnated state by virtue of the hypostatic union. Here there is no exchange of properties between the natures but only verbally predicated communication at the level of the person. This latter understanding is what I consider to be the correct approach. The Calvinist approach appears to be the view which leads J.M. Drickamer to his definition. He says, "The communication of attributes means that whatever can be attributed to (said about) either the divine or the human nature in Christ is said to be attributed to the entire person" (Walter A. Elwell, ed., *Evangelical Dictionary of Theology* [Grand Rapids: Baker, 1984], s.v. "Communication of Attributes, Communicatio Idiomatum," by J.M. Drickamer).

[42] Gerald O'Collins, *Christology: A Biblical, Historical, and Systematic Study of Jesus* (New York: Oxford University Press, 1995), 16.

Chapter 1. Christology: An Introduction

B.6. Conclusion

I offer my own thoughts as part of the ongoing contribution of ideas that delve into contemplating the one we worship as God incarnate. I hope to produce for myself "understanding and awe." My explorations will take me on the path of investigating how others in church history have pondered the "how" of the incarnation. Because of the constraints of this project selectivity is the order of the day. In light of these investigations my own proposal of how to conceive of the incarnation will emerge.

C. Thesis

The thesis of this book is that as part of a model[43] of a two-natured Christology, the Lord Jesus Christ as fully God in the incarnate state had and exercised the divine attribute of omnipresence during his earthly sojourn and beyond. By focusing attention on omnipresence, the neglected attribute, this perspective also serves as a focal point for conceptualizing the incarnation and understanding the relationship Christ has with *all* the divine attributes.[44] In defending this

---

[43] See the excellent discussion of Christological models in John McIntyre, *The Shape of Christology: Studies in the Doctrine of the Person of Christ* (Edinburgh: T and T Clark, 1998), 49-80. A focused study of the "two-natures" type model is covered by McIntyre, *Shape of Christology*, 83-113. More recently Jonathan Hill has provided a fantastic selection of models in "Introduction," in Anna Marmadoro & Jonathan Hill, eds., *The Metaphysics of the Incarnation* (New York: Oxford, 2011), 1-19. Rather than the use of models Colin E. Gunton prefers the use of *concepts*. "For concepts," Gunton observes, "enable us to express that which we believe to be true, so that a decision may be made about the rationality, and possibly also the truth, of that which is asserted or preached" (*Yesterday and Today: A Study in Continuities in Christology* [London: Darton, Longman and Todd, 1983], 152). Also helpful in evaluating some differing models of God and Christ, see Bertrand de Margerie, *Christ for the World: The Heart of the Lamb* trans. Malachy Carroll (New York: Franciscan Herald Press, 1973); John F. O'Grady, *Models of Jesus Revisited* (New York: Paulist, 1997); William J. Ladue, *Jesus Among the Theologians: Contemporary Interpretations of Christ* (Harrisburg, PA: Trinity, 2001); and Bruce McCormack, ed., *Engaging the Doctrine of God: Contemporary Protestant Perspectives* (Grand Rapids: Baker, 2008).

[44] Omniscience and omnipotence, the other two so-called relative attributes, will be seen to be both possessed and used by Jesus also. Often evangelicals will distinguish between possession and use of the relative attributes. For example, Erickson utilizes this very distinction with regard to Christ's knowledge. Erickson claims that Jesus possesses all knowledge in the sub-conscious. This knowledge is due to Christ's being divine. Yet in Erickson's proposal, Jesus is subject to his Father and therefore obtains consciously only that which his Father permits (see Erickson, *The Word Became Flesh*, 558-60). Thomas Morris has also made a similar type of argument based on his "two minds" view of the person of Jesus. Morris's framework is helpful but his specific solution to omniscience is incorrect. For example, he must posit that Jesus does not have knowledge of his necessary goodness. The reason for his insistence on this proposal appears to be not so much his desire to safeguard the various scriptural data on Christ's knowledge, as it is to defend a libertarian concept of freedom for the man Jesus to be able to explain how Jesus is genuinely tempted. See Thomas V. Morris, *The Logic of God Incarnate* (Ithaca, NY: Cornell University Press, 1986), 146-62. For a critique of Morris on this point, see John S. Feinberg, "The Incarnation of Jesus Christ," in *In Defense of Miracles: A Comprehensive Case for God's Action in History*, ed. R. Douglas Geivett and Gary R. Habermas. (Downers Grove, IL: InterVarsity, 1997), 241-42. One must concede the possibility of Jesus possessing omnipotence but not using it. However, what is contested here is that the said distinction works with the doctrine of omnipresence. It clearly cannot. I believe that Jesus draws on his omnipotence to perform miracles and to continue to up-

particular type of evangelical Christology, a non-kenotic view emerges. With a commitment to a Reformed emphasis on the *communicatio idiomatum*, as developed in the early church era, and best exemplified in John Calvin,[45] coupled with the *enhypostatic* insights of Leontius of Byzantium and John of Damascus, this view best represents the data of the New Testament. The teaching on the omnipresence of Jesus becomes a test case for articulating a sound conception of the incarnation, and becomes the focal observation for unlocking the *kenosis* issue. It is directly the matter of omnipresence that gives evangelicals, and others, the most trouble in explaining the relationship of the two natures in Jesus Christ.[46] It is common among evangelical scholars to claim that the Son of God does not give up any attribute of deity in becoming man as this would preclude Jesus' status as God. Omnipresence has both been denied and neglected in evangelical Christology. In much of the thinking on the person of Christ among evangelicals, the avowal of kenotic or sub-kenotic models necessarily leads to the dismissal that Jesus exercised omnipresence (as well as omniscience and omnipotence), although it is also claimed that Jesus still *had* these attributes in some kind of suppressed manner, or he had them in potency rather than in actuality. The end result is that Jesus was not omnipresent because this directly

---

hold the world by his powerful word. This does not deny the truth that Jesus on occasion does work through the Holy Spirit (e.g., Matt 12:28), but it is incorrect to state that *all* Jesus does he accomplishes through the Holy Spirit.

[45] Alasdair Heron explains that "*communicatio idiomatum* or . . . the perichoretic exchange of attributes between the divine and human natures of Christ, was not originally a main or central topic in the classical Reformed teaching of the sixteenth century. It was in fact a theme which Calvin and others treated with considerable reserve, even distrust" ("Communicatio Idiomatum and *Deificatio* of Human Nature: A Reformed Perspective," *GOTR* 43 [1998]: 367). Of course, Heron has in mind the debates centering on the Lord's Supper. Heron's historical insight is appreciated. However, Calvin nonetheless presents one of the most sophisticated expositions of the *communicatio idiomatum*. It was this Christological commitment which lay at the foundation that caused differences between the Lutherans and the Reformed. A classic example was the debate between Theodore Beza, who utilized Calvin's Christology, and Jacob Andreae. In her masterful study of this debate, Jill Raitt states, "The problem of the Lord's Supper cannot be separated from the fundamental theological doctrine of the person of Christ" (*The Colloquy of Montbéliard: Religion and Politics in the Sixteenth Century* [New York: Oxford University Press, 1993], 83). Furthermore, she adds, "The doctrine of Christ became the major theological sticking point between Reformed and Lutheran theologians in the second half of the sixteenth century. From the Maulbronn Colloquy of 1564 through the bitter battles about the meaning of kenosis in the first quarter of the seventeenth century, discussions of the Lord's Supper, which meant discussions of the manner of Christ's presence, became Christological arguments" (*Colloquy of Montbéliard*, 110). For more on Beza's Christology, see Jill Raitt, "The Person of the Mediator: Calvin's Christology and Beza's Fidelity," *OPASRR* 1 (1977): 53-80. Calvin's approach will be evaluated in a subsequent chapter.

[46] This will be demonstrated in Erickson's position. What is *prima facie* obvious to most people is that Jesus could not be omnipresent for he was a man restricted by the body he was in possession of, and therefore could not be everywhere simultaneously. This assumption, I believe, is a major ground for the doctrine's neglect. Because of the biblical data on Jesus' knowledge being more widespread, and given the direct statements concerning Jesus' lack of knowledge on several occasions, omniscience has become the point at which debate on the nature of the incarnation is focused. Omniscience will be dealt with summarily in aid of the exposition of the thesis.

would contravene his genuine humanity.⁴⁷ As a man, Jesus could only be in one place at a time. By proposing that Jesus both had and exercised omnipresence, I am rejecting both kenotic and sub-kenotic "solutions" and reaffirming the view made classical at the time of Chalcedon, and which has admirably been expounded by John Calvin. This theological retrieval is promising in itself and may point the way forward by looking back at the superiority of pre-modern theology in comparison to much theologizing of today. What emerges from these considerations is a "picture" of Jesus Christ who is fully God and truly man, a single person who is truly God and fully man. Because the incarnation must be seen in terms of an addition of a human nature to the already existing Son of God, and not a transformation or metaphysical alteration of the divine nature in the becoming man, the deity retains all its prerogatives as prior to the incarnation. It just so happens that now we may posit statements such as "Jesus Christ is omnipresent" or "God died on the cross" without recounting absurdities because of the unique constitution of the incarnate Christ.

D. Outline of the Book

I propose in chapters 2, 3 and 4 to set the context for a presentation of specific evangelical voices by broadly surveying the Modern era. The Christological contributions of selected scholars will be presented allowing their own position to emerge with little interaction from me in this early stage. In chapter 5 a survey of the Patristic era, with its important Christological developments, will be exhibited, especially noting where any of the Fathers advocated the omnipresence of Jesus. The Christology of Calvin will be explored in chapter 6, highlighting the famous *extra Calvinisticum*. These insights will provide backdrop for chapter 7, which will present the biblical evidence for the doctrine of the omnipresence of God, and the theological justification for the deity of Christ, and hence, the omnipresence of Jesus Christ. Chapter 8 will take a look at Philippians 2:5-8, and also evaluate various forms of kenotic type Christology by

---

⁴⁷ For a classic example, one would do no better than to examine the contribution of Gottfried Thomasius. In discussing the issue of omnipresence in relation to the incarnate Christ, Thomasius asserts, "As concerns the presence, the supposition that during this stage [incarnation] he existed outside the limitation of space would patently destroy the truth of his whole historical life; for such a mode of existence would not only contradict the natural restriction and conditionality of the earthly material body, but would also entirely contradict the condition of spiritual-corporeal human nature as this is now determined in everyone" ("Christ's Person and Work, Part 2: The Person of the Mediator," in *God and Incarnation in Mid-Nineteenth Century German Theology: G. Thomasius, I.A. Dorner, A.E Biedermann*, ed. and trans. Claude Welch [New York: Oxford University Press, 1965], 71). Evangelical scholar Gerald Hawthorne echoes these concerns: "If the Logos enters time and space omniscient, omnipotent, omnipresent, his entrance is a theophany. He certainly is not a human being like us" (Gerald F. Hawthorne, *The Presence and the Power: The Significance of the Holy Spirit in the Life of Jesus* [Dallas: Word Publishing, 1991], 212). Suffice to note here that within the two-natured model adopted in this book, one of the natures is obviously the human nature. Christ's genuine humanity is a basic and non-negotiable axiom. Without genuine humanity, salvation is impossible. Walvoord perhaps said it best, and speaks for many: "The humanity of Christ is evident . . . in the fact that He possessed a true human body composed of flesh and blood. . . . The evidence for His human body in the Scriptures is seemingly more compelling than the evidence for His deity" (John F. Walvoord, *Jesus Christ our Lord* [Chicago: Moody, 1969], 110).

modern evangelical voices who have addressed the matter of divine attributes in relation to the incarnate Christ, particularly omnipresence. A final brief concluding chapter will close the book showing the superiority of the pre-modern view of Christ drawn up at Chalcedon, developed by John of Damascus, and defended by Calvin.

E. Conclusion

I exhibit a great interest in the subject matter of Christology which stems from its compelling nature as a theological discipline inviting probing and re-examination. As indicated at the outset of this chapter, I will pursue this study out of the context of faith. In writing out my research a constant desire to articulate a thesis that honors the Lord is paramount. What will ensue is a Christian's attempt to "explain" something of the *how* of the incarnation with biblical fidelity, historical sensitivity, and hopefully enough sensible humility. I have no illusions of a final or definitive statement, which, will be accepted by all, but I need to be clear in my own mind precisely what I believe Scripture teaches as the truth on this issue. I am not telling, but re-telling a story that I have overheard from many.

CHAPTER 2

CHRISTOLOGY: CURRENT STATUS OF RESEARCH

Introduction

People are drawn to speculate on Jesus as moths to a flame. His name has a certain magnetic appeal. From the popular treatments by John Stott, Tim LaHaye, Lee Strobel, Stuart Olyott, Arthur Rowe, Gregg Allison, Joel McDurmon, and Bart Ehrman; to the scholarly endeavors of Gerald O'Collins, Hans Schwarz, Larry Hurtado, Michael McClymond, Stephen Holmes & Murray Rae, Joerg Rieger; Andreas Schuele & Günther Thomas; Anna Marmodoro & Jonathan Hill, Edward Oakes, and Oliver Crisp & Fred Sanders, for example, Jesus is back in vogue.[1] So it should not surprise us that Christology is on the resurgence. Even classic studies on Jesus are gaining new lease on life through

---

[1] John Stott, *The Incomparable Christ* (Downers Grove, IL: InterVarsity, 2001); Tim LaHaye, *Jesus: Who is He?* (Sisters, OR: Multnomah, 1996); Lee Strobel, *The Case For Christ: A Journalist's Personal Investigation of the Evidence for Jesus* (Grand Rapids: Zondervan, 1998); idem, *The Case For the Real Jesus: A Journalist Investigates Current Attacks on the Identity of Christ* (Grand Rapids: Zondervan, 2007); Stuart Olyott, *Jesus is Both God and Man: What the Bible Teaches About the Person of Christ* (Darlington: Evangelical Press, 2000); Arthur Rowe, *The Essence of Jesus* (Edison, NJ: Chartwell, 2006); Gregg R. Allison, *Jesusology: Understanding What You Believe About Jesus and Why* (Nashville: Broadman & Holman, 2005); Joel McDurmon, *Manifested in the Flesh: How the Evidence of Jesus Refutes Modern Mystics and Skeptics* (Powder Springs, GA: American Vision, 2007); Bart D. Ehrman, *How Jesus Became God: The Exaltation of a Jewish Preacher From Galilee* (New York: HarperCollins, 2014), and note the response volume released at the same time: Michael F. Bird, Craig A. Evans, Simon J. Gathercole, et al, eds., *How God Became Jesus: The Real Origins of Belief in Jesus' Divine Nature* (Grand Rapids: Zondervan, 2014); Gerald O'Collins, *Christology: A Biblical, Historical, and Systematic Study of Jesus*, 2d. ed. (Oxford: Oxford University Press, 2009 [1995]); Hans Schwarz, *Christology* (Grand Rapids: Eerdmans, 1998); Larry Hurtado, *Lord Jesus Christ: Devotion to Jesus in Earliest Christianity* (Grand Rapids: Eerdmans, 2003); idem, *How on Earth Did Jesus Become God? Historical Questions about Earliest Devotion to Jesus* (Grand Rapids: Eerdmans, 2005); Michael J. McClymond, *Familiar Stranger: An Introduction to Jesus of Nazareth* (Grand Rapids: Eerdmans, 2004); Stephen R. Holmes & Murray A Rae, eds, *The Person of Christ* (London: T & T Clark, 2005); Joerg Rieger, *Christ and Empire: From Paul to Postcolonial Times* (Minneapolis: Fortress, 2007); Andreas Schuele & Günther Thomas, eds, *Who is Jesus Christ for Us Today: Pathways to Contemporary Christology* (Louisville: Westminster John Knox, 2009); Anna Marmodoro & Jonathan Hill, eds, *The Metaphysics of the Incarnation* (New York: Oxford, 2011); Edward T. Oakes, *Infinity Dwindled to Infancy: A Catholic and Evangelical Christology* (Grand Rapids: Eerdmans, 2011); Oliver D. Crisp & Fred Sanders, eds, *Christology Ancient and Modern: Explorations in Constructive Dogmatics* (Grand Rapids: Zondervan, 2013).

reissues.[2] These and several newer publications show that incarnation theology is crucial, vibrant, and contemporary, certainly worthy of current reflection. Among the plethora of publications on Christology, the following works are particularly noteworthy.[3]

---

[2] For example, John Martin Creed, *The Divinity of Jesus Christ* (New York: Cambridge, 2011 [1938]) Also, see I. Howard Marshall, *I Believe in the Historical Jesus* (Iowa Falls, IA: World Bible, 2002), was originally released in 1977; and James Stalker, *Studies on the Person of Christ* (Chattanooga: AMG, 1995), includes the three texts, *The Life of Christ*; *Imago Christi*; and *The Teaching of Jesus Concerning Himself* written in the 1890s.

[3] Tyron L. Inbody, *The Many Faces of Christology* (Nashville: Abingdon, 2002). Inbody covers historical Jesus research and adds chapters on various contemporary approaches to Christology. I am not in agreement with his pluralist perspective, but his work needs to be noted. Other important works include, Peter C. Hodgson, *Jesus—Word and presence: An Essay in Christology* (Minneapolis: Fortress, 1971, 2007); Stephen T. Davis, ed., *Encountering Jesus: A Debate on Christology* (Atlanta: John Know, 1988); David H. Jensen, *In the Company of Others: A Dialogical Christology* (Cleveland, OH: The Pilgrim's Press, 2001); David Peterson, ed., *The Word Became Flesh: Evangelicals and the Incarnation* (Carlisle: Paternoster, 2003); Clive Marsh, *Christ in Focus: Radical Christocentrism in Christian Theology* (London: SCM, 2005); Paul D. Molnar, *Incarnation and Resurrection* (Grand Rapids: Eerdmans, 2007); Edwin Chr. Van Driel, *Incarnation Anyway: Arguments for Supralapsarian Christology* (New York: Oxford University Press, 2008); F. LeRon Schults, *Christology and Science* (Grand Rapids: Eerdmans, 2008). See my review of Shults (*JETS* 54 [2011], 877-79); Richard Swinburne, *Was Jesus God?* (New York: Oxford University Press, 2008); F. LeRon Shults & Brent Waters, eds., *Christology and Ethics* (Grand Rapids: Eerdmans, 2010); and Christopher W. Morgan & Robert A. Peterson, *The Deity of Christ* in Christopher W. Morgan & Robert A. Peterson, eds., *Theology in Community* (Wheaton, IL: Crossway, 2011). Impressive books have appeared from the pen of Oliver Crisp. See his *Divinity and Humanity: The Incarnation Reconsidered* (New York: Cambridge University Press, 2007); idem, *God Incarnate: Explorations in Christology* (London: T & T Clark, 2009). Also see Velli-Matti Kärkkäinen, *Christology: A Global Introduction. An Ecumenical, International, and Contextual Perspective* (Grand Rapids: Baker, 2003); and Alan Spence, *Christology: A Guide for the Perplexed* (Edinburgh: T and T Clark, 2008). Kärkkäinen's text contains shorter chapters and therefore covers a lot more ground than Inbody's. This is a truly ecumenical work. Yet it strengths lie in its avowed christocentricity of theological discourse, and its grounding in Trinitarianism. A comprehensive attempt is seen in Colin J. Greene, *Christology in Cultural Perspective: Marking out Horizons* (Grand Rapids: Eerdmans, 2004) and Edward T. Oakes, *Infinity Dwindled to Infancy: A Catholic Evangelical Christology* (Grand Rapids: Eerdmans, 2012). The future in Christological work lies in dialog with other faiths, Kärkkäinen suggests. Helpful treatments of this engagement with our postmodern world are found in Christopher Wright, *The Uniqueness of Jesus* (London: Monarch, 2001); Sun Wook Chung, ed, *Christ the One and Only: A Global Affirmation of the Uniqueness of Jesus Christ* (Grand Rapids: Baker, 2005); and the superb work by Todd L. Miles, *A God of Many Understandings: The Gospel and a Theology of Religions* (Nashville: Broadman & Holman, 2010). On the biblical material, see Frank J. Matera, *New Testament Christology* (Louisville: Westminster John Knox, 1999); Ben Witherington III, *The Many Faces of the Christ: The Christologies of the New Testament and Beyond* (New York: Crossroad/Herder, 1998); and especially Gordon D. Fee, *Pauline Christology: An Exegetical-Theological Study* (Peabody, MA: Hendrickson, 2007), which, in my opinion is a stand-out contribution, and has given his

Thousands of years since the time of Solomon the wise, his words about the making of many books, seem to have been spoken of our day rather than his own.[4] Indeed, in *The Life of Jesus*, author David Holdaway cites the editor of *World Christian Encyclopedia*, David Barrett, as saying: "The total number of book titles on Jesus in the world's libraries is an amazing 65,571 with 53,094 having Jesus in the title. Last year alone there were 1,500 new titles on Jesus."[5] Scot McKnight speaks of his own budding collection of works written on Jesus in the modern era alone filling two large bookcases from floor to ceiling.[6] He has since produced a special study of Jesus.[7] This fact of an ever increasing wealth of material on Jesus in and of itself surely justifies the humble words of even an able scholar such as David Wells: "I marvel now at the ease with which I accepted the invitation to write this volume [*The Person of Christ*]. I should have known better. I rapidly discovered myself sinking–at times irretrievably so–in the quagmire of scholarly discussion."[8] Thankfully, Wells persevered and produced one of the best volumes on this grandest of all subjects from an evangelical pen.[9] Before we take a closer look at evangelical contributions to Chris-

---

usual deep and careful exegetical studies in this tremendous resource. Matera's balance of a healthy tension between unity and diversity is well presented. However, I am inclined to see a greater ability inherent in the text of the New Testament for conceptual unity than does Matera. Similarly to Fee, I affirm a consistent unity without any irreconcilable differences among the various writers of the New Testament books. On this score Witherington is closer to Fee than Matera. The theological work of John Macquarrie has turned the thoughts of many in the academic world back to fundamental Christological issues. See *Jesus Christ in Modern Thought* (London: SCM; Philadelphia: Trinity Press International, 1990); and idem, *Christology Revisited* (Harrisburg, PA: Trinity Press International, 1998). Recently a thorough examination of Macquarrie's own proposal has come from Vernon L. Purdy, *The Christology of John Macquarrie* (New York: Peter Lang, 2009).

[4] Eccl 12:12.

[5] David Holdaway, *The Life of Jesus* (Kent: Sovereign World, 1997), 16. One may wonder what that number would be today! In this same year a publication emerged from a conference held at the Roehampton Institute London in 1996. The work contains a vast array of writers from different continents. Jesus is appealing to those outside the Christian faith it seems. See Stanley E. Porter, Michael A. Hayes, and David Tombs, eds. *Images of Christ: Ancient and Modern* (Sheffield: Sheffield Academic Press, 1997). And more recently from another academic symposium has come: James H. Charlesworth and Petr Pokorny, eds. *Jesus Research: An International Perspective* (Grand Rapids: Eerdmans, 2009).

[6] See Scot McKnight, "Who is Jesus? An Introduction to Jesus Studies," in *Jesus Under Fire: Modern Scholarship Reinvents the Historical Jesus*, ed. Michael J. Wilkins and J.P. Moreland (Grand Rapids: Zondervan, 1995), 52. An indispensable guide through this vast terrain is found in Craig Evans, *Jesus* (Grand Rapids: Baker, 1992). I suspect McKnight has a few more bookshelves today!

[7] Scot McKnight, *The Story of the Christ* (Grand Rapids: Baker, 2006).

[8] David F. Wells, *The Person of Christ: A Biblical and Historical Analysis of the Incarnation* (Alliance OH: Bible Scholar, 1992), vii.

[9] The most impressive works on Christology by evangelicals, in addition to David Wells, include G.C. Berkouwer, *Studies in Dogmatics: The Person of Christ*, trans. John

tology, there is need for a selective survey of scholarly research as a context for our more narrow focus.

B. The Modern Era

Subsequent chapters will survey the Patristic era to John of Damascus, and examine the Reformation contribution, especially looking at John Calvin. With this in mind it seems proper to start this highly selective perusal with the modern era, noting as is commonly stated, [the] "Enlightenment changed everything."[10] The period of the Enlightenment is broadly speaking that era between 1648, the end of the Thirty Years War (1618-1648), which has been characterized as the most devastating of the wars of religion, and Kant's famous work *Critique of Pure Reason*, published in 1781.[11] Although this is the time frame

---

Vriend (Grand Rapids: Eerdmans, 1955); John Blanchard, *Meet the Real Jesus* (Darlington, England: Evangelical Press, 1989); Donald G. Bloesch, *Jesus Christ: Savior and Lord* (Downers Grove, IL: InterVarsity, 1997); Robert M. Bowman, Jr. & J. Ed Komoszewski, *Putting Jesus in His Place: The Case for the Deity of Christ* (Grand Rapids: Kregel, 2007); Gordon H. Clark, *The Incarnation* (Jefferson, MD: The Trinity Foundation, 1988); Millard J. Erickson, *The Word Became Flesh: A Contemporary Incarnational Christology* (Grand Rapids: Baker, 1991); Michael S. Horton, *Lord and Servant: A Covenant Christology* (Louisville: Westminster John Knox, 2005); Donald Macleod, *The Person of Christ* (Downers Grove, IL: InterVarsity, 1998); Joel McDurmon, *Manifest in the Flesh: How the Evidence of Jesus Refutes Modern Mystics and Skeptics* (Powder Springs, GA: American Vision, 2007); Robert L. Reymond, *Jesus Divine Messiah: The New and Old Testament Witness* (Fearn: Christian Focus, 2003); Alan Spence, *Christology: A Guide for the Perplexed* (New York: Continuum/T & T Clark, 2008); and Bernard Ramm, *An Evangelical Christology: Ecumenic and Historical* (Nashville: Thomas Nelson, 1985). Also, see the helpful essay, which, chronicles several modern evangelical contributions to Christology, by Douglas Jacobsen and Frederick Schmidt, "Behind Orthodoxy and Beyond It: Recent Developments in Evangelical Christology," *SJT* 45 (1992): 515-42.

[10] A most helpful work on this era is Peter Gay, *The Enlightenment: An Interpretation. The Rise of Paganism* (New York: Alfred A. Knopf, 1966). For an insightful look at how the modern emphases of the Enlightenment have affected the theological enterprise, one will do no better than David F. Wells, *No Place for Truth Or Whatever Happened to Evangelical Theology?* (Grand Rapids: Eerdmans, 1993); and idem, *God in the Wasteland: The Reality of Truth in a World of Fading Dreams* (Grand Rapids: Eerdmans, 1994). There is also a helpful collection of essays in Philip Sampson, Vinay Samuel, and Chris Sugden, eds., *Faith and Modernity* (Oxford: Regnum, 1994). For a different perspective, see Calvin O. Schrag, "Rationality between Modernity and Postmodernity," in *Life-World and Politics Between Modernity and Postmodernity: Essays in Honor of Fred R. Dallmayr*, ed. Stephen K. White (Notre Dame, IN: University of Notre Dame Press, 1989), 81-106.

[11] "Perhaps the enlightenment is best understood . . . ," notes Davies, "by reference to the darkness which this 'light of reason' was trying to illuminate. The darkness was provided, not by religion as such, which was taken by the *philosophes* to be filling a basic human need, but by all the unthinking, irrational, dogmatic attitudes with which European Christianity had become encrusted" (Norman Davies, *Europe: A History* [Oxford: Oxford University Press, 1996], 596). For all aspects of this era of "Enlightenment," Davies' chapter, "Lumen: Enlightenment and Absolutism," is very helpful (Da-

usually associated with the modern era, seeds for it lay in an earlier period. This flowering age from twelfth through the fifteenth century is known as "Rebirth" or *Renaissance*.[12] With a reappraisal of classical texts based on the *ad fontes* cry, a recovery of the Greek and Roman heritage spawned a need for renewal in literature, politics, and art.[13]

Though aspects of autonomy were evident during the Renaissance, it is with the Enlightenment proper that we find some lasting changes that are still with us. A basic description of modernity is thus: the age where man replaces God in the center of the story.[14] This is due to the following factors. Religious fanaticism led to bloodshed, so doctrinal matters were deemed the culprit. Philosophical certainty of knowledge was supposedly achieved by René Descartes by first doubting everything, except the fact that he was himself doubting.[15] This skeptical approach would lead to the undermining of scriptural authority. Finally, with Immanuel Kant, the thinking subject was placed in center stage and a "Copernican Revolution" ensued. With the emerging certainties of the scientific method and the philosophical contributions of men like John Locke, George Berkeley, and David Hume, man emerged as the measure of all things. Alexander Pope's pithy precept said it all: "Know then thyself, presume not God to scan, The proper study of mankind is Man."[16]

The quest for certainty, the desire for harmony, and the assumption of autonomy would lead to the progress of humanity as man came of age. It is no surprise therefore that the doctrine of Christ as developed in the early centuries of the church age would fall on hard times during this secular humanistic period.

---

vies, *Europe*, 577-674). For a well-written succinct presentation of the beginnings of the modern era, see Stanley J. Grenz, *A Primer on Postmodernism* (Grand Rapids: Eerdmans, 1996), 57-81. For an attempt to rehabilitate the Enlightenment project's main thesis of free and creative enquiry and wed it to distinctively Christian concerns, see John Thornhill, *Modernity: Christianity's Estranged Child* (Grand Rapids: Eerdmans, 2000).

[12] See Herbert J. Muller, *Freedom in the Western World: From the Dark Ages to the Rise of Democracy* (New York: Harper and Row, 1963), 105-50. Colish is bold to suggest that the Medeival traditions from the fifth century on are the real contributors of genius, and laid the ground for the West's intellectual tradition as opposed to the Greek, Roman, and Christian heritage. See Marcia L. Colish, *Medieval Foundations of the Western Intellectual Tradition 400-1400* (New Haven: Yale University Press, 1997). For a lucid introduction to the Renaissance see Paul Johnson, *The Renaissance: A Short History* (New York: Modern Library, 2002).

[13] Bruce L. Shelley, *Church History in Plain Language* (Nashville: Thomas Nelson, 1995), 312; and Johnson, *Renaissance*, 25-165. Excellent resources for study are found in the double volume work, Lewis W. Spitz, *The Renaissance and Reformation Movements* II Volumes, rev. ed. (St. Louis: Concordia, 1987, [1971]).

[14] William C. Placher, *A History of Christian Theology: An Introduction* (Philadelphia: Westminster, 1983), 238.

[15] Grenz, *Primer on Postmodernism*, 63-67.

[16] Davies, *Europe*, 597.

B.1. Introduction

The early testimony to Jesus Christ found in the New Testament documents was basically uniform in its avowal that a consistent singular Christ emerged from its pages. Of course, there were debates about what this Christ "looked like," but the essential belief that an authoritative Scripture presented a single Christ was in-tact. The basis for this consensus was an axiomatic conviction that God revealed his word in the Bible and this revelation was the highest court of appeal. Moreover, as the Bible was believed to be a record of God's very thoughts, there could be no contradiction or internal inconsistency within this divinely inspired record. That is precisely what was challenged in the Enlightenment.[17] In place of revelation, reason became supreme. As Brown has said:

> Although he was not one of its early pioneers, the critical Königsberg philosopher Immanuel Kant (1724-1804) provides us with the best definition of the Enlightenment, one particularly appropriate for the understanding of its influence on Christian thought . . . . "Enlightenment," he writes, "is the emergence of man from his self-inflicted immaturity. Immaturity is the inability to use one's reason without making use of the guidance of another." Inasmuch as Christianity is by its very nature a religion of divine revelation, one that presupposes that human reason needs guidance and in fact is guided by God's revelation, it is apparent that Kant's principle is totally incompatible with Christianity as it had been understood.[18]

Kant cried out in his monumental work, "An Answer to the Question: What is Enlightenment?" betraying his belief in inherent abilities of humanity: "The motto of enlightenment is therefore: *Sapere aude* (Dare to be wise)! Have the courage to use your *own* understanding."[19]

B.2. From Revelation to Reason

Revelation was now subject to the observing dissection of the rational mind.[20] The new focus was not the mere use of reason, but the autonomy of reason.[21]

---

[17] A Helpful volume on this era is James M. Byrne, *Religion and the Enlightenment: From Descartes to Kant* (Louisville, KY: Westminster John Knox, 1997).

[18] Harold O.J. Brown, *Heresies: Heresy and Orthodoxy in the History of the Church* (Peabody, MA: Hendrickson, 1998), 397. For an introduction to some of the most important German writers of this era in their own words, see Edward T. Oakes, ed., *German Essays on Religion* (New York: Continuum, 1994), 1-84.

[19] Cited in Thornhill, *Modernity*, 9. A good introductory text on Kant is C.D. Broad, *Kant: An Introduction.* ed. C. Lewy (Cambridge: Cambridge University Press, 1978). To Read Kant himself one may begin with Immanuel Kant, *The Metaphysics of Morals*, ed. Mary Gregor, Intro. Roger J. Sullivan (Cambridge: Cambridge University Press, 1996).

[20] See the helpful analysis of this rational challenge to traditional Christianity and its aftermath in Alasdair I.C. Heron, *A Century of Protestant Theology* (Philadelphia: Westminster, 1980); Hendrikus Berkhof, *Two Hundred Years of Theology: A Report of*

With the newly established foundation of humanity's rational capabilities as the highest authority, the attack on miracles began, and as a result the New Testament picture of Jesus became very blurry indeed. "After Reason had accomplished its work of effacing all higher glory from the image of the Redeemer," Dorner asserts, "it seated itself on the throne which the faith of the Church had assigned to Christ as King, and placed the degraded one in the circle of sinners, to the end that it might pronounce over again His sentence of condemnation."[22] As Mackintosh shows, the significance of the person of Christ was almost non-existent within the Enlightenment project. "The background of the modern movement," writes Mackintosh, "is furnished by the uninspired Rationalism of the *Aufklärung*. [Johann Friedrich] Röhr, a characteristic exponent of its temper, declares that Christology has no place in the system of Christian doctrine, since we are concerned not with a religion for which Jesus is object of faith, but only with that which Jesus taught."[23] Specific problems arose within this new framework of conducting biblical studies.[24] Particularly, the issue of the historicity of the factual claims of the source material of the New Testament was a major matter in dispute.[25]

---

a Personal Journey (Grand Rapids: Eerdmans, 1989); and Gerald R. Cragg, *The Church and the Age of Reason 1648-1789* (Aylesbury: Penguin, 1960; reprint 1974). For a helpful survey with Christology at the forefront, see Oliver J.D. Greene, *Christology in Cultural Perspective: Marking out the Horizons* (Grand Rapids: Eerdmans, 2003), 74-167.

[21] Grenz, *Primer on Postmodernism*, 69.

[22] J.A. Dorner, *History of the Development of the Doctrine of the Person of Christ*, div. 2, vol. 3 (Edinburgh: T & T Clark, 1878), 29.

[23] H.R. Mackintosh, *The Doctrine of the Person of Jesus Christ* (New York: Charles Scribner's, 1912), 249.

[24] A valuable survey of the various writers that make up this crucial era of scriptural interpretation is found in Gerald Bray, *Biblical Interpretation: Past and Present* (Downers Grove, IL: InterVarsity, 1996), 321-75. Also helpful is Donald K. McKim, ed., *Historical Handbook of Major Bible Interpreters* (Downers Grove, IL: InterVarsity, 1998), esp., 257-80, which is the historiographical essay by G.T. Sheppard, "Biblical Interpretation in the Eighteenth and Nineteenth Centuries." The most helpful treatment of historical insight to the leading Continental thinkers who wrote specifically about Jesus and his place in Christianity is Colin Brown, *Jesus in European Protestant Thought 1778-1860* (Durham, NC: Labyrinth, 1985; reprint, Grand Rapids: Baker, 1988).

[25] See Millard J. Erickson, *The Word Became Flesh: A Contemporary Incarnational Christology* (Grand Rapids: Baker, 1991), 89-110, esp. 102-07, where he narrows the issue to biblical theology. In summarizing the contribution of Norman Perrin, Erickson discusses three types of knowledge. These are (1) Historical Knowledge, basic and general where the knowledge of Jesus is akin to knowledge of Socrates. This is *Historie*, as Martin Kahler or Rudolf Bultmann would explain it; (2) Historic Knowledge, this is different as it has direct influence on the present. This is when historical knowledge, under certain conditions, may come to have contemporary significance; and finally (3) Faith Knowledge, which is itself trans-historical. For example, knowledge of Jesus death moves beyond the bare facts of Jesus dying with confidence in God, to suggesting specific meanings for the work of God in Christ, such as Jesus bore my sins on the cross. This latter reason is not accessible to the historian, and thus requires faith. Also see Marshall, *I Believe in the Historical Jesus*, 27-147, esp., 43-52.

B.3. Modern Christologies

John Macquarrie surveys three types of Christologies that were prominent at the height of this modern era. They are: (1) Rationalist, (2) Humanist, and (3) Idealist Christologies. For our purposes we will briefly review the first two types.[26] This selection is so for Friedrich D.E. Schleiermacher (humanist Christology), rather than Georg W.F. Hegel[27] (idealist Christology), helps transition to the contemporary scene with the emerging emphasis on experience as chronicled here.

B.3.1. Immanuel Kant

Kant is singled out to illustrate the rationalist approach. Within this religion of rationality, one could suppose that there was no place for Jesus at all.[28] Yet the significance of Jesus, which the gospel records faintly reveal, according to Kant, becomes the "archetype of a life well pleasing to God."[29] Macquarrie suggests that this bare concept of an ideal humanity without concrete personal instantiation really challenges the dogma of this school, which claims that the accidental truths of history can never serve to prove the necessary truths of reason. It appears, Macquarrie believes, that Kant must have the historical Jesus, who will appeal to the imagination, in order to spur one on to emulation so that the "ought" of obligation is realized in practice in a life pleasing to God.[30] Otherwise, there is no one to imitate. However, in Kant's overall approach, the historical personage of Jesus is largely irrelevant. Kant even uses imagery of descent language–echoing John's Gospel–in speaking of the archetype having "come down to us from heaven and [having] assumed our humanity."[31] Yet it must be borne in mind that a radical difference in meaning is assigned to all of these familiar theological terms such as "revelation," "Christ," and even "incarnation." For Kant, revelation is really natural–this worldly, and can be appropriated by all or anyone with human faculties. Christ is merely the archetype that antecedes and in some sense renders unnecessary the historical person of

---

[26] Beyond Macquarrie's analysis of "ideology," one is well advised to see the very interesting article by Nikolaus Lobkowicz, "Christ and the Ideologies," in *Crisis in Christology: Essays in Quest of Resolution*, ed. William R. Farmer (Livonia, MI: Dove, 1995), 93-113. I appreciate this methodology of beginning with the conception of the God-Man by Lobkowicz (this is reminiscent of Donald Bloesch), and the clear warning not to let our Christology result in mere ideology; it is a person we follow, not a dogma. Also helpful on this need for a worshipful attitude throughout our Christologizing is Thomas G. Weinandy, *Does God Change? The Word's Becoming in the Incarnation* (Still River, MA: St. Bede's Publications), xi-xviii. Nonetheless, a correct understanding of the person of Christ is still essential.

[27] For Hegel's Christology, see James Yerkes, *The Christology of Hegel* (New York: State University of New York Press, 1983).

[28] Macquarrie, *Jesus Christ in Modern Thought*, 181. Also see Mackintosh, *The Doctrine of the Person of Jesus Christ*, 249-50; and Dorner, *History*, 30-50.

[29] Macquarrie, *Jesus Christ in Modern Thought*, 181.

[30] Macquarrie, *Jesus Christ in Modern Thought*, 182.

[31] Macquarrie, *Jesus Christ in Modern Thought*, 184.

Jesus and thus lends a docetic strain to his view, which directly contradicts the earlier observations of his thought concerning the avowal and need for the historical Jesus. And finally, in this schema incarnation is not metaphysical but moral, resulting in a degree Christology. Jesus differs from all other men not in kind, but in degree.

B.3.2. Friedrich D.E. Schleiermacher

Humanistic Christology is illustrated by Schleiermacher in Macquarrie's survey.[32] Schleiermacher was truly a child of his times. He was born on November 21, 1768. He lived in an age when the Enlightenment flourished, yet at the same time an emerging dissatisfaction with the perceived cold rationalism began to bloom in the Romantic movement. Berkhof's comment regarding Schleiermacher's lifelong work is noteworthy. He says, "Like Kant and [Johann Gottlieb] Fichte, so also Friedrich Daniel Ernst Schleiermacher (1768-1834) started his journey in theology. Unlike them . . . he always remained a theologian."[33] No doubt, Schleiermacher's pioneering spirit as a theologian will keep his memory alive. When in 1821 he published the first edition of *The Christian Faith*, he wanted to present a system of theology which would be a "Church Dogmatics." Schleiermacher states, "We must begin with a conception of the Christian Church, in order to define in accordance therewith what Dogmatics should be and should do within that Church."[34] In this systematic theology, like his previous work, *On Religion: Speeches to its Cultured Despisers*, Schleiermacher sought to show that the religious feeling of utter dependence was a characteristic of all authentic self-consciousness. Moreover, in his theology text, he wants to move away from rationality and morality. To these two ways, he puts his own approach in clear opposition as he declares, "As regards Feeling . . . [which] simply takes place in the subject, and thus, since it belongs altogether to the realm of receptivity, it is an abiding-in-self; and in this sense it stands in antithesis to the other two–Knowing and Doing."[35] As Sell notes, "Though not entirely divorced from being and doing, feeling is distinguished from them; certainly it is not derived from them–it is immediate."[36] Perceptively, Grenz and Olson issue a warning so as not to confuse Schleiermacher's understanding of this "Feeling" of absolute dependence with mere emotion. They assert, "The German original, *Gefühl*, does not connote a sensation, as its English rendering [feeling] would suggest; but a deep sense of awareness." Grenz

---

[32] Macquarrie, *Jesus Christ in Modern Thought*, 192-211. Also see Mackintosh, *The Doctrine of the Person of Jesus Christ*, 250-56; and Dorner, *History*, 174-213.

[33] Berkhof, *Two Hundred Years of Theology*, 30.

[34] Friedrich D.E. Schleiermacher, *The Christian Faith*, English transl. of 2nd German ed., ed. and trans. H.R. Mackintosh and J.S. Stewart (Edinburgh: T & T Clark, 1989), 3. Schleiermacher's thesis § 2 claims, "Dogmatics is a theological discipline, and thus pertains solely to the Christian Church. . . ." (*The Christian Faith*, 3).

[35] Schleiermacher, *The Christian Faith*, 8.

[36] Alan P.F. Sell, *Theology in Turmoil: The Roots, Course and Significance of the Conservative–Liberal Debate in Modern Theology* (Grand Rapids: Baker, 1986), 16.

and Olson continue, "'Feeling,' therefore, lies on the pre-reflection plane of consciousness–that is beneath and before explicit thought or sensation."[37]

Schleiermacher's whole endeavor can be summed up from his proposition § 15, where he claims: "Christian doctrines are accounts of the Christian religious affections set forth in speech."[38] Hence, this means that Christian testimony about God is really attestation about our own experience or feeling of total dependence. In Christology, the importance of Jesus Christ is not the metaphysical constitution of his person, it is rather that in Jesus the "feeling" of dependence reaches its zenith. Schleiermacher undertakes his Christological development firmly rooted in this world of human experience, and it is a radical "Christology from below" that we encounter in his thought.[39] As Macquarrie reminds us: "[Schleiermacher] explicitly rejected as illogical and incoherent the traditional two-nature christology."[40] In the place of traditional teachings and conceptions, Schleiermacher issues forth what Macquarrie calls, "a conscientious . . . [attempt] to say in his own words what classical christology had said." That is summed up in his proposition § 94, which states, "The Redeemer, then, is like all men in virtue of the identity of human nature, but distinguished from them all by constant potency of His God-consciousness, which has a veritable existence of God in Him."[41] Christ thus becomes the ideal Christian.[42]

B.3.3. Summary

Both Schleiermacher and Kant leave us with a mere human Jesus. This "reduced" Christology has become virtually axiomatic in modern mainstream Christology.[43] And so out of the matrix of the enlightenment age the Chalcedonian two nature doctrine of Jesus Christ has been jettisoned. A conception of Jesus Christ's omnipresence is therefore impossible given the intellectual assumptions of the modern age.

---

[37] Stanley J. Grenz and Roger E. Olson, *20th Century Theology: God and the World in a Transitional Age* (Downers Grove, IL: InterVarsity, 1992), 44.

[38] Schleiermacher, *The Christian Faith*, 76.

[39] A nice introductory text to Schleiermacher's thought on Jesus Christ is Catherine L. Kelsey, *Thinking About Christ with Schleiermacher* (Louisville, KY: Westminster John Knox, 2003).

[40] Macquarrie, *Jesus Christ in Modern Thought*, 192.

[41] Schleiermacher, *The Christian Faith*, 385.

[42] Schleiermacher, *The Christian Faith*, 385-89.

[43] For example, the emergence of the Jesus Seminar and its portrayal of Jesus is clearly reminiscent of the merely human Jesus which emerged from the Enlightenment era. See how two of the most famous fellows of the Jesus Seminar, Marcus Borg and John Dominic Crossan, have taken their views to the public, in dialog with scholars of more conservative stance, in the following volumes: Paul Copan, ed., *Will the Real Jesus Please Stand up? A Debate between William Lane Craig and John Dominic Crossan Moderated by William F. Buckley, Jr.* (Grand Rapids: Baker, 1998); and Marcus J. Borg and N.T. Wright, *The Meaning of Jesus: Two Visions* (San Francisco: HarperCollins, 1999).

B.4. From Doctrine to Experience & Modern Critical Methods

With this emerging worldview Scripture was perceived as a merely human work and radical re-reading of the Bible commenced with a strong anti-supernatural bias and use of the new hermeneutic of suspicion.[44] Academic theology has since been dominated by the liberal wing and the expected foundation as a norm for theology is no longer a supreme revelation but the experience of a believing community.[45] This is precisely how the "History-of-Religions" school dominated the scene of biblical studies as exemplified in figures such as William Wrede.[46] After the abandonment of doctrine as the goal for study in Scripture, the "historical" approach, utilizing the critical methodologies encompassed in this enterprise, presented in its findings a plethora of conflicting and contradictory "experiences" in the biblical data. New Testament scholars have presented their views and the general conclusion, which has been widely accepted, is that the proclaimer (Jesus) had become the proclaimed (Christ), as made eminently famous by Rudolf Bultmann.[47]

Bultmann's approach was directly opposed by Roman Catholic scholar William Most. He charts a way between twentieth century Fundamentalist bibliology and modern existentialist impositions on the Bible, advocating that we can trust the documents of the New Testament to give us reliable historical data about Jesus.[48] Moreover, Reginald Fuller also countered much of Bultmann's theology, but from within protestant ranks.[49] Fuller was prepared to allow for a self-understanding of Jesus that contained a messianic content, even if couched,

---

[44] See Gerhard Hasel, *New Testament Theology: Basic Issues in the Current Debate* (Grand Rapids: Eerdmans, 1978; reprint, 1993), 19-28.

[45] For a contemporary approach in this vein, see the now classic volume, Peter C. Hodgson and Robert H. King, eds., *Christian Theology: An Introduction to Its Traditions and Tasks*, updated ed. (Minneapolis: Fortress, 1982, 1994). For an evangelical theology that quite successfully accomplishes this, see Stanley J. Grenz, *Theology for the Community of God* (Nashville: Broadman and Holman, 1994).

[46] See Stephen Neill and Tom Wright, *The Interpretation of the New Testament 1861-1986*, 2nd ed. (Oxford: Oxford University Press, 1960; reprint, 1988), 266-68; and Hasel, *New Testament Theology*, 46-51. For a helpful survey of the "history of religions" approach to the life of Jesus, see John K. Riches, *A Century of New Testament Study* (Valley Forge, PA: Trinity Press International, 1993), 14-30. A full refutation of Wrede's approach is found in Geerhardus Vos, *The Self-Disclosure of Jesus: The Modern Debate about the Messianic Consciousness* (George H. Doran, 1926, reprint, Phillipsburg, NJ: P & R, 2002).

[47] Peter Balla, *Challenges to New Testament Theology: An Attempt to Justify the Enterprise* (Tübingen: Mohr Siebeck, 1997; reprint, Peabody, MA: Hendrickson, 1998), 155. An attempt to regain insights from Bultmann and to rehabilitate his Christology can be found in James F. Kay, *Christus Praesens: A Reconsideration of Rudolf Bultmann's Christology* (Grand Rapids: Eerdmans, 1994).

[48] William G. Most, *The Consciousness of Christ* (Front Royal, VA: Christendom College Press, 1980).

[49] See Reginald H. Fuller, *Christ and Christianity: Studies in the Formation of Christology* (Valley Forge, PA: Trinity Press International, 1994).

The Omnipresence of Jesus Christ

in his opinion, in non-messianic expressions.[50] Thus the radical disjunction between pre and post-resurrection Jesus was lessened to some degree.[51] Only by moving in this direction of seeing greater continuity between the Jesus of history and the Christ of faith can one ever attain to the heights of the classical doctrine of Christology as evidenced at Chalcedon. Still, it was no longer fashionable to use John's gospel to try to understand who Jesus was; indeed the New Testament as a whole was not to be trusted.[52] After all, it was written by people with a serious theological and apologetic agenda. Form Criticism sought the oral traditions behind the text, source criticism was bent on study of other documents, such as Q, and redaction criticism claimed that the drafters of the New Testament writings used a "cut and paste" method to present their own beliefs.[53] This radical disjunction between the original message of the historical Jesus, and the dogmatic formulations of the Catholic church culminating in the

---

[50] Fuller, *Christ and Christianity*, 44-45.

[51] A helpful work which reaches very conservative conclusions despite a radical higher critical methodology is found in J.C. O'Neill, *Who Did Jesus Think He Was?* (Leiden: E.J. Brill, 1995). Apart from some kenotic concerns, and other "red flags" such as the view that certain teachings in John's gospel were given without a steadfast knowledge of Jesus' resurrection, indeed, that John's gospel contains much Jewish theology which preceded Jesus' birth, this is a fine treatment which affirms that Jesus knew himself to be the Son of God. This is a rare book from within the ranks of New Testament scholarship.

[52] E. Earl Ellis, "Background and Christology of John's Gospel: Selected Motifs," in *Christ and the Future in New Testament History* (Leiden: Brill, 2001), 70-88, shows how the same theology is found in both the Synoptic Gospels and John. Several of Ellis' essays in this text are helpful for understanding the New Testament portrayal of Jesus Christ. For an excellent attempt at developing a Christological doctrine based on the constraints of the text of the New Testament, yet grounded in faith, see Robert Morgan, "The Historical Jesus and the Theology of the New Testament," in *The Glory of Christ in the New Testament: Studies in Christology in Memory of George Bradford Caird*, ed. L.D. Hurst and N.T. Wright. (Oxford: Clarendon Press, 1987), 187-206.

[53] Evangelicals are divided on the value of the higher critical methods. A wide-section of evangelical scholars, some of whom have become world renowned in these fields of critical methodology, can be found in David Alan Black and David S. Dockery, eds., *New Testament Criticism and Interpretation* (Grand Rapids: Zondervan, 1991); and I. Howard Marshall, *The Origins of New Testament Christology* (Leicester: Apollos, 1993). See also Darrell L. Bock & Gregory J. Herrick, eds. *Jesus in Context: Background Readings for Gospel Study* (Grand Rapids: Baker Academic, 2005) Those challenging the use of the historical critical methodology include Eta Linnemann, *Historical Criticism of the Bible: Methodology or Ideology?* trans. Robert W. Yarbrough (Grand Rapids: Baker,1990); idem, *Is There a Synoptic Problem? Rethinking the Literary Dependence of the First Three Gospels*, trans. Robert W. Yarbrough (Grand Rapids: Baker, 1992); and Robert L. Thomas and F. David Farnell, eds., *The Jesus Crisis: The Inroads of Historical Criticism into Evangelical Scholarship* (Grand Rapids: Kregel, 1998). Helpful critique of the critical methodologies is found in Thomas C. Oden, *After Modernity. . . What?* (Grand Rapids: Zondervan, 1990), 109-20; and Reymond, *Jesus Divine Messiah*, 53-62.

proclamation of the Christ of faith, according to the critical scholars, put evangelicals on the defensive.[54]

B.5. Reactions to the Modern

In recent years entire denominations have felt the need to issue a statement on Christology. For example the Anglican community produced a volume containing a selection of articles by prominent churchmen.[55]

The conservative Wisconsin Evangelical Lutheran synod also produced a book with several essays, some of which challenge the widespread Reformed emphasis in Christology.[56] Moreover, some publications draw together contributors from different backgrounds, such as the interdenominational mix of articles reflecting on Christology, which resulted in a volume already cited in this chapter.[57] A gap in evangelical presentations on the life of Christ was admirably filled by a very helpful text by New Testament scholar Robert Stein.[58] Also

---

[54] The challenge from Modernity's perspective has been met by evangelicals. Examples of this engagement in broad categories include J. Gresham Machen, *Christianity and Liberalism* (Grand Rapids: Eerdmans, 1924; reprint 1974); and Nigel M. de S. Cameron, ed., *The Challenge of Evangelical Theology: Essays in Approach and Method* (Edinburgh: Rutherford House, 1987); on Christology specifically, one must digest the Bampton Lectures for 1866: Henry Parry Liddon, *The Divinity of Our Lord and Savior Jesus Christ: Eight Lectures Preached before the University of Oxford in the Year 1866*, 2nd ed. (New York: Scribner, Welford, 1868); and Warfield, *The Person and Work of Christ*.

[55] Donald Armstrong, ed., *Who Do You Say That I Am? Christology and the Church* (Grand Rapids: Eerdmans, 1999). The articles are written at an accessible level yet reveal the highest scholarship. Most important are the contributions of Richard Reid, who claims: "A biblical Christology is necessary because of the nature of the Christian faith. That faith is not based on an idea or an ideology. We are not talking about a "Christ principle." We are talking about a revelation from God which comes in and through historical events" (*Who Do You Say?*, 45); N.T. Wright, who distinguishes between self-involving language and self-referring language to show that there is an objective reality about which our discourse is conducted despite its reverential and worshipful attitude (*Who Do You Say?*, 66-67); and Alister McGrath, who writes an engaging historical essay showing that "the past illuminates the present by letting us see our own christological concerns and strategies in a much broader context" (*Who Do You Say?*, 90). Also noteworthy, dealing with theology generally, is the text by Peter Toon, *The End of Liberal Theology: Contemporary Challenges to Evangelical Theology* (Wheaton, IL: Crossway, 1995).

[56] Curtis A. Jahn, ed., *We Believe in Jesus Christ: Essays on Christology* (Milwaukee: Northwestern, 1999). Particularly significant essays in this volume, are Paul O Wendland, "Now that God is One of Us: A Study of the Communication of Attributes in the Person of Christ," and James R. Janke, "'We (Still) Do Not Have the Same Spirit': A Critique of Contemporary Reformed Christology and Its Impact on the Doctrine of the Lord's Supper."

[57] Farmer, *Crisis in Christology*.

[58] Robert H. Stein, *Jesus the Messiah: A Survey of the Life of Christ* (Downers Grove, IL: InterVarsity, 1996). On Christology in this text, see 141-54. Stein uses academic criticism and is a leading scholar for the Marcan priority thesis among Evangelicals. My own views on this issue are somewhat divergent from the Evangelical and wider aca-

in an anthology of evangelical voices, a defense of the traditional form of belief is presented on several fronts by New Testament scholars.[59]

Furthermore, a continuing dialogue on theological issues among Protestants and Greek Orthodox has focused on Trinitarian and Christological issues.[60] None of these contributions, however, have made evangelical voices and opinions more palatable to academic theology. Moreover, a marked absence of any focus on the attribute of omnipresence betrays the very need for an engagement with this issue. In very few instances have evangelicals obtained a hearing in broader scholarly circles concerning Christology in general. However, in *Semeia* 30 (1984): 3-235, several articles explored "Christology and Exegesis: New Approaches," as the title of the volume indicates. Grant Osborne and James Dunn were included among the scholars who wrote the essays. Osborne, "Christology and New Testament Hermeneutics," showed his familiarity with the broad spectrum of scholarship and concluded his article applauding insights from David Tracy, yet his words of faint hope that Christologies from above might still be drawn upon seem as an anti-climax. Dunn has not lacked criticism since the publication of his 1980 volume, *Christology in the Making*.[61] It seems that Dunn is not the best representative of traditional evangelical Chris-

---

demic community's "assured results of criticism." I hold to Matthean priority, and I believe the documents of the NT were composed much earlier than is generally supposed. See, for example, the following helpful works: Hajo Uden Meijboom, *A History and Critique of the Origin of the Marcan Hypothesis 1835-1866: A Contemporary Report Rediscovered*. Trans. John J. Kiwiet, ed. (Macon, GA: Mercer University Press, 1993); Henry Clarence Thiessen, *Introduction to the New Testament* (Grand Rapids: Eerdmans, 1943); John A.T. Robinson, *Redating the New Testament* (London: SCM, 1973); William R. Farmer, *The Synoptic Problem* (Dillsboro, NC: Western North Carolina Press, 1976); idem, *The Gospel of Jesus: The Pastoral Relevance of the Synoptic Problem* (Louisville, KY: Westminster John Knox, 1994); John Bernard Orchard, *A Synopsis of the Four Gospels in Greek: Arranged According to the Two-Gospel Hypothesis* (Edinburgh: T and T Clark, 1983); Eta Linnemann, *Is There a Synoptic Problem? Rethinking the Literary Dependence of the First Three Gospels*. Trans. Robert W. Yarborough (Grand Rapids: Baker, 1992); John Wenham, *Redating Matthew, Mark and Luke: A Fresh Assault on the Synoptic Problem* (Downers Grove, IL: InterVarsity, 1992); David Alan Black, *Why Four Gospels: The Historical Origins of the Gospels* (Grand Rapids: Kregel, 2001); and Robert Thomas, ed. *Three Views on the Origins of the Synoptic Gospels* (Grand Rapids: Kregel, 2002).

[59] Wilkins and Moreland, *Jesus under Fire*.

[60] See Thomas F. Torrance, ed., *The Incarnation: Ecumenical Studies in the Nicene-Constantinopolitan Creed* (Edinburgh: Handsel, 1981); and especially, *GOTR* 43 (1998): 221-480, which includes several articles on Trinity, Christology and Christological ecclesiology.

[61] See Dennis Johnson's review of Dunn, *Christology in the Making, WTJ* 44 (1982):164-69; and C.E.B. Cranfield, "Some Comments on Professor J.D.G. Dunn's *Christology in the Making* with Special Reference to the Evidence of the Epistle to the Romans," in *The Glory of Christ in the New Testament: Studies in Christology in Memory of George Bradford Caird*, ed. L.D. Hurst and N.T. Wright (Oxford: Clarendon, 1987), 267-80; This essay is now available in C.E.B. Cranfield, *On Romans and Other New Testament Essays* (Edinburgh: T & T Clark, 1998), 51-68.

tology as he has offered alternate exegetical options which undermine traditional supports of Jesus Christ's status as God.[62]

While evangelicals have tried to exposit the "Faith once delivered" as an excellent option for our emerging post-modern and post-postmodern world, liberals have tended not to take them seriously.[63] Particularly when it comes to the evangelical insistence that in Jesus of Nazareth, one encounters God manifest in the flesh, a clear disdain emerges, as is evidenced in recent years. Macquarrie, while questioning some of the bold assertiveness of Enlightenment thinking which had a severe distaste for revealed religion, nonetheless himself sounds rather confident with a touch of hubris when he says,

> We remain inevitably children of the Enlightenment. Some of its lessons can never be unlearned. We cannot go back to the mythology of a former age, or to its supernaturalism, or to its spiritual authoritarianism of an infallible church or an infallible Bible. So if we want to ask the question about Jesus Christ and think it worth asking, we have to confront not only all the difficulties and complexities [involved]. . . but the equally difficult problems of making sense of it all within the constraining framework of modern thought.[64]

C. Stephen Evans has provided a broadly apologetic work, which tackles the whole modern worldview, particularly as it appears in critical biblical studies. As a philosopher, he has written a helpful volume, if at times it is highly abstract. His contention is that the "Church's Story" or "Incarnational Narrative" is reasonable even though it is held in faith. This will be persuasive, particularly to those who have a similar faith commitment.[65]

B.6. Christology: A Myth?

In 1977 a bombshell fell. This time it did not explode on the playground of the theologians, but it made its mark directly in the hearts and lives of worshiping Christian lay-people, and it attracted the world of the mass media, causing shockwaves that are still felt today. That bomb was a book entitled *The Myth of*

---

[62] Rare examples of recognition of evangelicals by the wider academic community include (at the time) the evangelical leaning Clark Pinnock, "Christology and the Reformation," in Joseph D. Ban, ed. *The Christological Foundation for Contemporary Theological Education* (Macon, GA: Mercer University Press, 1988), 122-36; the popular scholar Millard J. Erickson, "Evangelical Christology and Soteriology Today," *Interpretation* 49 (July 1995): 255-66; and Gerald L. Bray, "Recent Trends in Christology" in *Constructive Christian Theology in the Worldwide Church*, ed. William R. Barr. (Grand Rapids: Eerdmans, 1997), 291-301.

[63] See Oden, *After Modernity. . . What?*, 21-70.

[64] *Jesus Christ in Modern thought*, (London: SCM; Philadelphia: Trinity Press International, 1990), 26. Here is an example of the triumphalism of the modern.

[65] C. Stephen Evans, *The Historical Christ and the Jesus of Faith: The Incarnational Narrative as History* (New York: Oxford University Press, 1995). For bold new attempt to argue about distinctly Christian experience in a philosophically sophisticated way, see Jeffrey S. Privette, *The Language of God Incarnate* (Austin, TX: Ancient Wisdom Books, 2010).

God Incarnate. This is a group of essays bound together as one volume. This work is the fruit of several years of gathering and interaction among seven scholars who have initiated what is known now as the "Myth debate."[66] David Wells remarks that the overnight notoriety achieved by the contributors was "out of all proportion to the intrinsic merit of the essays."[67] Wells must not be misunderstood here. He is alluding to the perception of the word "myth" in the minds of the public at large. He is not saying that the contributors were poor writers. Because the authors used the term "myth" which has a unique theological meaning, although in everyday language it means something different, a misunderstanding occurred. Although it is possible that an undesired confusion arose because of this book, one must also note that this word, "myth" was a carefully selected term which had positive controversial overtones, as understood by even trained theologians. In one of the follow-up books that constituted a part of the ongoing dialog with the *Myth* volume, Brian Hebblethwaite cordially invited the original writers of the essays in the *Myth of God Incarnate* to continue the exchange of ideas within the confines of the church as, according to him, all involved were Christians. However, Hebblethwaite forcefully expressed his view that the *specific teachings* in the *Myth* text were questioning long-held beliefs, and these doctrines denied essentially both Trinitarian and incarnation theology, and as such these teachings themselves categorically were *not* Christian.[68]

John Hick, the original editor of the *Myth of God Incarnate*, has himself written more extensively on the modern Christology found in the original book. He has employed a new term–metaphor. Hick says,

> A good metaphor – Jesus as "son of God", one in whom the divine Spirit was powerfully present and whose life has revealed to others the reality and claim of God – was turned into the metaphysical theory that Jesus had two natures, one human and the other divine. That theory has never been able to be formulated in a coherent and intelligible way that is also religiously acceptable.[69]

---

[66] John Hick, ed., *The Myth of God Incarnate* (London: SCM, 1977). This book has been reprinted six times prior to its reissue in 1993 with a new preface. This alone shows the continuing relevance of the issues. There was an almost immediate response to this work in the following volume: Michael Green, ed., *The Truth of God Incarnate* (London: Hodder and Stoughton, 1977). Also see George Carey, *God Incarnate: Meeting the Contemporary Challenges to a Classic Christian Doctrine* (Downers Grove, IL: InterVarsity, 1978); and Klaas Runia, *The Present-Day Christological Debate* (Downers Grove, IL: InterVarsity, 1984).

[67] Wells, *The Person of Christ*, 1.

[68] See Brian Hebblethwaite, "*The Myth* and Christian Faith," in *Incarnation and Myth: The Debate Continued*, ed. Michael Goulder (London: SCM, 1979), 15-16.

[69] John Hick, *The Metaphor of God Incarnate: Christology in a Pluralistic Age* (Louisville: Westminster John Knox, 1993), 79. This book has since been issued in a second edition.

Obviously, Hick feels that the notion of two natures in one person to be an invention of the church. As he states, he is not "religiously" satisfied with such classic conceptions. In this, he, along with many moderns, rejects Chalcedon. With Hick's commitment to a merely human Jesus, the very idea of an incarnation explicated in a Christology from above will never be acceptable to his modern mind. Although John Hick discusses Thomas Morris in his book, he still believes that those who argue for a two natured God-Man are really incoherent.[70] It is not my goal to investigate the *Myth of God Incarnate* debate, it is merely mentioned to illustrate that some contemporary writers, who have drunk deeply at the wells of modern theology, clearly reject Chalcedonian Christology. As will be shown shortly, even evangelicals have been influenced by Enlightenment thinking, and as a result of pressure from the modern age, they are unwittingly attempting to re-define Chalcedon so that its so-called incoherence is eliminated.[71]

C. Conclusion

This survey has provided a context for examining some evangelical voices on the person of Jesus. Now an investigation of some contemporary Christologies with a special emphasis on *kenosis* will occupy our attention. This will explain, to some extent, the preferred option of a *kenotic* type of Christology by many contemporary evangelical writers.

---

[70] For Morris's views on this matter one may consult the following: Thomas V. Morris, "The natures of God Incarnate," *CSR* 14 (1984): 35-44; idem, *The Logic of God Incarnate* (Ithaca: Cornell University Press, 1986; reprint, Eugene: Wipf and Stock, 2001); idem, "Rationality and the Christian Revelation," in *Anselmian Explorations: Essays in Philosophical Theology*, ed. Thomas V. Morris. (Notre Dame, IN: University of Notre Dame Press, 1987), 213-41; and idem, "The Metaphysics of God Incarnate," in *Trinity, Incarnation, and Atonement: Philosophical and Theological Essays*, ed. Ronald J. Feenstra and Cornelius Plantinga, Jr. (Notre Dame, IN: University of Notre Dame Press, 1989), 110-27. With the use of certain distinctions, such as the difference between Jesus being a real man yet not a mere man, and the difference between common human properties and essential human properties, coupled with a two minds approach to the incarnation, Morris shows that it is possible to be rational about belief in Jesus as God incarnate. Therefore, Hick's charge is based on an *a priori* settlement about what is possible and what is not possible metaphysically. This approach, exemplified in Hick, will never be countered convincingly by rational argument alone. But Morris's view does allow one with philosophical ingenuity to make some "sense" of revealed religion concerning the incarnation.

[71] See A.N.S. Lane, "Christology beyond Chalcedon," in *Christ the Lord: Studies in Christology Presented to Donald Guthrie*, ed. Harold H. Rowdon (Leicester: Inter Varsity, 1982), 257-81. This is a bold and critical appraisal seeking to move beyond the Chalcedonian framework. Also, see Ronald W. Leigh, "Jesus: the One-natured God-man," *CSR* 11, no. 2 (1982): 124-37 for a vigorous attack on the coherence of the two-nature model.

CHAPTER 3

CONTEMPORARY CHRISTOLOGY AND KENOSIS

A. Introduction

To begin, a short look at the history of *kenotic* thought will be followed by an investigation of its main theological affirmations.[1] This will lay a foundation before examining some modern approaches to kenotic and sub-kenotic Christology today, which are at the heart of the widespread explicit re-definitions of Jesus Christ as one person in two natures, and thus entail the implicit denial of Christ's omnipresence.

B. History

"The historical origins of kenoticism," notes David Wells, "lie mainly within the debates generated by post-Reformation Lutheranism and Calvinism."[2] Most helpful is Hoogland's work. It contains a section on the Tübingen-Giessen controversy. He notes,

> The Giessen theologians felt that the Biblical portrayal of the man Jesus in His humiliation does not allow for a theology which presents Him as exercising the full divine power in governing the world or as being everywhere present in His human nature during His humiliation. The true human development of Christ, which involved also a lack of knowledge, they insisted, must be taken seriously, so that recognition is given to the fact that as man Christ developed according to the laws of His nature. The possibility of weakness and development was explained by the idea of kenosis.[3]

---

[1] For a survey of the contribution of various theologians to this type of explanation of the incarnation one would do well to consult the following: H.R. Mackintosh, *The Doctrine of the Person of Christ*, 264-78; A.B. Bruce, *The Humiliation of Christ in Its Physical, Ethical, and Official Aspects* (Grand Rapids: Eerdmans, 1955), 134-91; Macquarrie, *Jesus Christ in Modern Thought*, 245-50; Dennis Edward Johnson, "Immutability and Incarnation: An Historical and Theological Study of the Concepts of Christ's Divine Unchangeability and His Human Development" (Ph.D. diss., Fuller Theological Seminary, 1984), 178-227; Vincent Taylor, *The Person of Christ in New Testament Teaching* (London: Macmillan, 1958), 260-76; I.A. Dorner, *History of the Development of the Doctrine of the Person of Christ*, trans. D.W. Simon, vol. 3 (Edinburgh: T & T Clark, 1886), 214-60; and idem, *Divine Immutability: A Critical Reconsideration*, trans. Robert R. Williams and Claude Welch (Minneapolis: Fortress, 1994).

[2] David Wells, *The Person of Christ: A Biblical and Historical Analysis of the Incarnation* (Alliance, OH: Bible Scholar, 1984), 133.

[3] Marvin Hoogland, *Calvin's Perspective on the Exaltation of Christ in Comparison with the Post-Reformation Doctrine of the Two States* (Kampen: Kok, 1966), 39. This is

Chapter 3: Contemporary Christology & Kenosis

A full account of kenosis, however, which cover the subject thoroughly, include Donald Dawe's historical survey, Moly Thomas's massive work which aims at aiding interreligious dialog and ecumenism, John Loubinos's recent essays, including his comparison of Christian and Buddhist spiritualities, the essays in a recent text edited by C. Stephen Evans, the classic from Father Lucien Richard, and the recent attempt by David Brown to rehabilitate British Kenotic teachings for today's use.[4] Dawe treats *kenosis* as an all-embracing theme. He consistently defines this kenosis idea with the self-emptying of God, or as God limiting himself to live a fully human life. Despite attempts to locate kenotic teaching in the early church, it is securely established that kenotic *Christology* is a phenomenon of recent origin. Even Mackintosh, who held to a modified *kenosis*, candidly exclaims, "No one would dream of saying that the Fathers had even begun to look in the direction of a Kenotic *theory*."[5] Ramm hence is unjustified in asserting, "The words *kenosis* and *kenotic* derive from the Greek verb in Philippians 2:7 which speak of Christ emptying himself to become in the form of the servant (*kenoo*) . . . Historically the text has been understood as a commentary on the incarnation . . . Hence some kenotic assumption *has always* [emphasis added] been part of historic Christology."[6] Dawe himself acknowledges a kenotic motif in the New Testament, and therefore believes it was clearly a part of Patristic theology beginning in the second century (and beyond throughout church history). Yet Dawe must admit that a fully developed kenotic Christology was not intended or evident in Patristic

---

an extremely helpful book.

[4] Donald G. Dawe, *The Form of a Servant: A Historical Analysis of the Kenotic Motif* (Philadelphia: Westminster, 1963); C. Stephen Evans, ed., *Exploring Kenotic Christology: The Self-Emptying of God* (Oxford: Oxford University Press, 2006); John L. Loubinos, *Self-Emptying of Christ and the Christian: Three Essays on Kenosis* (Eugene: Wipf and Stock, 2011); Lucien Richard, *A Kenotic Christology: In the Humanity of Jesus the Christ, the Compassion of our God* (Lanham, MD: University Press of America, 1982); idem, *Christ: The Self-Emptying of God* (Mahwah: NJ: Paulist, 1997); Moly Thomas, *Christology in Context: Kenotic Perspectives* (New Delhi: Intercultural Publications, 2005); and David Brown, *Divine Humanity: Kenosis and the Construction of a Christian Theology* (Waco, TX: Baylor University Press, 2011). These more recent works by Thomas, Evans, and Brown have not compelled me to accept a kenotic type of Christology despite their valiant attempts. The arguments in these books need to be listened to, but they also must be answered. Perhaps a more direct engagement and response to these particular books may be forthcoming in days ahead.

[5] Macintosh, *The Doctrine of the Person of Jesus Christ*, 269.

[6] Bernard Ramm, *An Evangelical Christology: Ecumenic and Historical* (Nashville: Thomas Nelson, 1985), 55. Ramm speaks for many when he comments on this famous text of Scripture. He asserts the normative status of a kenotic notion of some kind in the following way: "Historic Christology has always taught a kenosis in the incarnation if for no other reason than the text of Philippians 2:5-11 asserts it" (58). Vincent Taylor says similarly, "Some form of *kenosis* is essential to any worthy doctrine of the Incarnation . . . . Christology, in short, is incurably kenotic" (Taylor, *The Person of Christ*, 270, 272).

writers, there was merely an attempt to argue for the truth of the incarnation.[7] Of course, there are different types of kenotic thought. We must be careful to distinguish the variations so as not to unnecessarily misrepresent a person's viewpoint.

One must focus on the modern era to see the first true kenotic Christologies. Macquarrie begins his survey with Gottfried Thomasius (1802-73).[8] As the most famous advocate of kenotic Christology, Thomasius divided the divine attributes into two kinds.[9] First, there were the immanent attributes such as love and mercy; righteousness and holiness. These, argued Thomasius, were maintained by the Logos in the incarnation. The second category, were the so-called relative attributes of omnipotence, omniscience, and omnipresence. These latter omni-attributes were really contingent on the creation of the world and, in Thomasius's thinking, could be dispensed with by God. Hence, Jesus did not have the omni-attributes since he emptied himself of these in becoming man.

A rather more extreme form of *kenosis* is encountered in W.F. Gess (d. 1891). Ironically, unlike Thomasius's Lutheran commitment, Gess was a Calvinist. Nevertheless, Gess affirmed that the Logos gave up *all* divine attributes. Bruce explains the position of Gess:

> These attributes, therefore, the Logos parted with in His descent from Heaven; nay, not only with these so-called relative attributes, but also with those which Thomasius by way of distinction names the immanent attributes of Deity. Incarnation involved the loss not only of the perfect knowledge of the world, called omniscience, but of the perfect vision of God . . . . For the Logos, in becoming man, suffered the extinction of His eternal self-consciousness, to regain it again after many months, as a human, gradually developing. . .[10]

Taylor mentions several British scholars that took up the kenotic mantle. Of those surveyed by Taylor, he believes D.W. Forrester, *The Authority of Christ*

---

[7] Dawe says, "The kenosis motif seems to have played a lively part in the Christology of the second century. *Although there was no fully developed kenotic Christology* [emphasis added] at the time, there appeared in much Christian piety a naive, nonspeculative type of kenosis doctrine to explain what God had done in Christ" (*The Form of a Servant*, 53).

[8] Macquarrie, *Jesus Christ in Modern Thought*, 245.

[9] Gottfried Thomasius says of the incarnation, "It is a revelation of the immanent divine attributes: absolute power, truth, holiness and love. For by the incarnation the Son did not surrender these divine essential determinations, which as such are inseparable from the essence of God, and no more does he, as the incarnate one, withhold their use. . . . None the less, humiliation is at the same time *divesting*, continuous divesting of the divine mode of being and activity which he renounced in becoming flesh, and precisely thus a divesting of the so-called relative divine attributes, in which the immanent attributes are outwardly manifested and make their appearance: omnipotence, omniscience, omnipresence. He waives claim to the possession of these attributes . . ." ("Christ's Person and Work, Part 2: The Person of the Mediator," in *God and Incarnation in Mid-Nineteenth Century German Theology: G. Thomasius, I.A. Dorner, A.E Biedermann*, ed. and trans. Claude Welch [New York: Oxford University Press, 1965], 67-68, 70).

[10] Bruce, *The Humiliation of Christ*, 145.

(1906), P.T. Forsyth, *The Person and Place of Jesus Christ* (1909), and H.R. Mackintosh stand out; and the greatest of these is Mackintosh.[11] No doubt, he is indebted to these writers for his own approach. And despite severe criticism against kenotic Christology from different quarters,[12] Taylor maintains the view that kenotic Christology is necessary.

C. Theology

Kenotic Christology is a theology of the incarnation not merely an interpretation of one passage, namely Philippians 2:5-11, from whence it derives its name. In Philippians 2:7 Paul states that Christ emptied himself (ἑαυτὸν ἐκένωσεν). It is this verse that gives the kenotic view its name.[13] Evangelicals have not embraced this flat-out rejection of the possession of some or all attributes by the incarnate Christ. What is probably the majority view among evangelical theologians and exegetes is a view known as sub-kenotic Christology.[14] At this point it is best to illustrate the views with examples.

D. Kenotic Theology

Despite the seeming abandonment of nineteenth-century kenotic Christology, some are attempting to revive it as a viable approach for today.[15] This is stun-

---

[11] Taylor, *Person of Christ*, 262. He refers to Mackintosh as expressing "Christology in its best form".

[12] For example, D.M Baillie, *God Was in Christ: An Essay on Incarnation and Atonement* (New York: Charles Scribner's Sons, 1948), 94-98, who draws on the work of J.M. Creed and William Temple for his attack on kenotic Christology. Taylor acknowledges these works yet feels that the criticisms are not compelling. For probing of Baillie's "paradoxical" solution to the puzzle of the incarnation, see J.L.M. Haire, "An Unresolved Tension in the Christology of D.M. Baillie," *SJT* 17 (1964): 303-08; and Peter McEnhill, "'Good Pleasure, Grace and the Person of God Incarnate': Interpreting the Christology of D.M. Baillie for Today," *SJT* 50 (1997): 61-81. One may agree with Baillie on the shortcomings of kenotic thought, yet his own approach is less than fully satisfying. His is a functional kind of Christology, which lacks the substantive element that would provide full rationale for why Jesus is worshiped. Nevertheless, Baillie affirms the uniqueness of Jesus.

[13] See in this book, Chapter 8: "An Exegetical and Theological Look at Philippians 2:5-8."

[14] For this categorization one may consult H. Wayne House, *Charts of Christian Theology and Doctrine* (Grand Rapids: Zondervan, 1992), 30. Sub-kenotic Christology claims that Christ *had* the attributes of deity but rather chose either *not to utilize* them, or *used them sparingly and always in dependence on the Father*. Hence, in evangelical sub-kenotic Christology, Christ is said to have given up the independent use of his divine attributes (kenosis) in the incarnation. In this work I challenge both kenotic and sub-kenotic Christology. My focus on the attribute of omnipresence will seek to show that even the sub-kenotic view ends up questioning, albeit unintentionally, the full deity of Christ.

[15] This is particularly troubling for evangelicals as it is they who are trying to argue that Jesus is indeed God. The problems of kenotic thought have been spelled out in several places. For example, Wells notes five problems of this theory: (1) it attempts to sever the attributes from the essence of deity, (2) it implies a disruption in internal Trini-

ning given some of the recent evaluations from theologians such as Berkouwer and Macquarrie. In his classic work, hailed by some[16] to be on the scale of Mackintosh's earlier textbook, John Macquarrie explains the partial, if not main reason, for kenoticism's failure."Kenotic christologies," he posits, "turned out to be no more than an episode of modern thinking about the person of Christ. Their authors were attempting to do justice to the humanistic demands of nineteenth-century thought."[17] As German idealism sunk, so did Christologies wedded to this era. Berkouwer, on the other hand, states matters differently. "The *kenosis*-doctrine," claims Berkouwer, "did not point the way out of the impasse supposedly present in the dogma of the church."[18] Berkouwer continues: "The question remained urgent whether Christ was and could be truly God and truly man. At the end of the road, when the reconstruction of Christology was undertaken, arose the danger of the *complete humanization of Christ* [emphasis supplied]."[19] This appears to be the net result of kenotic thinking, yet some evangelicals are trying to reassert a kenotic theology. To these writers we turn.

D.1. Ronald Feenstra

Feenstra has attempted to explain the incarnation within a kenotic model.[20] What is interesting in this essay is that Feenstra begins with the Formula of

---

tarian relations, (3) the divine contraction affects the love of God, which gradually returned to Jesus, (4) the conversion of Godhead into manhood violates the Nicene Creed, and (5) it misplaced the element of humiliation by focusing on the incarnation rather than the cross (see David F. Wells, *The Person of Christ*, 138-39). Colin Gunton also states that a kenotic theory inevitably leaves us with a "mythical demi-god" that encounters us in Christ (see Colin E. Gunton, *Christ and Creation* [Carlisle: Paternoster, 1992], 83). Gerald O'Collins asserts that "the Council of Chalcedon declared that the properties or essential features of both the divine and human nature are *preserved* in the incarnation . . . . This teaching seems to rule out even a cautious form of kenotic theory, which proposes that the divine properties were, at least temporarily, not preserved after the incarnation, or at least not preserved in action" (O'Collins, *Incarnation* [New York: Continuum, 2002], 62-63). Hence, evangelicals advocating Chalcedonianism need to abandon kenoticism.

[16] See McIntyre, *The Shape of Christology*, 259.

[17] Macquarrie, *Jesus Christ in Modern Thought*, 250. Macquarrie goes on to assert that in the face of radicals such as Strauss and Feuerbach, the kenoticists tried desperately to continue to hold onto a Christology from above. Macquarrie believes this to be incorrect, and partially to blame for the ever present docetism he feels is still evident. He prefers the approach like that of Pannenberg, which starts from below with the man Jesus.

[18] G.C. Berkouwer, *Studies in Dogmatics: The Person of Christ*, trans. John Vriend (Grand Rapids: Eerdmans, 1955), 31.

[19] Berkouwer, *Person of Christ*, 31. Berkouwer also mentioned F.W. Korff, who challenged kenotic Christology as precluding the actual coming of God into the world, which Korff [and Berkouwer] deem as the "secret of Christology" (30).

[20] Ronald J. Feenstra, "Reconsidering Kenotic Christology," 128-52, in *Trinity, Incarnation and Atonement*, ed. Feenstra and Plantinga. He has also advocated for a more robust version of Kenotic Christology in Ronald J. Feenstra, "A Kenotic Christological Method for Understanding the Divine Attributes," in C. Stephen Evans, ed. *Exploring*

Chalcedon. In light of the 1500 years that Chalcedon has served the church, as Feenstra observes, his stated goal is thus an attempt which "presents kenotic Christology as one important modern attempt to articulate a theology of the Incarnation that comports with the Chalcedonian affirmation that Jesus Christ is truly divine and truly human."[21] Next, Feenstra outlines and presents the essence of the view earlier advocated by Thomasius. Here, Feenstra explains the concern that Thomasius had to maintain both natures for the incarnate Christ. Some interesting matters come to the fore and issues which Feenstra senses are of paramount importance include the question of whether the kenotic view described can do justice to the deity of Christ during the period of his earthly life. The issue has reached an impasse according to Feenstra because there is simple disagreement on what constitutes the divine nature. Can the distinction that Thomasius made stand or have the critics of kenotic thought won the day by including the so-called relative attributes as part of the divine nature, and therefore constitute them as essential to deity? Feenstra claims that those like Dorner, Baillie, and more recently, Pannenberg, who have challenged kenotic exposition, have not argued and therefore proved their view, but have merely asserted it. The matter therefore, issues forth in a new proposal as Feenstra ponders, "Perhaps the doctrine of the divine attributes must be revised in the light of the Incarnation."[22] To proceed with this part of his essay, Feenstra decides to deal mainly with omniscience. This is regrettable since the doctrine of omnipresence is therefore neglected. Feenstra, however, notes:

> Omnipresence can safely be eliminated from consideration both because there may be a sense of omnipresence according to which the kenotically incarnate Christ is omnipresent and because omnipresence appears to be conceptually secondary to questions of God's knowledge and power.[23]

It would be very helpful for an explanation to show *how* a "kenotically incarnate Christ is omnipresent." Alas, Feenstra provides no such aid. He remains on his course to discuss the question of omniscience. The fact that Feenstra summarily dismisses omnipresence is because he wants to show that it is really the

---

Kenotic Christology: The Self Emptying of God (New York: Oxford University Press, 2006), 139-64.

[21] Feenstra, "Reconsidering," 128.

[22] Feenstra, "Reconsidering," 135.

[23] Feenstra, "Reconsidering," 135. Certain matters trouble me as I reflect on some of Feenstra's discussion of Thomasius. Feenstra explains that Thomasius believed that after Jesus obeyed God he was once more taken into that glorious mode of existence and therefore re-possessed the relative attributes, including omniscience. This is not to say that the humanity is eliminated by Jesus as he enters again that mode of being that he enjoyed before the incarnation. This begs the question of why the incarnation necessitates an abandoning of these attributes in the first place. Furthermore, a more perplexing issue emerges as Feenstra asserts that Thomasius claimed that the relative attributes in fact are not intrinsically contradictory to true human existence. Moreover, regenerated Christians begin to experience partially the relative attributes themselves even now (see Feenstra, "Reconsidering," 131-33). I cannot imagine how Christians "possess [omnipresence] to a limited extent."

attributes of knowledge and power that drive one to an avowed kenotic position. This is an incorrect procedure. One may not relativize omnipresence in such a manner. On the contrary, I believe it is the truth of Christ's omnipresence that precludes the very notion of a kenotically conceived Christ. If anything, it is Christ's omnipotence that can conceptually be thought of in a kenotic way by maintaining a distinction between possession and use. However, Feenstra's proposal is not sub-kenotic but fully kenotic. This is so for his understanding of omniscience. Feenstra does not subsume omnipresence under omniscience as others do, but just brushes it off with a concession that it may even be possible that a kenotically conceived Christ is, "in some way," omnipresent. Nevertheless, he does not allow for omniscience. I will revisit this aspect of his view in a later chapter. His discussion on this attribute of knowledge will suffice for now. Feenstra interacts with Stephen T. Davis and Thomas V. Morris.[24] Two key questions drive the discussion for Feenstra. The first asks whether true deity may be maintained of the incarnate Christ. The second question centers on the possibility of genuine humanity of the exalted Christ. The solution to the first question for Feenstra focuses on a possibility that each person within the Trinity may possess the attribute of "omniscient-unless-kenotically-and redemptively-incarnate . . ." as essential to deity, yet once the Son, who has so become in the incarnation, it is ". . . no longer a live option for either the Father or the Holy Spirit to become incarnate in this way."[25] In this model, therefore, there really is no rescinding of anything to preclude genuine deity, for the doctrine of omniscience is wedded to a carefully phrased caveat. This certainly begs the question of whether this is justifiable biblically. Along with Davis, Feenstra cannot conceive of a view which allows Jesus to be both omniscient [without the caveat] and at the same time to be non-omniscient.

Feenstra's second issue attempts to deal with the objection to kenotic Christology that it necessarily entails the denial of the genuine humanity of Christ after the ascension. This is telling, for if it is necessary for a kenosis to occur, that is for the Son of God to actually give up certain attributes (e.g., omniscience) to become man, then a claim that Christ *now* posseses omniscience must cast doubt on his genuine humanity. Feenstra grants the legitimacy of this objection. The significance of his admission to the weightiness of this challenge will be re-visited later. At this point we must note how Feenstra diffuses the contention against his model of the incarnation. Essentially, he does this by positing a distinction between kenosis and incarnation. He feels that one may assert that the incarnation was merely the Son of God becoming man [taking human nature, no doubt], whereas kenosis involves the assumption of self limitation in sharing our finiteness as part of the redemptive strategy of God. While this is significant and *prima facie* allows Feenstra to ward off suggestions that kenotic Christology cannot affirm the genuineness of Christ's humanity since the ascension, it does not aid any approach, kenotic or sub-kenotic which equates *kenosis* with the incarnation or at least makes the *kenosis* the *sine qua*

---

[24] Davis is an advocate of a kenotic Christology. Morris is critical of kenoticism.
[25] Feenstra, "Reconsidering," 142.

non of incarnation.[26] Many questions emerge at this point which Feenstra recognizes:

> Fortunately we need not answer all these questions at this time. The central point here is simply that kenotic Christology does not require Christ's loss of humanity as exalted. If Christ's being human continues even when his kenosis ceases, then his incarnation, or being human, and kenosis are conceptually distinct.[27]

Feenstra makes this distinction and says that "the kenosis of the Son of God involves . . . his ceasing to possess certain attributes, such as omniscience," then continues, "[he] divests himself of these attributes, not in order to become *human* or to become *incarnate*, but in order to share our lot or condition during his life on earth."[28]

Overall, the positive contribution of Feenstra's kenotic proposal is found in his admission that the sub-kenotic proposal cannot work with reference to omniscience. This is due to the way Feenstra defines omniscience. He says: "Omniscience is . . . the attribute of knowing every true proposition."[29] What is devastating for the sub-kenotic position is what follows. Feenstra continues,

> So if a certain being, S, is omniscient, then the proposition, "S is omniscient," is true. Since S, being omniscient, knows every true proposition, S knows the proposition, "S is omniscient." Thus, if S is omniscient, then S must be aware of S's omniscience. So if Christ was omniscient during his life on earth, then he knew he was. It therefore seems unreasonable to suggest that the incarnate Christ retained his omniscience, having merely given up his use or awareness of it.[30]

This reasoning forces Feenstra to embrace a fully kenotic explanation of the relative attributes as previously explained, rather than to adopt a modified form such as sub-kenotic approaches commonly found in evangelical theology.

D.2. C. Stephen Evans

Evans also echoes a Kenotic Christology. In his book emphasizing the historicity and rationality of the Christian understanding of the New Testament, he includes a chapter expressing his view of the possibility of an incarnation. First, Evans dismisses the notion that the "incarnational narrative," as he calls the New Testament testimony, is internally logically incoherent. This is significant as a starting point as Evans claims, "If the incarnational narrative embodies logical contradictions at central points then it cannot be a true, historical account."[31] Evans acknowledges the able work of Thomas Morris in showing the

---

[26] Moreover, what Feenstra assumes in this line of reasoning by making a distinction between incarnation and kenosis is very close to the view I develop concerning the correct understanding of Phil 2:5-8. The incarnate Christ is the subject of the action involving kenosis. Rather than equating kenosis with self-limitation as Feenstra does, however, I prefer the option of seeing this as a reference to the death of Christ.
[27] Feenstra, "Reconsidering," 149.
[28] Feenstra, "Reconsidering," 148.
[29] Feenstra, "Reconsidering," 136.
[30] Feenstra, "Reconsidering," 136.
[31] Evans, *The Historical Christ*, 117.

coherence of the Chalcedonian doctrine of the incarnation, on which he relies, but Evans also states, "unlike Morris, I incline towards a kenotic view of the orthodox view." Second, after presenting a distinction between the traditional form and the kenotic model of the incarnation, Evans shows that with respect to divine attributes "it is essential only for a divine being to have such properties as 'being-omnipotent except when one freely chooses to relinquish this power.' " Evans claims, "The kenotic view thus allows for the possibility that Jesus, though a divine being, may actually have 'emptied himself,' and divested himself of such properties as omnipotence and omniscience *simpliciter*."[32]

E. Sub-Kenotic Theology

The main difference between kenotic and sub-kenotic approaches is the claim by adherents of the latter that the Son of God remained in possession of all divine attributes after the incarnation. The kenosis, in this model, has primarily been developed along three similar yet distinct proposals.[33] These sub-kenotic views are (1) the giving up of the *use* of relative divine attributes; (2) the giving up of *independent* use of relative divine attributes; and (3) the giving up of the "insignia of Majesty, the glories [and] the prerogatives of Deity."[34] Of these three types it is the second that has become very prominent in evangelical Christological doctrine.[35] To these we now turn taking a look particularly at Millard Erickson, Gerald Hawthorne, and Loring Prest.

---

[32] Evans, *The Historical Christ*, 129. Also see C. Stephen Evans, "The Self-Emptying of Love: Some Thoughts on Kenotic Christology," in *The Incarnation: An Interdisciplinary Symposium on the Incarnation of the Son of God*, ed. Stephen T. Davis, Daniel Kendall, and Gerald O' Collins (Oxford: Oxford University Press, 2002), 246-72.

[33] As already mentioned, Wayne House is my primary source for this categorization and terminology. See also the helpful article Robert E. Picirilli, "He Emptied Himself," *BV* 3, no. 1 (1969): 23-30. Picirilli lists five kenotic views and three sub-kenotic views. I am indebted to House, *Charts of Christian Theology and Doctrine*, 57, who brought my attention to this article. Though not completely compatible with the view advocated in this book, Picirilli's view does, however, sense the same kinds of problems that I have struggled with in both kenotic and sub-kenotic approaches. He is cautious to claim that he cannot solve the perennial Christological problem but offers suggestions to ponder. His basic contention is that the kenosis question is primarily to be understood as ". . . not in what he [Jesus] laid aside, but in what He took up" (Picirilli, "He Emptied Himself," 29). This is helpful, as far as it goes, affirming incarnation by addition, but it still holds on to what I continue to contest, namely that kenosis *is* co-extensive with incarnation.

[34] Picirilli, "He Emptied Himself," 25. This expression, as Picirilli notes, has its origin in Lightfoot's famous commentary on Philippians. Both House and Picirilli feel that it is vague and meaningless.

[35] For example, one may consult the following: Augustus Hopkins Strong, *Systematic Theology: A Compendium Designed for the use of Theological Students* (Valley Forge, PA: Judson, 1907), 701-706; John F. Walvoord, *Jesus Christ our Lord* (Chicago: Moody, 1969), 143-45; Paul Enns, *The Moody Handbook of Theology* (Chicago: Moody, 1989), 228-29; Donald Macleod, *The Person of Christ* (Downers Grove, IL: InterVarsity Press, 1998), 212-20; Gerald F. Hawthorne, *The Presence and the Power: The Significance of the Holy Spirit in the Life of Jesus* (Dallas: Word, 1991), 199-225; Robert P. Lightner, *Handbook of Evangelical Theology: A Historical, Biblical, and Con-

Chapter 3: Contemporary Christology & Kenosis

E.1. Millard J. Erickson

Erickson is one of the best known contemporary evangelical theologians. His evangelical contribution to Christological thinking has been taken notice of in the wider academic community. In the July 1995 issue of the theological journal *Interpretation*, Erickson joined other scholars in contributing to Christological discussion in a volume emphasizing the resurgence of systematic theology. In fact, Millard Erickson's first venture to develop a full scale treatment of one of the theological *loci*, after completing the first edition of his now famous *Christian Theology*,[36] was to write the important book *The Word Became Flesh: A Contemporary Incarnational Christology*.[37] It is this latter book that shall be our basis for analyzing his Christological position.

Millard J. Erickson says of his approach, "the view we have been introducing is a species of *kenotic theology* . . ." (emphasis added).[38] There are two places where Erickson addresses omnipresence. First, in discussing "Divine Self-Limitation," Erickson proposes that the incarnation is analogous to God's entering into covenant to redeem his people, or analogous to God's creation of the world. This strategy is significant for Erickson, as these examples show that God curtailed his freedom by becoming obligated in some way. This obligation for God is not a problem, however, Erickson maintains, as this was "freely chosen in the first place."[39] The reasoning continues in this manner:

> The incarnation can be thought of along those lines. While giving up the divine nature would be a surrender of deity, and even giving up certain attributes might well be, a voluntary decision to restrict the independent exercise of some divine attributes is not necessarily a forfeiture of deity. The limitations accepted in the incarnation are like those accepted in the promises and covenants made by God.[40]

Given this framework, Erickson mentions omnipresence. He claims, "The divine ability to be everywhere (or omnipresence, as theologians prefer) was not lost by the Second Person of the Trinity."[41] At this point the argument is subtle. Erickson continues, saying, "In that sense, what he was [as the Second Person of the Trinity prior to the Incarnation] did not diminish."[42] Yet, Erickson also

---

temporary Survey and Review (Grand Rapids: Kregel, 1995), 81-84; and Gordon R. Lewis and Bruce A. Demarest, *Integrative Theology: Historical, Biblical, Systematic, Apologetic, Practical* (Grand Rapids: Zondervan, 1996), 2:285-86 (Lewis and Demarest espouse a combination of views no. 2 and no. 3 mentioned above). The sub-kenotic view has been defended at length by Loring A. Prest, "The Disposition of the Divine Attributes of Omniscience, Omnipresence and Omnipotence in the Incarnate Christ" (Th.M. thesis, Grace Theological Seminary, 1984).

[36] Millard J. Erickson, *Christian Theology* 2nd ed. (Grand Rapids: Baker, 1998).
[37] Millard J. Erickson, *The Word Became Flesh: A Contemporary Incarnational Christology* (Grand Rapids: Baker, 1991).
[38] Erickson, *The Word Became Flesh*, 551.
[39] Erickson, *The Word Became Flesh*, 549.
[40] Erickson, *The Word Became Flesh*, 549.
[41] Erickson, *The Word Became Flesh*, 549.
[42] Erickson, *The Word Became Flesh*, 549.

The Omnipresence of Jesus Christ

posits, "He did, however, limit himself to exercising that power only in connection with restrictions imposed by a human body, which meant that he could be in only one physical location at a time."[43] In his second mention of omnipresence, Erickson further suggests, "Omnipresence is the attribute where the necessity of limitation involved in the incarnation is perhaps clearest. As God, Jesus had the capability of being everywhere." But Erickson, continues, "Yet, for the period of his earthly incarnation, he limited himself to the restrictions in location which having a physical human body entailed." It is here, again that Erickson denies what he affirms in the same paragraph. Finally, Erickson concludes, "He had possessed the capability of active omnipresence: being pure spirit, he was not limited to any particular place and time. But as part of the decision to become incarnate, he also decided not to exercise that capability, or to make it latent, for a period of time."[44]

Here we see clearly Erickson's commitment to a Christology that claims that Jesus possessed divine [relative] attributes in a latent manner, choosing not to exercise them. His observations concerning the "problem" of omnipresence highlights that it is incorrect, as Ronald Feenstra attempted, to brush off omnipresence with hardly a second thought. At least Erickson attempts to deal with this significant attribute.

E.2. Loring Prest

Prest is included as he has written a thesis dealing directly with the issues pertinent to this book. Prest attempts to solve the puzzling relation of divine attributes to the incarnate Christ. Although his final conclusion is basically the same as Erickson's, Prest has articulated his view rather differently. First, Prest claims,

> An examination of Jesus reveals that he is God. Jesus limits Himself. Therefore God can limit Himself. By virtue of His deity Jesus never lost the possession of His divine attributes. In order to be the God-man, however, Jesus humbled himself and gave up the exercise of all His attributes that were disconsonant with being a man.[45]

Second, Prest argues for a monothelite understanding of the person of Christ.[46] This is the view that claims that Jesus had but one will. Prest makes himself expressly clear as he goes on to state,

> Jesus is only one person, with one consciousness . . . . By virtue of the fact that Jesus never lost his deity, He never lost the possession of the attributes of omniscience, omnipresence, or omnipotence. However, for the sake of accomplishing

---

[43] Erickson, *The Word Became Flesh*, 549.
[44] Erickson, *The Word Became Flesh*, 561.
[45] Prest, "The Disposition of Divine Attributes," i. This assumption leads to the question of the genuineness of Christ's humanity now since the ascension. This matter will be taken up in a subsequent chapter.
[46] Prest, "The Disposition of Divine Attributes," i.

the grand scheme of redemption of man Jesus was willing to voluntary desist from the exercise of these attributes and live a normal human life.[47]

This view is a single mind and single will position, which is problematic in itself.[48] Erickson had quoted favorably the decision of the Sixth Ecumenical council of the Church which ruled this as a heresy.[49] Subsequently, dyothelitism has been the orthodox position regarding the person of Christ among the vast majority of confessing Christians. In this Erickson and Prest differ. Furthermore, Prest eliminates the impact of his denial of omnipresence by subsuming omnipresence as a function of omniscience.[50]

E.3. Gerald F. Hawthorne

Hawthorne is perhaps best known for his famous commentary on Paul's letter to the Philippians.[51] His exegesis in this commentary is in line with his explicit Christology found in his work on the person of Christ. Like Erickson, Hawthorne also classifies himself as embracing a form of kenotic Christology.[52] Nonetheless, Hawthorne goes on record early in his book on Jesus to show his commitment to an incarnationalist perspective. He says, "It is my studied opinion that the New Testament clearly teaches that the preexistent, eternal Son of God entered into history in the person of Jesus Christ and . . . this Jesus was, in the ancient words of Melito of Sardis (ca. A.D. 190), "by nature both God and man."'[53] His second main presupposition, as can be gathered from the first, is Hawthorne's conviction about the Bible. He says: "I hold a high view of Scripture. . . . I affirm that the Bible, of which the New Testament is one part, is God's special revelation to people . . . it is trustworthy, authoritative, essential . . . and that it was inspired by the Spirit of God."[54] Hawthorne especially wants it noted that he, along with several other scholars, affirms that "Jesus was *truly* God, *fully* God, God undiminished by emptying himself of even a single attribute!"[55] In continuation: "I refuse," Hawthorne stresses, "to say that in the incarnation the eternal Son of God gave up, surrendered, laid aside a single attribute belonging to deity, as if the attributes of God were like garments that could be

---

[47] Prest, "The Disposition of Divine Attributes," 129-30.

[48] Gerald F. Hawthorne, in his chapter "The Spirit as the Key to Kenosis," valiantly argues for a sub-kenotic view of Christ, and in his own words betrays his approach defending *monothelitism*. He posits, "Thus, I choose to side with [Vincent] Taylor, who advocates his own modified version of the unfashionable kenotic theory. His view of the person of Christ, including his explanation about the need for positing a single will in Jesus, may be the nearest that it is possible to get to a solution of this the greatest of all mysteries, the mystery of Jesus" (Hawthorne, *The Presence and the Power*, 214).

[49] Erickson, *The Word Made Flesh*, 75.

[50] Prest, "Disposition of Divine Attributes," 30-40.

[51] See Gerald F. Hawthorne, *Philippians* (Dallas: Word, 1983).

[52] Hawthorne, *The Presence and the Power*, 207.

[53] Hawthorne, *The Presence and the Power*, 5.

[54] Hawthorne, *The Presence and the Power*, 5-6.

[55] Hawthorne, *The Presence and the Power*, 207.

taken off and hung up somewhere until needed again."⁵⁶ It is helpful to grasp Hawthorne's approach to the kenosis passage in Philippians 2:6-9, however, to appreciate his specific teaching on the incarnation. In summarizing his view, he says:

> When Philippians 2:7 is looked at through this lens [of Chalcedonian Christology], one discovers that the expression, "emptied himself," does not say that he emptied himself of anything. Hence, one should not think that the phrase means that Christ discarded divine substances, essences or attributes. Quite the contrary [sic]. The series of participles immediately following the description of this event–"he emptied himself *by taking* the form of a slave, *by becoming* in the likeness of human beings, *by being found* in human form"– indicates quite emphatically, although paradoxically, that Christ's self-giving was accomplished by taking, that his self-emptying was achieved by becoming what he was not before, that his kenosis came about not by subtraction but by addition, that his *kenosis* (an emptying) was in reality a *plerosis* (a filling).⁵⁷

It is clear how Hawthorne views the passage of Philippians 2, and in some measure, how he conceives the incarnation. It is, on first reading, a healthy looking concept of incarnation by addition. This is innocently deceptive, however, as he goes on to explain the idea driving his concept. Hawthorne also says, "Divine attributes, including those of omniscience, omnipotence, and omnipresence, are not to be thought of as being laid aside when the eternal Son became human but rather thought of as becoming potential or latent within this incarnate One–present in Jesus in all their fulness, but no longer in exercise."⁵⁸ Again, the familiar distinction is noted here in Hawthorne. This approach has the merit of defending the genuineness of Jesus' humanity. This is the programmatic rationale for Hawthorne's endeavor.⁵⁹ Specifically referring to the attribute of omnipresence, while speaking of the incarnate Christ and drawing attention to the scriptures, Hawthorne posits, "Certainly the man, Jesus of Nazareth, was confined to time and space, and thus he was not omnipresent–no opponent of *any form of kenotic theory* [emphasis added] would say that he was omnipresent."⁶⁰

---

⁵⁶ Hawthorne, *The Presence and the Power*, 207.

⁵⁷ Hawthorne, *The Presence and the Power*, 207.

⁵⁸ Hawthorne, *The Presence and the Power*, 208.

⁵⁹ Hawthorne, *The Presence and the Power*, 210-11. For example, Hawthorne says, "Only if one assumes that the divine attributes were potential rather than active does it seem possible to talk about a real incarnation. If the Logos enters time and space omniscient, omnipotent, omnipresent, his entrance is a theophany. He certainly is not a human being like us" (212).

⁶⁰ Hawthorne, *The Presence and the Power*, 211. It is indeed possible to affirm that the Man, Jesus Christ is omnipresent, with the use of the concept *communicatio idiomatum* as has been done throughout the ages, while maintaining the denial that Jesus' humanity is omnipresent in the same way. For example, the debate about these very matters between Theodore Beza and Jacob Andreae resulted in Beza, as summarized by Jill Raitt, claiming this very notion of the interchange of properties (*communicatio idiomatum*). She says, "The communication of properties of burning iron and even in the soul's

Chapter 3: Contemporary Christology & Kenosis

---

animation of the body cannot be taken as duplicates of the hypostatic union. In the similes, Beza explained, both elements are created; in the hypostatic union, a finite reality is united to an infinite being. Beza concluded that the two natures (*ousiae*) must be kept distinct but not separate in the person of Christ. There is one Christ, Beza argued, who possesses two wills and actualities (*energiae*), two realizations (*energemata*), but only one result (*apotelesma*) since the person is unique. This is the way to understand Athanasius and therefore to remain orthodox" (Jill Raitt, *The Colloquy of Montbéliard: Religion and Politics in the Sixteenth Century* [New York: Oxford University Press, 1993], 114). Furthermore, Jill Raitt, once again gleans the clear Christological teaching of Beza, who "distinguished abstract and concrete predications. Thus one could say that Christ is omnipresent, omnipotent, or even that *the man Christ is omnipresent* [emphasis added] and omnipotent because such a concrete subject refers to the person. On the other hand, one may not say that the humanity is omnipresent and omnipotent because this would abolish the distinction between the human and the divine natures. So one can say God suffers, but only *kat' allo* or according to the other nature, the passible human nature, possessed by the Person of Christ . . ." (121).

49

CHAPTER 4

CONTEMPORARY EVANGELICAL CHRISTOLOGY AND CHALCEDON

A. Introduction

After presenting various attempts of evangelical Christology with a focus on kenosis, it will also be helpful to show attempts by evangelicals to re-conceptualize the incarnation with conscientious regard for the Chalcedonian framework. In his helpful survey of recent contributions to Christological thinking, John McIntyre suggested that the revision of his work should not forsake the emphasis on Chalcedon, even in the wake of process Christologies that are evidently popular in the twentieth century, "for some of these process christologies, as they might be called, sought a kind of validation in showing their conformity with, or at least their non-violation of, the main thrust of Chalcedon."[1]

At the conclusion of his fine work on the identity of Jesus, Carl F.H. Henry, quoting Oskar Skarsaune, gives his own historically sensitive account of Christology and suggests that Chalcedon has a magnetic appeal, and that any meaningful Christology will have to reckon with it, not necessarily as a concluding statement, but certainly a starting point or a "prelude to a new phase in the Christological controversy."[2] Here is another devastating blow to the Bultmannian thesis regarding the origins of New Testament faith. Skarsaune eloquently shows the true roots of incarnation teaching to be the Old Testament wisdom tradition, and he furthermore argues this is precisely how Jesus understood himself. It is therefore the intent of this section to survey some contemporary approaches at articulating a Christology for today, especially those with a conscious reflection on Chalcedon. To do this an evaluation of proposals by Anthony Lane and Ronald Leigh will be made. Studies on Chalcedonian Christology will be identified in our survey of Patristic theology. Some works are noted here for reference illustrating the continuing importance of, and the touchstone nature of Chalcedon for various traditions.[3] In particular, two rela-

---

[1] John McIntyre, *The Shape of Christology: Studies in the Doctrine of the Person of Christ* (Edinburgh: T & T Clark, 1998), ix.

[2] Carl F.H. Henry, *The Identity of Jesus of Nazareth* (Nashville: Broadman, 1992), 112. Also, see idem, "New Dimensions in Christology," in *New Dimensions in Evangelical Thought: Essays in Honor of Millard J. Erickson*, ed. David S. Dockery (Downers Grove, IL: InterVarsity, 1998), 299-316. For Skarsaune's contribution one may consult: Oscar Skarsaune *Incarnation: Myth or Fact?*, trans. Trygve R. Skarsten (St. Louis: Concordia, 1991).

[3] For a presentation of Catholic, Orthodox, and Protestant views reflecting on Chalcedon see Paul Fries and Tiran Nersoyan, eds., *Christ in East and West* (Macon, GA: Mercer University Press, 1987). Also helpful are the following: Tadros Y. Malaty, "The

tively important studies will provide the data for our analysis.[4] These are significant in that they are self-confessed evangelical writers.

B. Anthony Lane

In his essay "Christology beyond Chalcedon," Tony Lane provides rationale for seeking to move beyond the definition established in 451, as his title suggests. He is careful to nuance his position, however, so that one does not feel that he seeks to abandon the positive contribution of Chalcedon. This is commendable.

B.1. Introduction

After explaining that the definition sought to avoid the classical errors of Apollinarianism, Nestorianism, and Eutychianism, Lane contends that there was a blending of four traditions that finally made up the definition.[5] In seeking to re-examine the council's intent, and therefore distilling what may still be legitimate, Lane seeks a distinction between the statement put forth in 451, and the "raw material," shall we say, of the New Testament. "To be committed to the biblical doctrine of the incarnation," notes Lane, "is not necessarily to be totally committed to the Chalcedonian exposition of it."[6] Furthermore, Lane explains that those who have shown the "inadequacies of Chalcedon," have not thereby discredited the incarnation itself. To equate the definition with the New Testament data, therefore is incorrect. It is to "confuse text with commentary."[7]

B.2. Objections to Chalcedon.

Lane's next section, after briefly mentioning the political aspirations of the drafters, deals with the classic objections to the Chalcedonian definition. These come under four broad categories: (1) hellenization, (2) immutability, (3) dualism, and (4) docetism. First, under hellenization, Lane allows that every age needs to contextualize its message, and that the Fathers who coined the defini-

---

Nature of God the Word Incarnate: Μία Φῆσις του Θεόυ Σεσαρκομένη," *CCR* 7 (1986): 4-14; Timothy Maschke, "Chalcedon: Renewed, Restored, or Rejected? A Comparative Study of Two Contemporary Lutheran Christologies with Implications for Worship," *ConJ* (January 1991): 49-62; Edmund Schlink, "Christology of Chalcedon in Ecumenical Discussion," *Di* 5 (1963): 134-38; Rowan Williams, "'Person' and 'Personality' in Christology," *Drev* 94 (1976): 253-60 (which is immensely helpful); and George W. Stroup III, "Christian Doctrine: I Chalcedon Revisited," *ThTo* 35 (1978): 52-64. For a recent re-evaluation of Chalcedon by a Roman Catholic Scholar that conscientiously rejects process metaphysics and desires to strongly re-affirm Chalcedonian Christology, see Donald J. Gelpi, *Encountering Jesus Christ: Rethinking Christological Faith and Commitment* (Milwaukee, WI: Marquette University Press, 2009), 417-79.

[4] See A.N.S. Lane, "Christology beyond Chalcedon," in *Christ the Lord: Studies in Christology Presented to Donald Guthrie*, ed. Harold H. Rowdon. (Leicester: InterVarsity, 1982), 257-81; and Ronald W. Leigh, "Jesus: the One-natured God-man," *CSR* 11, no. 2 (1982): 124-37.

[5] He says, "The positive statement blends together four traditions: the Alexandrian, drawn from Cyril; the Antiochene, from the *Formula of Reunion*; the Constantinopolitan, from Flavian; and the Western, from Leo's *Tome*" (Lane, "Christology beyond Chalcedon," 261).

[6] Lane, "Christology Beyond Chalcedon," 258.

[7] Lane, "Christology Beyond Chalcedon," 258.

tion did nothing wrong *per se* in utilizing philosophical concepts at their disposal in the fifth century. "Of course," Lane hastens to add, "the . . . question then arises concerning their fidelity to the biblical message in the process of contextualizing it."[8] Next, under the same category, Lane shows the objection using the famous ontological/functional disjunction.[9] Again, giving warning against a *prima facie* understanding that the New Testament is exclusively functional, Lane permits the use of substantive language to describe the "who" of the incarnate Christ in ontological terms. The assumption of those who utilize the objection against substantive language is itself incorrect, according to Lane.[10] The second category of objection, namely, immutability is a particularly strong one according to Lane. Rather than accepting the Fathers' ". . . Greek concept of God [which] meant that he was essentially static and unchanging,"[11] Lane prefers the view of "Professor Moltmann [who] has a better approach."[12] Suffering love is posited as a superior attribute than immutability, and as reflecting the real teaching of the Scripture. "If God cannot change or suffer," says Lane, "it is hard to see how he could become man and suffer for us."[13] The third category of objections focuses on an overt dualism centered in the Chalcedonian statement. "Jesus," Lane explains, "has a dual existence, as God and as man. He acted sometimes as God, sometimes as man."[14] Lane's answer to this proposal is forthright. "This dualism," he dismisses, "is foreign to the New Testament portrait of Christ." With this aversion Lane grants full force to this particular objection. Lastly, the problem of docetism is touched upon. Lane links these objections previously discussed, and shows what he considers to be the undeniable outcome, namely docetism. "If the immutability and impassibility of God inevitably led Chalcedon to a dualistic portrait of Christ the most serious consequence of this dualism is the undermining of his true humanity."[15] Lane has placed this objection last not for its position of descending importance, but for rhetorical emphasis showing the deepest problems which

---

[8] Lane, "Christology Beyond Chalcedon," 263.

[9] Richard Bauckham has attempted to move beyond this impasse with his "Christology of Divine Identity," in *God Crucified: Monotheism and Christology in the New Testament* (Grand Rapids: Eerdmans, 1998), 26-42. While not addressing his Christology to matters of being or nature, Bauckham does focus the question on divine identity which includes Jesus in the identity of Israel's God. This approach has some promise for explaining the deity of Christ without recourse to the debates of the early church. Yet, as Bauckham has admitted that Jesus must be incorporated into the transcendence of God, this goal cannot be meaningful without discussing his nature as God, and therefore articulating a substantive Christology, which is what Chalcedon was ultimately about.

[10] The scholar who made this a basic axiom in his understanding of Jesus Christ was the French-born Oscar Cullmann. See Cullmann, *The Christology of the New Testament*, rev. ed., trans. Shirley C. Guthrie and Charles A.M. Hall (Philadelphia: Westminster, 1963).

[11] Lane, Christology beyond Chalcedon," 265.

[12] Lane, Christology beyond Chalcedon," 266.

[13] Lane, Christology beyond Chalcedon," 267.

[14] Lane, Christology beyond Chalcedon," 268.

[15] Lane, Christology beyond Chalcedon," 268-69.

Chalcedon may succumb to.[16] This issue of docetism is pursued by Lane along three distinct yet related avenues of thought. These are (1) human limitations, (2) knowledge, and (3) impersonal humanity. To evaluate these objections it is essential to probe the matters a little so as to grasp their intended effect, and their significance in discounting Chalcedon. Beginning with a biblical premise that Christ was made like his brethren in every respect, Lane asserts that ". . . it is essential that he shared in human limitations."[17] Here Lane cites with approval a famous line from Donald Guthrie who claimed, "all that Jesus did during his earthly ministry was governed by that limitation."[18] It is with this concept, that a truly limited Christ is the only correct understanding of Scripture, that Lane challenges the insufficiency of Chalcedon. "While the Chalcedonian Definition may allow a theoretical acknowledgment of human limitation," Lane concedes, "in practice," he now charges, "it denies them."[19] This dissatisfaction with Chalcedon goes hand in hand with Lane's dismissal of a "dualism" in the New Testament documents. Chalcedon fails in ascribing true limitations because it maintains that Christ was limited as man yet remained unlimited as God. Lane protests,

> These criticisms are not to be construed as a rationalistic attack on paradox. The problem with Chalcedon is not that it affirms the biblical paradox of God accepting human limitations but that it effectively denies these limitations. The affirmation that the historical Jesus was omniscient and omnipotent, which undermines his participation in human weakness and limitations, is not one half of a biblical paradox but an alien intrusion foreign to the New Testament.[20]

B.3. Omniscient or not?

From a general discussion of human limitations, Lane moves to the specific question of knowledge. "The issue of human limitation," indeed, asserts Lane, "is felt most acutely in the area of Christ's knowledge."[21] Of course, here is where the apparent biblical data are strongly in Lane's favor. He cites Luke 2:52 as well as Mark 13:32. He uses the latter to show that "he [Jesus] himself explicitly denied his omniscience."[22] Then Lane categorically blasts, "The affirmation of the omniscience of the historical Jesus has *no biblical basis* (emphasis added) and indeed runs counter to the clear teaching of the Gospels."[23]

---

[16] Lane is sure to point out that some errors in judgment about the person of Christ spring from misinformation and misinterpretation. "But," notes Lane, "to some extent the fault lies not simply in ignorance of or misinterpretation of the Chalcedonian Definition but in the Definition itself" (Lane, "Christology beyond Chalcedon," 269-70).

[17] Lane, Christology beyond Chalcedon," 270. Later on in the article, Lane proposes his preference for a Christology "from below," which, he contends is the biblical model. This is becoming more and more considered the norm.

[18] Lane, Christology beyond Chalcedon," 270.

[19] Lane, Christology beyond Chalcedon," 270.

[20] Lane, Christology beyond Chalcedon," 270.

[21] Lane, Christology beyond Chalcedon," 270.

[22] Lane, Christology beyond Chalcedon," 271.

[23] Lane, "Christology beyond Chalcedon," 271. It is very interesting and somewhat ironic to note that in the same volume in which Lane's essay appears is a helpful treat-

Lane continues, "It does not make sense to speak of the same one person being simultaneously ignorant and omniscient."[24]

B.4. Enhypostatic Christology

Lane moves to his final point concerning the so-called "Impersonal humanity." Unfortunately, as Lane concedes, many critiques of the enhypostatic concept appear to have failed to grasp the meaning of this notion, and therefore misrepresent it in the following way. "To say today that Christ's humanity was 'impersonal,'" says Lane, by way of illustration, "sounds blatantly docetic."[25] Then immediately following this assertion, Lane quotes, as an example, a maxim cited by D.M. Baillie attributed to R.C. Moberley: "Human nature which is not personal is not human nature."[26] What Lane finally claims about this misunderstanding, is that it is prevalent concerning the enhypostatic Christology. As such, he shows this as a proof that Christology needs to move beyond Chalcedon and be exposited in contemporary idiom.[27] To this Lane now proceeds in his own suggestions as to what a modern Christology might look like. His proposal will allow us the opportunity to complete our analysis of this writer.

B.5. Abiding value of Chalcedon

Lane argues that the criticisms which have been leveled against Chalcedon force us to the conclusion "that it cannot be accepted without reservation."[28] Its

---

ment of Incarnation Christology by I. Howard Marshall. He claims, "Our modern tendency is to insist that Jesus was every bit as man, just the same as one of us. This may perhaps cause us to do less than justice to the New Testament representation of him as primarily the Son of God who took on the form of man. Where modern discussion emphasizes the fullness of his humanity, the New Testament emphasizes the fullness of his divinity" (I. Howard Marshall, "Incarnational Christology in the New Testament," in *Christ the Lord: Studies in Christology Presented to Donald Guthrie*, ed. Harold H. Rowdon. [Leicester: InterVarsity, 1982], 7). Also see I. Howard Marshall, *The Origins of New Testament Christology*, updated ed. (Downers Grove, IL: InterVarsity, 1990), 126-29.

[24] Lane, "Christology beyond Chalcedon," 272.
[25] Lane, "Christology beyond Chalcedon," 272.
[26] Lane, "Christology beyond Chalcedon," 272.
[27] Rather than abandoning the enhypostatic idea one should seek to expound it. It is not clear that Lane wishes to dispense with the enhypostasia notion, but he appears to lean in that direction. Enhypostatic Christology is the only way to maintain the identity of Jesus with the Logos and avoid Nestorianism. Berkouwer gives a prod in the right direction by stating, "[When] the term 'anhypostasy' is used, the issue is not one of *truncating* human nature but one of uniting it with the Logos . . . . Hence in evaluating the idea of 'anhypostasy' one must always ask whether the rationale behind it is sound . . . . In view of the dangers of monophysitism . . . people gave preference to the expression 'enhypostasy' to avoid the undesirable connotation of the word 'impersonal.' By means of the term 'enhypostasy' they intended to oppose Ebionitism . . . and Nestorianism . . . . We must remember . . . that the church must . . . watch closely the *import* of the terms used to give expression to the mystery of the Christian faith" (G.C. Berkouwer, *Studies in Dogmatics: The Person of Christ*, trans. John Vriend [Grand Rapids: Eerdmans, 1954], 312-13).
[28] Lane, Christology beyond Chalcedon," 273.

Chapter 4: Contemporary Christology & Chalcedon

abiding value, however, is seen in the following claims. First, it prevails as a negative Christology ruling out specific heresies. What Christ is not, according to Chalcedon, has permanent value. Second, its positive statements, although in need of modification, because of adherence to immutability and impassibility, are still helpful and necessary.[29] Finally, because of its antiquity, just as with the Bible itself, Lane believes that Chalcedon needs to be updated by translation into contemporary form.[30] Now Lane moves to his specific proposals.

B.6. Christological Method

Here Lane is forthright in asserting a methodology. "The New Testament writers," he posits, "did not start with belief in the pre-existent divine Son and then identify this being with Christ."[31] Of course, Lane does not discount the Trinity, but merely hopes that a fully "precise" view of the Trinity should not hamper our understanding of the fully human Jesus.[32]

Lane's next suggestion follows on the heels of his discussing the Trinity. He believes that the historic Christ be our starting point. This is really the same matter as before. Here, also, Lane moves to make assertions that are troubling.

---

[29] It is difficult to see what Lane really considers to be binding in this regard. He grants that today Christology need not start from scratch, but must build upon Chalcedon.

[30] Lane, "Christology Beyond Chalcedon," 273-74.

[31] Lane, "Christology beyond Chalcedon," 275. Of course, this begs the question for us who have the entire Bible. What role, if any, should a fully biblical doctrine of God inform and shape our Christology? Trinitarianism and Christology stand next to each other and must frequently be examined in the hermeneutical process as one develops biblical teaching on either of these issues. No doubt, the one *will* inform the other. Lane suggests something quite unacceptable. See the following footnote.

[32] The desire for a doctrine of Christ informed by a doctrine of the Trinity that is *imprecise* is suspiciously troubling. Lane is trying desperately to save face here. He notes in the discussion that "to work from the doctrine of the Trinity to the person of Christ is to work from the unknown to the known" (Lane, "Christology Beyond Chalcedon," 275). In the footnote, Lane presents us with a caveat: "It is not, of course, being suggested that Christology be done as if there were *no* doctrine of the Trinity. It is the use of a *precise* doctrine of the Trinity to control Christology that is wrong" (275, n.70). It appears that Lane will be happy to utilize *his* view of the Trinity if it does not lead to a distorted (per Lane) view of Christ. To do this Lane exclaims, "In the New Testament the economic Trinity is primary. God is known to be three because of his action for our salvation as Father, Son and Holy Spirit" (275). One might ask, "Is this not precise?" A corrective to this popular notion is found in Henri Blocher. He asserts: "Transcendence and immanence in relation to the world do not change the divine identity when the world is created. They do not make God *correlative*; the glory of the ontological Trinity radiates in fullness, while it assures us that we . . . know God *himself* when he reveals himself: his revelation as the transcendent and immanent God is no alteration of his essence. We know him in grace and truth. This is the logic, theo-logic, of John 1:18: the ontological Trinity is the ground of effective revelation–the only-begotten God who is in the bosom of the Father was free as such to explain God, in grace and truth" (Henri Blocher, "Immanence and Transcendence in Trinitarian Theology," in *The Trinity in a Pluralistic Age: Theological Essays on Culture and Religion*, ed. Kevin J. Vanhoozer [Grand Rapids: Eerdmans, 1997], 123).

After stating that traditional Christology moved from the miracles that Jesus performed to the conclusion that these proved his deity, Lane counters, by saying, "this interpretation runs into a number of difficulties."[33] The miracles "can be paralleled in other biblical characters," says Lane.[34] Finally, Lane speaks of the relation of Jesus to the triune Godhead by mentioning three proposals that express that identity. He briefly mentions a "kenotic" view. He dismisses this approach while insisting that it has provided help for those beyond its immediate circle who wish to claim human limitations in their Christology. Next, Lane mentions a "double life of the logos" view that has been associated with H.L. Martensen. Lane dismisses this view as separating the two natures counter to the Chalcedonian definition.[35] Lastly, Lane briefly mentions another "kenotic" view but claims it should better be labeled the "self-restraint" view.[36] It is fairly self-explanatory. Christ retained the possession of all divine attributes but ceased from actually exercising them. Thus Christ did not "empty himself but rather limited himself during the incarnation."[37] All of the approaches start with the assumption that the pre-existent Logos has his own divine omniscience and omnipotence. Lane thinks it best to redefine our notion of the Trinity by starting to look at God through the lens of a limited Jesus.

B.7. Conclusion

Lane ends by stating that the answers provided by our various Christologies can only be for the "who" question and not of the "how" question. Lane has argued for a view of God as passible and mutable. Only in this way can he begin to

---

[33] Lane, "Christology beyond Chalcedon," 276.

[34] Lane, "Christology beyond Chalcedon," 277. One must concede that in some sense this is true. However, the specific purpose of the miracles that Jesus performed had the goal of identifying him as the Son of God. In John 20:30-31 which is clearly a purpose statement for the life ministry of Jesus as recorded by John, it is the signs (miracles) that were instrumental in leading to a correct insight into Jesus' person so faith in him would bring eternal life. Lane's thesis betrays this explicitly scriptural reason for the miracles Jesus performed. See also John 5:36; 10:25, 37-38; and 14:11.

[35] Lane, however, does admit that this double life view is consistent with the previously discussed presentation of Jesus' humanity. Rather than rejecting this approach, I believe it is on the right track in articulating a Christology of *one person in two natures*. What is in question, however, is whether this is really H. Martensen's view. Thomas Schultz associates Martensen with a "Kenotic" Christology. On this reading of Martensen's view, Shultz says, "The Incarnate Christ still possessed His true deity but only within the restricted confines of human consciousness. Before the incarnation the Logos had an infinitely divine relationship to the universe, but when He became the mediator His divine functions and attributes were limited to the extent of the capabilities of His manhhood" (Thomas Schultz, "The Doctrine of the Person of Christ with an Emphasis upon the Hypostatic Union" [Th.D. diss., Dallas Theological Seminary, 1962], 90). This seriously undermines the designation "double life" approach. If there is a divine life exercised by the incarnate mediator, according to Martensen's position, then it is a very different God from the one displayed throughout the pages of Scripture. For an alternative view of the kenotic approaches, one may consult the discussion in Schultz (84-92).

[36] I refer to this approach as *sub-kenotic*.

[37] Lane, "Christology beyond Chalcedon," 279.

grasp the possibility of an incarnation to begin with. This is a spirited defense of a Christology that attempts at preserving the Chalcedonian heritage, yet allowing for modern restatement of the concept of the incarnation.

C. Ronald Leigh

A very different kind of recommendation appears in the work of Ronald Leigh. Although there are similarities with Lane, ultimately this is a different approach to Christology.

C.1. Introduction

Whereas Lane sought to move beyond Chalcedon, Leigh seeks to abandon it completely. In this argument, Leigh does not seek to neglect either the true humanity or the true deity of Jesus, rather his intent is "to demonstrate the incoherence of the two-nature model of the person of Christ and the coherence of the one-nature model."[38]

C.2. Nature . . . What is it?

Leigh's first point is the matter of the "Logical Impossibility" of the two-nature model. He defines the terms "individual" and "nature." Again, "An individual," says Leigh, "is an extant, single, indivisible entity."[39] "*Nature*," Leigh continues, "is the set of essential characteristics (qualities or attributes) of any given individual or class of individuals, that is, the set of characteristics which that individual must have in order to be included in its class."[40] On this identification Leigh claims it is impossible for one individual to have two natures.[41] Leigh still adheres to a unique Jesus, just not a two-natured Jesus. "His uniqueness," claims Leigh, "can easily be maintained simply on the grounds that he is the only individual with the single set of characteristics which he has."[42] This

---

[38] Leigh, "Jesus" 125. Leigh believes his view presents logical consistency in regard to classification, coheres with the doctrine of *imago Dei*, and is sound in hermeneutics. Our analysis will follow his self-paved path.

[39] Leigh, "Jesus," 125.

[40] Leigh, "Jesus," 125.

[41] "The fact that one individual cannot have two natures," Leigh asserts, "underlies the long-standing problem created by those who claim that Jesus is one person *with* two natures" ("Jesus: the One-Natured God-man," 126, emphasis added). Two observations need to be briefly noted at this point. First, the designation "one person *with* two natures," may be the popular way of expressing Chalcedonian commitments, but technically it is "one person *in* two natures." This keeps us from speaking of the person as one thing or entity, and thereby allowing the natures to be abstractly described as an addition to the basic framework of person. The correct notion is that the person of Christ is *in* two natures, not permitting his person to be abstractly disassociated from the natures in which he exists. Thus the enhypostatic Christology does justice to the way Christ is described in the New Testament as God and as man. Second, the problem of Christology has not been caused by those who have formulated the Chalcedonian definition, as if the New Testament itself is so pristine in its portrayal of a one-natured Jesus. The very formula has been fashioned as a solution or explanation of the very difficulty inherent in the New Testament documents themselves. Chalcedon is not the problem; Jesus is the problem.

[42] Leigh, "Jesus," 125.

single set of characteristics is the same as a description of Christ's one nature, according to Leigh. This is key in his proposal. "The problem of the two natures of Jesus," posits Leigh, "is really a problem of two descriptions of Jesus. One individual [as defined earlier], having only one nature, needs only one description."[43]

C.3. Antinomy–Not Sufficient

After succinctly surveying views throughout church history, Leigh next dismisses the notion of "antinomy" for helping to solve the Christological question. He quotes the well-known definition as given by J.I. Packer:

> An antinomy exists when a pair of principles stand side by side, seemingly irreconcilable, yet both undeniable. There are cogent reasons for believing each of them; each rests on clear evidence; but it is a mystery to you how they can be squared with each other. You see that each must be true on its own, but you do not see how they can both be true together.[44]

Packer's famous discussion centers on the issue of divine sovereignty and human responsibility. It is fairly obvious how Leigh intends to proceed in his discussion of Christology. He cites Lorraine Boettner, Lewis Sperry Chafer, and Louis Berkhof as representatives of "antinomy Christology." For example, the Reformed theologian Louis Berkhof said, "the person of Christ can be said to be omniscient, but also have limited knowledge; can be regarded as omnipresent, but also as being limited at any particular time to a single place."[45] Leigh does not object to this approach by showing how the position of Berkhof and others is incorrect. Rather, Leigh counters by stating that other evangelical writers, primarily theologians and apologists, use the "law of non-contradiction," to expose falsehood. Leigh mentions and cites Charles Hodge, E.J. Carnell, J. Oliver Buswell, and Paul Little. The law of non contradiction basically asserts that you cannot affirm and deny the same thing in the same way at the same time. As a formula: A cannot be simultaneously non-A. Hence for Leigh, the law of non-contradiction shows that antinomy is "not wanted."[46] Furthermore, the concept of antinomy is "not needed because the New Testament data do not require it."[47] Leigh continues:

> The New Testament never speaks of the nature of Jesus as an antinomy. Nor does it give any basis for an antinomy. In other words, it does not say in one place that Jesus knew everything, while also saying in another place that Jesus did not know something.[48]

In addition, to this strong and categoric assertion, in a footnote Leigh relates the following:

---

[43] Leigh, "Jesus," 125. Evidently, this will become a rather complex *single* description of Jesus Christ if all the data are accounted for.
[44] Leigh, "Jesus," 128.
[45] Cited by Leigh, "Jesus," 129.
[46] Leigh, "Jesus," 130.
[47] Leigh, "Jesus," 130.
[48] Leigh, "Jesus," 130.

Jesus himself indicates that he did not know the timing of his own return (Matt. 24:36; Mark 13:32). However, the New Testament never says that Jesus knew everything. Although Peter's statement about Jesus, "you know all things" (John 21:17), is inspired in the sense that it is a reliable record of what Peter said, it is not necessarily an inspired statement in itself. Even if it is an inspired statement in itself, it can be considered to be a generalization while Jesus' own statements on the subject provide the exception to the generalization (similar to the generalizations that no one is righteous except Jesus). Other passages such as Mark 2:8 and John 2:24-25 may indicate superhuman knowledge, but superhuman knowledge is not the same as omniscience. Colossians 2:3 is probably an indication of the believer's fulness of wisdom and knowledge in Christ, rather than an indication of Christ's omniscience.[49]

C.4. One Nature Not Two

After rejecting the notion of antinomy, Leigh moves to the argument for the legitimacy of a description of Christ as one-natured. In this ingenious section, Leigh uses an analogy of a chair desk. He rejects the charge that this makes Jesus a *tertium quid*. "A genuine *tertium quid*," notes Leigh in his illustration, "given the classifications of desks and chairs, could be a pencil, or a glove, or a key."[50] "All of these items," he continues, "fail to fit into either of the two given classifications and thus each one forms a genuine *tertium quid*. The difference with the chair desk is that it qualifies for *both* of the two given classifications."[51] The analogy serves Leigh for he believes the best and most comprehensive classification of Jesus is God-man. Just like the chair desk, so the God-man fits in both categories.[52] This can be sustained as Leigh draws on the teaching concerning the *imago Dei*. Leigh believes that the incarnation took place by addition. I agree; this is helpful. It leads in the right direction. "The additions that were accomplished through the Incarnation," claims Leigh, "were sufficient to qualify him to be called human, but they were not sufficient to disqualify him from being called God."[53] This is so for Leigh believes there is "a degree of similarity [and] . . . that these two classifications are overlapping classifications."[54]

C.5. Method and Hermeneutics

Finally, Leigh discusses the issue of method under the heading of "theological-hermeneutical procedure." Here Leigh echoes similar concerns advocated by Lane. We should not allow our pre-determined notions of what God is like to shape our understanding of Jesus. Rather, Leigh continues, "As part of the Son's mission was to supply concrete information about the Father (John 1:18, 14:7-9) . . . . [so] the proper procedure [is] to build our picture of Jesus and at

---

[49] Leigh, "Jesus," 130. n. 23.
[50] Leigh, "Jesus," 132.
[51] Leigh, "Jesus," 132.
[52] Leigh explains in a footnote that his view differs from traditional Monophysitism. This is granted in my interpretation of his view and will not be a further problem at this point.
[53] Leigh, "Jesus," 133.
[54] Leigh, "Jesus," 133.

least part of our picture of the Father on the New Testament description of Jesus."[55]

C.6. Conclusion

Leigh's proposal *per se* is quite justified given the nature of the theological task, and its hermeneutical grounding. But it strikes me that it is not merely this that is leading to the result of a one-natured Jesus in conclusion of the argument. Something more is at stake here.

D. Conclusion on Contemporary Thinkers

Obviously the dissatisfaction with the Chalcedonian definition and the way it has been defended by proponents over the years has led to a need to re-examine the view. Has Leigh made a compelling case to abandon the two-nature model? Does in fact the New Testament present Jesus as deity without omniscience, and thus without omnipotence and omnipresence? Are the descriptions of Jesus' manhood the hermeneutical filter for understanding his deity, as Lane appears to favor, and therefore for grasping the constitution of his person? Are the evangelical positions of a kenotic or sub-kenotic Christology the right and only ones for making sense of the New Testament data? We will need to return to these and other questions. Before that, however, it is helpful to show how Christians thought about the incarnation in other eras. To do this we shall survey the early church, then focus in on the Christological commitment of John Calvin and the so-called *extra Calvinisticum*. After this historical presentation, an evaluation of the contemporary evangelical contribution can be made, as well as the positive exposition of the thesis concerning the omnipresence of Jesus Christ.

---

[55] Leigh, "Jesus," 136.

CHAPTER 5

PATRISTIC CHRISTOLOGY:
A SURVEY OF THE EARLY CHURCH

A. Introduction

The second through the sixth century is where the debates about Christology were most formative.[1] Discussion about the relation between the Father and the Son were primary during the first three to four hundred years. Also, discussion moved to the natures of Christ, which, predominated in the fourth and fifth centuries. Then in the sixth century and beyond the question of Christ's will or wills became significant. Despite the continuing nature of Christological debate, the conclusions reached by the time of the Chalcedonian formula of AD 451 have remained the standard. "One Person in Two Natures" has been considered the touchstone for orthodoxy ever since. Therefore, no in-depth study of Christology is complete without a survey of the early church. This chapter will sketch some of the leading contributions to Christological development from the time of Irenaeus through to the advances proposed by Leontius of Byzantium and John of Damascus.

B. Ante-Nicene Theology

The apostolic Fathers who chronologically followed the apostles focused on the Christian life, especially on ethics. Other concerns involved apologetics. Christology, though not prominent, is sometimes noted in their writings.[2] This sur-

---

[1] Lewis Ayres, *Nicaea and Its Legacy: An Approach to the Fourth-Century Trinitarian Theology* (New York: Oxford University Press, 2004); James Bethune-Baker, *An Introduction to the Early History of Christian Doctrine to the Time of the Council of Chalcedon* (London: Methuen, 1903); Glenn F. Chestnut, *Images of Christ: An Introduction to Christology* (San Francisco: Harper & Row, 1984); John Behr, *The Way to Nicaea: Formation of Christian Theology*, volume 1 (Crestwood, NJ: St Vladimir's Seminary Press, 2001); idem, *The Nicene Faith: Formation of Christian Theology*, volume 2, parts 1 & 2 (Crestwood, NJ: St Vladimir's Seminary Press, 2004); and Stephen W. Need, *Truly Divine and Truly Human: The Story of Christ and the Seven Ecumenical Councils* (Peabody, MA: Hendrickson, 2007).

[2] Ignatius had a tendency to refer to Jesus as God. Harris, speaks of the "boldness of Ignatius in designating Jesus as ὁ θεος . . ." (Murray J. Harris, *Jesus as God: The New Testament Use of* Theos *in Reference to Jesus* [Grand Rapids: Baker, 1992], 9). Harris cites the following from the Ignatian corpus: *Eph.* 1:1; 7:2; 19:3; *Rom. prooem*; 3:3; and *Poly.* 8:3. For Ignatius's Christology one may consult Johannes Quasten, *Patrology*, vol.1, *The Beginnings of Patristic Literature* (Allen, TX: Christian Classics, n.d.), 65-66; Aloys Grillmeier, *Christ in Christian Tradition*, vol.1, *From the Apostolic Age to*

vey begins with the first biblical/systematic theologian, Irenaeus, followed by a look at contributions from Tertullian and Origen.

B.1. Irenaeus (ca. 115-ca. 202)

Known as the first biblical theologian of the church, Irenaeus is therefore considered first.[3] Cyril Richardson notes, "He [Irenaeus] provided the framework of formal theology and indicated the topics that later theology and Christian philosophy would have to take up."[4] His desire to refute the heretical teaching of Gnostics in his day is well known.[5] As part of his anti-Gnostic biblical theology, a marked literalism is evident.[6] Irenaeus allowed no allegorical exegesis as would later become prominent in Origen. This emphatic biblical literalism plays a significant role in the development of his Christology as it functions as a part of Irenaeus's claim that the one and only true God is creator and therefore has united himself with creation. The incarnation serves as a building block of the grand edifice of recapitulation, or the summing up of all things in Christ.[7] "The heart of Irenaeus' Christology and indeed of his entire theology,"

Chalcedon (451), trans. John Bowden (Atlanta: John Knox, 1975), 86-89; Walter H. Wagner, *After the Apostles: Christianity in the Second Century* (Minneapolis: Fortress, 1994), 146-50; and, especially, Thomas G. Weinandy, "The Apostolic Christology of Ignatius of Antioch: The Road to Chalcedon," in Andrew F. Gregory & Christopher M. Tuckett, *Trajectories Through the New Testament and the Apostolic Fathers* (New York: Oxford University Press, 2005), 71-84. A most enlightening study is Vasilliou P. Stogianou, "Η Χριστολογια των Επιστολων Ιγνατιου του και Θεοφορου," in Σπού δαστηριον Ιστορικής Θεολογιας Πανεπιστημιον Θεσσαλονικης Συμποσιον εις τον Καθηγητην Παναγιωτην Κ. Χρηστου, ed. George Mantzarides (Thessaloniki: University of Thessaloniki, 1967), 71-110. The author denies that Ignatius was influenced by Hellenistic ideas, and maintains the faithfulness of Ignatius to the "Rule of Faith."

[3] Clark says, "Irenaeus was the first great Catholic theologian" (Everett Ferguson, ed., *Encyclopedia of Early Christianity* [New York: Garland, 1998], s.v. "Irenaeus," by Mary T. Clark).

[4] Cyril C. Richardson, ed., *Early Christian Fathers*, trans. and ed. Eugene R. Fairweather, Edward Rochie Hardy, and Massey Hamilton Shepherd, LCC 1 (Philadelphia: Westminster, 1953), 352.

[5] His most famous work is *Against Heresies*. The complete text in English translation is available in vol. 1 of the Ante Nicene Fathers. See Irenaeus, *Against Heresies*, trans. A. Roberts and W.H. Rambaut, ANF, American ed., vol. 1 (Buffalo: Christian Literature, 1885; reprint, Grand Rapids: Eerdmans, 1975). Another known work of importance is *The Proof (Demonstration) of the Apostolic Preaching*. This work is available in English translation in the series Ancient Christian Writers, vol. 16. See *St. Irenaeus, Proof of the Apostolic Preaching*, trans. and ed. Joseph P. Smith. Ancient Christian Writers (London: Longmans, Green and Co., 1952).

[6] See the helpful discussion in Thomas F. Torrance, *Divine Meaning: Studies in Patristic Hermeneutics* (Edinburgh: T & T Clark, 1995), 56-74. "Irenaeus gives immense attention to typological interpretation of prophetic testimonies culled from the Old Testament," observes Torrance, "in order to show the continuity of God's redemptive purposes in history. At no point, however, does he engage in allegorical exegesis (such as we find in Origen's writings)" (Torrance, *Divine Meaning*, 66).

[7] Gustaf Wingren, expresses as well as anyone how Irenaeus utilizes the idea of reca-

Chapter 5: Patristic Christology. A Survey of the Early Church

notes Quasten, "is his theory of recapitulation (ἀνακεφαλαιωσισ)."[8] Quasten continues,

> Although he borrowed the idea from the Apostle Paul, he developed it considerably. Recapitulation is for Irenaeus a taking up in Christ of all since the beginning. God rehabilitates the earlier divine plan for the salvation of mankind which was interrupted by the fall of Adam, and gathers up his entire work from the beginning to renew, to restore, to reorganize it in his incarnate Son, who in this way becomes for us a second Adam.[9]

In *Adversus Haereses* Irenaeus shows the connection between salvation, recapitulation, and the incarnation. He states, "When he [the Word or Son of God] became incarnate and was made man, he recapitulated in himself the long history of man, summing up and giving us salvation in order that we might receive again in Christ Jesus what we had lost in Adam, that is, the image and likeness of God."[10] Wingren has noted, "Christ alone is the subject of recapitulation, and there is nothing which He does from His birth until the end which is not part of the ἀνακεφαλαιωσις."[11] No doubt, the Incarnation is a key doctrine and in Irenaeus we have a high Christology.[12] In discussing the incarnation, Irenaeus states,

> Not one among the sons of Adam is called God or Lord. It is evident, however, to all who possess even a moderate bit of the truth, that unlike all men of the past the Christ is properly proclaimed as God, Lord, eternal King, Only-begotten, and incarnate Word, by all the prophets and apostles and the Spirit itself.[13]

---

pitulation: "The use of ἀνακεφαλαιωσις and *recapitulatio* is an attempt by Irenaeus to embody the whole of the Biblical proclamation about the work of Christ in a single word .... Recapitulation means the accomplishment of God's plan of salvation, and this accomplishment is within history, in a time-sequence, and is not an episode at one particular point of time. It is a continuous process in which the οἰκονομια, *dispositio*, of God is manifested by degrees. First, and most important of all–and the basis of our whole salvation–is the event of the birth of Jesus when the Son of God became an actual man" (Wingren, *Man and the Incarnation: A Study in the Biblical Theology of Irenaeus*, trans. Ross Mackenzie [Philadelphia: Muhlenberg, 1959)], 80-81). According to Robert Grant, Irenaeus believed the expression "recapitulation" meant "that Christ reenacted all earlier events, leading them to their destination" (Grant, *Jesus After the Gospels: The Christ of the Second Century* [Louisville: Westminster John Knox, 1990], 106).

[8] Quasten, *Beginnings of Patristic Literature*, 295.

[9] Quasten, *Beginnings of Patristic Literature*, 295-96.

[10] *Adversus Haereses*, 3.18.1. Cited in Quasten, *Beginnings of Patristic Literature*, 296.

[11] Wingren, *Man and the Incarnation*, 82.

[12] This point is brought out by Grant, *Jesus after the Gospels*, 98-108, esp. 101-102. See also Denis Mins, *Irenaeus* (Washington, DC: Georgetown University Press, 1994), 94-100.

[13] *Adversus Haereses* 3.19.2. For this translation consult Robert M. Grant, *Irenaeus of Lyons* (New York: Routledge, 1997), 137. This volume contains two parts. The first is an introduction to Irenaeus. The second section, which is much longer, is a fresh translation of many portions from *Adversus Haereses*.

He affirms that the Logos was made man. Christ has both divine and human natures. Wingren's insight into the importance of the Incarnation is noteworthy. He explains:

> Irenaeus lays a very great deal of emphasis on the fact that it is the Son from all eternity, and therefore *God Himself*, who assumes human flesh in Jesus. The One who has created everything from nothing enters into His corrupt Creation in the Incarnation in order to renew it.[14]

Irenaeus claims of Jesus Christ that "as man he is without beauty and capable of suffering (Is. 53:2-3) . . . . On the other hand he is holy Lord, marvelous Counselor (Is. 9:6), beautiful in appearance (Ps. 44:3), Mighty God (Is. 9:6) . . . ."[15] In addition, Irenaeus asserts, "For as the Lord was man in order to be tested, so also he was Word in order to be glorified . . . This is [the] Son of God . . . and son of man."[16] Irenaeus makes a statement in his *Demonstration of the Apostolic Preaching* which shows that Jesus Christ is omnipresent. In a section speaking about the work of the Son of God who has become incarnate, Irenaeus claims: "By His obedience unto death on the cross, He wiped out the ancient disobedience wrought on the tree. He is Himself the Word of almighty God, who in His invisible form pervades us all and encompasses the breadth and length, the height and depth, of the whole world, for by God's Word all things are guided and ordered."[17] There is no ambiguity about whom Irenaeus makes such statements. He is speaking of the incarnate Christ. Jesus pervades all. As the transcendence of the Son of God is not rescinded in the incarnation, the Word made flesh can guide the world in power. Also because he is everywhere present, he fills the cosmos.[18]

B.2. Tertullian (ca. 160-ca. 220)

Our survey will continue by evaluating the contribution of Tertullian.[19] He is known as the father of Western theology. Although Tertullian wrote about many issues, we are chiefly concerned with his contribution to Christology.[20]

---

[14] Wingren, *Man and the Incarnation*, 86.

[15] *Adversus Haereses* 3.19.2, cited in Grant, *Irenaeus of Lyons*, 137.

[16] *Adversus Haereses* 3.19.3. Ibid., 138.

[17] John Saward, trans., *The Scandal of the Incarnation: Irenaeus Against the Heresies*, selected and introduced by Hans Urs von Balthasar (San Francisco: Ignatius, 1990), 15. The passage quoted is from *Demonstration* 34. This helpful volume by Saward draws together many texts on the significance of Jesus Christ and his work in the theology of Irenaeus.

[18] Reist claims, "The essence of Irenaeus' proclamation is that Jesus Christ is divine, God Himself" (Irwin W. Reist, "The Christology of Irenaeus," *JETS* 13 [1970]: 247).

[19] For the Christology of the Apologists one should consult the following works: Comprehensive coverage is found in V.A. Spence Little, *The Christology of the Apologists: Doctrinal* (New York: Charles Scribner's Sons, 1935). An important book dealing with the totality of the thought of the Apologists is Robert M. Grant, *Greek Apologists of the Second Century* (Philadelphia: Westminster, 1988). Also, see Grant, *Jesus after the Gospels*, 58-95.

[20] Two important works by Tertullian on Trinitarianism and Christology are: Q. Sep-

As Kelly notes, "The central feature of Tertullian's Christology was its grasp of the two natures in Christ."[21] This important aspect of his Christology is not without difficulty for readers of Tertullian to grasp due to the nuances in terminology at the precise time Tertullian wrote and because of the debates among scholarly interpreters of his thought. Despite these challenges, we will attempt an evaluation of the contribution that clearly stands out in Tertullian's Christological exposition, namely that the Savior was composed of "two substances." The classic passage where this expression is found is in *Adversus Praxean* 27.[22] Norris explains the reason for Tertullian's language in this section. He says, "His [Tertullian's] defense . . . in the treatise *Against Praxeas*, was directed by Tertullian the Montanist against people who wanted to assert the absolute unity of the divine in face of the apparent division and plurality which the Logos-doctrine introduced into the divine nature."[23] Tertullian asserts:

> We see plainly the twofold state, which is not confounded, but conjoined in one person–Jesus, God and Man . . . so that the property of each nature is wholly preserved that the Spirit on the one hand did all its own things in Jesus such as miracles, and mighty deeds and wonders; and the flesh, on the other hand, exhibited the affections which belong to it . . . Forasmuch, however, as *the two substances* (emphasis added) acted distinctly, each in its own character, there necessarily accrued to them severally their own operations and their own issues.[24]

Quasten, commenting upon this very passage, argues that "[Tertullian] clearly announces the two natures in the one person of Christ . . . . We recognize in these statements the formula of the Council of Chalcedon (A.D. 451) of the two substances in one person."[25] Yarnold, however, states matters slightly differently. Instead of the later "two natures," he believes "the phrase," *videmus duplicem statum* (we see the twofold status), "is not two *natures*, but 'duplex status', which perhaps means something like 'two modes of being.'"[26] This insight is significant enough, given Tertullian' insistence that each "nature" retains its own properties. Yet one must also see that Quasten's observation that Chalcedon is anticipated here in Tertullian is surely justified. Tertullian states, "videmus duplicem statum, non confusum sed coniunctum, in una persona deum et

---

timii Florentis Tertulliani, *Adversus Praxean Liber* (*Tertullian's Treatise Against Praxeas*, ed. and trans. Ernest Evans [London: SPCK, 1948]); and idem, *De Carne Christi Liber* (*Tertullian's Treatise on the Incarnation*, ed. and trans. Ernest Evans [London: SPCK, 1956]).

[21] J.N.D. Kelly, *Early Christian Doctrines* (San Francisco: Harper Collins, 1978), 150.

[22] An English translation is available in Richard A. Norris, Jr., *The Christological Controversy* (Philadelphia: Fortress, 1980), 61-64. The quote is from 13.

[23] Norris, *The Christological Controversy*, 13.

[24] Cited in Johannes Quasten, *Patrology*, vol. 2, *The Ante-Nicene Literature after Irenaeus* (Allen, TX: Christian Classics, n.d.), 328.

[25] Quasten, *Patrology*, vol. 2, 328.

[26] Edward J. Yarnold, "Videmus Duplicem Statum": The Visibility of the Two Natures of Christ in Tertullian's *Adversus Praxean*," in *StPatr* 19 (Leuven: Peeters, 1989), 286.

hominem Iesum . . . . Salva est utriusque proprietas substantiae."[27] The clear language of two *substances* (Kelly), *natures* (Quasten), or *modes of being* (Yarnold) are without confusion.[28] Tertullian rejects the notion of any type of transformation of the deity of the Word into that of humanity. There is rather a conjunction, not a mixture resulting in some form of a *tertium quid*. Yarnold argues that Tertullian, utilizing Stoic philosophical concepts prefers the idea of inter-penetration. He notes that scholars have pointed out

> Tertullian's predilection for the verb *induere* for expressing the assumption by the Word of human nature. . . .The metaphor of the 'putting on' humanity like a coat seems to suggest a very superficial Christology, but Tertullian gives the word new dimension . . . suggest[ing] that in Christ the humanity and the divinity compenetrate.[29]

Grillmeier, on the other hand, does not give a glowing endorsement like those of Kelly and Quasten. Grillmeier goes to much greater length in evaluating Tertullian's Christology. He notes Tertullian's commitment to the unity of divine substance, while also noticing Tertullian's avowal of a differentiation within the unity.[30] In commenting on Tertullian's concept of the "threeness" (an economical dynamic threeness) of God, Grillmeier states, "Only the Father remains completely transcendent."[31] This singling out of the Father alone as

---

[27] Cited in Yarnold, "Videmus Duplicem Statum," 286. Grillmeier suggests that this is a difficult passage as scholars have differed in the translation (even the punctuation) and interpretation of Tertullian at this point (Grillmeier, *From Apostolic age to Chalcedon*, 123).

[28] Norris' translation asserts, "not compounded but conjoined, in one person, Jesus, who is God and a human being" (Norris, *Christological Controversy*, 63).

[29] Yarnold, "Videmus Duplicem Statum," 290. This idea anticipates the perichoresis notion found in John of Damascus' Christology.

[30] Grillmeier, *From the Apostolic age to Chalcedon*, 119.

[31] Grillmeier, *From the Apostolic age to Chalcedon*, 120. Despite Grillmeier's fine treatment of Tertullian, on this specific point he makes, there is no text that he points to in order to substantiate that in Tertullian "Only the Father remains transcendent," (120). After surveying carefully the treatise *Adversus Praxean*, the conclusion that is reached by this writer is very different. That the Word remains immutable even after the incarnation is observed from the following passage: "Who, being God was born in her [Mary]? The Word, and the Spirit who with the Word was born by the Father's will. Therefore the Word is in flesh; while we must also enquire about this, how the Word was made flesh, whether as transformed into flesh or as having clothed himself with flesh. Certainly as having clothed himself. God however must necessarily be believed to be immutable and un-transformable, as being eternal. But change of form is destruction of what was there first: for everything that is transformed into something else ceases to be what it was and begins to be what it was not. But God neither ceases to be, nor can be anything else. And the Word is God, and *the Word of God abideth for ever*, evidently by continuing in his own form" (Tertulliani, *Adversus Praxean* [27], trans. and ed. Ernest Evans [London: SPCK, 1948], 173). For an analysis of the Stoic background that may have influenced Tertullian's choice of options concerning the "how" of the incarnation, see Eric Osborne, "Tertullian as Philosopher and Roman," in *Die Weltlichkeit des Glaubens in der Alten Kirche: Festschrift für Ulrich Wickert zum siebzigsten Geburtstag*, ed.

Chapter 5: Patristic Christology. A Survey of the Early Church

transcendent is problematic, as it is the total immutability of the Word which keeps Tertullian from espousing any form of transformation in the incarnation.[32] This is certainly the case as can be seen by Tertullian's earlier work *De Carne Christi*. We must quote him at length to grasp the nature of his argument. Tertullian, in contrast to Gnostic speculation, asserts:

> For God runs no risk of ceasing to be what he is. 'But,' you say, 'the reason why I deny that God was really and truly changed into man, in the sense of being both born and corporated in flesh, is that he who is without end must of necessity also be unchangeable: for to be changed into something else is an ending of what originally was: therefore change is inapplicable to one to whom ending is inapplicable.' I admit that the nature of things changeable is bound by that law which precludes them from abiding in that which in them suffers change–the law which causes them to be destroyed by not abiding, seeing that by process of change they destroy that which they once were. But nothing is on equal terms with God: his nature is far removed from the circumstances of all things whatsoever.[33]

Tertullian next shows that God would be as mere created things, which are subject to the law of change that he mentions, if he is mutable. So to safeguard God's divinity one must not put God in the same category of created things. To complete his argument, Tertullian then shows that angels have in the past changed into human form yet remaining what they were, and then he makes the *a fortiori* claim concerning God. "Well then," forcefully asserts Tertullian, "that which was permitted to the angels of the inferior God when changed into human corporeity, the faculty of none the less remaining angels–will you deny this to the more mighty God, as though his Christ had not the power, when truly clothed with manhood, of continuing to be God?"[34]

Moreover, in further challenging Grillmeier's observation about only the Father being transcendent, one must ask: how could the Word continue to rule the world for the Father in the sole *monarchia* during the period of the incarnation (something Grillmeier already accepts[35] as part of Tertullian's view), if the incarnate Word is not transcendent above the created order even after the Word became flesh? Tertullian was clear that the belief in a Trinity in no way jeop-

---

Dietmar Wyrwa (Berlin: Walter de Gruyter, 1997), 231-47, esp. 239-41.

[32] See Kelly, *Early Christian Doctrines*, 151.

[33] Tertulliani, *De Carne Christi* [3], trans. and ed. Ernest Evans (London: SPCK, 1956), 11.

[34] Tertulliani, *De Carne Christi*, 11. There is a possible allusion to Christ's omnipresence in Tertullian, which is related to this discussion. In showing that there must of necessity be two "persons" as Christ on earth addresses his Father in heaven, Tertullian adds some pertinent remarks: "You have the Son on earth, you have the Father in Heaven. That is no separation, but a divine ordinance. Yet we know that God is even within the depths, and takes up his position everywhere–though in function and power–and that the *Son also, as inseparable, is with him everywhere* [emphasis supplied]" (*Adversus Praxean* 23).

[35] Grillmeier explains: "The monarchia of God is preserved because the Son exercises only the one rule of the Father and gives it back to the Father at the end of this world period" (*From the Apostolic age to Chalcedon*, 120).

ardizes the sole *monarchia*, even if the Son rules in behalf of the Father.³⁶ Although Grillmeier in continuing his exposition of Tertullian's view shares some insights made by others, he nonetheless believes Tertullian's approach is "not very deep."³⁷

Given the difficult issues being dealt with and the complexity of portraying biblical insight (remaining true to the *regula fidei*) with contemporary terminology, Tertullian passes the test with his Christology. It is true that his concept of the Trinity, although he was the first to introduce the term *trinitas* into use, has some problems, especially subordinationism.³⁸ Yet his Christology, as Quasten reminds us, "has all the merits of his teaching on the Godhead and none of its defects. He clearly announces the two natures in the one person of Christ."³⁹

B.3. Origen (ca. 185-ca. 251)

With Origen we return to Greek Christianity.⁴⁰ No doubt, Origen was a controversial figure, and is well known for his "speculative" theological proposals. Again, many interesting issues must be left aside to focus on Origen's Christology.⁴¹ Grillmeier's comment will set the tone for our brief investigation. "There

---

³⁶ See *Adversus Praxean* 3-4. What must be conceded in Grillmeier's assertion, is that a strain of subordinationism is evident in Tertullian. It is this observation, no doubt, coupled with certain expressions, such as the sun and the sunbeam, that have moved Grillmeier to assert that only the Father is truly transcendent.

³⁷ Grillmeier, *From the Apostolic age to Chalcedon*, 123. Grillmeier's discussion is very important. Although he suggests that the Chalcedonian question does not really surface (contra Kelly and Quasten), he agrees that Tertullian is "primarily the theologian of two natures or two substances" (129).

³⁸ See Quasten, *Ante-Nicene Literature*, 326.

³⁹ Quasten, *Ante-Nicene Literature*, 328. For more on Tertullian's Christology, see Dennis K. House, "The Relation of Tertullian's Christology to Pagan Philosophy," *Dio* 12 (1988): 29-36.

⁴⁰ Speaking of Clement of Alexandria and Origen, Sellers notes, "They were Christians living in an atmosphere of Greek thought–but Christians they remained" (R.V. Sellers, *Two Ancient Christologies: A Study in the Christological Thought of the Schools of Alexandria and Antioch in the Early History of Christian Doctrine* [London: SPCK, 1940], 3).

⁴¹ A full account of this important subject is found in J. Nigel Rowe, *Origen's Doctrine of Subordination: A Study in Origen's Christology* (Berne: Peter Lang, 1987). Helpful too is Ayres's magnificent achievement in Lewis Ayres, *Nicaea and its Legacy*: An Approach to Fourth-Century Trinitarian Theology (New York: Oxford University Press, 2004), 20-30, where he elegantly explains the tension in Origen concerning the relationship between the Father and the Son. Also note a less well-known resource for investigating Origen's Christological contribution: Harold J. Fickett, Jr., "A Comparative Study of the Christology of Origen and Calvin Based on the Περι Αρχων and The Institutes of The Christian Religion" (Th.D. diss., Eastern Baptist Theological Seminary, 1949). For a through re-examination of Origen we are indebted to the innovative work of Ilaria L.E. Ramelli, "Origen's Anti-Subordinationism and its Heritage in the Nicene and Cappadocian Line." *VC* 65 (2011): 21-49 for a claim that Origen was the direct influence on Nicene Christology.

Chapter 5: Patristic Christology. A Survey of the Early Church

is a real traditional basis to his [Origen's] christology," posits Grillmeier, "which is . . . expressed particularly clearly, as for example in his recognition of the two natures of the Lord."[42] Origen was first and foremost a biblical exegete and therefore it is not surprising that in his thought we find a *biblical* theology committed to the *regula fidei*.[43]

Origen was wise to admit, "For it is impossible to put into writing all that belongs to the Saviour's glory."[44] This was so, for Origen acknowledged the clear scriptural teaching of two natures in the person of Jesus Christ. He said, upon reflecting on this duality, that one is "baffled and struck with amazement at so mighty a wonder . . . ."[45] Nevertheless, Origen would attempt to "say" something about this greatest of all mysteries. However, one must appreciate his candor as he claims:

> It is then in no spirit of rashness, but solely in response to the demands of our inquiry at this stage, that we shall state in the fewest possible words that we may term the content of our faith concerning him rather than anything which needs to be proved by arguments of human reason, bringing before you our suppositions rather than any clear affirmations.[46]

Surprisingly, at this juncture Origen begins his exposition of his Christology with an appeal to the theory about the pre-existence of souls.[47] The one soul which did not fall but remained faithful would be joined to a body and therefore it was this soul which is in union with the Logos of God that is involved in the

---

[42] Grillmeier, *From the Apostolic age to Chalcedon*, 138-39.

[43] L.W. Barnard, makes this observation: "Origen based his Christology on Tradition as this was embodied in the Church and the Scriptures" (L.W. Barnard, "Origen's Christology and Eschatology," *AthR* [1964]: 315). In evaluating Origen, Bray's warning should be heeded: "It would be easy, but wrong, to dismiss Origen as a fantasizer who used the Bible as a quarry for fashioning his own ideas. He firmly believed that the Scriptures were an accurate record of a God who could be known and experienced by men" (Gerald Bray, *Creeds, Councils and Christ: Did the Early Christians Misrepresent Jesus?* [Fearn: Mentor, 1997], 80). For the exact opposite approach, note Rowe's comment. He says, "It appears ludicrous to regard Origen as a devotee of Scripture. His knowledge of the Bible may well have been unrivaled, but in all honesty let us admit that he simply uses it as a peg on which to hang his own preconceived ideas" (Rowe, *Origen's Doctrine of Subordination*, xix). Another writer who cautions against a rash condemnation of Origen is Crouzel. He argues that one needs to be conversant with the entire corpus of Origen's extant material before passing a quick and negative judgment. Crouzel also reminds his reader that Origen was far from a "systematic" theologian, though often thought of in that way, and more importantly that later theological criteria should not be used to criticize his speculations made in his own day. See Henri Crouzel, *Origen*, trans. A.S. Worrall (Edinburgh: T & T Clark, 1989), 46-49, 163-79 (esp. 163-67).

[44] Origen, *On First Principles,* trans. G.W. Butterworth (Gloucester, MA: Peter Smith, 1973), 109.

[45] Origen, *On First Principles*, 109.

[46] Origen, *On First Principles*, 110.

[47] See Kelly, *Early Christian Doctrines*, 154-58. Kelly sees this approach as the "key" to Origen's theology of the Incarnation.

incarnation.[48] Origen refers to this entity as the "God-man, the medium being . . . whose nature it was not contrary to assume a body."[49] So Origen appealed to the human soul, which was essentially the Logos joined to a human body, to explain the person of Jesus.

In this schema it is tempting to assume that Origen did not embrace a true incarnation of God. Jesus is merely the image of the image.[50] Of course, Origen did not believe it was possible for the one true God to somehow embrace a body, so his appeal, to the soul of the Logos functions as an escape from attributing something unworthy to God. Nevertheless, Origen affirmed the deity of the Logos. This whole matter is troubling, for as Madden observes, "In Origen's Christology the preexisting soul leaves the bosom of the Father at the Incarnation, while the Word remains there always in his place, withal being in a certain way present on earth in his soul."[51] This idea is very attractive as it appears to assert that Jesus Christ was omnipresent, even in the incarnate state prior to the ascension. Origen is saying something similar here, according to Madden. As Madden utilizes the traditional kenosis notion of the incarnation, he sees a potential problem with Origen's conception of the mechanics of the incarnation. The troubling feature, Madden asserts, is that Origen seems to hold to a *kenosis* of the soul rather than the Logos proper.[52] This may not be the case as Crouzel has evaluated the issue. In drawing one's attention to what Origen stated in the preface to the *Peri Archon*, Crouzel says, "His kenosis did not put an end to his divine character."[53] Origen appears clear. He says,

> Then again: Christ Jesus, he who came to earth, was begotten of the Father before every created thing. And after he had ministered to the Father in the foundation of all things, for 'all things were made through him', in these last times he emptied himself and was made man, was made flesh, although he was God; and being made man he still remained what he was, namely God.[54]

It follows here that Crouzel is correct. There is no way to restrict the *kenosis* (as traditionally understood), which Origen takes to be the incarnation itself, merely to the soul. It is spoken of in relation to the Word who is the creator (language drawn from John 1:3), who also became flesh (John 1:14) in such a way that he still remained absolute God.[55] This is further borne out when one sees

---

[48] See Barnard, "Origen's Christology and Eschatology," 317.

[49] Origen, *On First Principles*, 110.

[50] The discussion in Nicholas Madden, "An Aspect of Origen's Christology," in *Studies in Patristic Christology*, ed. Thomas Finan and Vincent Twomey (Portland, OR: Four Courts, 1998) is particularly illuminating.

[51] Madden, "An Aspect," 27.

[52] Madden, "An Aspect," 27.

[53] See Crouzel, *Origen*, 186.

[54] Origen, *On First Principles*, 3.

[55] Origen held to a form of the *communicatio idiomatum*, which was necessary for his explication of the death of Christ. This is found in *Peri Archon* 2.6. Origen states, "The Son of God is said to have died, in virtue of that nature which could certainly admit of death, while he of whom it is proclaimed that 'he shall come in glory of the Father and

the clear affirmation Origen made concerning the omnipresence of the Word. Following his discussion of the eternity of the Word, Origen says, "After this it will be appropriate for us to make mention of the bodily coming of and incarnation of the only-begotten Son of God. And here we must not suppose that all the majesty of his godhead was confined within the limits of a tiny body."[56] To provide a rationale for his reasoning Origen appeals to the words of John the Baptist in John 1:26, 27. The Baptizer spoke of one who stood in the midst of the people he addressed even though Jesus, according to Origen, was physically absent. Origen rounds off his discussion stating the matter plainly, "This shows that the Son of God was both wholly present in his body and also wholly present everywhere."[57]

C. Nicene Theology

Our survey will continue with a look at the Christology of Nicea[58] and particularly that of Athanasius of Alexandria.[59] Despite pious claims that "Athanasius

---

the holy angels' is called Son of man. . . . while the divine nature is spoken of in human terms the human nature is in its turn adorned with marks that belong to the divine prerogative" (Origen, *On First Principles*, 111).

[56] Origen, *On First Principles*, 317. Origen continues connecting the omnipresence of the Word with the "essence of the Father," which is also omnipresent.

[57] Origen, *On First Principles*, 317. See Fickett, "A Comparative Study of the Christology of Origen and Calvin," 94-95. Also Origen states, "Even, then, if the God of the universe descends with Jesus into human life by his power, and even if the Word who 'was in the beginning with God', and who was himself God, comes to us, he does not go away from where he was, nor does he leave his throne, as though one place were deprived of him, and another which previously did not possess him were filled . . . ." (Origen, *Contra Celsum*, trans. Henry Chadwick, cited in Torrance, *Divine Meaning*, 355-56).

[58] Most important in evaluating the Christological attempts of the Nicene council is Basil Studer, *Trinity and Incarnation: The Faith of the Early Church*, trans. Mathias Westerhoff, ed. Andrew Louth (Collegeville, MN: Liturgical, 1993), 110-114. For the history between Nicaea (325) and Ephesus (431) with a theological focus, one should consult Georges Florovsky, *The Byzantine Fathers of the Fifth Century* (Vaduz, Liechtenstein: Büchervertriebsanstalt, 1987), 136-93; Leo Donald Davis, *The First Seven Ecumenical Councils (325-787): Their History and Theology* (Collegeville, MN: Michael Glazier, 1983), 33-169; and Stephen Need, *Truly Divine & Truly Human: The Story of Christ and the Seven Ecumenical Councils* (Peabody, MA: Hendrickson, 2008). For exhaustive treatments of all things theological during the tumultuous fourth century, R.P.C. Hanson, *The Search for the Christian Doctrine of God: The Arian Controversy 318-381* (Edinburgh: T & T Clark, 1988); Ayres, *Nicaea and its Legacy*; Franz Dünzl, *A Brief History of the Doctrine of the Trinity in the Early Church*. Trans. John Bowen (Edinburgh: T and T Clark, 2007); Khaled Anatolios, *Retrieving Nicaea: The Development and Meaning of Trinitarian Doctrine* (Grand Rapids: Baker, 2011); and Donald Fairbairn, *Life in the Trinity: An Introduction to Theology with the Help of the Fathers* (Downers Grove, IL: InterVarsity, 2011) are highly recommended.

[59] Two important studies in Greek need to be noted at this point. Constantine Karakoli, "Η ΟΙΚΟΥΜΕΝΙΚΗ ΣΥΝΟΔΟΣ ΤΗΣ ΝΙΚΑΙΑΣ ΚΑΤΑ ΤΟΝ ΜΕΓΑΝ ΑΘΑΝΑΣΙΟΝ" in Σπουδαστηριον Ιστορικης Θεολογιας Πανπιστημιον Θεσσαλονικης

was the champion at Nicea," this was not the case.⁶⁰ Athanasius attended the famous council of 325 but was merely an attendant and aid to his bishop Alexander. To begin this phase we must start with the so-called Arian crisis.

C.1. The Search for the Christian God

Richard Hanson has painstakingly documented the central issues surrounding what is now known as the Arian crisis.⁶¹ The controversy began when a Presbyter, Arius contested the eternity of the Son of God. This was a result of debating the meaning of Proverbs 8, which all participants at the time took to be a teaching about Christ.⁶² This text became a virtual battle-ground. Athanasius later deals with it in *Contra Arianos* book II. The whole debate flared up with a disagreement between Arius and his Bishop Alexander. "Soon," according to Clayton, "'the Lord created me' reverberated through every street and alleyway in Alexandria, and wherever else those sympathetic to Arius's notions wished to prove that the Son was a creature."⁶³ The way out of this difficulty for those wishing to maintain the eternity of the Son was to argue for divine generation.⁶⁴ This was a theological idea going back to Origen and it finally became the orthodox understanding of the relations in the Trinity. Athanasius himself goes to

---

Χαριστηριον εἰς τον καθηγτην Παναγιωτην Κ. Χρηστου, ed. George Mantzarides, (Thessaloniki, 1967), 113-18; and Stylianos G. Papadopoulos, *ΑΘΑΝΑΣΙΟΣ Ο ΜΕΓΑΣ ΚΑΙ Η ΘΕΟΛΟΓΙΑ ΤΗΣ ΟΙΚΟΥΜΕΝΙΚΗΣ ΣΥΝΟΔΟΥ* (Athens, 1975). In this latter work especially, one notes how Athanasius dealt with the Christological matters in conjunction with the issue of the "Theology of Synod" for the church at large.

⁶⁰ See Alvyn Petterson, *Athanasius* (Harrisburg, PA: Morehouse, 1995), 7.

⁶¹ R.P.C. Hanson, *The Search for the Christian Doctrine of God: The Arian Controversy 318-381* (Edinburgh: T & T Clark, 1988). Also extremely helpful is Rowan Williams, *Arius: Heresy and Tradition* (Grand Rapids: Eerdmans, 2002). Williams interacts with critiques of the first edition published in 1987, and remains adamant about the misgivings of so called "Arianism," as he says, ". . . there is a growing sense that Arianism is a very unhelpful term to use in relation to the fourth- century controversy (247). His study is indispensable for understanding this era of theological controversy.

⁶² On this whole matter of Proverbs 8, one should consult Allen L. Clayton, "The Orthodox Recovery of a Heretical Proof-Text: Athanasius of Alexandria's Interpretation of Prov. 8:22-30 in Conflict with the Arians" (Ph.D. diss., Southern Methodist University, 1988).

⁶³ Clayton, "The Orthodox Recovery," 2.

⁶⁴ Athanasius, however, was one of the few to settle on the opinion that Proverbs 8 taught about the incarnation of the Logos. In this he followed Marcellus of Ancyra. See Clayton, "The Orthodox Recovery of a Heretical Proof-Text," 206-18 for Marcellus, and 255-93 for Athanasius. This is a fascinating study of the interaction of biblical interpretation, dogmatic formulation, and apologetic contention. Athanasius includes elements of incarnation and divine eternal generation in his exposition of Proverbs 8. "Athanasius' first exegesis of Proverbs 8:22 ff," as Clayton observes, "relates vv. 22 and 23 to the incarnation and vv. 25-30 to the pre-cosmic generation of the Son from the Father" (Clayton, "The Orthodox Recovery of a Heretical Proof-Text," 274). On Marcellus, see Joseph T. Lienhard, *Contra Marcellum: Marcellus of Ancyra and Fourth-Century Theology* (Washington, DC: Catholic University Press, 1999).

Chapter 5: Patristic Christology. A Survey of the Early Church

lengths to sustain the eternal nature of all three persons in the divine Triad.[65] The driving force was an approach which necessitated a fully divine savior otherwise salvation was not guaranteed. An eternal Christ was thus required to provide eternal life. The debate reached a high point at the famous council of Nicea (AD 325) but far from a solution, this was merely a slowing down of the theological merry-go-round so many more could jump on and join in the discussion.[66] From the issue concerning the relations within the Godhead, we must forego further investigation at this juncture to concentrate particularly on Christology. R.P.C. Hanson has evaluated the specific issue of Christology according to the broader concerns of Arian theology. He says,

> Arianism in all its forms assumed that the Incarnation was a dispensation on the part of God which necessitated a reduction or a lowering of God so that it had to be undertaken by a being who, though divine, was less than fully divine. The inferiority of the incarnate Logos to God the Father was necessary for an Incarnation to take place at all.[67]

For "Arius, the Alexandrian Presbyter," in particular, notes Norris, "[his] public teaching after A.D. 318 occasioned the trinitarian and christological debates of

---

[65] See Roland Chia, "ΜΙΑ ΟΥΣΙΑ ΤΡΕΙΣ ΥΠΟΣΤΑΣΕΙΣ: St. Athanasius and the Doctrine of the Holy Trinity," *JianDao* 9 (1998): 27-48.; Petterson, *Athanasius*, 36-90; Thomas Torrance, "The Doctrine of the Holy Trinity According to St. Athanasius," in *Trinitarian Perspectives: Toward Doctrinal Agreement* (Edinburgh: T & T Clark, 1994), 7-19; Quasten, "The Theology of Athanasius," in *Patrology*, vol. 3, *The Golden Age of Greek Patristic Literature from Nicaea to Chalcedon* (Allen, TX: Christian Classics, n.d.), 66-70; and, especially, Peter Widdicombe, "Athanasius and the Making of the Doctrine of the Trinity," *ProEccl* 6 (1997): 456-78.

[66] "It must be granted," Robert Wilken has noted, "that the trouble began with Arius and the varying responses to his teaching. To be sure, his doctrine had been condemned at Nicaea long before the time of Cyril and Nestorius, but this was only a prelude to the violent battle stretching across the fourth century" (Wilken, "Tradition, Exegesis and the Christological Controversies," in *Studies in Early Christianity*, vol. 9 [New York and London: Garland, 1993], 143). Please note that pagination is from the volume in which this article is reprinted: 141-63. Hanson's study, *The Search for the Christian Doctrine of God*, is particularly helpful in tracking the developments after Nicaea. The creed itself which was adopted does not deal with the two natures in a Christological manner per se, but it addresses the nature of the Son as God. The Nicene watchwords are ἐκ τοῦ πατρός γεννηθέντα and ὁμοούσιον τῷ πατρί. As Christ is generated by the Father, He has the same substance as the Father, and he is fully God.

[67] R.P.C. Hanson, "The Arian Doctrine of the Incarnation," in *Arianism: Historical and Theological Reassessments. Papers from the Ninth International Conference on Patristic Studies. September 5-10, 1983, Oxford, England*, ed. Robert C. Gregg (Philadelphia: The Philadelphia Patristic Foundation Ltd., 1985), 182. This essay is very helpful for all stages of Arian Christology. For a consideration as to how metaphor influenced these theological/christological debates see Catherine Osborne, "Literal or Metaphorical? Some Issues of Language in the Arian Controversy," in eds. Lionel Wickham & Caroline P. Bammel, assist. Erica C.D. Hunter, *Christian Faith and Greek Philosophy in Late Antiquity: Essays in Tribute to George Christopher Stead in Celebration of his Eightieth Birthday 9th April 1993* (Leiden: E.J. Brill, 1993), 148-70.

the fourth century."[68] Norris is in agreement with Hanson's observation about the Arian commitment to the transcendence of God. "[Arius] was a firm believer not only in the unity of God," Norris states, "but also in a doctrine of divine transcendence which saw God's way of being as inconsistent with that of the created order."[69]

A look at the Nicene Creed shows that Christology needs to be discerned between the lines.[70] This was the beginning of a "scientific theology," as Torrance puts it; its ablest defenders were Hilary in the West and Athanasius in the East.[71] To Athanasius we must now turn.

C.2. Athanasius of Alexandria's Christology

Athanasius became bishop in 328.[72] Soon after he found himself in exile where he was afforded opportunity to write. *Contra Gentes* and *De Incarnatione* probably emerged at this time between 335-37.[73] It is noted that no specific mention of the Arian crisis is found in these works.[74] Later during his second exile, Athanasius begins his anti-Arian literature. These writings were probably intended for more mature theological students such as monks, but later became public records.[75] However, there emerges a clear pastoral concern as Athanasius is seeking to keep Christians from embracing Arian theology, and he also seeks to win back those deceived by the Arian arguments. Athanasius writes on

---

[68] See Norris, *The Christological Controversy*, 17.

[69] Norris, *The Christological Controversy*, 17.

[70] Norris, *The Christological Controversy*, 18.

[71] See Torrance, "The Relation of the Incarnation to Space in Nicene Theology," in *Divine Meaning*, 343-73; and "The Nicene Theology of Athanasius and Hilary," in Basil Studer, *Trinity and Incarnation*, 115-25.

[72] For a recent volume which attempts at filling an obvious void in comprehensive Athanasian studies, see the very well written and eminently documented book by Khaled Anatolios, *Athanasius: The Coherence of His Thought* (New York: Routledge, 1998). Christology is highlighted in the section "The Redeemed Relation between God and Creation as a Christological Problem," 138-61.

[73] John Kaye, *Some Account of the Council of Nicaea in Connexion with the Life of Athanasius* (London: Francis & John Rivington, 1853), follows the classical studies of Bernard de Montfaucon, the Father of Greek Paleography, in dating these two works to A.D. 318. This date is also posited by Archibald Robertson in *St. Athanasius: Select Works and Letters*, NPNF 2, vol. 4 (New York: Christian Literature, 1892; reprint, Grand Rapids: Eerdmans, 1998), lxiii. Hanson, *Search for the Christian Doctrine of God*, 418, opts for the later date [A.D. 335-336]. For a balanced treatment of this issue, see Anatolios, *Athanasius*, 26-30. Anatolios finally opts for a "fairly credible combination of [a] *terminus post quem* [335] and [a] *terminus ante quem* [328]" (Anatolios, *Athanasius: Coherence*, 27, 29).

[74] On this see especially Richard J. Voyles, "The Fear of Death and a False Humanity as the Human Dilemma: The Argument of Influence in Athanasius' Christology," *Pat-ByzR* 8 (1989): 135-44. Voyles considers it a mistake to read *On the Incarnation* as an anti-Arian polemic.

[75] See *Encyclopedia of Early Christianity*, ed. Ferguson, s.v. "Athanasius" by Charles Kannengiesser.

Chapter 5: Patristic Christology. A Survey of the Early Church

this false teaching "so that those who are distant from her might flee her, and those deceived by her might repent." (*Contra Arianos* I, 1).

The works *Orationes Contra Arianos* books I-III, are the most mature reflections by the Alexandrian bishop on the matter of the relationship between the Father and the Son, and therefore implicitly of a Christology that is grounded in Trinitarianism. The books consisting of *Contra Arianos* I-III were probably written, as Hanson says, "between 339 and 345, [and] perhaps [we can] envisag[e] their production as a fairly long-drawn-out process over that period."[76] These discourses against the Arians include, albeit not in a systematic way, teaching on Christology proper.[77]

---

[76] Hanson, *Search for the Christian Doctrine of God*, 419. Anatolios suggests that the entire Anti-Arian polemic of Athanasius is to be dated "between the 340s and the early 370s, from the issue of the relation of the Son to the Father, to that of the relation of the Spirit to Father and Son, to Christological questions" (Anatolios, *Athanasius*, 93).

[77] See Craig Alan Blaising, "Athanasius of Alexandria: Studies in the Theological Contents and Structure of the 'Contra Arianos' with Special Reference to Method" (Ph.D. diss. University of Aberdeen, 1987). This dissertation is invaluable as a running commentary on the three books of Athanasius known as *Contra Arianos*. When Blaising discusses the "Christological" material in book three, he explains that the broader concern was clearly about the relationship of the Son with the Father, yet "[it] does not mean that it is illegitimate to attempt to discern Athanasius' Christology as much as possible in these [Book III:30-35] and the following sections" (394-95). It should be noted that there are actually four volumes or books entitled *Contra Arianos*. Among the foremost Athanasian scholars today there is difference of opinion regarding the genuineness of all four books. George Dragas and Thomas F. Torrance accept book four as genuine, whereas this is a minority view. Charles Kannengiesser, on the other hand, rejects book three as not part of the original composition of Athanasius, He sees *Contra Arianos* I and II as a compositional unity involving some redactional additions by Athanasius. He also holds book four as spurious. Many, including Blaising, accept book three as truly from Athanasius's pen (see 1-11). The following studies are particularly helpful in assessing the Christological contribution of Athanasius: Grillmeier, *From the Apostolic age to Chalcedon*, 308-28 (especially 326-28); Kelly, *Early Christian Doctrines*, 284-89; Petterson, *Athanasius*, 109-35; Thomas F. Torrance, *Theology in Reconciliation: Essays Towards Evangelical and Catholic Unity in East and West* (Grand Rapids: Eerdmans, 1975), 215-66; George Dion Dragas, "ΕΓΕΝΕΤΟ ΑΝΘΡΩΠΟΣ" and "The Eternal Son," in *Athanasiana: Essays on the Theology of Saint Athanasius* (London, 1980), 9-73; idem, *Saint Athanasius of Alexandria: Original Research and Perspectives* (Rollinsford, NH: Orthodox Research Institute, 2007), which is a veritable treasurehouse including an exhaustive bibliography of Athanasian studies; Thomas G. Weinandy, *Athanasius: A Theological Introduction* (Burlington, VT: Ashgate, 2007); Jon M. Robertson, *Christ as Mediator: A Study in the Theologies of Eusebius of Caesarea, Marcellus of Ancyra, and Athanasius of Alexandria* (New York: Oxford University Press, 2007), 137-216; Peter Widdicombe, *The Fatherhood of God From Origen to Athanasius* (New York: Oxford University Press, 2000, [1994]), 145-222; Charles Twombley, "The Nature of Christ's Humanity: A Study in Athanasius," *PatByzR* 8 (1989): 227-41; Richard J. Voyles, "The Fear of Death and a False Humanity as the Human Dilemma: The Argument of Influence in Athanasius' Christology," *PatByzR* 8 (1989): 135-44; Ellen T. Charry, "The Case for Concern: Athanasian Christology in

Many of the concentrated studies on Athanasius's Christology center on the question of whether he affirmed a human soul for the man Jesus Christ. This will have to be treated briefly.[78]

Alvyn Petterson has challenged a growing consensus concerning the infamous label of "spacesuit Christology," made popular by Richard Hanson.[79] Hanson argued that the incarnation was much like an astronaut putting on a spacesuit. What this would appear to mean is that Athanasius merely uses his "external" body just like a space traveler uses his "external suit." This is decidedly an attempt to read certain passages in Athanasius with modern sensibilities. Our modern predisposition to a more Antiochene type Christology, that emphasizes the genuine humanity is admitted by Frances Young, and would certainly characterize Hanson's own presuppositions that color his reading of Athanasius. Young, however, has at the same time given the Alexandrian tradition a fair hearing (unlike Hanson in my opinion), and concludes that "[t]he Alexandrian tradition insisted throughout that the Logos was the sole subject of the incarnate experiences; this alone could be called a real Incarnation of the Logos."[80] This was linked to the need for the Savior to be fully divine and the sole actor in redemption. Young adds: "In spite of docetic tendencies in their attempts to do justice to this belief [the real Incarnation], the Alexandrines in fact, gave a better account of traditional Christian belief than the Antiochene school, which divided the natures and failed to expound their unity in the Incarnation."[81] Athanasius himself claimed that the body that was assumed by the logos was not ἄψυχον.[82] Furthermore, George Dragas has shown that the classification of Athanasius's though within a logos-flesh (sarx) framework must be questioned.[83] Dragas has conclusively shown that for Athanasius flesh (sarx) in

---

Pastoral Perspective," *ModTheol* 9 (1993): 265-83; Charles Kannengiesser, "Athanasius of Alexandria and the Foundation of Traditional Christology," *TS* 34 (1973): 103-13; and Chauncey R. Daley, "Christology of Athanasius of Alexandria" (Ph.D. diss., Southern Baptist Theological Seminary, 1954).

[78] On this issue Grillmeier and Quasten are very thorough. See also Christopher Stead, "The Scriptures and the Soul of Christ in Athanasius," *VC* 36 (1982): 233-50. Stead focuses on the influence of Eusebius and his changing Christology as he combats Marcellus, and on his direct influence on Athanasius. In opposition to Grillmeier's approach, Khaled Anatolios, "'The Body as Instrument': A Reevaluation of Athanasius' Logos-Sarx Christology," *CCR* 18 (1997): 78-84, challenges the 'Logos-Sarx' framework and offers an admirable attempt at reading Athanasius without traditional prejudice. This is a superb article!

[79] See Hanson, *Search for the Christian Doctrine of God*, 448. For a more balanced view, See Petterson, *Athanasius*, 109-117; and Frances M. Young, "A Reconsideration of Alexandrian Christology," *JEH* 22, no. 2 (April 1971): 103-114.

[80] Young, "Reconsideration of Alexandrian Christology," 113.

[81] Young, "Reconsideration of Alexandrian Christology," 113.

[82] Young, "Reconsideration of Alexandrian Christology," 108. Though admittedly, this was later in Athanasius's career, after the Apollinarian controversy was well under way.

[83] See Dragas, *Athanasiana*, 9-32, especially 12-14, where Dragas puts much data in chart form.

essence means "man." In this study, Dragas conclusively treats Athanasius's Christology showing that the eternal Logos becomes "humanized" without ceasing to be divine. Furthermore, Anatolios has masterfully discredited the traditional approach evident in Hanson, by showing conclusively that Athanasius's own arguments lead in another direction.[84] It is a "model of predication," that Anatolios garners from the primary materials. This must lead us to investigate the "double account" teaching of Athanasius that he garnered from within the biblical material.

C.2.1. Double Account of the Savior

Athanasius certainly held a view embracing two distinct but joined natures in one person, and therefore clearly anticipated Chalcedon. Petterson has demonstrated that Athanasius, in his anti-Arian polemics, shows what is proper to each nature nevertheless also retaining that the actions are performed by the one subject.[85] This is particularly highlighted in *Contra Arianos* III. Scripture "contains as we have often said," repeats Athanasius, "a double account of the Savior."[86] It is here that Athanasius grounds his specific Christological methodology in the Scope of Scripture.[87] We must investigate this. While noting the

---

[84] "With regard to the subjectivity of the Incarnate Word," notes Anatolios, "it has become commonplace among modern commentators on Athanasius to say that, according to the Egyptian bishop, the divine Word is the sole subject of all the acts of Jesus Christ and the humanity of Christ is conceived as an instrument by which the Word acts. While it is indeed true that Athanasius speaks of Christ's humanity as an instrument, the interpretation of this concept within the framework of an agent—instrument model is *highly misleading* [emphasis supplied]. It is simply not the case that Athanasius relates the divinity and humanity of Christ in terms of subjectivity and instrumentality, with the implied extrincism of this model. Rather . . . it is typical of Athanasius's logic to refer the act back to the subject in the same way he refers will to being, and to the task of redemption to One who is adequate for the task. . . . The important thing to see is that this commonality [the Word with our human nature] is expressed by Athanasius not primarily within the framework of an agent using an instrument that is "extrinsic" to that agent, but much more fundamentally within the framework of predicating the humanity of Christ to the divine Word." See Anatolios, *Athanasius: Coherence of his Thought*, 140. This entire discussion (138-163) is masterful, and, in my opinion, settles the issue regarding Athanasius's Christology. Also see Khaled Anatolios, *Athanasius* (New York: Routledge, 2004).

[85] Petterson's comments acknowledge that some have read Athanasius too woodenly, yet he maintains that Athanasius is misunderstood in this way. See his discussion in Petterson, *Athanasius*, 112-13.

[86] This translation is found in Norris, *The Christological Controversy*, 87. In the Greek, the passage reads: Σκοπός τοινύν ούτος καὶ Χαρακτηρ τῆς Αγιας Γραφῆς ὡς πολλάκις εἴπομεν διπλῆν ειναι τὴν περι τοῦ Σωτῆρος ἐπαγγελίαν ἐν αὐτή. For the Greek text see ΑΘΑΝΑΣΙΟΥ ΑΛΕΞΑΝΔΡΙΑΣ ΤΟΥ ΜΕΓΑΛΟΥ ΑΠΑΝΤΑ ΤΑ ΕΡΓΑ 3 ΔΟΓΜΑΤΙΚΑ Β ΕΛΛΗΝΕΣ ΠΑΤΕΡΕΣ ΤΗΣ ΕΚΚΛΗΣΙΑΣ 12 (Θεσσαλονικη: Πατερικαι Εκδῶσεις, 1975), 94. Also see J.- P. Migne, ed. PG 45: 385 A.

[87] Hall has nicely captured the essence of this in his fine intro to Patristic hermeneutics. See, Christopher A. Hall, *Reading Scripture with the Church Fathers* (Downers Grove, IL: InterVarsity, 1998), 56-64, esp. 62. For an insightful look at this concept in

possibility that Athanasius was not the author of the third oration, Clayton, nevertheless had this to say about 3.29: "Whether or not Athanasius was the author of the third oration, the above passage [cited above] *accurately reflects his concept of the* skopos *of scripture* [emphasis added]."[88] Clayton also sees the exegetical value that Athanasius placed on the double account formula. He concludes,

> Athanasius insisted that Scripture's one *skopos* was a 'double account of the savior,' i.e., *skopos* was the means by which economic statements could be sorted out from the absolute ones. It is the 'nature' of Christ (pre-existent or incarnate) that gives meaning to the 'terms' of scripture. Discover the 'person' of a text and it can be interpreted correctly.[89]

What becomes clear from Athanasius's discussion is that there are two kinds of language describing the Son of God. These are linked to the two natures that constitute the person of Jesus Christ. Let us take another look at this important passage in a slightly lengthier context and draw out his main argument.

> Now the scope and character of Holy Scripture, as we have often said, is this, – it contains a double account of the Saviour; that He was ever God, and is the Son, being the Father's Word and Radiance and Wisdom; and afterwards for us He took flesh of a Virgin, Mary Bearer of God, and was made man. And this scope is to be found throughout inspired Scripture, as the Lord Himself has said, "Search the Scriptures, for they are they which testify of Me." But lest I should exceed in writing, by bringing together all the passages on the subject, let it suffice as a specimen, first John saying, "In the beginning was the Word, and the Word was with God, and the Word was God. The same was in the beginning with God. All things were made by Him, and without Him was made not one thing;" next, "And the Word was made flesh and dwelt among us, and we beheld His glory, the glory as of one Only-begotten from the Father."[90]

Athanasius goes on to explain:

> Consequently, when the flesh was suffering, the Logos was not apart from it. That is why the suffering also is said to belong to him. When he was doing the works of the Father in a divine way, the flesh was not external to him. On the contrary, the Lord did these things in the body itself . . . . Thus, when it was necessary to

---

addition to other interpretive matters in Athanasius, see James D. Ernest, "Athanasius of Alexandria: The Scope of Scripture in Polemical and Pastoral Context," *VC* 47 (1993): 341-62. On the practice of Athanasius's exegesis, see idem, "The Uses of Scripture in the Writings of Athanasius of Alexandria," (Ph.D. diss., Boston College, 2000); for a *précis* of James Ernest's argument in his dissertation I am dependent on his paper, presented at a North American Patristics Society conference meeting, entitled: "Athanasius as Exegete?" (Presented at Loyola University, Chicago, May 26, 2001). The dissertation is now published as James D. Ernest, *The Bible in Athanasius of Alexandria* (Leiden: Brill, 2004).

[88] Clayton, "Orthodox Recovery of a Heretical Proof-Text," 233.

[89] Clayton, "Orthodox Recovery of a Heretical Proof-Text," 253.

[90] *St. Athanasius: Select Works and Letters* in NPNF 2, vol. 4, "Four Discourses Against the Arians", 409 (Book III: 29).

Chapter 5: Patristic Christology. A Survey of the Early Church

raise up Peter's mother-in-law, who was suffering from a fever, it was a human act when he extended his hand but a divine act when he caused the disease to cease.[91]

Athanasius leaves us with a maxim in *Contra Arianos* III. 35, when he states, "If we recognize what is proper and peculiar to each [acts according to a specific nature], while at the same time perceiving and understanding that both sets of deeds come from one [agent], we believe rightly and shall never be led astray."[92] This observation shows the truth of Quasten's comment: "A . . . consequence of the personal unity of Christ is the *communicatio idiomatum*."[93]

Within this exegetical procedure, Petterson has caught Athanasius's commitment to the omnipresence of Jesus. "The Logos transcends the body and the world of which it is a part," notes Petterson, "and consequently is not handicapped by it; and yet he is immanent in it, his transcendence not precluding his ubiquitous presence in the finite world."[94] This approach to the incarnation was not new, however. Athanasius held to this concept in his earlier work *De Incarnatione Verbi Dei*. "For He was not, as might be imagined," posits Athanasius, "circumscribed in the body, nor, while present in the body, was He absent elsewhere."[95]

Commenting on this specific text from Athanasius's *De Incarnatione*, Torrance states, "A fundamental point here is that when the Word or Son of God became man, assumed from us a human body, and therefore shared our physical space, *he remained* what he ever was."[96] And in a note on this very matter, Torrance further shows the source and influence of this idea: "This was the point made by Origen [already demonstrated]," notes Torrance, "and was later taken up by the whole Church."[97] The other concern Athanasius has, according to Torrance, is with regard to Christ as Mediator. Because of the distinction

---

[91] Norris, *The Christological Controversy*, 90.

[92] Norris, *The Christological Controversy*, 94.

[93] Quasten, *Golden Age of Greek Patristic Literature*, 75.

[94] Petterson, *Athanasius*, 110. Anatolios also grasps exceptionally well the paradoxical nature of Athanasius's statements that provide us with the raw data for exacting a Christology proper. In discussing the possibility / impassibility question, Anatolios posits "Paradoxical Christological statements of this kind [in Athanasius] can be dismissed as simply nonsensical and meaningless. While we will not attempt to 'explain away' the paradoxical element, what we can do is go beyond glib assertions that Athanasius simply does not take Christ's humanity seriously and try to see how such statements were intelligible for Athanasius himself." See Anatolios, *Athanasius*, 148. The answer according to Anatolios is to see that the whole "Christological" issue is grounded in the "logic of Redemption [where] seemingly contradictory statements ha[ve] to do with the asymmetrical and teleological character of the unity of humanity and divinity in Christ" (148).

[95] See Athanasius, "On the Incarnation of the Word," in *St. Athanasius: Select Works and Letters*, NPNF 2, vol. 4 (New York: Christian Literature, 1892; reprint, Grand Rapids: Eerdmans, 1975), 45.

[96] Torrance, *Divine Meaning*, 366 (emphasis in original).

[97] Torrance, *Divine Meaning*, 366, n. 93.

between creator and creature, the Logos makes it possible for the Father to dwell fully in the Son bodily because of the nature of the triune Godhead. The doctrine of *perichoresis*, interpenetration, or mutual indwelling, safeguards the distinction of persons while allowing their inseparable relations to be observed. Only the Logos made flesh, not a mere human, could serve as a mediator.[98] However, Christ is still the Logos filling the world. This notion of Jesus' omnipresence is also found in *Contra Arianos* I. 42, where we read: "Although he is the same one having become man and called Jesus, nonetheless he has all creation under his foot."[99] What is evident in Athanasius is that the absolute transcendence of the Logos is what allows Jesus (the Logos made flesh) to remain unchanged in one very specific sense. Here the concept of Incarnation by addition is paramount.[100] What Athanasius sees as essential for the Logos is exemplary, indeed as Torrance claims, it has been adopted by the whole church.

D. Post-Nicene Theology

As we continue our examination of Christology towards Chalcedon and beyond many issues must be set aside.[101] It is not that other disputes were unimportant,

---

[98] See the brief but helpful discussion in Torrance, *Divine Meaning*, 366-67. For an in-depth analysis of interpenetration (*perichoresis*), see Thomas F. Torrance, *The Christian Doctrine of God, One Being Three Persons* (Edinburgh: T & T Clark, 1996), 168-202. Torrance's comments in this latter work are significant, and they help to counter insufficient or incorrect notions of *perichoresis*. Oliver Crisp has recently defended a use of *perichoresis* not only as a Trinitarian concept (person *perichoresis*), as he names this idea, but also within Christology itself (nature *perichoresis*). I am somewhat hesitant at this stage of adopting anything like a perichoretic explanation of the person of Christ, Crisp's essay notwithstanding. See Oliver Crisp, *Divinity and Humanity: The Incarnation Reconsidered* (New York: Cambridge University Press, 2007), 1-33.

[99] This translation is taken from William G. Rusch, ed. and trans., *The Trinitarian Controversy* (Philadelphia: Fortress, 1980), 106.

[100] "What has taken place," Sellers observes, "is that He, the Logos who is eternal with the Father, has in these last days assumed flesh–but He is still the same person both before and after the Incarnation. Aaron is still Aaron, [Athanasius] says, after he had put on the high-priest's vesture. Here, clearly, Athanasius is drawing near to the thought that the incarnate life of the Logos is an "addition to" the life which is His by nature" (Sellers, *Two Ancient Christologies*, 35).

[101] For the Apollinarian controversy, see Sellers, *Two Ancient Christologies*, 45-65. Sellers comments, "'Two separate principles of mind and will' [Apollinaris] says, 'cannot dwell together without one striving against the other', 'such a subject would be in a state of perpetual turmoil'" (61). Also see Grillmeier, *From the Apostolic Age to Chalcedon*, 329-60. Also helpful are Hall, *Doctrine and Practice*, 154-56, 159-60; Kelly, *Early Christian Doctrines*, 289-95; Norris, *Christological Controversy*, 21-23, and esp. 103-11 for a translation of Apollinaris' comments on Christology which survive; Charles Gordon Brown and James Edward Swallow, trans., "Letters on the Apollinarian Controversy" in *Christology of the Later Fathers*, ed. Edward Rochie Hardy, with Cyril C. Richardson. LCC 3 (Philadelphia: Westminster, 1954), 215-32; Georges Florovsky, *The Byzantine Fathers of the Fifth Century*, 181-85; G.L. Prestige, *Fathers and Heretics: Six Studies in Dogmatic Faith with Prologue and Epilogue, Being the Bampton Lectures for 1940* (London: SPCK, 1948), 94-119; and Quasten, *Golden Age of Greek*

Chapter 5: Patristic Christology. A Survey of the Early Church

but we will resume our survey at this time by focusing briefly on Augustine, as the great bishop of Hippo wrote important contributions to the doctrine of omnipresence. Then, prior to an examination of Chalcedon itself, we will look at the Nestorian controversy. This is so because it was in the debate with Nestorius that Cyril of Alexandria was forced to come to terms with an adequate Christological interpretation, which itself paved the way to Chalcedon.

D.1. Augustine of Hippo (354-430)

Augustine's influence is still felt today.[102] Both the Catholic and Protestant traditions claim him as their own. His life was lived during changing times, and the best biographies of his life and teaching have caught the dynamic of his thought as it has developed and deepened with the passage of time.[103]

Patristic Literature, 377-83. General Antiochene Christology is covered by Hans J.W. Drijvers, "Early Forms of Antiochene Christology," in *After Chalcedon: Studies in Theology and Church History*, ed. C. Laga, J.A. Munitz, and Lucas Van Rompay (Leuven: Peeters, 1985), 99-113, and Camillus Hay, "Antiochene Exegesis and Christology," *ABR* 12 (1964): 10-23. For Chrysostom's approach, see Melvin E. Lawrence III, *The Christology of John Chrysostom* (Lampeter: Edwin Mellen, 1996). Theodore of Mopsuestia's Christology may be pursued in the following works: L. Patterson, *Theodore of Mopsuestia and Modern Thought* (London: SPCK, 1926), 23-46; Richard A. Norris, *Manhood and Christ: A Study in the Christology of Theodore of Mopsuestia* (Oxford: Clarendon, 1963); Rowan A. Greer, "The Analogy of Grace in Theodore of Mopsuestia's Christology," *JTS* 34 (1983): 82-98; and John S. Romanides, "Highlights in the Debate over Theodore of Mopsuestia's Christology and Some Suggestions for a Fresh Approach," *GOTR* 5, no.2 (Winter 1959-1960): 140-85. And on Theodoret, see Paul B. Clayton, *The Christology of Theodoret of Cyrus: Antiochene Christology from the Council of Ephesus (431) to the Council of Chalcedon (451)* (New York: Oxford University Press, 2007).

[102] See the classic article by Henri Marrou, "St. Augustine and His Influence through the Ages," in *Personalities of the Early Church*, ed. Everett Ferguson (New York: Garland, 1993), 271-347. Many of Augustine's themes are well captured in the volume entitled *Collectanea Augustiniana*, ed. Joseph C. Schnaubelt and Frederick Van Fleteren (New York: Peter Lang, 1990). A sure guide through the vast terrain of Augustinian scholarship is available in Allan D. Fitzgerald, ed., *Augustine through the Ages: An Encyclopedia* (Grand Rapids: Eerdmans, 1999).

[103] For example, the following works have made an impact in Augustinian scholarship. Gerald Bonner, *St. Augustine of Hippo: Life and Controversies* (London: SCM, 1963). A much-praised biography in English is Peter Brown, *Augustine of Hippo: A Biography* (Berkeley: University of California Press, 2000, [1967]). For Augustine as a theologian, one may begin with Eugene TeSelle, *Augustine the Theologian* (London: Burn and Oats, 1970). Other significant works include Mary T. Clark, *Augustine* (Washington, DC: Georgetown University Press, 1994); Henry Chadwick, *Augustine* (Oxford: Oxford University Press, 1986), which is brief but brilliant; Carol Harrison, *Augustine: Christian Truth and Fractured Humanity* (Oxford: Oxford University Press, 2000); and the magnificent work, Serge Lancel, *Saint Augustine*, trans. Antonia Nevill (London: SCM, 2002). For an Eastern evaluation of the Bishop of Hippo, see Aristotle Papanikolaou & George E. Demacopoulos, eds. *Orthodox Readings of Augustine* (Crestwood, NY: St. Vladimir's Seminary Press, 2007).

The Omnipresence of Jesus Christ

"It is significant," notes Harrison, "that Augustine did not write a work specifically on the incarnation or Christology."[104] This should not disappoint or deter us in an attempt at articulating Augustine's views on this topic, however, for as Daley reminds us, "Augustine's thought is always Christocentric."[105] His specific doctrine on the incarnation must be sought out by looking at various strands of his writings.[106]

Augustine was converted to the faith in 386, in what may be described as a sudden and dramatic conversion.[107] One must also note, however, that there had been a growing dissatisfaction with his Manichaean beliefs, and a steady appreciation of Neoplatonist thinking, which Augustine encountered both in his study of philosophy, and from the preaching of Ambrose, bishop of Milan. He was finally won to the faith of his mother, Monica, who had dedicated the young child to the ways of Christ. Jesus filled a void in the Platonist framework of his thinking. "Augustine [now] saw Christ," explains Chadwick, "as able to bring redemption because in one person he is both God and man."[108] Furthermore, notes Chadwick, for Augustine:

> The God-Man is the way and the ladder by which God enables us to rise from the temporal to the eternal. He is both road and goal, Jacob's ladder. By knowing the Son of Man in history, we may come to discern the eternal wisdom of God (T [*De*

---

[104] Harrison, *Augustine*, 30.

[105] Fitzgerald, ed., *Augustine Through the Ages*, s.v., "Christology" by Brian E. Daley. For more on Augustine's Christology, see Fitzgerald, ed., *Augustine Through the Ages* , s.v., "Jesus Christ," by William Mallard; Agostino Trapè, "Saint Augustine," in *Patrology*, vol. 4, *The Golden Age of Latin Patristic Literature from the Council of Nicea to the Council of Chalcedon*, ed. Angelo Di Berardino, with an introduction by Johannes Quasten, trans. Placid Solari (Allen, TX: Christian Classics, n.d.), 430-32; Clark, *Augustine*, 58-72; Studer, *Trinity and Incarnation*, 167-85; idem, *The Grace of Christ and the Grace of God in Augustine of Hippo: Christocentrism or Theocentrism* trans. Matthew J. O'Connell (Minnesota: Michael Glazier, 1997); TeSelle, *Augustine the Theologian*, 146-56; and Grillmeier, *From the Apostolic age to Chalcedon*, 405-13.

[106] This is admirably achieved by Clark, *Augustine*, 58-65.

[107] Augustine's account of this is nicely presented in *Confessions* xviii, 28. "I returned to the place where Alypius was sitting," notes Augustine after hearing the child's voice, in the memorable garden scene, say: 'take up and read,' believing this to be a command from God, "for on leaving it I had put down there the book of the apostle's [Paul's] letters. I snatched it up, opened it and read in silence the passage on which my eyes first lighted: *Not in dissipation and drunkenness, nor in debauchery and lewdness, nor in arguing and jealousy; but put on the Lord Jesus Christ, and make no provision for the flesh or the gratification of your desires* [Rom. 13:13-14]. I had no wish to read further, nor was there any need. No sooner had I reached the end of the verse than the light of certainty flooded my heart and all dark shades of doubt fled away" (St. Augustine, *The Confessions*, introduction, translation and notes, Maria Boulding, ed. John E. Rotelle, in *The Works of Saint Augustine: A Translation for the 21st Century*, vol. 1.1 [Hyde Park, NY: New City, 1997], 207).

[108] Chadwick, *Augustine*, 53-54.

Trinitate] xiii. 24). He is both example and gift, our pattern and our expiation; the Mediator for whom Porphyry had no room . . .[109]

Augustine spells out his Christological commitments in a letter known as *ad Volusianum*.[110] He clearly embraces an orthodox understanding of the incarnation. "He [Jesus Christ] has so appeared as the Mediator between God and men," notes Augustine, "that, uniting the two natures in one person, He both exalted what was ordinary by what was extraordinary, and tempered what was extraordinary by what was ordinary in Himself."[111] This union in no way destroys the respective natures of divinity and humanity, however, Augustine declares, and continues in a series of penetrating questions:

> And do we suppose that something incredible is told us regarding the omnipotence of God when it is affirmed that the Word of God, by whom all things were made, did so assume a body from the Virgin, and manifest Himself with mortal senses, as neither to destroy His own immortality, nor to change His eternity, nor to diminish His power, nor to relinquish the government of the world, nor to withdraw from the bosom of the Father, that is, from the secret place where He is with Him and in Him?[112]

Furthermore, in speaking of the assumed humanity of Jesus Christ, Augustine explicitly affirms its genuineness and its integrity after the union. "The fact that He took rest in sleep, and was nourished by food, and experienced all the feelings of humanity," states Augustine, "is the evidence to men of the reality of that human nature which He assumed but did not destroy."[113]

It is in this specific epistle to Volusianus that we also hear Augustine specifically affirm the omnipresence of Christ. In reply to the questions posed by Volusianus, which were directly aimed at the perceived incoherence of the incarnation, Augustine expresses the faith of the Catholic Church. "I wish you to understand that the Christian doctrine," explains Augustine, "does not hold that the Godhead was so blended with the human nature in which He was born of the virgin that He either relinquished or lost the administration of the universe, or transferred it to that body as a small and limited material substance."[114] The bishop of Hippo also adds these pertinent comments:

---

[109] Chadwick, *Augustine*, 53-54. For an impressive analysis of how Augustine's growing appreciation for Jesus' Mediatorial status influenced the bishop's hermeneutics, see Michael Cameron, "The Christological Substructure of Augustine's Figurative Exegesis," in *Augustine and the Bible*, ed. and trans. Pamela Bright (Notre Dame, IN: University of Notre Dame Press, 1999), 74-103.

[110] See St. Augustin[e], *To Volusianus* (epistle 137), trans. J.G. Cunningham, ed. Philip Schaff, under the title *The Confessions and Letters of St. Augustin, With a Sketch of His Life and Work*, NPNF 2, vol. 1 (New York: Christian Literature, 1892; reprint, Grand Rapids: Eerdmans, 1956), 473-81. For the historical context of this writing, see Lancel, *Saint Augustine*, 314-22.

[111] Augustine, *ad Volusianum*, 9 (NPNF 2, vol. 1), 477.

[112] Augustine, *ad Volusianum*, 9, 475.

[113] Augustine, *ad Volusianum*, 9, 476.

[114] Augustine, *ad Volusianum*, 9, 474.

Understand the nature of the Word of God, by whom all things were made, to be such that you cannot think of any part of the Word as passing, and from being future, becoming past. He remains as He is, and *is everywhere in His entirety* [emphasis supplied]. He comes when He is manifested, and departs when He is concealed. But whether concealed or manifested, He is present with us as light is present to the eyes both of the seeing and of the blind.[115]

Augustine's thoughts on the question of God's presence are presented in another letter (to Dardanus) known as the treatise *On the Presence of God*.[116] Here, Augustine further expresses his Christology in conjunction with discussing the ways of God's presence. Grabowski captures the emphasis of Augustine very well. He says:

His treatise *On the Presence of God* bears ample evidence to the fact that St. Augustine considered the presence of God predominantly as a dynamic presence. The occasion of this disquisition was a misconception by Dardanus and others of the way Christ is present. Christ as God is everywhere present; but it does not follow, Augustine contends, that Christ's humanity is everywhere present. He solves this difficulty by pointing to the existence of a twofold nature in Christ: the divine, which is everywhere, and the human, which is circumscribed in space. Augustine explains this by way of comparison. As the operative inbeing of God in man according to what is said in the Acts [17:28] does not make man everywhere present, so likewise because the divinity of God dwells in the humanity of Christ, it does not follow that His humanity is everywhere as the divine nature is.[117]

Also, in this famed epistle Augustine argues for the full humanity of Jesus. He speaks of Christ as a "perfect man." The bishop's explanation follows. "Obviously, when you say perfect man," notes Augustine, "you mean that the whole human nature is there, for a man is not perfect if either a soul is lacking to the body or a human mind to the soul."[118] It is, therefore, clear that Augustine's

---

[115] Augustine, *ad Volusianum*, 9, 475.

[116] See St. Augustine, "On the Presence of God" (epistle 187), in *Saint Augustine: Letters*, trans. Sister Wilfrid Parsons, 4:165-203 in *The Fathers of the Church: A New Translation*, ed. Joseph Deferrari, vol. 30 (New York: Fathers of the Church, Inc., 1955), 221-55. A most thorough study of this topic of God's presence in Augustine's theology is that of Stanislaus J. Grabowsky, *The All-Present God: A Study in St. Augustine* (London: Herder, 1954). "Because the work [epistle 187] was written at a mature period of the Saint's [Augustine's] life, and because it is an *ex professo* treatment of the subject," Grabowski claims, "it commands an authority of the first rank on the topic" (75).

[117] Grabowski, *All-Present God*, 158-59.

[118] St. Augustine, "On the Presence of God" (epistle 187. 4), in *Saint Augustine: Letters*, trans. Sister Wilfrid Parsons, 4:224. TeSelle, commenting on Augustine's conception of the hypostatic union, alerts us to what may be seen as an anticipation of a two-minds Christology in Augustine. "But it is just as clear," notes TeSelle, "that Augustine thought in terms of two minds, human and divine, and two wills, joined, to be sure, without any possibility of falling away, but still with a distinct human life, even a 'private' life . . . and experiencing all the temptations arising from it, though always being sustained because of the unity with God" (TeSelle, *Augustine the Theologian*, 151).

Christology both anticipates and matches that which is later codified in Chalcedonianism.

From this brief look at Augustine, we must take our sights back to Greek Christianity. It is in the East that Christology continued as a hotbed of discussion. To see the really important precursors to Chalcedon, one must look at the Nestorian controversy.

D.2. Nestorius of Constantinople (ca. 381-451)

One would think that after Nicea (325) and Constantinople (381), all would be quiet on the Eastern front. Far from it; indeed, the theological battles raged on. In particular, the Trinitarian issue was still being discussed. Arianism was far from dead. In this anti-Arian climate, the debate between Cyril of Alexandria and Nestorius[119] was carried on fiercely.[120]

Nestorius became bishop in Constantinople in 428.[121] Soon he began preaching in polemical fashion against Arianism and sparked the heated debate about the *theotokos*.[122] The word signified how the Virgin Mary was the bearer of [Christ as] God. Although it was designed to express a Christological truth, popular piety was desirous of maintaining its use because of the developing Mariolatry and Mariology.[123] For Nestorius's concerns one must understand the problem he had with the idea of mutability. Whatever the *theos* meant in *theotokos*, it was a mutable *theos*, a *theos* subject to change, and only an Arian would revel in such language of a God who was borne within the womb of a

---

[119] For Nestorius's life and work, see Friedrich Loofs, *Nestorius and His Place in Christian Doctrine* (Cambridge: The University Press, 1914); Prestige, *Fathers and Heretics*, 120-49; and Florovsky, *Byzantine Fathers of the Fifth Century*, 210-49. For his Christology, see Grillmeier, *Christ in Christian Tradition: From the Apostolic Age to Chalcedon*, 447-72, 501-19; Carl E. Braaten, "Modern Interpretations of Nestorius," *Church History* 32 (1963): 251-67; J.F. Bethune-Baker, *Nestorius and His Teaching: A Fresh Examination of the Evidence* (Eugene, OR: Wipf and Stock, reprint, 1998); Paul Gavrilyuk, "*Theopatheia*: Nestorius's Main Charge Against Cyril of Alexandria," *SJT* 56 (2003): 190-207; J.A. McGuikin, "The Christology of Nestorius of Constantinople," *PatByzR* 7 (1988): 93-129; and idem, "The Christology of Nestorius" [an update of his 1988 essay], in *St. Cyril of Alexandria: The Christological Controversy: Its History, Theology and Texts* (Leiden: E.J. Brill, 1994) now released under the same title by (Crestwood, NY: St. Vladimir's Seminary Press, 2004). This resource is invaluable for appreciating all facets of this turbulent historical episode. And most importantly, see *Nestorius: The Bazaar of Heracleides*, ed. and trans. G.R. Driver and Leonard Hodgson (Oxford: Clarendon, 1925).

[120] Wilken in particular has drawn attention to the theological climate in which the war was waged between these church men. He claims, "In terms of the controversy between Cyril and Nestorius this situation meant that the immediate background and presupposition of the controversy was not so much a question of Christology, but of the Trinity" (Wilken, "Tradition, Exegesis and Christological Controversies," 145).

[121] Quasten, *Golden age of Greek Patristic Literature*, 514.

[122] This dislike for the term *theotokos*, Nestorius surely inherited from his teacher, Theodore of Mopsuestia. See Hall, *Doctrine and Practice in the Early Church*, 212-14.

[123] Hall, *Doctrine and Practice in the Early Church*, 212.

woman, no matter how pious she was. Linking the teaching of both Arians and Apollinarians, Nestorius, according to Grillmeier, feared that

> In their Christology the Logos enters into physical, natural unity with the flesh, [therefore] he is also involved in whatever happens to the body, such as birth, suffering and death. The Arians [especially] seek to spread the title *Theotokos* so as to have opportunity of attacking the very divinity of Christ.[124]

Although Cyril and Nestorius had a common foe in Arianism, they combated the dreaded heresy with weapons honed from two diverse traditions. An immensely helpful book addresses the interconnections of Christ and grace during this era fully appreciative of the different concerns of both the Antiochenes and the Alexandrians. These alternative perspectives tended to complicate matters as terminology did not have a fixed meaning for both.[125] Wilken has captured well their respective approaches.[126] The major Trinitarian issue undergirds the question about "how God could become man." In citing a syllogism provided originally by Francis Sullivan, Wilken puts it thus:

(1) The Word is the subject of the human operations and sufferings of Christ,
(2) Whatever is predicated of the Word must be predicated of him according to his own nature (*kata physin*),
(3) *ergo*, the nature of the of the Word is limited and affected by human operations and sufferings of Christ, and is subordinate to the Father.[127]

In the Alexandrian tradition, the Logos was seen as completely God, with a humanity assumed, yet without change. This allowed the Alexandrian theologians to speak of the Logos himself as suffering, but only according to the human nature. The Antiochene school viewed matters slightly differently. They accepted only the minor premise of the syllogism–that is, the man suffers and is subject to change in that the Logos is impassible. Any reference to suffering therefore had to be stated of the man Jesus of Nazareth.[128] At the time when Cyril and Nestorius are on the scene these approaches hardened, and neither side was able to fully grasp the other's major concerns.[129]

---

[124] Grillmeier is drawing from F. Loofs' *Nestoriana* (Halle, 1905). This has been republished as *Nestoriana: Die Fragmente Des Nestorius* (Charleston, SC: Nabu, 2011); See Grillmeier, *From the Apostolic age to Chalcedon*, 452.

[125] See Donald Fairbairn, *Grace and Christology in the Early Church* (New York: Oxford University Press, 2003). For the confusion of terminology, see Norris, *Christological Controversy*, 27-28; and especially McGuikin, "The Christology of Nestorius of Constantinople," 105ff.

[126] Wilken, "Tradition, Exegesis and Christological Controversies," 142-54.

[127] Wilken, "Tradition, Exegesis and Christological Controversies," 146.

[128] Wilken, "Tradition, Exegesis and Christological Controversies," 146-48.

[129] The issues involved are far more complex than can be examined here. One is referred to the discussion in McGuikin, *St. Cyril of Alexandria*, 127-226; Florovsky, *Fathers of the Fifth Century*, 246-49, 267-88; and for more on Cyril's Christology, see Steven A. McKinion, *Words, Imagery, and the Mystery of Christ: A Reconstruction of Cyril of Alexandria's Christology* (Leiden: Brill, 2000); Thomas G. Weinandy & Daniel A. Keating, eds. *The Theology of Cyril of Alexandria: A Critical Appreciation* (London:

D.2.1. One Son or Two?

"In Nestorius' heresy," observes Florovsky, "St. Cyril saw a denial of the most true and ontological combination of Divinity and human nature in Christ, a denial of the single Christ, and a rending of him into a 'duality of Sons.' "[130] This was so for Nestorius utilized the same type of language as Theodore had before him, about the "assumed man."[131] Cyril countered by arguing for a unity of person. As Hall expresses, "The union is indescribable but personal (or hypostatic; Gk *kath' hypostasin*); he [Cyril] means that the humanity of Jesus Christ belongs to the person of the Word, and is not another person distinct from or alongside him."[132] At this point the debate is squarely Christological. How do we explain the incarnate one? Nestorius was adamant that the suffering be attributed to the man, while Cyril was clear that the Logos himself suffered. It appears that Cyril confuses the natures, at least in the eyes of Nestorius, and that Nestorius separates them, at least in the eyes of Cyril. After a church council held at Ephesus in 431, the condemnation of Nestorius followed. This was a time when politics was thickly in the mix. Instead of coming together to discuss the matter in 431, each side met separately and anathematized the other. The imperial authorities needed some stability and sided with Cyril. Nestorius' teaching of "two Sons," was branded as heresy.[133]

In the wake of this debate, Cyril's letters to Nestorius have proved very important documents for the church's view of the person of Christ.[134] Although

---

T & T Clark, 2001), 23-147; and Norman Russell, *Cyril of Alexandria* (New York: Routledge, 2000). More recently an exceptionally excellent resource is Hans van Loon, *The Dyophysite Christology of Cyril of Alexandria* (Leiden: Brill, 2009) Supplements to *Vigiliae Christianae*. See also Susan Wessell, *Cyril of Alexandria and the Nestorian Controversy: The Making of a Saint and of a Heretic* (New York: Oxford University Press, 2004).

[130] Florovsky, *Fathers of the Fifth Century*, 279.

[131] See Nestorius' "First Sermon Against the Theotokos," in Norris, *Christological Controversy*, 123-31.

[132] Hall, *Doctrine and Practice*, 214.

[133] See Norris, *Christological Controversy*, 28. Following his exile, Nestorius proceeded to ponder the Christological matter with some diligence. He later published the work *Bazaar of Heracleides*, in which he speaks of his own life and defends a Christology which many today consider orthodox. See especially, Milton V. Anastos, "Nestorius was Orthodox," in *Doctrine of God and Christ*, ed. Everett Ferguson, 195-216. Grillmeier too, despite a candid critical look at Nestorius' teaching, goes to great lengths to exonerate him. In this, Grillmeier is dependent on Loofs, and is especially indebted to the work of L.I. Scipioni, *Nestoriano e il Concilio di Efeso* (Milan, 1974). Nestorius does not speak specifically of the omnipresence of Christ, but he does defend his Christology as compatible with the orthodox tradition. "But I say," Nestorius asserts, "that the union of God the Word is neither passible nor mortal nor changeable. . . . I have kept without blemish the faith of the [318]. . . who were assembled at Nicaea, saying that God the Word is unchangeable [and] immortal, that he is continuously that which he is in the eternity of the Father" (Nestorius, *Bazaar*, 181-82).

[134] Hall especially draws attention to the Second letter to Nestorius. He states, "The *Second Letter to Nestorius* was to become one of the documents annexed to the Chalce-

there is some advancement in his thought, as Florovsky contends, his early approach is just as sound as his later more mature reflections.[135] It appears that because of his commitment to the transcendence of Christ, Cyril too held to the teaching concerning the omnipresence of Jesus Christ. In his *Third Letter to Nestorius*, Cyril says,

> [Christ took] flesh of the holy virgin, and making it his own, from the womb, he underwent a birth like ours, and came forth a man of a woman, not throwing off what he was, but even though he became [man] by the assumption of flesh and blood, yet still remaining what he was, that is, God indeed in nature and truth. . . . But when seen as a babe and wrapped in swaddling clothes, even still in the bosom of the Virgin who bore him, he filled all creation as God, and was enthroned with him who begot him.[136]

Christ's immanence is affirmed in that he filled creation, and his transcendence is defended for he rules on the throne high above the world with God the Father.

D.2.2. Extreme Cyrillism and Leo's *Tome*

Not long after the famous *Formula of Reunion* 433, where Cyril affirmed the "two natures" in Christ,[137] a defender of Cyril's (earlier?) view concerning one incarnate nature came on the scene. Eutyches (c. 378-454) was an Archmandrite of a monastery in Constantinople who was accused of heresy at a synod of Bishops in Constantinople (November, 448).[138] After his condemnation, Eutyches appealed to several authorities for help including Alexandria.[139] His case was taken up by Dioscorus the bishop of Alexandria, who convened a council

---

donian Formula" (*Doctrine and Practice*, 215).

[135] Well known is the truth that Cyril appealed to Athanasius as an authority. However, at one crucial point in defending that Jesus was "one incarnate nature," he was reading a work written not by Athanasius, but by Apollinarius. See Hall, *Doctrine and Practice*, 221-22; and Quasten's discussion in *Patrology: The Golden Age of Greek Patristic Literature from Nicaea to Chalcedon*, 139-40. Nevertheless, Cyril paved the road to Chalcedon.

[136] Translated by Edward Rochie Hardy, *Christology of the Later Fathers*, 350.

[137] There was a difference, however, between affirming Christ as "from" two natures, and the later Chalcedonian "in" two natures. The matter involving Eutyches brings out how language could be manipulated. Eutyches affirmed the two nature doctrine but only under pressure, yet spoke of Christ as "from two natures." In this matter is the famous dispute that before the incarnation, Christ is said to be two natures, after the union only one. Leo would directly challenge this in the famous *Tome*.

[138] Grillmeier, *From the Apostolic Age to Chalcedon*, 523-26. See also Hall, *Doctrine and Practice*, 226. This council was termed the σύνοδος ένδημουσα, "home synod," a type of local assembly which met periodically to address various matters. See the brief but helpful discussion in Florovsky, *Byzantine Fathers of the Fifth Century*, 291-92.

[139] Grillmeier claims, "[Eutyches] launched a systematic campaign to avenge himself on his opponents and lead the Alexandrian cause to victory" (*From the Apostolic age to Chalcedon*, 526). In attempting this, Eutyches called on people "all over the world," including the bishop of Rome.

Chapter 5: Patristic Christology. A Survey of the Early Church

in Ephesus the following year (449).[140] Not only was Eutyches defended but an anathema was placed on any who affirmed the "two natures" doctrine of the earlier *Formula of Reunion* of 433. Florovsky is no doubt right that Eutyches' position "contains the source of genuine monophysitism."[141] As the Greek word implies, Monophysitism, is a belief that Jesus Christ incarnate had only one nature; its battle-cry was: "only one nature after the union." All was still not settled.

The West was involved at this time as Flavian patriarch of Constantinople was picked out for special condemnation at the "Robber Synod" in attempts at completely defeating Nestorianism, and Pope Leo of Rome came to his defense. Leo's famous letter known as the *Tome of Leo* proved to be a very significant document.[142] Although it made no impact at Ephesus in 448, Leo later

---

[140] This gathering was later dubbed, "the Robber Council" by Pope Leo the Great.

[141] Florovsky, *Fathers of the Fifth Century*, 292. Monophysitism would not simply go away after Chalcedon. For a very informative summary history, see John Chapman, "Monophysites and Monophysitism," transcribed by Michael T. Barrett, *The Catholic Encyclopedia,* vol. 10 (New York: Robert Appleton, 1911) [on-line]; accessed 12 August 2002 available from http://www.newadvent.org/cathen/10489b.htm; Internet. Also noteworthy is John Meyendorff, *Christ in Eastern Christian Thought* (Washington, DC: Corpus Books, 1969), 17-31. For an in-depth treatment, consult Georges Florovsky, *The Byzantine Fathers of the Sixth to Eighth Century,* vol. 9 of *The Collected Works of Georges Florovsky*, ed. Richard S. Haugh, trans. Raymond Miller, Anne-Marie Döllinger-Labriolle and Helmut Wilhelm Schmiedel (Vaduz, Liechtenstein: Büchervertriebsanstalt, 1987), 35-190; and A.A. Luce, *Monophysitism: Past and Present* (London: SPCK, 1920).

[142] *Tomus ad Flavianum* is available in translation in *Christology of the Later Fathers*, ed. Hardy, 360-70 (trans. William Bright). Grillmeier refers to this as a virtual "synthesis of what Leo had to say on the Christological question before the Council of Chalcedon" (*From the Apostolic age to Chalcedon*, 530). There is a docetic strain in the doctrine of Eutyches (see Florovsky, *Fathers of the Fifth Century*, 292; for the view that docetism was not really inherent in Eutyches' position, see the discussion in Kelly, *Early Christian Doctrines*, 330-34, who nonetheless refers to him as a "muddle headed archmandrite"). Leo (apparently) acknowledges this Eutychian docetic content, in his letter: "Possibly his [Eutyches'] reason for thinking that our Lord Jesus Christ was not of our nature [docetism] was this. . . because the Virgin's conception was caused by a divine act, therefore the flesh of him whom she conceived was not of the nature of her who conceived him" (Hardy, *Christology of Later Fathers*, 363). Leo further comments, "On which mystery of the faith this Eutyches must be regarded as unhappily having no hold whatever; for he has not acknowledged our nature to exist in the only-begotten Son of God . . ." (367). Leo counters by stating, "What was assumed from the Lord's mother was nature, not fault; and the fact that the nativity of our Lord Jesus Christ is wonderful, in that he was born of a virgin's womb, does not imply that his nature is unlike ours" (364). A strong affirmation of two nature in one person is found in this document: ". . . the distinctness of both substances is preserved . . . both meet in one person . . ." (363). Leo kept a single subject at the center of theological language while allowing predicate statements to be applied to the respective natures. This was the genius of Leo which is found enshrined in Chalcedonian Christology.

sent it along with extracts from the Fathers to the East for consideration among leaders during the turmoil.

Grillmeier, taking the analysis of C. Silva-Tarouca, offers a survey:

> (1) vv. 1-15: Introduction (Eutyches' disregard of scripture and creed in which he shows himself to be *multum inprudens et nimis inperitus*).
> (2) vv. 16-53:1. The origin of the two natures in Christ shown in creed and scripture.
> (3) vv. 54-93: 2. The co-existence of the two natures of Christ in the unity of the person.
> (4) vv. 94-120: 3. The mode of operation of the two natures.
> (5) vv. 121-76: 4. The *communicatio idiomatum*.
> (6) vv. 177-205: Conclusion (the *inprudentia hominis inperiti*, Eutyches, who was insufficiently censured at the synod of 448).[143]

"The unity of the two modes of action is stressed," notes Grillmeier, "as much as the distinction of the divine and human activity" in Leo's Tome.[144] In particular, one encounters a form of the *communicatio idiomatum* in Leo:

> Accordingly, on account of this unity which is to be understood as existing in both natures we read, on the one hand, that "the Son of Man came down from heaven" (John 3:13), inasmuch as the Son of God took flesh from that Virgin of whom he was born; and, on the other hand, the Son of God is said to have been crucified and buried, inasmuch as he underwent this, not in his actual Godhead, wherein the Only-begotten is coeternal and consubstantial with the Father, but in the weakness of human nature. Wherefore we all, in the very Creed, confess that "the only-begotten Son of God was crucified and buried," according to that saying of the apostle, "For if they had known it, they would not have crucified the Lord of majesty" (I Cor. 2:8).[145]

Based on this careful espousal of *communicatio idiomatum* Leo endorses the position concerning the omnipresence of Christ from this passage. This is so because the sufferings of Christ can only be spoken of the person in reference to his human nature. Jesus' Godhead remains unaltered in the incarnation. The omnipresence of Jesus is emphasized in the following quote. Leo puts the matter this way: "The Son of God, descending from his seat in heaven, yet not departing from the glory of the Father, enters the lower world, born after a new order, by a new mode of birth."[146] Also, Leo claims,

> The same who, remaining in the form of God, made man, was made Man in the form of a servant. For each of the natures retains its proper character without defect; and as the form of God does not take away the form of a servant, the form of a servant does not impair the form of God.[147]

---

[143] Grillmeier, *From the Apostolic age to Chalcedon,* 530.
[144] Grillmeier, *From the Apostolic age to Chalcedon,* 553.
[145] Hardy, *Christology of the Later Fathers,* 366.
[146] Hardy, *Christology of the Later Fathers,* 364.
[147] Hardy, *Christology of the Later Fathers,* 364.

Kelly cites a phrase from one of Leo's sermons underscoring yet again this crucial idea. "It is the one and the same Son of God," says Leo, "Who exists in both natures, taking what is ours to Himself without losing what is His own."[148]

Despite Leo's theological contribution, it would take a change of events in the political arena to foster change and to provide a hope for Christological unity. It was the death of Emperor Theodosius in July of 450, and the emergence of Marcian as his replacement that occasioned the famous Council of Chalcedon in 451. "The whole object of the council, from the imperial point of view," as Kelly notes, "was to establish a single faith throughout the empire."[149] We must now turn to this important meeting.

E. Chalcedonian Christology

It is widely held that Chalcedon was a magnificent achievement of theological significance which has echoed down the centuries to our own day.[150] Indeed, the model espoused in this book is unashamedly Chalcedonian.[151] Perhaps the question surrounding a sound conception of the incarnation centers on whether one affirms chalcedonianism or kenoticism. Even detractors, who are not entirely in agreement with the Chalcedonian approach, nonetheless attempt at a kind of fidelity to its basic structures.[152] It remains a normative statement as a

---

[148] Cited in Kelly, *Early Christian Doctrines*, 338.

[149] Kelly, *Early Christian Doctrines*, 339.

[150] Blaising claims, "The definition of faith at Chalcedon has now taken its place in a tradition of Christological formulation that includes other elements that have also taken their place during the history of theology. The basic reason Protestant evangelicalism has continued to make use of these formulations is not because of a doctrine of the authority of tradition, but because those formulations are in fact descriptive of what is in Scripture" (Craig A. Blaising, "Chalcedon and Christology: A 1530th Anniversary," in *The Bib Sac Reader*, ed. John F. Walvoord and Roy B. Zuck [Chicago: Moody, 1983], 102). Writing from another perspective, Grillmeier, nevertheless, arrives at the same conclusion. His final words concerning his evaluation of the Patristic achievement at Chalcedon are clear. "At all events," Grillmeier asserts, "the Fathers believed that they were fighting for the pure picture of Christ, as it was drawn by the Bible" (Grillmeier, *From the Apostolic age to Chalcedon*, 557).

[151] For a sympathetic review of Chalcedonian Christology, see John S. Marshall, "The Christology of Chalcedon," *AthR* (1960): 117-25; Basil Studer, *Trinity and Incarnation*, 211-219; and Stephen Need, *Truly Divine & Truly Human*, 93-108. For a critical appraisal seeking to move beyond the Chalcedonian framework, see A.N.S. Lane, "Christology beyond Chalcedon," in *Christ the Lord: Studies in Christology Presented to Donald Guthrie*, ed. Harold H. Rowdon (Leicester: InterVarsity, 1982), 257-81. For a vigorous attack on the coherence of a two-natures model, see Ronald W. Leigh, "Jesus: the One-natured God-man," *CSR* 11, no. 2 (1982): 124-37. I shall interact with Lane and Leigh in a later chapter.

[152] As an example, note contemporary theologian John Macquarrie's attempt at maintaining Chalcedon's "governing intention." He realizes that abandoning Chalcedon completely would be to forfeit our Christian heritage and therefore our claim to stand in that tradition. Yet, evidently, he appears to want to distance himself from the obvious substantive content of Chalcedon. See the helpful discussion and analysis in John McIntyre, *The Shape of Christology: Studies in the Doctrine of the Person of Christ* (Edin-

Christological regulative principle.[153] "Chalcedon," posits Brown, "is the second great high-water mark of early Christian theology: it set an imperishable standard for orthodoxy."[154]

We will provide a brief analysis of its content and a discussion of its importance. The significance of Chalcedon in contemporary theology will be noted in a subsequent chapter. It must suffice for now to grasp the history and theology of Chalcedon. This will show, one may argue, how any theology of Christ that is consistently Chalcedonian should also affirm without hesitation, the omnipresence of the incarnate Lord Jesus Christ. To the specific definition we now turn.

E.1. The Chalcedonian Definition

This ecumenical council[155] was supposed to be held at Nicea. Due to military problems Marcian the newly appointed emperor was unable to leave Constanti-

---

burgh: T & T Clark, 1998), 259-82.

[153] This appears to be the position of Richard Norris, Jr., when he says, "There is a sense . . . in which it is true that the Council of Chalcedon solves the christological problem by laying out its terms. Its formula dictates not a Christology but formal outlines of an adequate christological language" (Norris, "Chalcedon Revisited: A Historical and Theological Reflection," in *New Perspectives on Historical Theology: Essays in Memory of John Meyerndorff*, ed. Bradley Nassif [Grand Rapids/Cambridge, U.K.: Eerdmans, 1996], 31). Norris's essay is stimulating reading, but contains elements that are troubling. Particularly his anachronistic reading of categories (eminently made famous by George Lindbeck) back onto the Chalcedonian achievement. See the rebuttal of some of Norris's problematic aspects in the helpful article: Sarah Coakley, "What Does Chalcedon Solve and What it Does Not? Some Reflections on the Status and Meaning of the Chalcedonian 'Definition,'" in *The Incarnation: An Interdisciplinary Symposium on the Incarnation of the Son of God*, ed. Stephen T. Davis, Daniel Kendall, and Gerald O'Collins (Oxford: Oxford University Press, 2002), 144-63, esp. 146-52.

[154] Harold O.J. Brown, *Heresies: Heresy and Orthodoxy in the History of the Church* (Peabody, MA: Hendrickson, 1998), 181.

[155] Among very helpful materials are the following: Grillmeier, *From the Apostolic age to Chalcedon*, 543-57; idem, *Christ in Christian Tradition*, vol. 2, pt. 1, *From Chalcedon to Justinian*, trans. Pauline Allen and John Cawte (Atlanta: John Knox, 1987); R.V. Sellers, *The Council of Chalcedon* (London: SPCK, 1953); Kelly, *Early Christian Doctrines*, 338-43; Leo Donald Davis, *The First Seven Ecumenical Councils*, 170-206; Philip Schaff, *The Creeds of Christendom: With a History and Notes*, vol. 1, *The History of the Creeds* (Grand Rapids: Baker, 1876; reprint,1998), 29-34; Hall, *Doctrine and Practice*, 230-36; Meyendorff, *Christ in Eastern Christian Thought*, 3-16; and Florovsky, *Fathers of the Fifth Century*, 293-99. For a very interesting history of the events prior to, and including the contents of the procedure at Chalcedon, one will do well to look at Peter L'Hullier, *The Church of the Ancient Councils: The Disciplinary Work of the First Four Ecumenical Councils* (Crestwood, NY: Saint Vladimir's Seminary Press, 1996), 181-205. Following this section there is an extended discussion of the Chalcedonian Canons (L'Hullier, *The Church*, 206-301). There are over 750 footnotes to this section on Chalcedon in L'Hullier's work (302-28). Also see the recently reprinted text by William Bright, *The Canons of the First Four General Councils of Nicaea, Constantinople, Ephesus and Chalcedon: With Notes* (Minneapolis: Filiquarian, nd, [Oxford:

Chapter 5: Patristic Christology. A Survey of the Early Church

nople so he changed the venue of the gathering to nearby Chalcedon.[156] According to L'Hullier, "the number of bishops who came from far or near . . . must have been close to 510."[157] No doubt this was an impressive array of participants. After several discussions throughout several days of meetings, a "committee" was appointed to produce a definitive Christological statement. Here is what was drawn up:

> We, then, following the holy Fathers, all with one consent, teach men to confess one and the same Son, our Lord Jesus Christ, the same perfect in Godhead and also perfect in manhood; truly God and truly man, of a reasonable [i.e. rational] soul and body; consubstantial [i.e. coessential] with the Father according to the Godhead, and consubstantial with us according to the Manhood; in all things like unto us, without sin; begotten before all ages of the Father according to the Godhead, and in these latter days, for us and our salvation, born of the Virgin Mary, the Mother of God, according to the Manhood; one and the same Christ, Son, Lord, Only-begotten, to be acknowledged in two natures, *inconfusedly, unchangeably, indivisibly, inseparably*; the distinction of the natures being by no means taken away by the union, but rather the property of each nature being preserved, and concurring in one person and one Subsistence, not parted or divided into two persons, but one and the same Son, and only begotten, God the Word, the Lord Jesus Christ, as the prophets from the beginning [have declared] concerning him, and the Lord Jesus Christ himself has taught us, and the Creed of the holy Fathers has handed down to us.[158]

After confessing solidarity with the earlier Creeds (primarily Nicea and Constantinople), the drafters express their distinctive Christological formula.[159] Repeatedly the formula speaks of the "one and the same," (ενα και τον αὐτον). This *one*, is described, for example, as, "Son and only-begotten, the divine Logos, [and the] Lord Jesus Christ." This is crucial for it keeps one subject at the center of the theological language. It is true it does not speak of the hypostatic union as Cyril had done, but it is compatible with that affirmation.[160] The

---

Clarendon, 1892]).

[156] Leo Donald Davis, *The First Seven Ecumenical Councils*, 180.

[157] L'Hullier, *The Church of the Ancient Councils*, 187. He indicates that when one considers that some may have been represented by proxy, the number of actual bishops was probably nearer 450.

[158] Taken from Schaff, *Creeds of Christendom*, 2: 62-63.

[159] It must be borne in mind that the drafters were drawing on several previous doctrinal affirmations of the incarnation. "An analysis of the Chalcedonian creed," notes Grillmeier, "shows that it is anticipated almost clause for clause in other documents. The documents which are chiefly used are the second letter of Cyril to Nestorius, Cyril's letter to the Antiochenes with the Formulary of Reunion of 433 (*Laetentur* letter), and the Tome of Leo to Flavian. Finally we must also add Flavian's *professio fidei*, which had been read out at the Council of Chalcedon in the context of the acts of the trial of Eutyches. One clause even seems to hint at a letter of Theodoret" (Grillmeier, *From the Apostolic age to Chalcedon*, 544).

[160] Davis claims: "Though the Definition insisted on the unity of the person in Christ by repeating the adjective "same' eight times, it still left the concept of hypostatic union unclear" (*First Seven Ecumenical Councils*, 188).

natures are two in *one* person. Furthermore, "the council of Chalcedon," as Studer notes, "established the distinction between the personal and natural levels."[161] More importantly as Studer continues:

> For in contrasting the trinitarian terms *physis* and *prosopon* (or *hypostasis*), and at the same time ascribing the function of union to the person, or hypostasis, the council opened the way for a later solution of the problem, even though it had not itself yet found the solution. According to this the unity of Christ must not be sought in that which makes the Trinity one, neither in nature, nor in essence, but rather in what distinguishes the persons from each other. The divine nature as such is not the bearer of the divine and human attributes, neither does the Godhead as such constitute the unity, nor is it as such the principle of all action. We must rather seek for the unity in the direction of the hypostasis.[162]

E.2. The Value of Chalcedon

The key section is found in the use of four Greek adverbs which deny any change or confusion of the natures in the incarnation. Particularly the words, "without confusion" (ἀσυγχύτως), and "without change" (ἀτρέπτως) safeguard against any mixing of the two natures into a *tertium quid*, and also keep one from affirming any diminution of the Deity. The other words, "without division" (ἀδιαιρέτως), and "without separation" (ἀχωρίστως), were carefully selected to counter any Nestorian tendencies. All in all, this is a well rounded and amazing set of boundary guidelines. "By using . . . [these] four Greek negative adverbs," says Davis, "the bishops showed their concern for the mysterious and incomprehensible nature of the subject matter with which they were dealing."[163] Most importantly for our study, one sees that because Chalcedon wholeheartedly stressed the inviolable integrity of both natures after the union, that this permits, and moreover, requires that Jesus Christ as God incarnate is omnipresent because of the divine nature.

The specific formula of acknowledging one Christ ἐν δύο φύσεσιν, "in two natures," as opposed to ἐκ δύο φύσεσιν, "out of (from) two natures" is of paramount significance.[164] "For the natures as such," as Grillmeier affirms, "remain preserved."[165] One is not to seek the unity at the level of the natures. Each nature remains unchanged after the union. Each nature is important as an unim-

---

[161] Studer, *Trinity and Incarnation*, 217.

[162] Studer, *Trinity and Incarnation*, 17.

[163] Davis, *First Seven Ecumenical Councils*, 187.

[164] See the brief discussion in Schaff on the views of Dorner and Baur, who thought that "from two natures" was the original wording. Schaff's view affirms that "in two natures" was the original reading. See Schaff, *Creeds of Christendom*, 64 n. 4. "[The Formula] insists," declares Norris, "not (with the Formula of Reunion) that Christ is "out of two natures" but "in two natures," which are neither divided from each other nor confused with each other. At the level of language, therefore, the "Definition" accepts the central emphases of both the Antiochene and the Alexandrian schools" (*Christological Controversy*, 30).

[165] Grillmeier, *From the Apostolic age to Chalcedon*, 549.

paired principle of distinction.¹⁶⁶ Although it is now clear that Chalcedon maintains both the unity of the person, and a distinction of the natures, it was not forward looking enough to include statements that would "safeguard against Monothelitism and Monergism."¹⁶⁷ The fact of the hypostatic union is evident in Chalcedon's statement, however, the nature and the specific "how" of the union is still unclear. Later Christological insights are still needed for a more complete picture for understanding the Incarnation. This is often referred to as the "mechanics" of the incarnation. Those additional insights needed to explain more adequately the constitution of the Person of Christ, can be detected in the writings of Leontius of Byzantium, to which we now turn.

F. Leontius of Byzantium (c. 475-543)

Scholarship on Leontius is divided. My initial probing into his thought uncovered a key in his supposed "enhypostatic" notion which I sought to utilize.¹⁶⁸ It

---

¹⁶⁶ Grillmeier, *From the Apostolic age to Chalcedon*, 549.

¹⁶⁷ Grillmeier, *From the Apostolic age to Chalcedon*, 550. In fact "the definition of Chalcedon," posits Davis, "was not the end but the intensification of controversy" (*First Seven Ecumenical Councils*, 194). One may follow the debates and developments in the excellent volumes by Aloys Grillmeier, *Christ in Christian Tradition*, vol. 2, *From the Council of Chalcedon (451) to Gregory the Great (590-604)*, pt. 1, *From Chalcedon to Justinian I*, trans. Pauline Allen and John Cawte (Atlanta: John Knox, 1975); Aloys Grillmeier, with Theresia Hainthaler, *Christ in Christian Tradition*, vol. 2, *From the Council of Chalcedon (451) to Gregory the Great (590-604)*, pt. 2, *The Church of Constantinople in the Sixth Century*, trans. John Cawte and Pauline Allen (London: Mowbray/Louisville: Westminster John Knox, 1995); and idem, *Christ in Christian Tradition*, vol. 2, *From the Council of Chalcedon (451) to Gregory the Great (590-604)*, pt. 4, *The Church of Alexandria with Nubia and Ethiopia after 451*, trans. O.C. Dean, (London: Mowbray/Louisville: Westminster John Knox, 1996). The stalwart Cyrillians formed the nucleus of the Monophysites (those affirming only one nature in Christ) subsequent to Chalcedon. They were not necessarily admirers of Eutyches, but the formula, once espoused by Cyril: "One nature after the union," was their battle cry. The subsequent historical and theological development of monotheletism (the view that Christ had one will) is well presented in John Chapman, "Monothelitism and Monothelites," transcribed by Douglas J. Potter, *The Catholic Encyclopedia*, vol. 10 (Robert Applteon, 1911) [on-line]; accessed March, 2002; available from http://www.newadvent.org/cathen/10502a.htm; Internet. It is Haire's contention, "That we may differ in our opinion about the extent to which the technical terms used at Chalcedon are final. We may wish more explicit reference in a statement on the person of our Lord to His Messianic acts. We may well desire to use the best of modern scientific terms to describe our Lord's human nature. But can we go beyond the conclusion reached here, beyond the *vere Deus, vere homo*? To do so will, I suspect, tend to Adoptionism or a monophysitism of the Eutychian type. I do not believe that the theologians whom I have dared to criticize intended to reach either of these positions. Indeed most of them make explicit disclaimers. But I believe that their assumptions lead them in the one direction or the other" (J.L.M. Haire, "On Behalf of Chalcedon," in T.H.L. Parker, ed. *Essays in Christology for Karl Barth* [London: Lutterworth, 1956], 111).

¹⁶⁸ What I supposed was originally expressed by Leontius of Byzantium, that is, the idea of "enhypostasia," in fact may have been coined by Leontius of Jerusalem. See U.

may be necessary to adjust the focus onto the idea rather than on the one who first coined it. Nevertheless, in agreement with some of the major authorities on Leontius's thought concerning his importance, I will endeavor to present findings here which will remain beneficial for this study.

F.1. Origenist or Cyrillian?

There is a scholarly debate concerning the person of Leontius of Byzantium.[169] Although one cannot enter the debate at this point or deal at length with the

---

M. Lang, "Anhypostatos–Enhypostatos: Church Fathers, Protestant Orthodoxy and Karl Barth," *JTS* 49 (1998): 630-57, esp., 654-55. Ilie Fracea, "Ο ΛΕΟΝΤΙΟΣ ΒΥΖΑΝΤΙΟΣ" Βιος καὶ Συγγραματα" (Ph.D. diss., University of Athens, 1984), argues that both Leontii are one and the same (following Loofs). This is a fascinating study which enters the debate about the Leontius corpus and balances the modern scholarly consensus with a credible alternative of Leontius' life and work. Whatever the actual case may be regarding the origin of this notion of *enhypostasia*, what is certain is that a use of this concept by John of Damascus in the eighth century solidifies it as an essential Christological doctrine which serves as a means of maintaining the union of two natures while explaining why there are, however, not two persons.

[169] The popularity of Leontius of Byzantium as a research subject was intensified with the work of F. Loofs, *Leontius von Byzanz und die gleichnachmigen Schriftsteller der griechischen Kirche* (Leipzig, 1887). It was Loofs who made popular the idea that Leontius made advancements in Christological thinking beyond Chalcedon by proposing the "enhypostasia" solution to the incarnation. According to Loofs, Leontius argued that each nature cannot be without its own hypostasis, yet the human nature of Christ was not *anhypostaton* (having no [independent] subsistence), but *enhypostaton* (having its subsistence "in" another), that is, the human nature of Christ subsisted only in its conjunction with the Word made flesh. Herbert M. Relton helped English-speaking readers to become familiar with Leontius and the approach of Loofs to this sixth-century theologian. See his book (originally a dissertation), *A Study in Christology: The Problem of the Relation of the Two Natures in the Person of Christ* (London: SPCK, 1917), esp. 69-93. This view of the origin of this notion of "enhypostasis" is widespread and has made its way into several textbooks. See Hardy, *Christology of the Later Fathers*, 376, where the editor on the extracts from Leontius argues the same way as Loofs. Also see John McIntyre, *The Shape of Christology: Studies in the Doctrine of the Person of Christ* (Edinburgh: T & T Clark, 1998, 1966), 96-98. McIntyre was the first to draw my attention to this way of expressing the solution as in Leontius' *enhypostasia* approach several years ago. This understanding has recently been challenged. Brian Daley in particular has shown that the "en" in *enhypostaton*, really is the opposite of an A-privative, and therefore the concept of *enhypostaton* merely affirms concrete existence, not existence "in" another. The locative meaning which Loofs ascribed to Leontius of Byzantium was a mistake. See Daley, "The Origenism of Leontius of Byzantium," *JTS* 27 (1976): 333-69. Grillmeier follows Daley in affirming this approach to Leontius of Byzantium. See Grillmeier and Hainthaler, *From Chalcedon to Gregory (Church of Constantinople in sixth Century)*, 181-229 esp. 193-200. Vigorous in asserting this point is F. LeRon Shults, "A Dubious Christological Formula: From Leontius of Byzantium to Karl Barth," *TS* 57 (1996): 431-46. For a response to Shults, see Matthias Gockel, "A Dubious Christological Formula? Leontius of Byzantium and the *Anhypostasis-Enhypostasis* Theory," *JTS* 51 (2000): 515-32. Gockel's article has been extremely helpful. Yet despite this new understanding which is surely assured by recent scholarship, the comment

arguments, some conclusions need to be held, however tentatively, in order to benefit from his thought.

Several dissertations have been written which deal with the thought of Leontius. We will take a brief look at two. The now famous (or infamous?) work of David Evans published in 1970 argued that Leontius of Byzantium was an Origenist in Christology who affirmed the pre-existence of an un-fallen soul which became Christ.[170] In this, it is claimed that Leontius was influenced by Evagrius Ponticus.[171] Not happy with the direction of Evans' study and totally opposed to the conclusions, Joseph Lynch has undertaken to show that Leontius was in fact a Cyrillian in Christology.[172] In this debate, Evans's position is so tentative that he has to resort to mere probability to show his case. In the light of Lynch's criticisms, which have also been made by Daley and Grillmeier, it is safe to conclude that Leontius of Byzantium was no Origenist in Christology.[173]

---

by Daley is nonetheless significant. Speaking of the manhood of Christ in Leontius's view, according to Daley, Leontius shows that it "'exists *in*' the hypostasis of the Logos, or that the single hypostasis of the Incarnate word *is* the Logos Himself." Furthermore, asserts Daley, "He [Leontius of Byzantium] does not deny the correctness of such statements, when properly understood" (Daley, "The Origenism of Leontius of Byzantium," 360). Based on this observation, and the subsequent use of the idea of the *enhypostaton* used by John of Damascus as really referring to the in-subsistence of Jesus' human nature, we will accept the doctrine as a significant and indispensable aspect of sound Christological thinking.

[170] David Beecher Evans, *Leontius of Byzantium: An Origenist Christology* (Washington, DC: Dumbarton Oaks, 1970). This is Evans's expanded version of his 1966 Harvard dissertation.

[171] Meyendorff agrees with Evans. In discussing Leontius's solution to the Christological dilemma between Chalcedonians and Monophysites, Meyendorff claims, "Leontius undertook then to offer his contemporaries *his* solution, an Origenist solution to the christological problem . . . thinking he thereby could show the usefulness of Evagrian metaphysics" (*Christ in Eastern Christian Thought*, 44).

[172] John Joseph Lynch, "Prosopon and the Dogma of the Trinity: A Study of the Background of Conciliar use of the Word in the Writings of Cyril of Alexandria and Leontius of Byzantium" (Ph.D. diss., Fordham University, 1973). See the essence of his argument in Lynch, "Leontius of Byzantium: A Cyrillian Christology," *TS* 36 (1975): 455-71.

[173] Evans's case rests on an unlikely identification of the "Nous" of Evagrian Cosmology with Jesus in Leontius's Christology. Direct refutation of this is to be found in Leontius's claim that the Word took a human soul (as well as a body) in the incarnation. It is God as Creator who takes up existence as a man not a preexisting "nous" which is merely joined to flesh to produce the human Jesus. See the Cyrillian like statements made by Leontius in Lynch, "Leontius of Byzantium: A Cyrillian Christology," 468-71. For example: "For it is my opinion that the soul was most in need of cleansing and for this reason it was *taken*" (Lynch, "Leontius of Byzantium," 470, emphasis added). Lynch's comments are important at this point. He says, "Note well: [the word] "taken." For an Origenist, the soul or nous, of Christ was united uninterruptedly to the Word from the moment of its origin before the creation of the material world; for a Cyrillian, the soul of Christ was taken simultaneously with the body at the moment of the Incarnation" (470).

F.2. The Christology of Leontius

Can a clear picture emerge from the battleground of the scholarly debate? It is certainly true that we know more about Leontius because of the focused attention on his writings than we would otherwise. The corpus of his writings is still a matter in dispute but from what is certainly genuine a not so hazy picture appears.

Aristotelian metaphysics were coming into vogue once more in the sixth century.[174] There was a widespread interest in re-interpreting Aristotle's categories. Specifically, the need to find clarification for the "principle of individuation" was wedded to an attempt to articulate a carefully defined notion of *hypostasis*. A desire to distinguish nature from hypostasis was crucial to maintain adherence to Chalcedon in the wake of Monophysite arguments. Leontius employs philosophical distinctions with some ingenuity. In the work known as *Contra Nestorianos et Eutychianos* I, Leontius provides his early reflections.[175] There is some debate whether Leontius affirmed an individual or particular human nature for Christ in this work.[176] Let us quote Leontius for a sampling:

> *Hypostasis*, gentlemen, and the enhypostatized (ἐνυπόστατον) are not one and the same thing. For *hypostasis* refers to the *individuum*, but hypostatic to the essence; and *hypostasis* defines the person (πρόσοπον) by means of the particular characteristics; the enhypostatized (ἐνυπόστατον) means, however, that it is not an *accident* – *it has its being in another and is not perceived in itself*; of this kind are all qualities, both those that are called properties of the essence as well as those which are added to the essence; none of the latter is *ousia* [i.e., an existing thing], but is al-

---

[174] See Nicholas J. Moutafakis, "Christology and its Philosophical Complexities in the Thought of Leontius of Byzantium," *HisPQ* 10 (1993): 99-119. He deals with the creative use of philosophy in Leontius who sought to solve a theological problem using Aristotelianism. Moutafakis draws on the work of Tatakis and Relton (affirming the Loofsian reading of Leontius), while also making use of Evans to further substantiate his findings.

[175] An extract which captures the approach of Leontius is found in *Christology of the Later Fathers*, 376-77.

[176] See the impressive analysis by Richard Cross, "Individual Natures in the Christology of Leontius of Byzantium," *JECS* 10 (2002): 245-65. This is a very difficult article to follow yet one that finally offers a plausible reconstruction of Leontius's concerns in the fictional debate encountered in the *Epilyseis*. A strong argument is made that Leontius rejects particular human nature yet maintains the idea of individual natures. For Leontius, "Christ's human nature," Cross argues "includes accidents, and is thus an individual nature . . . . the rejection of particular natures confirms that the human nature that is a component of this individual nature is universal or common, and Christ's human nature is thus a bundle of universal nature + universal accidents" (258). Immediately following this description, Cross continues, "[Leontius] posit[s] that Christ's human nature is individual, [therefore], does not entail accepting that it is divided from the Word: it does not, in other words, entail accepting that Christ's human nature is itself a hypostasis. Again we see Leontius consciously using his new insight to avoid Nestorianism" (258). This study is a valuable balance to the challenge against Loofs in contemporary Leontian scholarship. Cross rehabilitates Loofs by arguing that Loofs was right all along, albeit, for other reasons.

Chapter 5: Patristic Christology. A Survey of the Early Church

ways perceived in combination with the essence, like colour in the body and knowing in the soul.[177]

In Lang's view what Leontius is attempting in this passage is a distinction between the hypostasis (in this case an individual) and the *enhypostaton* (in this case a specific person). Hence the *enhypostaton* is that which exists by itself; it is not an accident. Rather, it is seen in itself. Later writers, such as Pamphilius, believed that for Leontius the *enhypostaton* was true for both natures of the Incarnate God–man.[178] It is evident that much speculation occurs in this work.

In the later work by Leontius of Byzantium entitled *Epilyseis*, he further elucidates this matter of hypostasis. This is brought out in a question that the Orthodox (Leontius) poses to his Severan interlocutor: "πῶς ουν μιαν Χριστοῦ φυσιν καλεῖς και ταυτην συνθετού τῆς Χριστοῦ προσηγοριας οὐ φυσιν ἀλλ' ὑποστασιν σημαινουτης περι ἠν αἱ φυσεις ὁρῶνταί και εν αι το προσωπον ἀφοριζεται[?]"[179] It is clear that Leontius keeps unity at the level of person and hypostasis in the Incarnation. Any plurality is kept for the *physeis* (natures) of Christ which are shown or defined in the hypostasis of the person. As Lynch observes, ""Christ" refers not to nature but to an ὑποστασις, which is that "around which the natures are seen," and the προσωπον that "which is distinguished in" the natures."[180]

In the end the aims of Leontius to justify Chalcedon are accomplished in his work. He argues that the "two," is in relation to *physis* (nature), so that Christ is one in two natures. Thus, he avoids the error of separating the person of Christ into two *hypostases* (subsistencies, persons). This is achieved with his reference to the *enhypostaton*. This means that a concrete existence of the subject [Christ as a union] is central to understanding the person. Leontius asserts,

> So then if the Godhead and manhood when united in substance, do not retain even the union of natural property of each, they are mixed together, and there remains neither Godhead nor manhood, but another kind of substance has been produced, formed out of them and yet not the same. What could be more impious or abominable than even to conceive of this, not to speak of affirming it and teaching it as a dogma? It remains, then, that from this examination of the character of substantial

---

[177] Cited in Grillmeier and Hainthaler, *From Chalcedon to Gregory*, 194. On this passage see Gockel, "Dubious Christological Formula?" 518-21; and U.M. Lang "Anhypostatos–Enhypostatos," 642-44. This was the text which Loofs used to substantiate his reading of Leontius's commitment to the solution of Christ's nature as existing in the subsistence of the Word. I Agree, that this is not the major burden, but it is certainly not the case that Leontius's theology precludes the notion. It has been argued that this is in fact consistent with his main concern of repudiating Monophysites in their insistence that the person of Christ had to be one nature only.

[178] See Lang, "Anhypostatos–Enhypostatos," 643.

[179] Cited in John Joseph Lynch, "Prosopon and the Dogma of the Trinity," 264. My translation is as follows: "How can you speak of a one-natured Christ, and that conjoined, when the proclamation/announcement is not about his nature but of Christ's subsistence wherein the natures are defined, in which natures, the person is distinguished?"

[180] Lynch, "Prosopon and the Dogma of the Trinity," 264.

union, we should grasp the unmixed [respective] identity of deity and humanity, according to the previous examples,[181] gathering a faint image from all these things of the truth which is above all things, which shows that one entity is produced out of these.[182]

His focus is in explaining the real existence of Christ as two natures in one person. One cannot speak of the human nature as independently existing without reference to the Word. He believes that *ousia* is a secondary principle, as he draws on Aristotelianism. The principle that an *ousia* cannot be without a *hypostasis* is countered by Leontius not by a term, but by the totality of his thought, which is, however, compatible with later interpretations of that very same term, *enhypostaton* as exhibited in John of Damascus.

G. John of Damascus (ca. 650-749)

In our survey we jump ahead one hundred years to the time of John of Damascus, often referred to as John Damascene.[183] His life, like that of Leontius, is a little mysterious. There are some "legendary" aspects to the biographical details available. Yet, his writings are securely established, save for one work entitled *Barlaam and Joasaph*, which, has been disputed throughout the centuries. His main work, for which he is well known, is the famous *Fount of Knowledge* in its three unequal parts: *Dialectics*,[184] *On Heresies*, and *Exact Exposition of the Orthodox Faith*. We will focus attention on the last of these, and particularly to book three of the *Exposition*.[185] It is here that we encounter the heart of his Christology.

---

[181] Leontius's examples were the torch which is on fire, showing the wood is made fiery and the fire wood, and the plain union of living beings, that is, humanity with a body-soul unity.

[182] Cited in Hardy, *Christology of the Later Fathers*, 377.

[183] John of Damascus' dates vary from scholar to scholar. For the above dates see Ferguson, ed., *Encyclopedia of Early Christianity*, s.v., "John of Damascus," by George C. Berthold. An excellent work on the Damascene's life and work, is Andrew Louth, *St. John Damascene: Tradition and Originality in Byzantine Theology* (Oxford: Oxford University Press, 2002).

[184] In the *Philosophical Chapters*, as *Dialectics* is also known, John lays the conceptual groundwork and foundation for his later theological thinking in the *Exposition*. For example, in *Dialectics* [*Peri Enhypostatou*] he writes, "In its proper sense . . . , the enhypostaton is either that which does not subsist in itself but is considered in hypostases, just as the human species, or human nature, that is, is not considered in its own hypostasis but in Peter and Paul and other human hypostases. Or it is that which is compound with another thing differing in substance to make up one particular whole and constitute one compound hypostasis . . . . Thus, [humans are] made up of soul and body, while neither the soul alone nor the body alone is called a hypostasis, but both are called enhypostata . . . . Again, that nature is called enhypostaton which has been assumed by another hypostasis and in this has its existence." Cited in Charles Craig Twombly, "Perichoresis and Personhood in the Thought of John of Damascus" (Ph.D. diss., Emory University, 1992), 92.

[185] An English translation by S.D.F. Salmond of the *Exposition* is available in John of Damascus, *Exposition of the Orthodox Faith*, NPNF 2, vol. 9 (New York: Christian

G.1. John Damascene's Christology

John's Christology draws on both Leontius of Byzantium and Maximus the Confessor.[186] "[He] discovers," notes Meyendorff, "their [the conceptions and ideas of earlier theologians] inner coherence, and with the help of supplementary sources . . . arrives at his final synthesis."[187] That final synthesis includes exposition of the two wills and two energies of the one person of Christ. Also prominent in his Christology is the idea of perichoresis, or interpenetration of the two natures.[188] What will occupy our analysis, however, will be his understanding of "Enhypostasia," which serves as the crown of Chalcedonian thinking about the person of Christ, and therefore serves as an answer to the "how" question left unanswered by the definition of 451.

"In the incarnation," Florovsky notes, echoing the Damascene, "God the Logos receives not abstract humanity, as it is perceived by pure speculation, for this would not be Incarnation but a phantom and deceit."[189] On the other hand we must also resist the idea that the Logos received "all of human nature as realized in the human race."[190] The truth is grasped rather in the affirmation that the Logos receives "manhood as it is in the indivisible." [191] "He received it," continues Florovsky, "however, in such a way that by itself it was not and is not a special or preexisting hypostasis but receives its very existence in his [the

---

Literature, 1899; reprint, Grand Rapids: Eerdmans, 1975), 1-101. The Greek text to which I am referring is Nikos Matzoukas, ed., Ἰωάννου Δαμασκηνοῦ: Ἔκδοσις Ἀκριβὴς τῆς Ὀρθοδόξου Πίστεως (Thessaloniki: S. Pournara,1998). For an introduction to John Damascene's life and work, see Georges Florovsky, *Byzantine Fathers of the Sixth to Eighth Century*, 254-92; John Meyerndorff, *Christ in Eastern Christian Thought*, 116-31, which is especially helpful for John's Christology; and John B. O'Connor, "St. John Damascene," transcribed by Anthony A. Killeen, *The Catholic Encyclopedia*, vol. 8 (New York: Robert Appleton, 1910) [on-line]; accessed February 2002; available from http://www.newadvent.org/cathen/08459b.htm; Internet.

[186] Beyond those works already mentioned, the following are also extremely helpful for John's Christology: Jaroslav Pelikan, *The Christian Tradition: A History of the Development of Doctrine*, vol. 2, *The Spirit of Eastern Christendom (600-1700)* (Chicago: University of Chicago Press, 1974), 68-83; K. Rosemond, *La Christologie de saint Jean Damascene* (Ettal: Buch Kuntsverlag, 1959); Twombly, "Perichoresis and Personhood in the Thought of John of Damascus," 82-152; and Richard Cross, "Perichoresis, Deification, and Christological Predication in John of Damascus," *MS* 62 (2000): 69-124.

[187] Meyendorff, *Christ in Eastern Christian Thought*, 116.

[188] Two notions need to be held in balance in understanding John on this matter. First, because of the reality of the incarnation, the flesh becomes literally God's flesh (in a divinized form), so that it is true that God the Word suffers in the flesh. However, one must maintain the distinctions (of which he is so fond) so as not to assert that the deity is somehow maimed. The illustration of the sun shining in the tree, which is nonetheless present and permeates the tree, remains free from the axe of the woodsman that chops the tree down, exemplifies John's faith on this matter. Both of these notions are held together by John.

[189] Florovsky, *Byzantine Fathers of the Sixth to Eighth Centuries*, 270.

[190] Florovsky, *Byzantine Fathers of the Sixth to Eighth Centuries*, 270.

[191] Florovsky, *Byzantine Fathers of the Sixth to Eighth Centuries*, 270.

Logos'] hypostasis." Now comes the crucial concept for this idea to surface completely: "Manhood in Christ is hypostasized in the very hypostasis of the Logos. It is *enhypostasized* to the Logos."[192] This is to be gleaned from John in his reply concerning the maxim that "no *physis* is without its *hypostasis*." The Damascene asserts:

> yet it does not necessarily follow that the natures that are united to one another in subsistence should have each its own proper subsistence. For after they have come together into one subsistence, it is possible that neither should they be without subsistence, nor should each have its own peculiar subsistence, but that both should have one and the same subsistence. For since one and the same subsistence of the Word has become the subsistence of the natures, neither of them is permitted to be without subsistence, nor are they allowed to have subsistences that differ from one another, or to have sometimes the subsistence of this nature and sometimes of that, but always without division or separation they both have the same subsistence–a subsistence which is not broken up into parts or divided, so that one part should belong to this, and one to that, but which belongs wholly to this and wholly to that in its absolute entirety. For the flesh of God the Word did not subsist as an independent subsistence, nor did there arise another subsistence besides that of God the Word, but as it existed in that became rather a subsistence which subsisted in another, than one which was an independent subsistence. Wherefore, neither does it lack subsistence altogether, nor yet is there thus introduced into the Trinity another subsistence. [193]

This passage contains several important points. It is here, where, despite John's agreement that a *physis* cannot be without a *hypostasis*, he nonetheless endeavors to claim that when we speak of the incarnation we cannot isolate the natures and discuss them individually without reference to the other nature. Moreover, one senses the desire to address the natures as having one and the same hypostasis. This is necessary to avoid Nestorianism. Furthermore, allowing the flesh described as God's own one is cautioned so as not to allow a new hypostasis to enter the equation. Rather, the humanity exists in the hypostasis of the Word. Here, John of Damascus explicitly affirms what is known now as the doctrine

---

[192] Florovsky, *Byzantine Fathers of the Sixth to Eighth Centuries*, 270.

[193] See John of Damascus, *Exposition of the Orthodox Faith*, trans. S.D.F. Salmond in NPNF 2, vol. 9, 53. In Greek it reads: "οὐκ ἀνάγκη τὰς ἀλλήλαις ἑνωθείσας φύσεις καθ' ὑπόστασιν ἑκάστιν ἰδίαν κεκτῆσθαι ὑποστασιν· δύναται γὰρ εἰς μίαν συνδρᾶ μοῦσαι ὑπόστασιν μήτε ἀνυπόστατοι εἶναι μήτε ἰδιάζουσα ἑκάστῃ ἔχειν ὑπόστασιν, ἀλλὰ μίαν καὶ τὴν αὐτὴν ἀμφότεραι. Ἡ αὐτὴ γὰρ τοῦ Λόγου ὑπόστασις ἀμφοτέρων τῶν φύσεων ὑπόστασις χρηματίσασα οὔτε ἀνυπόστατον μίαν αὐτῶν εἶναι συγχωρεῖ οὔτε μὴν ἑτεροϋποστάτους ἀλλήλων εἶναι παραχωρεῖ, οὐδὲ ποτὲ μὲν τῆσδε ποτὲ δὲ ἐκείνης, ἀλλ' ἀεὶ ἀμφοτέρων ἀδιαιρέτως καὶ ἀχωρίστως ὑπάρχει ὑπόστασις οὐ μερί ζομένη καὶ διαιρουμένη καὶ μέρος μὲν αὐτῆς τῇδε, μέρος δὲ τῇδε διανέμουσα, ἀλλὰ πᾶσα ταύτης καὶ πᾶσα ἐκείνης ἀμερῶς καὶ ὁλοσχερῶς ὑπάρχουσα. Οὐ γὰρ ἰδιοσυσ τάτως ὑπέστη ἡ τοῦ Θεοῦ Λόγου σὰρξ οὐδὲ ἑτέρα ὑπόστασις γέγονε παρὰ τὴν τοῦ Θεοῦ Λόγου ὑπόστασιν, ἀλλ' ἐν αὐτῇ ὑποστᾶσα ἐνυπόστατος μᾶλλον καὶ οὐ καθ' αὑτὴν ἰδιοσύστατος ὑπόστασις γέγονε. Διὸ οὐδὲ ἀνυπόστατός ἐστιν οὐδὲ ἑτέραν ἐν τῇ Τριάδι παρεισφέρει ὑπόστασιν" (Matzoukas, Ιωαννου Δαμασκηνοῦ, 242).

Chapter 5: Patristic Christology. A Survey of the Early Church

of the assumption by the Logos of an "Inpersonal" (*enhypostaton*) human nature.[194] The humanity does not have its own hypostasis but neither is it without hypostasis (*anhypostaton*); rather it exists *enhypostaton* (in [locative prepositional sense] the Word's subsistence). Finally, this does not insert a foreign or extra subsistence into the Trinity, for it is the person, God the Son, who is incarnate. One subject remains at the center. In this scheme, notes Meyerndorff, "According to John of Damascus, the enhypostatization of human nature into the Logos can give that human nature a properly human or "carnal" principle of individuation."[195] Because of this, one can see that John Damascene improves the formula found in Leontius of Byzantium [Jerusalem?].[196] More clearly than before, we see one subject at the center. Also a philosophical analysis of terms allows John to argue that the Word assumed a human nature into the hypostasis of that very Word as it became flesh. No mixing of natures nor of separation is found here, although distinctions abound. Chalcedon was finally justified and bettered.

"It may seem somewhat one-sided," concedes Studer, "if the whole wealth of late patristic theology, usually too little regarded, is considered under the aspect of the development of the concept of hypostasis."[197] Studer continues by saying: "Yet, after what has been said, it could hardly be doubted that the decisive contribution of the theologians of that time consisted in the clarification of

---

[194] One should not read into this term the idea of *im*personal, that is that the human Jesus did not have a character, personality, or an "internal human make up" so to speak. The "in-personal" notion safeguards the unity of the person in the incarnation while allowing that the natures which constitute the Incarnate Christ are both complete and inseparable without confusion. In other words, when the second person of the Trinity became flesh (John 1:14), the Logos was not adding a full grown person into His being, but the nature of the human Jesus came into being as the Word underwent a union with a human nature at conception. The person throughout is the Logos who became flesh, otherwise it would be both untrue and blasphemous for Jesus of Nazareth to claim: "Before Abraham was, I am!" (John 8:58).

[195] Meyendorff, *Christ in Eastern Christian Thought*, 120.

[196] We note here a comment by Twombly which again draws attention to the fact that Patristic writers affirmed that the divine nature of Christ retained its presence in the whole of creation, hence adhering to the concept advocated in this book, namely the omnipresence of Jesus Christ. After the incarnation, notes Twombly, "The divine nature not only has a certain kind of relationship with its own human nature but is also related to the rest of creation in a way that might be termed mutually immanent. It is said to 'pervade all things'" (Twombly, "Perichoresis and Personhood," 96). He is referring to *Exposition* 3 (7), where John discusses the union of two natures but also keeps them distinct. The divine nature is said to "penetrate all, as it [Divine nature] wills without itself being penetrated" (my translation; see Matzoukas, Ιωαννου Δαμασκηνου, 238). I see John's emphasis not only on immanence, though this no one can deny, but also on transcendence. The Word as God is impassible and is not subject to material objects or spiritual entities influencing or manipulating its being; the Word cannot be threatened or coerced forcibly from without, except that it wills to be so moved as in the death of Christ.

[197] Studer, *Trinity and Incarnation*, 238.

this concept [hypostasis], dogmatized by Chalcedon."[198] The *theoria* of speculative theology, and the *oikonomia* of salvation history finally had a well rounded "contemplation of the trinitarian God, who in the incarnation of his word had revealed his glory."[199] Only a fully divine Jesus could manifest this glory as the only begotten Son of the Father, and only an omnipresent Christ could be the Word, who though incarnate as genuinely human, still ruled the universe that he created, and came to redeem, as the true God.

H. Conclusion

Our survey has stretched many years. Clearly, this overview has been selective.[200] Despite some omissions it is hoped that the chapter has clearly shown the relevance Christology played in the outworking of the Church's theological commitments. For the Fathers, Christology is centrally significant. In the exposition of the person of Christ, many have affirmed the omnipresence of Jesus after the incarnation. Particularly noteworthy contributions on the attribute of omnipresence are found in Irenaeus, Tertullian, Athanasius, and Augustine. The affirmation of the ubiquity of the person of Jesus Christ therefore has patristic precedent.

The early church hammered out its doctrines not as dry academic exercises but in the heat of battle for the very life of the church. For this reason, in a very real sense one cannot fathom the issues involved at a distance from worship in community with fellow pilgrim Christians. Our union with those who went before is as real as the union we have with those who share the common cup with us in our celebration of the Lord's Table today. We profess, along with countless saints before us, one and the same Jesus Christ, both fully God and fully man. Jesus is one person in two natures, God the Son. Furthermore, our survey shows that Christological exposition was an attempt to interpret the raw materials of the New Testament documents. By the time of the Council of Chalcedon, a framework, in which to ground biblical exposition was sorely needed. Too many different Christs were being proclaimed. The desires of Church leaders to remain faithful to the witness of the Scriptures prompted council after council, and debate after debate. We too, must strive that a right, albeit not exhaustive, understanding of the person of Jesus Christ be maintained

---

[198] Studer, *Trinity and Incarnation*, 238.

[199] Studer, *Trinity and Incarnation*, 238.

[200] The Cappadocians, who are famously associated with giving us the Eastern definition of the Trinity, which clearly distinguishes between the one nature (essence or *ousia*) of God and the three *hypostases* (persons or subsistencies), were not included in our survey. However, one may note a very helpful article on Gregory of Nyssa for another clear affirmation that the church Fathers viewed the doctrine of omnipresence as possessing great significance and importance. See L.R. Wickham, "Soul and Body: Christ's Omnipresence (De Tridui Spatio p. 29o, 18-294, 13)" in *The Easter Sermons of Gregory of Nyssa: Translation and Commentary*, ed. Andreas Spira and Christoph Klock (Cambridge, MA: Philadelphia Patristic Foundation, 1981), 279-92. Also, see George D. Dragas, "The anti-Apollinarist Christology of St. Gregory of Nyssa: A First Analysis," *GOTR* 42 (1997): 299-314, for more on Gregory's Christology.

and defended. What is at stake may be our salvation (a widespread patristic concern), as the gospel of salvation hinges on the person of Jesus. But more importantly than our own redemption is God's own honor; we must think of Christ no less than who he is. The early church set the Christological standard. As we attempt to theologize today in faithfulness to scripture, we should also seek to adhere to the patristic Christological achievement. The enhypostatic idea must supplement Chalcedonian Christology to provide a coherent view of Jesus Christ. This should be required for Christological orthodoxy today.

CHAPTER 6

REFORMATION CHRISTOLOGY: CALVIN'S *EXTRA CALVINISTICUM*

A. Introduction

At the time of the Reformation developments in the Trinitarian and Incarnational theological tradition were made.[1] John Calvin, in particular, is credited with path-breaking emphases that have affected later generations, even down to the present-day evangelical milieu. It seems appropriate, therefore, to include a chapter on John Calvin's Christology as he makes a significant contribution to Christology, especially the matter of Jesus' omnipresence.[2] In this chapter we

---

[1] The central aspects of Reformed Christology may be investigated in various works. For an introduction see H.R. Mackintosh, *The Doctrine of the Person of Jesus Christ* (New York: Charles Scribner's Sons, 1912), 230-46 (this chapter is entitled, "The Christology of the Reformation Churches"). Comprehensive coverage is found in J.A. Dorner, *History of the Development of the Doctrine of Christ*, vol. 2, trans. D. W. Simon (Edinburgh: T & T Clark, 1886); and especially helpful is A.B. Bruce, *The Humiliation of Christ in Its Physical, Ethical, and Official Aspects* (Grand Rapids: Eerdmans, 1955), 82-132. For Christ's humanity in particular, see Jaroslav Pelikan, *The Christian Tradition: A History of the Development of Doctrine*, vol. 4, *Reformation of Church and Dogma (1300-1700)* (Chicago/London: University of Chicago Press, 1984), 350-62; Geoffrey W. Bromiley, "The Reformers and the Humanity of Christ," in *Perspectives on Christology: Essays in Honor of Paul K. Jewett*, ed. Marguerite Shuster and Richard Muller (Grand Rapids: Zondervan, 1991), 79-104; and David Foxgrover, "The Humanity of Christ: Within Proper Limits," in *Calviniana: Ideas and Influence of John Calvin*, ed. Robert V. Schnucker (Kirksville, MO: Sixteenth Century Journal Publishers, 1988), 93-105.

[2] For an introduction to Calvin's Christology, see the following works: Stephen Bud Edmondson, "Christ the Mediator: Calvin's Eclectic Christology" (Ph.D. diss., Yale University, 1999) idem, *Calvin's Christology* (New York: Cambridge University Press, 2004). This book is based on his dissertation; Richard A. Muller, *Christ and the Decree: Christology and Predestination in Reformed Theology from Calvin to Perkins* (Durham, NC: Labyrinth, 1986), 17-38; John Frederick Jansen, *Calvin's Doctrine of the Work of Christ* (London: James Clarke, 1956); Paul Van Buren, *Christ in Our Place: The Substitutionary Character of Calvin's Doctrine of Reconciliation* (London: Oliver and Boyd, 1957); Klauspeter Blaser, "Calvins Lehre von den drei Ämtern Christi," *ThStu* 105 (1970): 3-52; Christian Link, "Die Entscheidung der Christologie Calvins und ihre theologische Bedeutung: Das sogenannte Extra-Calvinisticum," *EvT* 47 (1987): 97-119; Wolfgang Kratz, "Christus – Gott und Mensch: Einige Fragen an Calvins Christologie," *EvT* 19 (1959): 209-19; and Kevin Dixon Kennedy, "The Union of God and Humanity

will examine John Calvin's contribution. A focused look at the teaching called *extra Calvinisticum* will occupy the attention of this part of the book. This will enable a later contrast of the contemporary evangelical voices with both the patristic era, and with the Christology of this great theologian, John Calvin.

B. Extra Calvinisticum

Throughout the history of Christian thought, a doctrinal position known now as the *extra Calvinisticum* was held by certain individuals.[3] E. David Willis offers an explanation regarding the origin of the term. The "Extra Calvinisticum" as a term may have first been introduced by Theodore Thumm in 1623. The synonymous term "Extra Calvinianum" appeared still earlier in a 1621 work of Balthazar Mentzer. The appearance of both terms, however, crystallized an idea long held among Lutheran theologians that it was characteristically Calvinist to teach that after the Incarnation the Eternal Son had an existence *etiam extra carnem*. This Lutheran sentiment appeared as early as the Colloquy of Maulbronn, in 1564. Already by that date "Calvinist" was becoming synonymous with, or was even replacing, "Zwinglian" as the most comprehensive term to describe the "sacramentarians," and the Reformed theologians were giving increased attention to the *etiam extra* affirmation.[4]

This doctrine, the *extra Calvinisticum*, has to do with the incarnated Son of God. Particularly, the question of the relationship of the two natures is paramount in the *extra* doctrine, and hence the matter becomes focused on how the attribute of omnipresence relates to him. "In the incarnation," states Peterson,

---

in Jesus Christ the Mediator," chapter 3 of "Union with Christ as Key to John Calvin's Understanding of the Extent of the Atonement" (Ph.D. diss., Southern Baptist Theological Seminary, 1999), 73-101; idem, *Union With Christ and the Extent of the Atonement in Calvin* (New York: Peter Lang, 2002). This book is Dixon's published dissertation. More recent work on Calvin's thought has emerged from the philosopher, Paul Helm. See his *John Calvin's Ideas* (New York: Oxford University Press, 2004), 35-57 (on the Trinity) and 58-92 (on the *Extra* doctrine); and idem, *Calvin: A Guide for the Perplexed* (London: T & T Clark, 2008), 36-74.

[3] Irenaeus, Athanasius, and Cyril, among others, are adherents from the early church. As discussed in the previous chapter, Augustine also affirmed this view. See E. David Willis, *Calvin's Catholic Christology: The Function of the So-Called Extra Calvinisticum in Calvin's Theology* (Leiden: E.J. Brill, 1966), 44-48, where Willis cites Epistle 137, 2 [*ad Volusianum*], where Augustine claims that it is not Christian teaching " that God was so poured into the flesh in which he was born of the Virgin that he either abandoned or lost the care of the government of the universe or that he transferred this care into that small body as into a gathered and contracted material" (46). Willis believes that Augustine was the major influence on Calvin concerning the *extra Calvinisticum*. In the Middle-Ages, Gabriel Biel was a proponent of the *extra Calvinisticum* (See 42-43). For Biel, see Heiko Oberman, *The Harvest of Medieval Theology* (Cambridge, MA: Harvard University Press, 1963; reprint, Grand Rapids: Baker, 2000), 264-65. Of course, the teaching was not called *extra Calvinisticum* in their writings. The content, however, was consonant with that which we find in Calvin.

[4] Willis, *Calvin's Catholic Christology*, 23.

"Jesus Christ is fully divine; none of his deity was set aside when the Word became flesh."[5] Moreover, adds Peterson, "Calvin affirms that God the Son was wholly incarnate in Jesus of Nazareth and yet wholly outside (extra) of him too. This is the *extra-calvinisticum*, the Calvinistic 'extra' or 'without.' God was 'without' Jesus as well as fully incarnate in him."[6] The scripture teaching regarding the transcendence of God is the driving force for the *extra* doctrine. This appears certain in Calvin, who keeps the Creator/creature distinction, which became so important for Reformed theology, as a basic axiom of his Christology. "God's majesty," notes Calvin, "is too lofty to be attained by mortal men, who are like grubs crawling upon the earth."[7] Moreover, Calvin says,

> The situation would surely have been hopeless had the very majesty of God not descended to us since it was not in our power to ascend to him. . . . Even if man had remained free from all stain, his condition would have been too lowly for him to reach God without a mediator.[8]

In his classic work on Calvin, Niesel asserts, "When Calvin says that God must meet us in Christ because we ourselves cannot bridge the gulf which exists between Creator and creation, he is no doubt thinking of the radical distinction between God and His creatures."[9]

Especially during the post-Reformation scholastic era, Lutheran dogmaticians decried, what was to them, a theological mistake which the Calvinists affirmed: "*illud extra calvinisticum*" (that calvinist "extra" or "beyond"), meaning the person of Christ had an existence *beyond* the body of Jesus (*etiam extra carnem*).[10] Calvin may have given prominence to this view, but he did not invent it.[11]

---

[5] Robert A. Peterson Sr., *Calvin and the Atonement* (Phillipsburg, NJ: P & R, 1983; reprint, Fearn: Christian Focus, 1999), 27.

[6] Peterson Sr., *Calvin and the Atonement*, 27.

[7] See John Calvin, *Institutes of the Christian Religion*, trans. Ford Lewis Battles, ed. John T. McNeill, LCC 20 and 21 (Philadelphia: Westminster, 1960), 1:352 (II.vi.4). All subsequent references to this work will be cited as *Institutes* (with section reference).

[8] *Institutes* II.xii.1.

[9] See Wilhelm Niesel, *The Theology of Calvin*, trans. Harold Knight (Philadelphia: Westminster, 1956), 112.

[10] Especially helpful is Marvin P. Hoogland, *Calvin's Perspective on the Exaltation of Christ in Comparison with the Post-Reformation Doctrine of the Two States* (Kampen: Kok, 1966), 11-44. I appreciate Hoogland's analysis and insight in distinguishing variations of Lutheran Christology. For a detailed investigation of the two natures issue from one strand of Lutheranism, see Martin Chemnitz, *The Two Natures of Christ*, trans. J.A.O. Preus (St. Louis: Concordia, 1971 [first published in 1578]). Also of note, Robert A. Kelly, "Tradition and Innovation: The Use of Theodoret's *Eranistes* in Martin Chemnitz' *De Duabis Naturis in Christo*," in *Perspectives on Christology: Essays in Honor of Paul K. Jewett*, ed. Marguerite Shuster and Richard Muller (Grand Rapids: Zondervan, 1991), 103-25; and Wilbert R. Gawrisch, "On Christology, Brenz and the Question of Ubiquity," in *No Other Gospel: Essays in Commemoration of the*

Chapter 6: Reformation Christology: Calvin's Extra Calvinisticum

This chapter will attempt to highlight Calvin's position, locate it within the context of his own Trinitarian thought. The genius of Calvin in re-articulating a nuanced exposition of the *communicatio idiomatum* becomes key in differentiating his thought from the Lutheran attempt to assign ubiquity to the body of Jesus Christ.[12] In all this retracing of historical theology it will become evident that the main concern is primarily Christological. The chapter will demonstrate that Calvin did indeed teach the *extra Calvinisticum* based on a certain methodology in his desire to be faithful to Scripture.

C. Calvin's Extra Calvinisticum

It is commonly accepted that Calvin indeed held to a doctrine which later was dubbed the *extra Calvinisticum*. There are two places in the *Institutes* where it is clearly affirmed. These are II.xiii.4, and IV.xvii.30.

> They thrust upon us as something absurd the fact that if the Word of God became flesh, then he was confined within the narrow prison of an earthly body. This is mere imprudence! For even if the Word in his immeasurable essence united with the nature of man into one person, we do not imagine that he was confined therein. Here is something marvelous: the Son of God descended from heaven in such a way that, without leaving heaven, he willed to be borne in the virgin's womb, to go about the

---

400th anniversary of the Formula of Concord 1550-1980, ed. Arnold J. Koelpin (Milwaukee: Northwestern Publishing, 1980), 229-53.

[11] See Donald K. McKim, ed., *Encyclopedia of the Reformed Faith* (Louisville: Westminster John Knox; Edinburgh: St. Andrew, 1992), s.v. "Extra Calvinisticum," by David Willis-Watkins. The most recent study on the *extra calvinisticum*, that I am aware of, is Andrew McGinnis, *The Son of God Beyond the Flesh: A Historical and Theological Study of the Extra Calvinisticum* (London: Bloomsbury, 2014), in which he discerns the contributions of Cyril of Alexandria, Thomas Aquinas, and Zacharias Ursinus to the doctrine and how they utilized it. Moreover, McGinnis shows how recent scholars have attempted to use the *extra* doctrine to further other theological concerns than Christology. I am very sympathetic to McGinnis's conclusion that the *extra calvinisticum* is a crucial doctrine that should be restricted to the sphere of Christology.

[12] Speaking of Luther, McLelland says, "One positive point in his favor should be remarked, that he did not rest in a logically simple doctrine of ubiquity (as others like Westphal and Brenz seemed to) but preferred the idea of multivalent presence ("present where he will") in Joseph McLelland, "Lutheran-Reformed Debate on the Eucharist and Christology," in Paul C. Empie and James I. McCord, eds. *Marburg Revisited: A Reexamination of Lutheran and Reformed Traditions* (Minneapolis, MN: Augsburg, 1966), 49. For more on Luther's Christology one should consult Marc Lienhard, *Luther: Witness to Jesus Christ*, trans. Edwin H. Robertson (Minneapolis: Augsburg, 1982); Ian D. Kingston Siggins, *Martin Luther's Doctrine of Christ* (New Haven: Yale University Press, 1970); and Norman E. Nagel, "*Martinus*: 'Heresy, Doctor Luther, Heresy!' The Person and Work of Christ," in *Seven-Headed Luther: Essays in Commemoration of a Quincentenary 1483-1983*, ed. Peter Newman Brooks (Oxford: Clarendon, 1983) For a statement of contemporary conservative Christology in the tradition of Luther one will be ably served by Curtis A. Jahn, ed., *We Believe in Jesus Christ: Essays on Christology* (Milwaukee: Northwestern Publishing, 1999).

earth, and to hang upon the cross; yet he continuously filled the world even as he had done from the beginning.[13]

But from Scripture we plainly infer that the one person of Christ so consists of two natures that each nevertheless retains unimpaired its own distinctive character. . . . There is a commonplace distinction of the schools to which I am not ashamed to refer: although the whole Christ is everywhere, still the whole of that which is in him is not everywhere. . . . Therefore, since the whole Christ is everywhere, our Mediator is ever present with his own people, and in the Supper reveals himself in a special way, yet in such a way that the whole Christ is present, but not in his wholeness. For, as has been said, in his flesh he is contained in heaven until he appears in judgment.[14]

From the first quote, it is of vital importance to note that in Calvin's thought, the omnipresence is true of the second person in the incarnate state *prior* to the ascension.[15] This is not an issue of a supposed rank or position that Jesus attained to, but what was true of Jesus because of the nature(s) of his person. Any discussion which focuses on the Lord's Supper, must take this serious Christological position into account. Commenting on this very passage in Calvin, Richard Muller says, "The transcendence of the divine nature provides Calvin with the conceptual background for his doctrine of the union of the divine with human nature in Christ."[16] One must concede that Muller has rightly under-

---

[13] *Insitutes* II.xiii.4.

[14] *Insitutes* IV.xvii.30.

[15] In her thesis, Eleanor Stonebraker states, "The *extra calvinisticum* is the calvinist belief that, *since the Ascension* [emphasis added], Christ's divinity is beyond the bounds of his humanity (Heidelberg Catechism, number 48)" ("Heroes and Beggars: A Lutheran Look at the Extra Calvinisticum, Inside and Out" [MTS thesis, Trinity Lutheran Seminary, 1991], iv). Two observations are needed at this point. First, it may be true that in the ensuing battles between the Lutherans and the Calvinists over the Lord's Supper, that a focus on the post-ascension Christ became the locus of investigation. This is not the point Calvin himself makes, although he had much to contribute to the debate about the Lord's Supper. Calvin makes it a matter of the *theology of Christ*. The *person* becomes the focus, not a position which he receives at the ascension. Second, the Heidelberg Catechism in Q. 48 affirms the *extra Calvinisticum* in the answer, yet no discussion of the supposed post ascension significance is noted. See Philip Schaff, *The Creeds of Christendom* (Grand Rapids: Baker, 1998), 3: 322. Also see Jan Rohls, *Reformed Confessions: Theology from Zurich to Barmen* (Louisville: Westminster John Knox, 1998). Rohls states, "The Incarnation cannot be understood in such a way that the Son of God would cease to be true God. The Incarnation is not a *kenosis* in the sense that the *Logos* actually *becomes* flesh. The incarnation is not a change of substance whose result would be that the Son of humanity takes the place of the Son of God. As the Son of Humanity Christ continues to be the Son of God" (104). We conclude that Stonebraker's definition though broadly correct includes a misleading element. Calvin maintained that the *extra Calvinistuicum* is true of the person of Christ both prior to and subsequent to the Ascension.

[16] Muller, *Christ and the Decree*, 20.

stood Calvin on this important point. Far from grounding the extra doctrine in a supposed (mere) immanence, Calvin rightly speaks of the "immeasurable essence" of divinity which is united with a human nature. It is the *transcendent* Christ that is omnipresent. This is not to deny immanence, but rather to ground the presence in the divine essence. Furthermore, as is characteristic of Calvin, it is true to say, therefore that Christ (incarnate) is truly omnipresent. Muller continues his thoughts on Calvin's passage. He asserts,

> The absolute transcendence of Christ's divinity represents on the one hand Calvin's ever present concern for maintaining the sovereignty of God while on the other it demonstrates his effort to underscore the reality of Christ's human nature and its identity with the nature of all men. The extra calvinisticum preserves the integrity of the natures and the mystery of the union.[17]

From the second quote by Calvin (*Institutes* IV.xvii.30), one can see that a prior Christological commitment is programmatic in delineating the significance of the presence of Christ in the Eucharist.[18] Here is evidence for Calvin's commitment to Chalcedonian Christology.[19] His emphasis is unmistakable. There is only "one person" who, nevertheless, "consists of two natures" notes Calvin. Moreover, the natures, both divine and human, in Christ retain their own distinctive character. Willis noted in his classic work on Calvin's Christology, that the latter reference (IV.xvii.30) appeared in the 1536 edition, under the treatment of the Eucharist, and found itself in a much expanded emphasis in the 1559 edition.[20] By the time of the final edition, Calvin incorporated the now famous first reference (II.xiii.4) in order to "forestall menacing Trinitarian and anti-trinitarian speculation."[21] It appears that Calvin had much on his mind

---

[17] Muller, *Christ and the Decree*, 20.

[18] In his fine book, Douglas Farrow, *Ascension and Ecclesia: On the Significance of the Doctrine of Ascension for Ecclesiology and Christian Cosmology* (Grand Rapids: Eerdmans, 1999), 165-264, the author has a chapter entitled "Where is Jesus." In this section Farrow treats Calvin (175-80), among others. Although some of his insights are helpful, there is an overall neglect of the *extra Calvinisticum* in this section where one would most expect it. This is most unfortunate as it could have made this good book much better. Nevertheless, Farrow's approach to Calvin's view of the Eucharist appears pristine.

[19] McCormack has said, "In the main, Calvin's Christology belonged to the Alexandrian-Cyrillian type" (Bruce L. McCormack, "For us and our Salvation: Incarnation and Atonement in the Reformed Tradition," *GOTR* 43 [1998]: 286). More specifically, Raitt admits Calvin's Chalcedonian commitment. See Jill Raitt, "The Person of the Mediator: Calvin's Christology and Beza's Fidelity," *OPASRR* (1977): 55, where she cites *Institutes* II.xiv.5-8, to show how Calvin countered Servetus's charges of Calvin as a Nestorian.

[20] Willis, *Calvin's Catholic Christology*, 27.

[21] Willis, *Calvin's Catholic Christology*, 27. Noteworthy is Willis's comment that Calvin actually was countering arguments posed by detractors who believed that the

when articulating this *extra Calvinisticum*. He has as a major concern to establish the correct view of Christ. This can be seen in his rebuttal of Francesco Stancaro concerning the mediatorial role of Christ.[22] Here, too, Trinitarianism is vital as Calvin is charged with Arianism.[23]

D. Calvin's Trinitarianism

Calvin's Christology is to be located within a Trinitarian theology.[24] Only when his Trinitarianism is appreciated, can the Christology of Calvin be evaluated for its function in the sacramental teaching on the Lord's Supper. Any misunderstanding on Calvin's view of either Christology or the Lord's Supper may be traceable to an inadequate grasp of Calvin's Trinitarianism. Yet, as with all Calvin's theology, the connection to soteriological themes is apparent in his approach to the Trinity. The focus will be on his "Substantial" Trinitarianism, however. In classic fashion, for Calvin the doctrine of the Trinity is the matrix out of which Christological teaching springs forth. This aspect of Calvin's thought in reality requires fuller attention than can be devoted to in this brief section. However, its importance will manifest itself in the subsequent discussion.

Trinitarianism is fundamental for Calvin's theology.[25] "[Calvin] was not interested in the metaphysical niceties of abstract theology," explains George,

---

emphasis on Christ's true incarnation would restrict him in a 'prison of the flesh,' so to speak, "within the limits of a small place" (27).

[22] Indispensable for understanding this episode are Tylenda's two articles. See, Joseph N. Tylenda, "Christ the Mediator: Calvin versus Stancaro [with translation of Calvin's First Treatise against Stancaro]," *CTJ* 8 (1973): 5-16; and idem, "The Controversy on Christ the Mediator: Calvin's Second Reply to Stancaro," *CTJ* 8 (1973): 131-57. Also see Edmondson, "Christ the Mediator," 35-81.

[23] In his masterful book on Calvin's life, Cottret claims of the Genevan reformer that "a terrible suspicion . . . dogged Calvin throughout his life, that of Arianism" (Bernard Cottret, *Calvin: A Biography*, trans. M. Wallace McDonald [Grand Rapids: Eerdmans; Edinburgh: T & T Clark, 2000], 125). Cottret's discussion is of the famous Lausanne disputation of 1536 where Calvin was accused by Pierre Caroli of not "believing in the dogma of the Trinity" (124). "The debate was not merely doctrinal," Cottret explains, "it raised a double question that would haunt Calvin for the rest of his days. Is the Trinity demonstrable from the sole standpoint of Scripture?" (126).

[24] It is interesting that Torrance sees that "Calvin's Trinitarian convictions were actually rather closer to those of the Greek Fathers, Athanasius, Gregory Nazianzen and Cyril of Alexandria" (Thomas F. Torrance, *Trinitarian Perspectives* [Edinburgh: T & T Clark, 1994], 58). On the other hand, Lane asserts that Calvin "reveals no significant knowledge of Athanasius's theology" (Anthony N.S. Lane, *John Calvin: Student of the Church Fathers* [Grand Rapids: Baker, 1999], 79). And finally, Lane's "survey has not encouraged the view that the Greek fathers greatly influenced Calvin" (85). The jury is still out it seems. However, at present, I am inclined to lean more with Torrance on this issue.

[25] See Jack Rogers, "Calvin and the Italian Anti-Trinitarians (A.D. 1558)," in *Calvin's Opponents*, ed. Richard C. Gamble (New York: Garland, 1992), 123-32, for a brief

"nor was he slavishly attached to traditional terminology. *The Trinity was crucial because it was a witness to the deity of Jesus Christ and thus to the certainty of salvation procured by Him* (emphasis in original)."[26] Again, we note Calvin's emphasis of linking divinity proper with practicalities. Correct notions of God are essential for God's own honor and for our salvation. "The purpose of Calvin's Trinitarianism," notes Niesel, "is to secure the biblical message 'God revealed in the flesh' against false interpretations."[27] Early in his discourse on the Trinity, Calvin boldly asserts:

> But God also designates himself by another special mark to distinguish himself more precisely from idols. For he so proclaims himself the sole God as to offer himself to be contemplated clearly in three persons. Unless we grasp these, only the bare and empty name of God flits about in our brains, to the exclusion of the true God.[28]

It is evident that Calvin believes that without a Trinitarian understanding of God, there is no real or true knowledge of the Holy.[29] Well known are Calvin's concerns against useless speculation. He, in place of mere "sophistry," will provide a biblical exposition to substantiate his position. Consider his rationale:

> And yet I will exert special effort to the end that they who lend ready and open ears to God's Word may have a firm standing ground. Here, indeed, if anywhere in the secret mysteries of Scripture, we ought to play the philosopher soberly and with great moderation; let us use great caution that neither our thoughts nor our speech go beyond the limits to which the Word of God itself extends. For how can the human mind measure off the measureless essence of God according to its own little measure, a mind as yet unable to establish for certain the nature of the sun's body, though men's eyes dimly gaze upon it? Indeed, how can the mind by its own leading come to search out God's essence when it cannot even get to its own? Let us then willingly leave to God the knowledge of himself. For as Hilary [of Poitiers] says, he is one fit witness to himself, and is not known except through himself. But we shall be "leaving it to him" if we conceive him to be as

---

but beneficial insight into the political ramifications of enforcing Trinitarianism in Calvin's Geneva. More recently a very informative and challenging article has emerged on Calvin's Trinitarianism. See Kurt Anders Richardson, "Calvin on the Trinity," in Sung Wook Chung, ed. *John Calvin and Evangelical Theology: Legacy and Prospect* (Louisville, KY: Westminster John Knox, 2009), 32-42.

[26] Timothy George, *Theology of the Reformers* (Nashville: Broadman, 1988), 200-201.

[27] Niesel, *The Theology of Calvin*, 57.

[28] *Institutes* I.xiii.2.

[29] Note Torrance's interpretation of Calvin's Trinitarianism. See Thomas F. Torrance, *Trinitarian Perspectives* (Edinburgh: T & T Clark, 1994), 41-76. "The 'Trinity'," Torrance says, "is not just a way of thinking about God, for the one true God is actually and intrinsically Triune and cannot be truly conceived otherwise" (43).

he reveals himself to us, without inquiring about him elsewhere than from his Word.³⁰

In a notable observation, Wendel said this of the Genevan Reformer, "Calvin had made the traditional trinitarian teaching his own, without the slightest reservation. The same attachment to the dogmatic tradition is prominent in his Christology."³¹ In relation to the doctrine of the Trinity it has been claimed that Calvin made a significant contribution to establishing a fully co-equal trinity.³² At times, Calvin maintains the view of rank or order in the Trinity.³³ This understanding of divine rank is not necessarily a problem *per se*, but along with his avowal of the doctrine of eternal generation, Calvin follows tradition and states that the Father is the *source* of the Son.³⁴ Nevertheless, the doctrine of the

---

³⁰ *Institutes* I.xiii.21. In this section Calvin continues, "And let us not take it into our heads either to seek out God anywhere else than in his Sacred Word, or to think anything about him that is not prompted by his Word, or to speak anything that is not taken from that Word."

³¹ François Wendel, *Calvin: Origins and Development of His Religious Thought*, trans. Philip Mairet (Preses Universitaires de France, 1950; reprint, Grand Rapids: Baker, 1997), 215.

³² In his famous essay "Calvin's Doctrine of the Trinity," Benjamin Warfield claims, "he [Calvin] conceives more clearly and applies more purely than had ever previously been done the principle of *equalization* in his thought of the relation of the Persons to one another, and thereby, as we have already hinted, marks *an epoch in the history of the doctrine of the Trinity* [emphasis added]" (B.B. Warfield, *Calvin and Augustine* [Philadelphia: P & R, 1956], 230). Richardson has done the church a great service in his study of Calvin on the trinity. See Kurt Anders Richardson, "Calvin on the Trinity" in Sung Wook Chung, ed., *John Calvin and Evangelical Theology: Legacy and Prospect* (Louisville, KY: Westminster John Knox, 32-42). See also the very good book by Gerald Bray, *The Doctrine of God* (Downers Grove: InterVarsity, 1993), makes a strong case that Calvin was the first to ascribe the full deity of all three persons without any hint of subordinationism. This insight is valid, in that Calvin established the notion that each person of the Trinity is *autotheos*, "God in and of himself," which struck at the heart of the traditional Patristic emphasis that the Father alone is *autotheos* and πηγή της θεότητος, "the source of the Godhead" (197-212). The definitive study on this now is Brannon Ellis, *Calvin, Classical Trinitarianism and the Aseity of the Son* (New York: Oxford, 2012).

³³ On this see Christoph Schwöbel, "The Triune God of Grace: The Doctrine of the Trinity in the Theology of the Reformers," in *The Christian Understanding of God Today*, ed. James M. Byrne (Dublin: Columba, 1993), 49-64. Schwöbel claims, "We find that for Calvin there is in the divine Trinity a certain order, dispositio vel oeconomica, which does not impair the unity of the divine essence, but nevertheless offers clear distinctions of the trinitarian persons through the inner-trinitarian relations" (51).

³⁴ For example, Calvin states, "The observance of an order is not meaningless or superfluous, when the Father is thought of as first, then from him the Son . . . . the Son is said to come forth from the Father alone" (*Institutes* I.xiii.18). Although Calvin says this in a context where he also maintains the co-eternality of the three persons, he still affirms a type of derivation of the Son from the Father (relationally not substantially). This type of assertion can be problematic despite its wide appeal within evangelical circles. It

Chapter 6: Reformation Christology: Calvin's Extra Calvinisticum

Trinity is the foundation for his Christology. In the *Institutes* I.xiii.1-29, his discussion of the Trinity includes some comments on the divinity of Christ. This paves the way for his Christology proper, beginning in II.xiv.1–II.xv.6. Calvin's teaching on the Trinity and the divinity of Christ also becomes the basis for his teaching concerning the Lord's Supper, in IV.xvii.1–IV.xviii.1-20.[35] Jones notes a remedial intention of the Genevan's approach to the Lord's Supper. "Correcting Luther's Christomonism," notes Jones, "which ascribed to the human nature of Christ the attribute of omnipresence (which properly belongs only to God), Calvin's eucharistic theology sought a broader theological base."[36]

Warfield perhaps expresses it best. When speaking of Calvin's trinitarian emphasis, he claims,

> If we look for the prime characteristics of Calvin's doctrine of the Trinity, accordingly we shall undoubtedly fix first upon its simplicity, then upon its consequent lucidity, and finally its elimination of the last remnants of subordinationism, so as to do full justice to the deity of Christ. Simplification, clarification, equalization – these three terms are the notes of Calvin's conception of the Trinity. And, of course, it is the last of these notes which gives above all else its character to his construction.[37]

Calvin's simplicity is found in a basic affirmation at the start of his discussion on Trinitarian matters. He says, "Although the heretics rail at the word person . . . they cannot shake our conviction that three are spoken of, each of which is

---

is beyond the scope of this study to discuss the difficulties in relation to this doctrine. Clearly, Calvin uses it, as did Augustine, in a relational sense as opposed to a substantial or accidental one. However, the passage from John's gospel which records the words of Jesus saying, "I have come forth from the Father" (John 16:28) is better understood as the economic ministry associated with the Incarnation, not an eternal coming forth from the Father in an eternal generation, albeit relational.

[35] In his section on the Trinity, a brief remark links the importance of the assumption of flesh with the mediatorial role. This anticipates Calvin's teaching that in the Eucharist there is a real impartation of Christ which links us to God. He says, "For from the time that Christ was manifested in the flesh, he has been called the Son of God, not only in that he was the eternal Word begotten before all ages from the Father, but because he took upon himself the person and office of the Mediator, that he might join us to God" (*Institutes* I.xiii.24).

[36] Paul H. Jones, *Christ's Eucharistic Presence: A History of the Doctrine* (New York: Peter Lang, 1994), 144. Important treatments of Calvin on the Sacrament of the Lord's Supper can be found in B.A. Gerrish, *Grace and Gratitude: The Eucharistic Theology of John Calvin* (Minneapolis: Fortress, 1993); and Thomas J. Davis, *This is My Body: The Presence of Christ in Reformation Thought* (Grand Rapids: Baker Academic, 2008).

[37] Warfield, "Calvin's Doctrine of the Trinity," 230.

entirely God, yet that there is not more than one God."[38] This includes the great Trinitarian affirmations. First, there is one God. This is the foundational truth concerning God as Creator. There is one God according to biblical religion. Second, there are three persons so designated, and according to revelation only three. The one God of the Bible is revealed as a fellowship of three persons. The three are revealed as God; Father, Son, and Holy Spirit are all God. Third, the full deity of each is tacitly assumed in the expression, "entirely God." Calvin certainly affirmed the full deity of all three persons. There is no notion of derived divinity or a lesser status for the Son and the Spirit. All three persons share fully in the divine essence. Lastly, this conviction is unshakeable. It is not a matter of speculation as if one may or may not adhere to this Trinitarian teaching. On the contrary, it is carefully provided by God's own revelation in the Word. As such it is an assured doctrine and one that we can firmly embrace. Calvin claimed in this same paragraph that this notion of a Trinitarian God is ". . . attested and sealed by Scripture."[39] Again, this denotes the reason for our certainty concerning the Triune God. From the Trinitarian concept of God we turn to the wonderful teaching concerning God's majesty. For "if Jesus Christ is to mean anything decisive to us," states Niesel, "we must encounter in Him the majesty of God and find in Him the One 'who is truly our God.'"[40]

E. Calvin on God's Majesty

Calvin cites Augustine favorably on this matter of the divine majesty[41] in the incarnate Christ. Calvin asserts:

> And Augustine explained it in the same way, with words not in the least ambiguous: "When Christ said, 'You will not have me with you always,' he was speaking of the presence of the body. For with regard to his majesty, to his providence, to

---

[38] *Institutes*, I.xiii.3. For a beautiful poem delineating the heart of Calvin's Trinitarian commitment, see Helen A. Zigmund, "Calvin's Concept of the Trinity," *HQ* 5 (1965): 58-64. This is as artistic as it is unique. Her insight appears clearly and correctly.

[39] *Institutes* I.xiii.3. To see how Scripture shaped both Calvin's mind and Theology, see the well-written essay by Ronald S. Wallace, "A Christian Theologian: Calvin's Approach to Theology," in *The Challenge of Evangelical Theology: Essays in Approach and Method*, ed. Nigel M. de S. Cameron (Edinburgh: Rutherford House, 1987), 123-50, esp. 132-40. On Calvin's salvific concerns within his overall theology, see Trevor Hart, "Humankind in Christ and Christ in Humankind: Salvation as Participation in our Substitute in the Theology of John Calvin," *SJT* 42 (1987): 67-84. Also the salvific work of Christ is mediated, according to Calvin through the proclamation of the Word of God. See the enlightening study on Calvin's preaching of Christ and his sacramental notion of the Word of God in Dawn DeVries, *Jesus Christ in the Preaching of Calvin and Schleiermacher* Theology (Louisville: Westminster John Knox, 1996), 1-43, 95-104.

[40] Niesel, *The Theology of Calvin*, 111.

[41] While discussing our need for a mediator, and the depths of human sin, Calvin states: "The situation would surely have been hopeless had the very *majesty of God* (emphasis added) not descended to us, since it was not in our power to ascend to him" (*Institutes* II.xii.1).

Chapter 6: Reformation Christology: Calvin's Extra Calvinisticum

his ineffable and invisible grace, he fulfilled what he said, 'Behold, I am with you even to the end of the age' [Matt. 28:20, Vg.]. But with regard to the flesh that the Word assumed. . . 'You will not always have me with you.' [Augustine next touches on the ascension, then adds] . . . . And yet he is here, for the presence of his majesty has not departed [Heb. 1:3]. According to the presence of his majesty, we have Christ always; but according to the presence of the flesh, it is rightly said, 'You will not always have me' [Matt. 26:11]."[42]

Although Calvin's discussion here will center on the third of Augustine's "modes of presence" (ineffable grace), it is nonetheless clear here that Calvin affirmed the majesty of God in the incarnate Christ. Christ is present (also) in his divine majesty as God. Wyatt has a statement which shows us the link between the previously discussed concept of the Trinity and the majesty of God. "As a trinitarian theologian," notes Wyatt, "Calvin has a concept of the divine majesty that necessarily includes Jesus Christ as he is the eternal Son of the Father."[43] Jones's comment, further claims that this divine majesty, seen as immutable, is hence untransferable from one nature to the other. "Contrary to Luther's Christological emphasis on the unity of the person of Christ and the communication of properties," says Jones, "Calvin stressed the immutability and incommunicability of Christ's divinity."[44] Calvin did have a certain understanding of the communication of attributes which was distinct from Luther's. It will be examined later. Suffice to note here that Jones, just cited above, in the same paragraph says, "the exchange of properties applied only the office of Christ as the Mediator and not to the ontological union of the two natures."[45]

Speaking of Calvin's teaching in the *extra Calvinisticum*, Wyatt expresses the concern that Calvin had to safeguard the majesty of God. "The theological stance adopted in the extra-calvinisticum derives," claims Wyatt, "in part, at least, from Calvin's conviction that the doctrine of the Incarnation should not imply change or diminution in the deity."[46] Wyatt adds a quote from Calvin's Commentary on the Gospel of John to sustain this insight. Wyatt says of Calvin,

---

[42] *Institutes* IV.xvii.26.

[43] Peter Wyatt, *Jesus Christ and Creation in the Theology of John Calvin* (Allison Park, PA: Pickwick, 1996), 29.

[44] Jones, *Eucharistic Presence*, 141.

[45] Jones, *Eucharistic Presence*, 141. This statement is only half correct. Certainly Calvin resisted any actual transference of properties between the natures in contrast to Luther, but also Calvin insisted on a lexical predication of the person of Christ in any action which would ordinarily be literally true of only one nature alone. Hence Jones's comment that the "exchange of properties applied to the office of Christ," needs further elaboration. See below in this chapter.

[46] Wyatt, *Jesus Christ*, 35. This concern that Wyatt traces in Calvin is also the driving force of my contention for the omnipresence of Christ.

Again, since he distinctly attributes the name of Word to the man Christ, it follows that when he became man Christ did not cease to be what he was before and that nothing was changed in that eternal essence of God which assumed flesh. In short, the Son of God began to be man in such a way that he is still that eternal Word who had no temporal beginning.[47]

Calvin, even in the famous passage in Paul's letter to the Philippians, does not capitulate to a type of kenotic Christology after the Incarnation. Contemporary evangelicals have assumed that because Christ was a man, by virtue of the incarnation, and so exercising attributes such as omnipresence and omniscience was incommensurate with the incarnate state. Calvin, however, would not agree. He says,

> [He] *Emptied himself.* This emptying is the same as the abasement, as to which we shall see afterwards. The expression, however, is used ἐμφατικοτέρως for being brought to nothing. Christ, indeed, could not renounce His divinity, but He kept it concealed for a time, that under the weakness of the flesh it might not be seen. Hence, He laid aside His glory in view of men, not by lessening it, but by concealing (supprimendo) it.[48]

Clearly, Calvin would consider a mere sophistry that Jesus could not exercise certain attributes because they were not consonant with his being human. Calvin's approach is rather refreshing given how he refers to the divine glory of Christ in his incarnate state. Of course, Jesus could be omnipresent. The *extra Calvinisticum* is a clear repudiation of such doctrines which imply a Christ who could not exercise omnipresence, shall we say, and was by implication confined to the body. Calvin, being steeped in Pauline theology, would exclaim: μὴ γένοιτο! It is now time to examine Christ's unity of the person of Christ. To do this we will examine Calvin's understanding of the *communicatio idiomatum*.

F. Calvin on *Communicatio Idiomatum*

It is on this issue that Calvin differed quite considerably from Luther.[49] Not only in the actual outworking of his thought on the communication of idioms, but also because he emphasized the immutability of God, which led him to where Luther could never go. Wendel's assessment is insightful. He says,

> Yet while he emphatically affirms the unity of Christ's divinity with his humanity, Calvin cannot go further into the question of communication of idioms without

---

[47] Calvin, *Commentary* on John 1:14, cited in Wyatt, *Jesus Christ*, 35.

[48] John Calvin, *Galatians, Ephesians, Philippians and Colossians*, CNTC, trans. T.H.L. Parker, ed. David W. Torrance and Thomas F. Torrance (Grand Rapids: Eerdmans/Carlisle: Paternoster, 1996), 248.

[49] The brief but helpful essay by Stephen R. Holmes, "Reformed Varieties of the *Communicatio Idiomatum*" is clear in distinguishing the position of both reformers. See Stephen R. Holmes & Murray A. Rae, eds. *The Person of Christ* (London: T & T Clark, 2005), 70-78.

much hesitation, and whenever he thinks he can concede something on this point, he automatically attaches the reservation that, in the person of Christ, divinity and humanity keep their own characteristics without reacting upon one another any more than is required for the existence of this union sui generis, and for the mediation of which it is the bearer.[50]

Wendel goes on to quote from Calvin's commentary on Luke 2:40. Calvin said, "Although in unity of person he was God and man together . . . it does not . . . follow that all that belonged to the divinity was communicated to the human nature . . ."[51] Next, Wendel cites the passage from the *Institutes* (II.xiii.4) which we have already quoted. Wendel comments, "These are the clearest formulations of what has since been called the *extra calvinisticum*: they vividly define the very basis of Calvinist thinking concerning the essential separateness of the two natures and the maintenance of their respective characters."[52] And finally, Wendel explains the difference between Calvin and Luther by stating,

> While Luther had taken the unity of the person of Christ as his starting point of departure and, by extending the traditional notions of communication of the idioms and of the ubiquity, finished by admitting the ubiquity not only of the divine, but also of the human nature of Christ, Calvin took his stand upon the immutability and incommunicability of the divinity, and thence arrived logically – or at least apparently so – at very different conclusions.[53]

Luther's position is well known[54] and to highlight Calvin's contrasting approach, one is well served to turn to Tylenda's article.[55] In this article, Tylenda notes that Calvin speaks of the "communication of attributes" in two sections in the *Institutes*. One of those is in Calvin's Christological treatment, and the other is, not surprisingly, in his exposition of the Lord's Supper.[56] There is certainly a deepening over time of Calvin's thinking on these significant issues, but as will be evident from the first edition of the *Institutes*, Calvin from the beginning embraced the pivotal teachings of the "extra" doctrine as seen in his advocacy

---

[50] Wendel, *Calvin*, 222-23.

[51] Wendel, *Calvin*, 223.

[52] Wendel, *Calvin*, 224.

[53] Wendel, *Calvin*, 224.

[54] For example, see Lienhard, *Luther: Witness to Jesus Christ*, 335-46.

[55] See Joseph N. Tylenda, "Calvin's Understanding of the Communication of Properties," in *An Elaboration of the Theology of Calvin*, ed. Richard C. Gamble (New York & London: Garland, 1992), 148-59.

[56] For a helpful analysis of the important points within the debate concerning the Lord's Supper, see Joseph C. McLelland, "Lutheran-Reformed Debate on the Eucharist and Christology," in *Marburg Revisited: A Reexamination of Lutheran and Reformed Traditions*, ed. Paul C. Empie and James I. McCord (Minneapolis: Augsburg, 1966), 39-54.

of the ancient teaching of *communicatio idiomatum*. Let us see what Calvin says before examining Tylenda's exposition. Calvin claims,

> We ought not to understand the statement that "the Word was made flesh" [John 1:14] in the sense that the Word was turned into flesh or confusedly mingled with flesh. Rather it means that, because he chose for himself the virgin's womb as a temple in which to dwell, he who was the Son of God became the Son of Man–not by confusion of the substance, but by unity of person. For we affirm his divinity so joined and united with his humanity that each retains its distinctive nature unimpaired, and yet these two natures constitute one Christ.

Also, from among the same section, Calvin adds,

> Thus . . . the Scriptures speak of Christ: they sometimes attribute to him what must be referred solely to his humanity, sometimes what belongs uniquely to his divinity; and sometimes what embraces both natures but fits neither alone. And they so earnestly express this union of the two natures that is in Christ as sometimes to interchange them. This figure of speech is called by the ancient writers "the communication of properties."[57]

Tylenda, also cites the first edition of the Institutes,[58] indicating Calvin's commitment to this teaching from the beginning. In the 1536 edition, Calvin states,

> Thus . . . the Scriptures speak of Christ; they sometimes attribute to him what must be referred exclusively to his humanity, sometimes, what refers particularly to his divinity; sometimes what embraces both natures but fits neither one alone. Finally, through "communication of properties" they assign to his divinity the things that belonged to his humanity, and to his humanity those that pertained to his divinity.[59]

Now, Tylenda conveniently classifies for us these four categories with examples. One can summarize his work in list form:

1. Scriptures attribute to Christ properties which belong solely to his humanity. Example: Christ "increased in age and wisdom" (Luke 2:52).
2. Scriptures attribute to Christ properties which belong uniquely to his divinity. Example: Christ said, "Before Abraham was, I am" (John 8:58).
3. Scriptures attribute to Christ characteristics which belong to both but not to one or other alone. Examples: Christ's power of remitting sins (John

---

[57] *Institutes* II.xiv.1.

[58] Tylenda cites the references to the section as found in the *Corpus Reformatorum* (1.66), and the *Opera Selecta*, eds. P. Barth and G. Niesel, (1.79). One may locate these references in a copy of the English translation by Ford Lewis Battles of the 1536 edition. See John Calvin, *Institutes of the Christian Religion*, trans. and annotated by Ford Lewis Battles (Grand Rapids: Eerdmans/The Henry H. Meeter Center for Calvin Studies, 1975; reprint 1989), 52.

[59] See previous note.

1:29). Christ raising to life whom he wills. Christ bestowing righteousness and holiness.⁶⁰
4. Scriptures attribute to the divinity that which is characteristic of the humanity, and they attribute to the humanity that which is characteristic of the divinity. Examples: "God purchased the church with his blood" (Acts 20:28). "The Lord of Glory was crucified" (1 Corinthians 2:8). "The Word of life was handled" (1 John 1:1). "No one has ascended into heaven but the Son of Man who was in heaven" (John 3:13). "God laid down his life for us" (1 John 3:16).⁶¹

Tylenda claims, "It is only in the fourth point that we encounter the communication of idioms."⁶² Tylenda then proceeds to ask if Calvin had a definition. What he does in answering this question is combine statements from both the first and definitive edition of the *Institutes* and notes also the "working definition" offered by John McNeill in a footnote in this section (II.xiv.1). Tylenda concludes, "we can perhaps adapt a tentative definition: for example, the communication of idioms, or properties, is the interchange of properties of the divine and human nature of Christ."⁶³ It is assumed that this is rather unsatisfactory because of its ambiguity. Tylenda suggests to better ascertain how Calvin conceived of this practice, one had to study the examples Calvin himself used. Then one could see how Calvin understood them. Let us hear Calvin's explanation:

> All these [examples of category 1] refer solely to Christ's humanity. In so far as he is God, he cannot increase in anything . . . . Yet he does not ascribe these qualities solely to his human nature, but takes them upon himself as being in harmony with the person of the mediator.⁶⁴

---

⁶⁰ Tylenda notes of this third category, "Christ had been endowed with these prerogatives when he was manifested in the flesh. It is true that along with the Father he held them before the creation of the world, but it had not been in the same manner or respect, and they could not have been given to a man who was nothing but a man."

⁶¹ This data is found in Tylenda, "Calvin's Understanding," *passim*.

⁶² Tylenda, "Calvin's Understanding," 151.

⁶³ Tylenda, "Calvin's Understanding," 151.

⁶⁴ *Institutes* II. xiv. 2. This is reminiscent of what Jones had asserted earlier. Tylenda also notes that some scholars have resisted equating Calvin's use with the Patristic doctrine. For example, Tylenda cites K. McDonnel, *John Calvin, the Church, and the Eucharist* (Princeton, 1967), where McDonnel says, "For Calvin the communication of idioms is not to be found in the ontological union of two integral natures but exclusively in the office of Christ the Mediator" (cited, 152 n.13). In this same footnote, Tylenda explains his view, with which I am in substantial agreement. He says, "My reading of the statement [*Institutes* II.xiv.2] is as given above, namely, Calvin is emphasizing the fact that the attributes are predicated of a *person*, a *subject* having that nature, and not solely of the nature itself. Furthermore, in the passage Calvin says nothing about the office of Mediator, and moreover, Calvin wrote that statement in explanation of the first

Calvin goes on to provide, what I believe is the key to understanding his own view of the matter of *communicatio idiomatum*. Calvin states [in the very next sentence from the previous quote],

> But the communicating of characteristics or properties consists in what Paul says: "God purchased the church with his blood" [Acts 20:28 p.], and "the Lord of glory was crucified" [I Cor. 2:8 p.]. John says the same: "The Word of life was handled" [I John 1:1 p.]. Surely God does not have blood, does not suffer, cannot be touched with hands. But since Christ, who was true God and also true man, was crucified and shed his blood for us, the things he carried out in his human nature are transferred improperly, although not without reason, to his divinity.

Now Tylenda's analysis will help clarify the importance of Calvin's expression. "In all of Calvin's five examples [from category 4]," notes Tylenda, "the divine or human property is said of a subject, a person (Jesus Christ), and that subject is designated either in function of his divine nature as "God," or "Lord of Glory," or in function of his human nature as "Son of Man." And the crucial insight follows this as Tylenda further explains, "In none of the examples is the property of one nature applied to the other *nature as such*; it is always applied to a *subject possessing that nature*.[65] In conclusion, we add a final remark summing up and also contrasting Calvin with Luther. "For Calvin," Tylenda asserts, "an attribute of one nature is assigned to the person of Christ, though designated by his other nature; for Luther, the attribute of one nature is granted to the other nature."[66] Given this insight and analysis we can see why Calvin strongly resisted the doctrine of the ubiquity of the body of Christ, something Lutherans

---

and not the fourth point where he treats the communication of idioms. True Christ's office of Mediator goes hand in hand with his Incarnation, with Christ's ontological constitution in unity of person and duality of natures. The fact that Christ may have been appointed to the office of Mediator prior to his Incarnation does not make the office of Mediator the *exclusive* basis for the communication of idioms. The Word who was Mediator, but not yet incarnate, could not have been the subject of the communication of properties; rather, only when he is in possession of both natures could he be the subject of such predication. Hence, the hypostatic union seems to be the proximate and immediate basis of such a communication" (153n.13). Also Willis states, "For Calvin, the *communicatio idiomatum* is primarily a hermeneutical tool to keep in balance the varied Scriptural witness to the one person; but it rests upon and presupposes the hypostatic union" (Willis, *Calvin's Catholic Christology*, 67).

[65] Tylenda, "Calvin's Understanding," 153. A point of clarification is added by Tylenda which is helpful. "Calvin does not mean that a human concrete attribute as 'blood' or 'dying' can be applied to divinity as such, or to the divine nature in the abstract, for example, 'divinity is mortal,' because he has already rejected such predication in his commentary on Acts 20:28. But he does mean, and so do the Scriptures, that 'blood' and 'dying' can be predicated of divinity *in the concrete*, of a *divine being*, if the divine being, is also human, and therefore has blood and is mortal. Hence, Christ is a single subject having two real natures (he is true God and true man) we can truthfully say by the communication of idioms that 'God purchased the church with his blood'" (154).

[66] Tylenda, "Calvin's Understanding," 158-59.

Chapter 6: Reformation Christology: Calvin's Extra Calvinisticum

still maintain. For Calvin, the whole of Christ is present in the Eucharist but not in his wholeness.[67] This affirmation along with his understanding of the communication of properties drew criticism, and especially the charge of Nestorianism. To this matter we now turn.

G. Calvin's Christology: Nestorian or Not?

Calvin's Christology, like later Reformed teaching on Christ, was charged with Nestorianism because he affirmed that Christ was present beyond his physical body.[68] A brief treatment of this question is therefore required. Given the insight of the *extra Calvinisticum* and a particular application of it in the matter of the Eucharist, Heiko Oberman provides an example in Calvin's thought and then asks an all-important question. He says,

> A typical example is Calvin's statement: "When we receive the water of Baptism it is as if (*c'est autant comme si*) the Blood of our Lord Jesus Christ flows down from heaven . . . when we receive the bread and wine in the Lord's supper, it is as if (*c'est autant comme si*) Jesus Christ descends from heaven and becomes our food . . . ." It can well be argued that this "*comme si*" is not to be regarded as a threat to Calvin's sacramental realism, since Christ as the true matter and the Spirit as the agent of salutary communion . . . are not in competition. They are to be seen as bound together in the light of a basic systematic principle . . . . Yet, if the "*comme si*" suggests that Christ can be on earth according to his divinity while remaining in heaven according to his humanity, can Calvin teach a real Incarnation; is not his Christology Nestorian?[69]

---

[67] Calvin uses the famous *totus/totum* distinction to enable this kind of commitment. This scholastic distinction was found in Thomas Aquinas and in Peter Lombard. Willis, discussing this matter, notes it as: "a distinction between *totus*, the Son as he is eternally, and *totum*, the Son as he is eternally but including also what he united to himself . . ." (Willis, *Calvin's Catholic Christology*, 36). This is a helpful comment but is also fraught with potential misunderstanding, hence Willis cites Aquinas for the explanation. "'Totus' does not apply to the person as a thing is called whole," says Aquinas, cited by Willis, "because it has parts, but 'totus' applies to the person in the same way a thing is called whole because it is perfect and has nothing missing from it. Thus he [Jesus Christ] is said to be everywhere in his entirety because there is nothing missing from his existence as a person which enables him to be everywhere. For since the 'totus' is of the masculine gender, it applies to the person. Insofar as he is everywhere, he is missing something of what pertains to the human nature, because according to the human nature he is not everywhere. And therefore it is said that he is not everywhere 'totum,' because 'totum' is of the neuter gender it applies to the nature" (37). Although in the *Institutes*, Calvin does not name his sources, in 1557 in his *Final Admonition to Westphal*, he specifically mentions this distinction and also names Peter Lombard as an authority (see 31).

[68] George, *Theology of the Reformers*, 218.

[69] See Heiko A. Oberman, "The 'Extra' Dimension in the Theology of Calvin," in *An Elaboration of the Theology of Calvin*, 171-72.

In this article, Oberman offers a possible solution to the above-stated problem. It is no surprise that Calvin would be accused of Nestorianism, given his insistence on the *extra Calvinisticum*. Oberman's solution is interesting in that he shifts the focus to another time reference in the history of the church. Oberman suggests that Calvin writes against the concept of Marcionite doceticsm. He says,

> It is of extreme importance to realize that the scopus of the extra calvinisticum is not a rejection of Cyril with possible Nestorian results. Indeed, it is not at all to be placed in the dimension of the alternatives Cyril-Nestorius, but in an earlier stage in the history of Christian thought, the period in which adoptionism and docetism were the decisive alternatives.[70]

This observation may be valid as far as the essence of his argument is concerned. Yet one wonders if Calvin's conclusions, albeit, designed to combat another heresy than Nestorianism, actually still fall into the error of Nestorianism? It would have to be supposed that they could. Moreover, Peter Wyatt, challenges Oberman's narrow focus, claiming rather that,

> the scopus of IV.17 is actually very broad; in this chapter. Calvin deals not only with the integrity of the *verus homo*, but also, among other things, with the manner in which we are fed in the sacrament by Christ's body, the secret power of the Holy Spirit to unite things separated in space (Christ's body at the right hand of the Father and his members on earth) and the integrity of Christ's divine nature. Oberman isolates one aspect of Calvin's wide-ranging discussion on the Supper and elevates it to pre-eminence, while apparently overlooking Calvin's explicit reference to the monophysite position of Eutyches.[71]

Oberman's attempted solution does not lessen the potential charge against Calvin. Hence the matter is not easily resolved. The problems with the *extra Calvinisticum* will not go away, yet the basic emphasis in the *extra* doctrine solves more problems than it creates. Wendel's observation at this juncture is helpful in eliminating the charge of Nestorianism by focusing on Calvin's intent. "Whenever Calvin comes to speak of the person of Christ," notes Wendel, "he takes care to place emphasis simultaneously upon the unity of the God-man and upon the distinction between the two natures."[72] Wendel's penetrating analysis into Calvin's purpose in the Christology undergirding the *extra Calvinisticum* is perhaps the answer to the charge of Nestorianism in Calvin's view of Christ. Wendel continues,

> What mattered above all to Calvin was to avoid anything that might be interpreted as a confusion of the divinity with the humanity, even at the centre of the person-

---

[70] Oberman, "The 'Extra' Dimension," 174.
[71] Wyatt, *Jesus*, 51 n. 25.
[72] Wendel, *Calvin*, 219.

Chapter 6: Reformation Christology: Calvin's Extra Calvinisticum

ality of Christ. From the very beginnings of his theological reflections he had felt the necessity of safeguarding the divinity of Christ from any contamination by humanity. Certainly Christ was both true God and true man and he conjoined the two natures in a single person, but that was not an exception, not even a unique exception, to the absolute transcendence of the divinity.[73]

Wendel's treatment appears to be sound indeed. Willis is in substantial agreement, yet arrives at similar conclusions from a slightly different path. "He [Calvin] views the Incarnation," states Willis, "as a reassertion of Christ's empire over the part of creation which had rebelled." How was this so? One may ask. Willis goes on to explain. He posits, that according to Calvin,

> In the Incarnation there was an ordering of the lesser by the greater, of the weak by the powerful, so that the Eternal Son's life and power during the period of the Incarnation were never exhausted by his fleshly Person or by his fleshly accomplishments. Others seek to avoid diminishing Christ's eternal reality during the period of the Incarnation by saying that eternal properties were shared by the humanity, but Calvin feels such a route would bypass the real humanity of Christ. The eternal properties were exercised by Christ during the Incarnation not by the humanity of the One Person but by the Divinity of the One Person. In the Incarnation, the Son of God left heaven only in such a way that he continued to exercise his dominion over creation; the Incarnation was the extension of his dominion, not the momentary abdication of it.[74]

Because we must finally settle the issue of whether Calvin was a Nestorian, by his actual intent and not on an overemphasis of one aspect of his thought at the expense of another, Willis is probably correct in stressing that "even when Calvin says the Son "indwelt" the flesh or "clothed" himself with the flesh, he explicitly wishes to avoid Nestorianism."[75] Calvin expressly rejects both Eutychianism and Nestorianism. He says,

> We therefore hold that Christ, as he is God and man, consisting of two natures united but not mingled, is our Lord and the true Son of God even according to, but not by reason of, his humanity. Away with the error of Nestorius, who in wanting to pull apart rather than distinguish the nature of Christ devised a double Christ! . . . . Let us beware, also, of Eutyches' madness; lest, while meaning to show the unity of the person, we destroy either nature.[76]

---

[73] Wendel, *Calvin*, 220.

[74] Willis, *Calvin's Catholic Christology*, 76.

[75] Willis, *Calvin's Catholic Christology*, 64.

[76] *Institutes* II.xiv.4. Holmes claims: "Calvin is particularly concerned to stress the unconfused and unmingled two natures of the mediator, but, properly understood, nothing he says can be taken as down-playing the unity of the person" (see Stephen R. Holmes, "Reformed Varieties of the *Communicatio Idiomatum*," in Holmes & Rae, eds.

Also, Wyatt opines that even Luther intended no heresy with his version of Christology. "One might be tempted," suggests Wyatt, "even to observe the "Nestorian tendency" in Calvin's christology, but he is no more Nestorian, strictly speaking, than Luther is Monophysite."[77] This appears to assess fairly the extant data for both the great reformers, and should cause Lutherans pause to reflect before challenging Calvin with Nestorian theology. "Calvin never intended that his teaching concerning the transcendence of Christ should imply a split in the identity of Christ, as if somehow there could be an incarnate *Logos* and a discarnate *Logos*."[78] This possible misunderstanding surfaces another problem in the *extra Calvinisticum*, the epistemological question posed by the *etiam extra carnem*. To this we now must turn.

H. Calvin's Doctrine of Knowledge of God the Redeemer: Through *Logos ensarkos* or *Logos asarkos*?

"Outside Christ," warns Calvin, "there is nothing worth knowing, and all who by faith perceive what he is like have grasped the whole immensity of heavenly benefits."[79] Calvin had a practical orientation to his doctrinal affirmations. He would applaud the famous saying of Melanchthon: "To know Christ is to know his benefits." Calvin held this because he knew that in Christ alone are all the treasures of wisdom and knowledge. Yet it is fair to ask, "in Calvin's Christology, is there a loophole permitting knowledge of God in a salvific sense, through the *Logos asarkos*?" A brief consideration of this important question will occupy this short section before concluding the chapter.

Eleanor Stonebraker, writing from a Lutheran perspective, posits the following,

> God With Us will not retreat into pure spirit nor into a haven where the flesh is spared our pain. Jesus is God taking us on, for keeps. In Jesus, God takes on our ugliest sin, our profoundest humiliation, our death. No part of God is left over; no part of God is safe; no part of God is uncommitted. For, writes Luther, "apart from Christ there is no God or Godhead at all."[80]

This surely betrays Luther's insistence that God is known only through Christ, but also the emphasis that the only God knowable is Christ. The idea that "there is no God left" over, suggests that the entire Trinity is taken up in the Incarna-

---

The Person of Christ, 74. This insightful essay addresses Calvin, Luther, Turretin, and Owen in dialogue with Cyril of Alexandria.

[77] Wyatt, *Jesus*, 49. Calvin clearly repudiated the Nestorian heresy: "Away with the error of Nestorius, who in wanting to pull apart rather than distinguish the nature of Christ devised a double Christ!" (*Institutes* II.xiv.4).

[78] Wyatt, *Jesus*, 49. Wyatt also states that the real distinction has to do with "two powers exercised by one Christ" (Wyatt, *Jesus*, 49). There is some merit to this proposal and it is worthy of further investigation. It is defended very well by Wyatt in this work.

[79] *Institutes* II.xv.2.

[80] Stonebraker, "Heroes and Beggars," 65.

tion.⁸¹ This is incorrect. Only the Son was joined to humanity in the Incarnation. Hence the Father retains his Godhead without humanity, so does the Spirit. The Word made flesh does have an economical aspect. Since the revelation of Jesus Christ in the incarnation, God is known only through Him. True, there is a Christocentrism which is common to both Calvin and Luther. The Lutheran view, however, appears to move beyond Christocentrism to a type of Christomonism.⁸² That God is known only through Christ, who in Calvin's view has existence beyond the flesh, does pose a possible misinterpretation of how one may know God. It was not Calvin's intent to suggest or to affirm that Christ is now a type of Cosmic Spirit beyond the flesh, whereby people may relate to God without the historical person of Jesus of Nazareth. As Stonebraker herself is aware, Calvin has stated categorically, "God has never manifested himself to man in any other way than through the Son."⁸³ Here is where Willis is very helpful. Within Willis's argument regarding Calvin's doctrine of the knowledge of God, the issue of "Natural Theology" arises. Willis highlights for us the epistemological priority of the Incarnate Christ as our means to knowing God. "The *Deus manifestatus in carne*," says Willis, "maintains his priority because he is the only all-sufficient source of our knowledge of God."⁸⁴ Yet it is also true "that the revelation really took place as the flesh directed man beyond itself to something higher, behind, or beyond it."⁸⁵ When one tempers the discussion

---

⁸¹ Of course, Luther really did not espouse this despite the unfortunate way Lutheran incarnational theology is cast by Stonebraker. Discussing the Trinity, Luther's biographer, Roland Bainton suggests Luther outdid his teachers in affirming the Trinity, which humanly speaking, cannot be explained philosophically. See Bainton, *Here I Stand: A Life of Martin Luther* (Nashville: Abingdon, 1950), 219. Commenting on Gen 19:24, Luther writes, "We may note also the fact that Moses here says that the Lord (Jehovah) rained fire and brimstone from the Lord (Jehovah). The mode of speaking greatly irks the Jews and they try in vain to explain it. But Moses mentions Jehovah twice to show that there is but one God, but that in this one God there are three distinct persons" (Quoted in Robert Morey, *The Trinity: Evidence and Issues* [Grand Rapids: World Publishing, 1996], 97). Also see Schwöbel, "The Triune God of Grace," 49-50.

⁸² See the conservative Lutheran essays in Curtis A. Jahn, ed., *We Believe in Jesus Christ: Essays on Christology* (Milwaukee: Northwestern Publishing, 1999). Especially significant contributions in this volume include Paul O. Wendland, "Now that God is One of Us: A Study of the Communication of Attributes in the Person of Christ," 65-90; and James R. Janke, "We (still) do not Have the Same Spirit. A Critique of Contemporary Reformed Christology and its Impact on the Lord's Supper," 247-312.

⁸³ *Institutes* IV.viii.5. Cited by Stonebraker, "Heroes and Beggars," 66.

⁸⁴ Willis, *Calvin's Catholic Christology*, 110.

⁸⁵ Willis, *Calvin's Catholic Christology*, 113. Notice how Willis has caught the important nuance in Calvin's thought. He says, "That the eternal Son of God was not restricted to the flesh does not mean he was not united to it. To confess the unity of the two natures in One Person is to confess that mysterious way in which he who was boundless in majesty and power joined himself to that which was weak and limited . . . . It is Calvin's clear intention, in his use of the expression *Deus manifestatus in carne*, to

with the sure intent of Calvin, not to speak of some "Cosmic Christ Principle," which is immanent without the body, but to emphasize greatly the immutability and the total transcendence of the Son of God, even after the Incarnation, one will not be tempted to think that Calvin's thought legitimizes knowledge of Christ (or God) without the incarnate Jesus Christ as revealed in Scripture.[86] No appeal to a religion outside of the "Incarnated One" will do. Christ has a presence beyond the flesh, but his Divinity is still united to it. "The *extra-calvinisticum*," states Robert Peterson, "does not open the door for a knowledge of God apart from the incarnate Word. Rather it serves to safeguard the fact 'that in Jesus Christ we are faced not merely by enhanced nature, but the fact that there God Himself stands revealed to us.'"[87]

So the ones who saw him in the flesh and did not believe are worse off than those who never have seen him in the flesh and yet have believed–the difference is that we have seen him in the "flesh" through the eyes of faith, which has led us to a realization of that heavenly and divine in Jesus as mediated by the

---

state the unity of the Person so unambiguously that all the Christological heresies threatening the Church might be avoided" (63).

[86] For Calvin's view of Scripture's role in our "Knowing God," see Ronald S. Wallace, "A Christian Theologian," 129-37. Well known is the famous Barth–Brunner debate concerning the role of "Natural Theology" in Calvin. This debate was perpetuated by another generation of Calvin scholars in the work of Edward A. Dowey, *The Knowledge of God in Calvin's Theology* (Grand Rapids: Eerdmans, 1994), who took up the Brunner mantle, and T.H.L. Parker, *Calvin's Doctrine of the Knowledge of God* (Grand Rapids: Eerdmans, 1959), who affirmed Barth's position. There is a sense in which Calvin taught both that there is "Natural Revelation," though not necessarily a (true) "Natural theology," and that our real knowledge of God comes mediated solely through Christ (God manifested in the flesh) as revealed in Scripture. It is beyond the scope of this chapter to enter the debate, but it is significant to note that Calvin's *extra* doctrine does serve " . . . as a constant reminder," as Willis, asserts, "that creation, redemption, and sanctification are the interpenetrating spheres forming the context which is presupposed by the Church's knowledge and service of God" (Willis, *Calvin's Catholic Christology*, 105). On Calvin's view of "Nature," see Susan E. Schreiner, *The Theater of His Glory: Nature and the Natural Order in the Thought of John Calvin* (Grand Rapids: Baker, 1995).

[87] Peterson, *Calvin and the Atonement*, 29. See also Stephen Bud Edmondson, "Christ the Mediator," 609-617. "Does Calvin threaten the unity of Christ," asks Edmondson, "and thereby turn Christians in some sense from the Incarnate Christ as sole image of God, the one through whom alone they can know God in the truth of God's being? In answer to this question we can say with assurance that at least within the context of Calvin's theology, this should not be a concern, for Calvin directs Christians nowhere other than to the *persona* of the Mediator, Christ in the unity of his two natures, to find and unite themselves to God as God has revealed Godself in God's love and mercy" (Edmondson, "Christ the Mediator," 615-16). Edmondson adds, "Calvin does not argue for the ubiquity of Christ's divinity outside of his humanity to in any way turn believers to this divinity apart from his humanity" (616).

very Word of God, the Scriptures.[88] Athanasius was right in saying, "No Salvation without the Word of God!" Calvin would agree. It is especially in the preaching of the Word that Christ is made present to the believers as they hear spiritually, according to Calvin. "The one thing that is necessary," claims DeVries, in Calvin's view, "is the Word that offers and presents Christ."[89] Calvin made this plain in his commentary on John's gospel: "As often as Christ calls us to the hope of salvation by the preaching of the gospel, he is present with us. For not without reason is the preaching of the gospel called Christ's descent to us."[90]

I. Conclusion

The *extra Calvinisticum* was definitely a Calvinist doctrine. It was not an invention of Calvin but was taught in the early church Fathers. Great theologians such as Athanasius developed a similar position. From the Schoolmen of the Middle-Ages, Gabriel Biel definitely held to it. The *extra Calvinisticum* is, for Calvin, an affirmation of which we should be proud. The doctrine was designed to uphold the distinction of the two natures in Christ, to also keep the unity of the person in full integrity, while at the same time maintaining the immutability of God. So within the framework of Calvin's theology of Christ, the omnipresence of the Lord Jesus is wholeheartedly affirmed by Calvin.[91] Calvin's ap-

---

[88] "The "extra Calvinisticum" functions to remind us that salutary knowledge from Christ as witnessed to in the Scriptures . . . when illumined by the Holy Spirit in the community of the faithful," Willis, reminds us, "derives not from flesh alone. For the Christ witnessed to in the Scriptures is precisely the Eternal Word through whom and with whose Spirit believers of the Old Testament knew God, and who, even in the incarnation, was not confined to the flesh. . . . Calvin's doctrine of the knowledge of God is exclusively Christological only in the sense that a saving knowledge of God is available through Christ alone, who as the Eternal Son of God cannot be isolated from or known without his manifestation in the flesh, but who is not restricted to the flesh" (*Calvin's Catholic Christology*, 130-31).

[89] DeVries, *Jesus Christ in the Preaching of Calvin and Schleiermacher*, 20-21.

[90] Quoted in DeVries, *Jesus Christ in the Preaching of Calvin and Schleiermacher*, 26. The soteriological purpose of the incarnation in Calvin's thought has not been dealt with in this chapter. This is not to lessen the importance of this theme, merely to keep the focus on our main purpose. For an insightful study of Calvin's Christology highlighting the soteriological concern, one may consult Randall C. Zachman, "Jesus Christ as the Image of God in Calvin's Theology," *CTJ* 25 (1990): 45-62.

[91] Because Calvin affirmed the Chalcedonian Christology which maintained that both natures in the incarnate Christ retained their properties, the reformer was adamant that Christ, by virtue of the divine nature, possessed and exercised the other so called relative attributes of deity as well. For example, he affirms Christ's omniscience. Calvin says: "In so far as he is God, he [Jesus Christ] cannot increase in anything, and does all things for his own sake; nothing is hidden from him; he does all things according to the decision of his will, and can be neither seen or handled" (*Institutes* II.xiv.2). These statements are made immediately following Calvin's concession that the incarnate Christ, because of genuine humanity, does indeed "increase in age and wisdom. . . with God

proach to the question of Jesus' omnipresence must be considered definitive, and as such is worthy of emulation.

---

and men . . . [and is said] not to know the Last Day" (*Institutes* II.xiv.2). Calvin also affirmed Jesus as omnipotent. He says: "Christ is brought forward by Isaiah both as God and adorned with the *highest power* [emphasis supplied], which is the characteristic mark of the one God" (*Institutes* I. xiii. ix). Calvin also claimed: "How plainly and clearly is his [Jesus Christ's] deity shown in miracles! Even though I confess that both the prophets and apostles performed miracles equal to and similar to his, yet in this respect there is the greatest of differences: they distributed the gifts of God by their ministry, but he showed forth *his own power* [emphasis added]" (*Institutes* I.xiii.13).

CHAPTER 7

BIBLICAL AND THEOLOGICAL EVIDENCE FOR JESUS CHRIST'S OMNIPRESENCE

A. Introduction

After having surveyed Christological contributions throughout various significant eras of church history it is time to present a case for the primary thesis of this book. To do this will involve providing arguments from the Bible as well as from theological reflection. Again, because of the abundance of literature selectivity is in order; yet, some interaction is necessary for the honing of Christological assertions. My assumptions concerning the Trinity, and deity of Jesus Christ are reiterated at this juncture as they are the foundation on which I seek to build. Moreover, it should also be clear now, that I affirm the Chalcedonian formula of AD 451 as a sound interpretation of the New Testament's witness to the person of Jesus Christ. Finally, it is also imperative to explain that the enhypostatic Christology, famously associated with Leontius of Byzantium (or Jerusalem) and John of Damascus, is the safest way of avoiding Nestorianism and Eutychianism, and therefore permitting the familiar model of "one person in two natures" as the clearest explanation of the "mechanics" of the incarnation. With this stated, to the biblical evidence for Jesus' omnipresence we now proceed. We begin by looking at the omnipresence of God.

B. Biblical Evidence for God's Omnipresence

At the outset of this section a preliminary overview of the teaching of the omnipresence of God is essential. Two key texts in the Old Testament provide the undisputable contention that God is omnipresent: Psalm 139 and Jeremiah 23.

B.1. Psalm 139

In this Psalm, the writer affirms the all knowing nature of the God of the Bible. In contradistinction from pagan deities, Yahweh is the all-knowing God. In the first six verses, this knowledge is explained from God's intimate personal acquaintance with the writer. In traditional poetic language, the Psalmist expresses God's knowing his "sitting down and his rising up." This knowledge is so encompassing that it includes words that the writer has not uttered yet. No wonder this is deemed as knowledge too high, unattainable for the Psalmist. In verse seven a change of topic enables the Psalmist to continue his exaltation in praise of God, by specifically addressing omnipresence. The words are familiar:

> Where can I go from your Spirit? Or where can I flee from your presence? If I ascend to the heaven, You are there; if I make my bed in hell [*Sheol*, the grave], behold You are there. If I take the wings of the morning, and dwell in the uttermost

parts of the sea, even there Your hand shall lead me, and Your right hand shall hold me.[1]

Admittedly, there is a connection of some sort between the all-knowingness of God and his omnipresence.[2] One way of expressing this is to see omniscience as primary, and therefore to deduce omnipresence as a function of omniscience. Loring Prest does just this.[3] Prest argues that because David first speaks about knowledge (vv.1-6), and only after mentions omnipresence (vv. 7-12), that one is the basis for the other to the point that "David did not see any major difference between the two concepts."[4] This explanation follows on the discussion that Prest makes trying to dismiss the "traditional" understanding of God's omnipresence as essential presence, and in its place argue for God's personal presence.[5] Prest follows this procedure for he thinks he can avoid pantheistic conclusions believed to be associated with the traditional definition. It is quite surprising that Prest charged Charles Ryrie with pantheism, based on Ryrie's definition of omnipresence.[6] For the present discussion it is assumed that Ryrie's definition is sound as he maintains the transcendence of God in his definition which naturally precludes pantheism. Prest is incorrect in charging Ryrie in this regard. Moreover, it is wrong to subsume omnipresence under omniscience.

---

[1] Ps 139:7-10.

[2] They are treated together by Brunner. See Emil Brunner, *The Christian Doctrine of God*, trans. Olive Wyon (Philadelphia: Westminster, 1950), 256-65; 297-300.

[3] See Loring Prest, "The Disposition of the Divine Attributes of Omniscience, Omnipresence and Omnipotence in the Incarnate Christ" (Th.M. thesis, Grace Theological Seminary, 1984), 35-40. Specifically, Prest asserts, "Omnipresence is to be understood as that aspect of God's omniscience whereby everything is within His presence" (40).

[4] Prest, "The Disposition," 35.

[5] Prest here follows Grace M. Dyck, "Omnipresence and Incorporeality," *RelS* 13 (1977): 85-91. By trying to establish a sense of presence which speaks of one's ability to be aware of happenings and to exhibit some influence as personal presence rather than asserting an essential presence, Dyck attempts to lessen the traditionally strong connection between God's omnipresence and His incorporeality. Dyck, to be sure, is not advocating that God is corporeal, but that it is not necessary that God is incorporeal based on her version of omnipresence. The examples she gives are illuminating. Suppose a student is in a room. He is present at the lecture given in the room, so his presence extends beyond his mere skin. In this manner Dyck attempts to argue that God is present in the sense of awareness and influence of all things in the world. I believe the matter of corporeality is settled by Jesus' statement that "God is Spirit." As pure Spirit, God does not have a body. The distinction between personal presence and essential presence seems unwarranted when applied to God as he has no skin to transcend with His so–called "personal presence." God is everywhere essentially *and* personally. The student is technically limited by her physico-spatial location, and as such it may be appropriate to utilize such a distinction in her case.

[6] Prest, "The Disposition," 28-29. Prest quotes from Charles C. Ryrie, *Survey of Biblical Doctrine* (Chicago: Moody, 1972), 24: "Omnipresence says God is everywhere present," Ryrie asserts, "(though separate from the world and things in it), while pantheism says that God is in everything. Omnipresence says that God is present in the room where you are reading this, while pantheism affirms that God is in the chairs and in the windows etc" (Ryrie, cited by Prest, 28).

Chapter 7: Biblical and Theological Evidence for Jesus Christ's Omnipresence

Despite the order that these two ideas appear in Psalm 139, Van Gemeren is surely correct in saying of verse 7, "The presence of God is everywhere; *hence* [emphasis added] he perceives all things in all places."[7] From this observation it appears that omniscience is possible because of omnipresence. Moreover, allowing Prest's way of defining omnipresence tends to confuse these distinct attributes. Erickson warns against this. He says, "This [identifying them as synonymous] does not appear to be what theologians have meant by 'omnipresence.'" Erickson continues, "[theologians] have generally understood it to mean a genuine presence with all objects, not merely knowledge of them or power over them."[8] This careful distinction must be maintained, but Prest has not exhibited clarity on this point. Erickson furthermore adds,

> This, in turn, is related to the biblical witness that God is actually present with us, not that he merely knows us. There is a difference, for example, between David's testimony in Psalm 139:7-12 to God's presence with him and his testimony regarding God's knowledge of him in the remainder of the Psalm. Jeremiah also sees God as filling the whole heaven and earth (Jer. 23:23-24).[9]

Commenting on this passage of Scripture, Psalm 139, John Frame draws attention to the reason for the notion of omnipresence. "David is not saying," Frame argues, "that God just happens to be wherever David chooses to go." This is rather simple and does not really express a distinctive concept about God. Frame continues, "Rather, David understands that the very nature of God as Lord makes him inescapable. The one who made and controls heaven and earth is necessarily present everywhere in the world he has made."[10] There is inherent truth within the concept of God as the Lord, revealed in Scripture, that he must be everywhere. "God's omnipresence," Frame states, "is an implication of his Lordship."[11] David thus knows God as Lord and therefore exclaims: "where can I go from your presence?"

B.2. Jeremiah 23

As Erickson linked the passage from Jeremiah to the verses from Psalm 139, it will be helpful to look also at this text to demonstrate the biblical foundation of the doctrine of omnipresence. Following this brief observation, an analysis of the doctrine of omnipresence will set the context for a specific look at the incarnation.

---

[7] Willem A. VanGemeren, *Pslams* (Grand Rapids: Zondervan, 1991), 837. For a careful exegetical study of the Psalm, see Th. Booij, "Psalm CXXXIX: Text, Syntax, Meaning" *VT* 55:1 (2005), 1-19. Booij notes concerning verse 6, "It is generally assumed that in v. 6 *da'at* refers to YHWH's knowledge of the speaker. The preceding verse, however, is not speaking about YHWH's knowledge, *but about his nearness*" (emphasis added), 3.

[8] Millard J. Erickson, *The Word Became Flesh: A Contemporary Incarnational Christology* (Grand Rapids: Baker, 1991), 560-61.

[9] Erickson, *The Word Became Flesh*, 561.

[10] John M. Frame, *The Doctrine of God* (Phillipsburg, NJ: P & R, 2002), 580.

[11] Frame, *The Doctrine of God*, 580.

In Jeremiah 23, the prophet is relaying the stringent warning from the Lord against the false prophets who speak lies in his name. It is at once woeful and wonderful, as it is in this chapter that God emphatically says he will drive away the infidel nation (people, priest, and prophet) from his presence (vv. 33; 39), yet also maintains that he will bless his people with a return from exile and the remnant will abide with the King who will reign wisely (vv. 5-6). Seeing the false messages of hope brought by the false prophets, in verse 16 (and following), Jeremiah records the direct response from God saying, "This is what the Lord Almighty says:" It is within this response that the rhetorical questions from God resound, which clearly affirm his omnipresence. The text reads thus: "Am I only a God nearby," declares the Lord, "and not a God far away? Can anyone hide in secret places so that I cannot see Him" declares the Lord. "Do not I fill heaven and earth?" declares the Lord.[12]

Again a connection is made concerning God's knowledge and his presence. This passage discusses the ontology of God. "These verses give expression," notes Thompson, "to both the transcendence and the immanence of God. The questions are rhetorical and demand a negative answer."[13] Only because the God of the Bible is both transcendent, so as not to be confused with the created order, and also immanent, so as not to be thought of as absent or unaware do the questions make sense. In their classic commentary Keil and Delitzsch state, "The force of the question: Am I a God at hand, not afar off? is seen from what follows." These writers continue, "Far and near are here in their local, not their temporal signification. . . . The question, which has an affirmative force, is explained by the statement of ver. 24: I fill heaven and earth."[14] There are some interpretive difficulties with these verses.[15] However, the best insights are those such as Thompson's that stress God declaring, albeit by rhetorical questions, his transcendence and immanence. The reason no one can escape from God's gaze is that he sees all. He sees all for he is high above the created order. "Yahweh is the transcendent one," notes Carroll, "who fills heaven and earth and from whom no one can hide."[16] The God who speaks in this text, therefore,

---

[12] Jer 23:23-24. For a helpful overview of the theology of the book, see H.G. Mitchell, "The Theology of Jeremiah," *JBL* (January, 1901), 56-76.

[13] J.A. Thompson, *The Book of Jeremiah* (Grand Rapids: Eerdmans, 1980), 501.

[14] C.F. Keil and F. Delitzsch, *Commentary on the Old Testament,* Vol. 8, *Jeremiah and Lamentations* (Peabody, MA: Hendrickson, 1989), 361.

[15] The options are nicely presented by Robert P. Carroll, *Jeremiah: A Commentary* (Philadelphia: Westminster, 1986), 464-68. The issues center on two matters. First, is the text assertion as in the Septuagint, and if so what does it mean that God is not distant but near? Is this spatial or temporal? Second, if as in the Masoretic text, the verses (23-24) are indeed rhetorical questions, should one link verse 23 with the preceding or following words? Carroll finally opts for a view which sees God's hiddenness in the rhetorical challenge from Yahweh. This draws on the paradox that the God who is impossible to hide from remains himself hidden. These notions may justifiably be seen in this text, without discounting that God still declares his own transcendence. As such, the text may speak about God's nearness and distance as well as implying that he is hidden (until revealed) and therefore not susceptible to manipulation, especially by the false prophets–which is a key theme throughout the chapter.

[16] Carroll, *Jeremiah,* 466.

asserts his own omnipresence by indicating no limit to his dwelling place. It is no surprise, therefore, that Charnock's classic statement on omnipresence begins with this text of Jeremiah.[17]

In case one might think that the teaching of Scripture is based on few verses, and therefore on "scanty evidence," it is imperative to take note of Levine's words. "In reading the Hebrew Bible with the question of God's whereabouts in mind," asserts Levine, "we observe that the concern with the presence of God and his nearness is a major theme."[18] Indeed if John Frame is correct in stressing the connection of these attributes such as omnipresence with the Lordship of God, then the declaration that God's presence is a major theme rings true, for the Lordship of God is discovered in every book of the Bible.

C. Omnipresence as Doctrine

Now that two of the several biblical verses have been seen to provide rationale for the theological assertion of omnipresence, it is important to see how this doctrine has been expounded.[19] Several concepts of God's presence are shown to give this teaching its comprehensiveness. A basic definition utilizing the term "immensity," would be as follows: Divine immensity [omnipresence or ubiquity] means on the one hand that God is necessarily present everywhere in space as the immanent cause and the sustainer of the created order, and on the other hand that this same God transcends the limitations of any actual or possi-

---

[17] Stephen Charnock, *The Existence and Attributes of God* (Grand Rapids: Baker, 1996), 1:363.

[18] Baruch A. Levine, "On the Presence of God in Biblical Religion," in *Religion in Antiquity: Essays in Memory of Erwin Ramsdell Goodenough*, ed. Jacob Neusner (Leiden: Brill, 1968), 72. Levine suggests that "Rarely does the biblical spokesman, be he priest, prophet, or Psalmist, assume the omnipresence of God" (72). Yet his article is replete with instances of God's people entering into his presence, calling for God's presence, experiencing God's presence in various situations–all these references would render the biblical God nothing more than a local deity such as is worshiped by Israel's enemies. Indeed, the presupposition that God's people "assume" God's omnipresence is the only way to make sense of the exclusivity of their God. See Paul R. House, *Old Testament Theology* (Downers Grove, IL: InterVarsity, 1998) for an approach that utilizes the greatness of God as the only God, and who is thereby the Creator, as the theme which unfolds throughout the canon of the Old Testament.

[19] Other Bible verses to support omnipresence would include the following: 1 Kgs 8:27 (see also Acts 7:44-50); Job 11:7-9; Isa 66:1; Matt 28:18-20; and Acts 17:22-31. Also, note Tozer's words concerning this doctrine. "Few other truths are taught in the Scriptures," he asserts, "with as great clarity as the doctrine of the divine omnipresence. Those passages supporting this truth are so plain that it would take considerable effort to misunderstand them" (A.W. Tozer, *The Knowledge of the Holy* [New York: HarperCollins, 1962], 80). For a survey of how the specific doctrine of omnipresence was handled from the early church though the time of Peter Lombard, see Adrian Fuesrt, *An Historical Study of the Doctrine of The Omnipresence of God in Selected Writings between 1220-1270* (Washington, D.C.: Catholic University of America Press, 1951), 1-20. Though I resist his conclusion that we must conceive of God spatially, I have profited from the following ThM thesis, David A. Wolfe, "The Omnipresence of God," (Winona Lake, IN: Grace Theological Seminary, 1981). There is a growing trend of thinkers that affirm some type of spatiality for God.

ble space/place, and as such cannot be circumscribed, divided, or measured by spatial relations. It is evident that I am affirming a spaceless or non-spatial view of God in relation to space, which is the counterpart to a timeless view of God, in relation to time.[20]

A helpful thesis on the question was penned by Patrick Ahern.[21] Though, I am not certain that his distinction between omnipresence and immensity is necessary, it is overall a competent proposal. His distinctions where actual presence may be seen in its various modes such as circumscriptive, definitive and repletive are good, though I prefer other ways of defining the niceties and variations of God's presence, as will be shown below.

One of the most sophisticated treatments of the doctrine of omnipresence has come from the continental theologian Luco J. van Den Brom.[22] He suggests that God exists in his own space, and thus can be conceived of as being spatially extended but not coinciding with the created order. In other words, God inhabits higher dimensions which include our universe. In this manner, van Den Brom avoids both pantheism and panentheism. His primary concern is that a spaceless God, in his estimate, cannot be considered as an agent that produces an effect in the space time world we know. After reviewing some of the classic conceptions of Divine presence, van Den Brom asserts: "It seems that nobody has been particularly successful in formulating God's nonspatial omnipresence in such a way that one can also speak of God's disembodied dynamic action."[23]

More recently we have the interesting work of Elizabeth Callender.[24] Her view is based on a reading, analysis, and interpretation of Karl Barth. Callender affirms that God is not a-spatial, but that he inhabits his own space. Rather than opting for the so-called "container" view of space, she adheres to a "relational" approach. Her definition echoing Barth is that God "is spatial, where spatiality

---

[20] For a defense of the timeless view, see Paul Helm, *Eternal God: A Study of God without Time* (Oxford: Oxford University Press, 1988); and idem, "Divine Timeless Eternity," in *God and Time: Four Views*, ed. Gregory E. Ganssle (Downers Grove, IL: InterVarsity, 2001), 28-60; and the essays in Gregory E. Ganssle & David M. Woodruff, eds. *God and Time: Essays on the Divine Nature* (New York: Oxford University Press, 2002). In regard to the question of how a timeless God can become incarnate, see Brian Leftow, "A Timeless God Incarnate," in *The Incarnation: An Interdisciplinary Symposium on the Incarnation of the Son of God*, ed. Stephen T. Davis, Daniel Kendall, and Gerald O' Collins (Oxford: Oxford University Press, 2002), 273-99; and Douglas K. Blount, "On the Incarnation of a Timeless God" in Ganssle and Woodruff, eds., *God and Time*, 236-48.

[21] Patrick Francis Ahern, "A Study of the Omnipresence and Immensity of God" MA, Thesis, (Loyola University, 1951).

[22] Luco J. van Den Brom, *Divine Presence in the World: A Critical Analysis of the Notion of Divine Omnipresence* (Kampen, The Netherlands: Kok, 1993).

[23] Luco J. van Den Brom, "As Thy New Horizons Beckon," in *Understanding the Attributes of God*, ed. Gijsbert van Den Brink and Marcel Sarot (Frankfurt: Peter Lang, 1999), 94.

[24] Elizabeth Jarrell Callender, "A Theology of Spatiality: The Divine Perfection of Omnipresence in the Theology of Karl Barth" (Ph.D. Thesis; University of Otago, Dunedin, New Zealand, 2011).

is defined as the characteristic way one being is determined to freely and lovingly exist in an intimate and properly ordered personal relationship with another distinct being. Stated more succinctly, spatiality means being fully co-present with others in ordered 'distinction and relationship.'"[25] More fully, Callender states:

> Barth's theology of God's spatiality challenges us to shift from anthropocentric definitions of what it means to be spatial to the relational spatiality enacted and revealed in God's triune being and work, most fully in Jesus Christ. How God is mutually present with Himself as Father, Son and Holy Spirit, and with the creation, especially human beings, is the basis of our new understanding of spatiality that is seen most fully in Jesus Christ. As the primal spatiality, God gives a corresponding spatiality to creatures, especially those made in His image. This originates in the particular and unique spatiality of Jesus Christ, in and through whom all other human beings are spatial. Spatiality is revealed in the way the Son Jesus Christ is present with His Father, and the Father is present with the Son, both in and through the presence of the Holy Spirit.

Callender continues,

> Spatiality is defined by the triune God as the loving and free being in act who elects to be the one God for humanity in the distinction of Father, Son and Spirit; by the Father's intra-trinitarian relationship and His covenant relationship with creation; by the unity of the one Person of Jesus Christ in two complete and distinct natures, elected to accomplish the reconciliation of the world with God; and by the Spirit as the empowering presence that unites God, unites human beings, and unites God and human beings in corresponding order while maintaining proper distinctions. [26]

From a rather different perspective, evangelical writer, Hugh Ross has attempted to address the notions of God, Trinity and Incarnation with this same approach of "extra-dimensions."[27] Hugh Ross is a scientist with keen theological interests. By suggesting that God inhabits other dimensions, Ross feels he can provide an answer to the troubling questions surrounding the difficult doctrines of the Trinity and the Incarnation, the matters of God's presence, and in addition even evil and suffering. Again, like van Den Brom's suggestion, this is attractive as a proposal. However, Ross appears to conceptualize the extra dimensions in such a way that God literally exists in them. This seems a little different and far short of the classic concept of God transcending the created order.[28]

---

[25] Callender, "Theology of Spatiality," 9.

[26] Callender, "Theology of Spatiality," 5.

[27] Hugh Ross, *Beyond the Cosmos: The Extra–Dimensionality of God. What Recent Discoveries in Astronomy and Physics Reveal about the Nature of God* (Colorado Springs: NavPress, 1996).

[28] See the insightful critique of Ross's proposal in William Lane Craig, "Hugh Ross's Extra-Dimensional Deity: A Review Article," *JETS* 42 (1999): 293-304.

It is becoming popular and common to perceive God's presence in terms of knowledge and power.[29] Yet by this procedure an important element is left out of the concept, if defined in this way. Rather than limiting or equating God's presence with ability to exert influence or ability to be aware, a genuine presence of God in light of his infinity is demanded. God is present not merely *per virtuten et operationem,* but *per essentiam.* God's essence or nature–God himself, is present in all parts of the created order without being divided, and what is furthermore essential is that God is present in his whole being, yet without being confined by the created order.[30] Once this is established as a necessary foundation, other ways of God being present may be explored. There is therefore, an *essential* presence as a foundational statement regarding this doctrine/attribute. Beyond the basic concept of the Lord's essential presence (omnipresence), are other ways of conceiving God's actual presence in scripture. There is a *moral* presence, a *heavenly* presence, and [now] a new *Christological* presence within the world.[31] We will look at each of these. The last aspect will help us transition to the theological rationale of Jesus Christ's omnipresence.

C.1. Essential Presence

Traditionally, God has been conceived as "pure spirit," not without biblical influence. Jesus once had a conversation with a Samaritan woman and categorically declared that "God is Spirit" (John 4:24). God is immense as Spirit, and therefore can be worshiped anywhere.[32] As John Feinberg puts it, "God's infin-

---

[29] See David A. Wolfe, "The Omnipresence of God" (Th.M. thesis, Grace Theological Seminary, 1981); and Douglas Keith Blount, "An Essay on Divine Presence" (Ph.D. diss., University of Notre Dame, 1997). Wolfe argues for a concept of omnipresence in which "everything everywhere at any given instance stands in the immediate presence of God . . . . In defining omnipresence in this manner, it actually became an essential part of omniscience" (i). Blount offers a similar approach that is heavily philosophical in which God has control by affecting and awareness. Blount's main concern throughout his "Essay" appears to be a defense of the eternity or timelessness of God. While Blount's concept of God generally is applauded for its Anselmian characteristics, God's omnipresence requires some more explication. Hence, this view is an insufficient development of the concept of theological omnipresence.

[30] Robert Oakes provides a helpful approach to omnipresence from a philosophical perspective. He also maintains the doctrine of simplicity. What is extremely helpful in his work is the way he avoids the idea that omnipresence must entail pantheism as the created order would be a part of God, in whom we exist. He thus posits a view in which the transcendence of God and his immanence are both upheld. See "Divine Omnipresence and Maximal Immanence: Supernaturalism Versus Pantheism," *APQ* 43 (2006): 171-79.

[31] Of course, in the Old Testament there had always been the Christological presence of the Son of God, who has existed from eternity. But now, Jesus of Nazareth is the literal embodiment of the Christ since his conception in the NT era.

[32] Frame's definition includes the following statement: "God's immensity is to space what his atemporal eternity is to time. This does not merely mean that God is omnipresent, but that he transcends space altogether" (Frame, *Doctrine of God,* 576).

Chapter 7: Biblical and Theological Evidence for Jesus Christ's Omnipresence

ity in relation to space is omnipresence and/or immensity."[33] St. Augustine argued that God was everywhere present "not only by power and knowledge, but also by nature."[34] The early church taught that "God's pervasion of all things [is] and [is] a mark of His divinity."[35] These are all ways of speaking about God's *essential presence*. God is present by virtue of being God, and being the infinite God revealed in Scripture, God is necessarily omnipresent. "It is as natural to think that God is everywhere," notes Charnock, "as to think that God is."[36] This essential presence itself has aspects or dimensions that must be recognized. In the following quote from Thomas Aquinas this can be seen. The example is as follows:

> A King, for example is said to be present in the whole kingdom by his power, although he is not everywhere present. Again, a thing is said to be by its presence in other things which are subject to its inspection; as things in a house are said to be present to anyone, who nevertheless may not be in substance in every part of the house. Lastly a thing is said to be substantially or essentially in that place in which its substance is.[37]

Although Aquinas in context may be considered an able exponent of the view that sees omnipresence strongly tied to knowledge and power it is unmistakable in the cited passage that Aquinas adheres to an essential presence of God which is ubiquitous. As there is no place where God's substance is not, God is necessarily present everywhere. As Charnock notes in his chapter on divine omnipresence, that God is present with a "repletive" presence.[38] This is true only for God. It means "He fills all places." And as Charnock further notes, "He is everywhere, because no creature, either body or spirit, can exclude the presence of his essence; for he is not only near, but in everything (Acts xvii. 28)."[39] In summarizing Augustine's concept of God's presence, Grabowski states:

> The divine presence is thus most perfect, and is expressed by the perfection of extension and the perfection of intensity. Extensively, God pervades the whole universe, and every minutest part of it, by being present to each particular thing. Intensively God is present to the whole universe and to each individual thing in the manner that the Creator and self-subsisting Being alone is able to be present to them, and without whom they would not be able to subsist. He is wholly and most present to all beings and to each one of them, and by the power of that presence keeps them together and sustains them in existence.[40]

---

[33] John S. Feinberg, *No One Like Him: The Doctrine of God* (Wheaton, IL: Crossway, 2001), 249.

[34] Stanislaus J. Grabowski, *The All-Present God: A Study in St. Augustine* (London: Herder, 1954), 32. This book is absolutely fascinating.

[35] Grabowski, *The All-Present God*, 33.

[36] Charnock, *Existence and Attributes*, 1:368.

[37] Thomas Aquinas, *Summa Theologica* I, q. 8, a. 3, quoted in Blount, "An Essay on Divine Presence," 16.

[38] Charnock, *Existence and Attributes*, 1:367-69.

[39] Charnock, *Existence and Attributes*, 1: 367.

[40] Grabowski, *The All-Present God*, 62.

God's essential presence thus involves the concept that God is necessarily present by virtue of his Godhead/infinity, and that this entails his sustaining of all else that is not God. Because he is transcendent and definitely not a part of the created order, God remains distinct from the universe; as God is also immanent, that is near, he is to be thought of as everywhere present, yet not identified by anything in the universe. So it is not entirely incorrect to speak in terms of God's presence suggesting this is so by virtue of his knowledge and power, God may indeed be thought of as present in some sense this way. It is incorrect to limit God's omnipresence to his mere knowledge and power to influence. God must be thought of as actually present in his whole being at all points in the created order. He is not extended as he is not spatial. But by being the creator who is greater than the universe he has made, God is spiritually present as the sole preserver of the created order.

C.2. Moral Presence

In addition to the notion of God's essential omnipresence, scripture also teaches other aspects of the Lord's presence. There is a moral presence of God.[41] This is a covenant closeness which is more experiential in nature. God manifests his special felt presence among his own people. A distinction is necessary to understand the significance of this type of presence. "God is ontologically [essentially] present in all places and with all people," notes Feinberg, "but he is not present *ethically* with nonbelievers."[42] Feinberg immediately adds a startling claim which is nonetheless true. "This means that God is ontologically present even in hell," he states, "but that does not mean hell's inhabitants have any awareness of God's presence or any moral or spiritual relation to him."[43] So an awareness or sense of God's immediate presence is reserved only for the saved.

In the Psalms, in a mood of worship, spiritual longing is a key component of pursuing God. In the famous passage of Psalm 46:1, God is spoken of as a "very present help in trouble." Moreover, his people, the righteous, dwell in his presence (Ps 140:13). It is in God's covenant closeness that the Psalmist happily confesses, "In Your presence is fulness of joy." These are all instances of

---

[41] Feinberg calls this type of presence *moral, ethical,* or *spiritual,* and defines it thus: "it means God has a spiritual relationship by saving faith with an individual and that no sin blocks fellowship and communion between God and that person" (Feinberg, *No One Like Him*, 250).

[42] Feinberg, *No One Like Him*, 251.

[43] Feinberg, *No One Like Him*, 251. It is best to conceive the situation in hell, not as the absence of God's presence (ontological/essential), but to the presence of God's absence (as paradoxical as it sounds). There will be a lack of awareness of the divine omnipresence, or any aspect of his presence. But there will be a presence of judgment, and a presence of the execution of punishment. Grudem suggests that in hell God will be present to punish (Wayne Grudem, *Systematic Theology: An Introduction to Biblical Doctrine* [Grand Rapids: Zondervan, 1994], 175). Furthermore, in a dispensation of God's felt moral presence, along with the physical presence of Jesus among His own in the eschaton, that non-elect humanity will stand before God at the great white throne evaluation (see Rev 20:11-14). Even there, unredeemed humanity will have no covenant closeness with God.

Chapter 7: Biblical and Theological Evidence for Jesus Christ's Omnipresence

this manifest moral/spiritual presence of God. As a pastor, it is this moral presence that I call out for in gatherings of corporate worship. As a Christian, it is God's moral presence, mediated fully by the Triune Godhead that one longs for in personal experience, and in private devotions. In distinction to God's essential or ontological presence, moral presence is manifest by God to those in covenant relationship with him. His essential presence is, however, the ground for his moral presence.

God himself spoke of this special type of manifest moral presence when encouraging Moses to lead the Israelites in God's way. To the questioning Moses, God replied: "My presence will go with you, and I will give you rest" (Exod 33:14). Of course, this is in context a theophany, where a physical manifestation is permitted by God for the sake of his saint. His closeness is not identical with the physical manifestation but is rather illustrated by it. When God is no longer permitting a physical theophany, it does not mean he is not morally present, yet this closeness is always something different or distinct from his essential or ontological omnipresence.

The most significant concept revealed to the people of God concerning God's manifest moral presence is in regard to the establishment of a specific structure for a dwelling place for God. In giving the instructions for how to build the tabernacle (Exod 25-27), and later the temple (2 Sam 7:13; 1 Kgs 5-6; 2 Chr 3-7), God was giving glimpses of truth concerning his moral presence.[44] "Solomon's Temple, where the Ark was in the Holy of Holies, was . . . conceived as a place where Jahweh was present in person (1 Kings viii. 12). This presence was always regarded as bestowing blessing."[45]

Israel faltered and turned the symbol into an object of worship, and this tendency has persisted throughout the Old Testament.[46] God allows certain events to transpire such as the capture of the ark of the covenant (1 Sam 4), the departure of the manifest Glory from the temple (Ezek 10), and ultimately for the temple and capitol city to be razed to the ground (Jer 25:1-14). All these and other similar events in the history of God's people are object lessons on the principle of God removing his moral presence because of his people's sin. In the New Testament this occurs when we grieve or quench the Spirit of God. When confession of sin is forthcoming, a renewed fellowship occurs and God's people can once again walk in the light of God's manifest moral presence (1 John 1:5-2:1).[47]

---

[44] See Elmer A. Martens, *God's Design: A Focus on Old Testament Theology* (Grand Rapids: Baker, 1981), 91-93; 226-29. "The manifestation of Yahweh," states Martens, "together with his presence and holiness sums up the theological implications of the tabernacle" (93).

[45] Gerhard von Rad, *Old Testament Theology* (Peabody, MA: Prince, 2005), I.237.

[46] Martens comments that "Israel's story shows how a community can seize upon a theological symbol such as the temple, and theologize upon it to the point of bringing blindness on themselves" (Martens, *God's Design*, 155).

[47] von Rad discusses aspects of theology in regard to the Ark, the Tent, the Tabernacle (which he sees as distinct from the Tent), and the Temple of Solomon. See von Rad, *Old Testament Theology* I.234-41. These comments are insightful, especially as he says, "The Tent is not in the least the place where Jahweh dwells on earth, as was the case

Before we examine God's heavenly abode it is important to note that God on occasion manifests his presence to people who are not part of his covenant community, but nonetheless does so to further his covenant plan. Thus there is a presence which is mediated to unregenerate people, which has specific covenant significance.

A classic case in point is the account of the writing on the wall that appeared to King Belshazzar in Daniel 5:1-31. In this particular instant it involves a judgment from God. The king is weighed and found wanting. Even as he celebrates, in a party designed to show the superiority of his gods, Belshazzar is unaware that the enemy is already within his camp. The Medes and Persians are to be the recipients of Belshazzar's kingly rule. God, who is supreme ruler of heaven and earth, is the one who truly governs the affairs of men. He enthrones emperors in their kingly functions, and he raises empires (cf. Dan 4:28-35).

There is another aspect of his presence among unregenerate people when God manifests himself to certain ones in certain times to bestow temporal worldly blessing. A case in point is Cyrus. In Isaiah 45:1-7, a truly amazing passage of scripture, God declares that Cyrus is God's anointed, though Cyrus does not know the Lord, and that earthly treasure will be given into this man's hands by Yahweh, Israel's God. God specifically states that he, himself, will hold Cyrus's hand. This is a manifestation of a covenant presence among a non saved person to bestow blessing, which will enable the outworking of the Lord's covenant plan of the ages.

In summary, this covenant-fulfilling significant presence is distinct from God's moral presence as it is associated with non-redeemed people or nations. In this sense God may manifest himself as the covenant God who blesses (materially/temporarily) or judges (temporarily and eternally) individuals or nations who do not have a saving relationship with him. And these manifestations are the presence of God to ensure the plan of God is fulfilled throughout history.

C.3. Heavenly Presence

The scriptures clearly declare God's dwelling place to be the heavens. In Deuteronomy, Moses exclaims, "Look down from your holy dwelling place in heaven" (Deut 26:15).[48] In Psalm 115, the writer contrasts Yahweh with the idols, and shows his sovereign majesty by emphatically stating: "Our God is in heaven; He does whatever He pleases" (v. 3). Later in the same Psalm, the Psalmist speaks of the particular dwelling place of God in terms of ownership in contrast to the earthly sphere as man's place of living. "The heaven, even the

---

later with, for instance, the Temple of Solomon" (I.236). He explains that the Tent was a temporary place of meeting. "After the settlement of Israel in Canaan," notes von Rad, "the Tent disappears from history" (I.236). On the Ark, he continues: "Israel thought of the Ark as the Throne of Jahweh. Wherever the Ark is Jahweh is there fully present" (I.237). God was mobile, however, according to von Rad. As the Ark was taken up, so did Jahweh rise to lead His people. "Thus," he informs us, "two completely different 'theologies' are connected with the Tent and with the Ark—with the former it is a theology of manifestation, but with the latter one of presence" (I.237).

[48] Von Rad notes, "according to the Deuteronomic theology, Jahweh dwells in heaven" (von Rad, *Old Testament Theology*, I.238).

heavens, are the Lord's," he cries, "But the earth He has given to the children of men" (v. 15). Indeed, "the Lord's Throne is in Heaven" (Ps 11:4), "the Lord looks down from heaven" (Ps 14:2), and speaking of the Lord, the Psalmist also declares: "Whom do I have in heaven but You?" (Ps 73:25).

This notion is also brought out in the New Testament. Jesus taught his disciples to pray by addressing God with these words: "Our Father in Heaven" (Matt 6:9). As the heavens are higher than the earth, this imagery is surely designed to teach God's people his eminently higher order of being than mankind who have been, nonetheless, created in his image. God is the Heavenly Father, who sends his Son (John 6:32, cf. Gal 4:4), who gives his Holy Spirit (Luke 11:13), and who speaks from his dwelling place on high (Matt 3:17; 17:5). God as the one inhabiting a heavenly realm therefore has a heavenly presence. It is this dimension of God's presence which the angels enjoy as they sing: "Holy, Holy, Holy." Yet, just as God dwells in the heavens, and he permits a manifestation of his glorious presence to be connected with both the tabernacle and the temple, one must not conclude that this exhausts the divine presence. Wayne Grudem speaks of God's various manifestations as "God's presence to punish, to sustain, or to bless."[49] Surely, God's heavenly presence is a blessing to all those privileged to share it.

In the same way God was still abiding in heaven while he was connected with both tabernacle and temple, yet without vacating heaven, God has identified with humanity in the strongest possible way in the incarnation yet without abandoning his presence in heaven. This time it is no mere temporal indwelling of a lifeless structure, but the incarnation of the Son of God, resulting in God's becoming man. God is not only among us, he is also one of us. This aspect of Christological presence must be examined.

C.4. Christological Presence

A biblical theology of God's presence finds its crowning concept in the incarnation.[50] Indeed, it is the name Immanuel that is given to this child who mediates God's presence to the world as never before. "God [is] with us," in a new sense. God with us as one of us. The incarnation of the Son of God is itself a revelation of God. In Hebrews the writer declares that God has spoken in the past, yet now through Christ Jesus, the Son of God, he speaks definitively and finally (Heb 1:1-4). The incarnation does not replace other concepts of God's revelation or of God's presence but it complements them, fulfills them, and

---

[49] Grudem, *Systematic Theology*, 175-77.

[50] On this see the helpful study by Jean Galot, *Who is Christ? A Theology of the Incarnation*, trans. M. Angeline Bouchard (Chicago: Franciscan Herald, 1981), 161-70. "Jesus defined himself," argues Galot, "by comparison with the Temple of Jerusalem, as the real temple: 'Now Here, I tell you, is something greater than the Temple' (Mt 12:6). He affirmed a superiority over Solomon and Jonah. As the essential value of the Temple lay in the divine presence within it, only this presence could be superior to the Temple. Thus, Jesus implied that in his person the authentic presence of God lay hidden." Furthermore, adds Galot, speaking of the incident with Nathanael (John 1:51), "The Son of Man is . . . the earthly place where God is present. He is concretely God's presence on the earth" (161).

finalizes God's means of revelation to his world.[51] There is a newness (and freshness) with the presence of Jesus among his fellow countrymen of God's presence among them. During Christ's so-called earthly ministry, God mediates his moral presence through is Son directly. In a voice beaming from the heavens, God declares: "This is My Son, in whom I am well pleased. Hear Him" (Matt 17:5). So a relationship to the Son is essential as the *sina qua non* of a relationship with God. He who honors the Son, honors the Father (see John 5:23), and he who has the Son, has eternal life (see 1 John 5:12). Indeed, eternal life is to know God through Jesus Christ the Son (John 17:3). The importance of one's relationship to Jesus Christ cannot be overstated.

Problems arise, however, when one discusses the Christological presence of God. This is so for the appearing in the flesh, and the dwelling as man in our midst was a historically conditioned event that is now long in the past. That is not to say that the incarnation was temporal.[52] Far from it; the Son of God added a human nature to himself and henceforth the Son of God will be none other than the Man Jesus Christ throughout eternity. Christ, furthermore, will re-visit the planet in the second coming to complete his mission. The fact that Jesus is not present in the flesh, however, places one in a difficult position of accepting that it is Jesus Christ who continues to mediate God's presence. Of course, there is an answer to this, which, is bound up with the central claims made throughout this dissertation concerning Jesus Christ's omnipresence. This will be examined shortly. What many seem to do, however, is to reverse the roles, we could say. Rather than Jesus mediating God's presence, theologians and other biblical commentators are fond of suggesting that it is in fact the Holy Spirit who mediates Jesus' presence to us. Let an illustration suffice to show this trend. In an otherwise excellent volume on the triune God, James R. White makes this fundamental mistake of role reversal. In a section where White is discussing "the Spirit as God," he mentions the notion of the "interpenetration" of the divine persons. He supports this contention with a quote from John 14:23, which states: "Jesus answered and said unto him, "If anyone loves Me, he will keep my word; and My Father will love him, and We will come to him and make Our abode with him.""

White's comments immediately following the citation are as follows: "Jesus promises that the Father and He will dwell with those who love Him and keep

---

[51] God is still revealed in nature, human conscience, and the Old Testament and New Testament Scriptures. The incarnation is a supreme revelation of God in the sense that to know God *now*, since the coming of Christ, is to know God only through the Son of God who was incarnate.

[52] Walvoord notes, "The act of incarnation was not a temporary arrangement which ended with His death and resurrection but, as Scriptures make evident, His human nature continues forever, His earthly body which died on the cross being transformed into a resurrected body suited for His glorious presence in heaven. The continuance of His humanity is reflected in such passages as Matthew 26:24 (ASV) where it is stated that Christ will sit on the throne of His glory and return to earth as the Son of Man: 'Henceforth ye shall see the Son of Man sitting at the right hand of Power, and coming on the clouds of heaven' " (John F. Walvoord, *Jesus Christ Our Lord* [Chicago: Moody, 1969], 112-13).

Chapter 7: Biblical and Theological Evidence for Jesus Christ's Omnipresence

His word (i.e., the true disciples). Yet how does the Lord do this? He does so by His Spirit, whom He sends in His place."[53] The concept of interpenetration or perichoresis as a theological doctrine expressing an important aspect of Trinitarianism is not in question. But the particular way of application of this perichoretic concept to this passage by White appears unnecessary, especially as it detracts from the fulfillment of Jesus' actual presence and has replaced it with the Spirit's presence. Christ explicitly stated that he, along with the Father, would come and dwell among these believers who exhibit this love for Christ. There is no reason to suggest that it is not really Christ himself who will be present but the Spirit that mediates Jesus' presence. If Jesus is not really with us but the Spirit is in his place, how is it that Jesus mediates God's presence? We are back at this problem. It would appear that we must either revise our concept that Jesus definitively reveals God or that this revelation is not final. Or one may have to revise the idea that Jesus is here only by proxy, that is, "in the Holy Spirit." In my estimation it is the notion of Jesus Christ's omnipresence which safeguards his continuing revelation of God.[54] To this claim we will now turn.

D. The Omnipresence of Jesus Christ

In this part of the project, the positive case will be set forth for the thesis. This will proceed in two broad sections. One will be the biblical evidence for the omnipresence of Jesus Christ. The second will be the specific theological arguments, which supplement this teaching. The specific contribution of this book will therefore be established to show how the doctrine of omnipresence serves as a *key* to solve the kenosis question. Beyond this positive presentation, an examination of some problems associated with this claim will be made, especially centering on the exposition of Philippians 2:5-8 in the next chapter. It is this Pauline passage which according to some renders the thesis impossible. At this juncture of evaluating some of the more important studies of the Philippians text, a return to some of the contemporary evangelical voices will be made in order to evaluate more specifically what appears to be the widespread consensus of a moderate form of kenosis in conceiving the incarnation, and hence of a denial of Jesus' omnipresence.

D.1. Biblical Evidence for Jesus' Omnipresence

There are several passages that support the doctrinal claim establishing Jesus Christ's omnipresence. These will be noted as a foundation for re-affirming Jesus' deity. As such there is a type of cumulative case that is established.

D.1.1. The Gospel of John

In John's gospel, which strongly teaches the deity of Jesus, it is not surprising to find material which undergirds the thesis. In John 1:48-49 the text asserts that Jesus had seen Nathanael under the fig tree before Nathanael approached

---

[53] James R. White, *The Forgotten Trinity: Recovering the Heart of Christian Belief* (Minneapolis: Bethany, 1998), 149-50.

[54] There is then an objective presence of Christ by virtue of the divine nature of the incarnate Son of God, but this presence becomes experientially felt or subjectively experienced through the proclamation of the gospel.

Jesus.[55] In his remarkable response to Jesus declaring that he saw him, Nathanael exclaims: "You are the Son of God! You are the King of Israel!" This is quite the reversal from his previous question asking if anything good can come out of Nazareth. What prompted this stunning response is the fact that a divine miracle occurred in Jesus "seeing" Nathanael. It was not merely the case that Jesus was a fair distance away, yet could still somehow "make him out," so to speak. The only satisfying explanation is that Jesus was present to Nathanael and therefore could see him well before he could have identified Nathanael with human eyes. Yet the only way Jesus could have been present is if he is not confined to the body. As the Son of God who is clearly deity, this should not alarm us. Another clue in the text supports this claim. Because Jesus spoke of Nathanael as one without guile, some have suggested that Nathanael was meditating on scripture, particularly the Jacob narrative. Hence there is a double reference in Jesus' words to Nathanael that underscore, not only him seeing Nathanael, but also knowing his deepest thoughts. Nathanael is unlike Jacob who was a man of guile. Furthermore, as Jacob saw the vision of angels ascending and descending on the ladder as he perceived the presence of God at Bethel, so now Jesus informs Nathanael, that he is the place where the angels of God will ascend and descend, which implies that he–Jesus himself is the place of God's manifestation to his people, and the mediator between heaven and earth. As such a one, Jesus could "see" Nathanael well before he was physically close, for he is omnipresent. Ravi Zacharias makes this same deduction concerning Jesus' omnipresence in the encounter with Nathanael.[56]

In John 2:19-21, an interesting confrontation scene emerges as Jesus speaks to crowds as he has cleansed the temple, asserting something quite stupendous: "Destroy this temple," Jesus says, "and in three days I will raise it up." Obviously a misunderstanding occurs and even his disciples did not fully understand Jesus' words until after his resurrection from the dead (v.22). Christ is here speaking of his body, but what is to be noted is that he implicates his person as the agent of resurrection, after the Jews "destroy [his] temple." This is reminiscent of John 10:17-18, where again Jesus speaks of his impending death but carefully instructs his listeners saying: "I lay down my life that I may take it again." As in 2:19-20, Jesus says, *he* will raise his dead body. Tenney's comment is helpful. "Anyone can lay down his life," Tenney asserts, "if that means simply the termination of physical existence; but only the Son of the Father could at will resume his existence."[57] The only way to make sense of this kind

---

[55] Walvoord mentions this very passage in answering kenotic Christology. He finds kenoticism problematic because of its denial of Jesus' deity. "The false theory of kenosis," claims Walvoord, "is in direct conflict with scriptures which affirm the omniscience of Christ (John 2:24; 16:30), assert *His omnipresence (John 1:48)* [emphasis added] and demonstrate His omnipotence as revealed in His many miracles" (Walvoord, *Jesus Christ Our Lord*, 142).

[56] See Ravi Zacharias, *Jesus among Other Gods: The Absolute Claims of the Christian Message* (Nashville: Word, 2000), 28-32, esp. 32.

[57] Merrill C. Tenney, *John* (Grand Rapids: Zondervan, 1981), 110. See also F.F. Bruce, *The Gospel and Epistles of John* (Grand Rapids: Eerdmans, 1983; reprint, 2001), 228-29. Bruce says of John's statement about Jesus raising himself from the dead: "Sim-

of categoric assertion is to see that the person of Jesus will somehow transcend the physical body, and moreover, once the body is killed, he as a person, though dead, in some sense can affect the body by causing it to rise from the dead.[58] That Jesus truly died, it must be asserted. Yet the divine nature did not, indeed, could not die (1 Tim 6:16), and the divine-human person is responsible for his own resurrection.

Also, in John's gospel, a clear affirmation of Jesus abiding presence in heaven is made while he is incarnate and speaking on the earth. In John 3:13 in the New King James Version, the text reads: "No one has ascended to heaven but He who came down from Heaven, that is the Son of Man *who is in heaven*" (emphasis added). This text, as we noted in an earlier chapter was a favorite text of John Calvin in supporting his *extra Calvinisticum* doctrine.[59] Many today do not consider it genuine as it stands in the King James tradition. The emphasized words "who is in heaven" are missing from the minority text tradition. A most important article by David Alan Black establishes the authenticity of the King James reading of the text.[60] Moreover, Black argues precisely that this text substantiates the omnipresence of Jesus Christ. Jesus as the incarnate one, is speaking to Nicodemus, and at the same time he addresses his listener, Jesus claims that he is simultaneously in heaven. William Hendriksen does not believe the expression "who is in heaven" is genuine, yet has this to say: "The idea contained in the omitted clause [who is in heaven] is, however, definitely scriptural (cf. 1:18)."[61] In Greek the expression, ὁ ὢν ἐν τῷ οὐρανῳ has the

---

ilarly, he [Jesus] is repeatedly said elsewhere in the New Testament to have been raised from the dead by God (Acts 2:32; Rom. 6:4; Heb. 13:20; 1 Pet. 1:21, etc.), but here *he rises of his own volition* [emphasis added]. John does not contradict the testimony of other NT writers; the difference is one of emphasis" (229).

[58] Morris' comments are apropos: "It is undoubtedly true that the New Testament prefers to speak of God raising Jesus, but Jesus several times predicted that he would rise (e.g., Mark 8:31; Luke 24:7) and some passages say that he did rise (Acts 10:41; 17:31; 1 Thess. 4:14). We ought not to put any opposition between the Father and the Son in this matter, nor should we doubt that the habitual New Testament form of expression is that the Father raised the Son. But we should not overlook the fact that there is also a strand of New Testament teaching that says that the Son 'rose.' The present passage [John 10:17-18] is part of this strand" (Leon Morris, *Gospel According to John* [Grand Rapids: Eerdmans, 1995], 456-57 n. 53).

[59] In his commentary on this passage, Calvin asserts, "It may be thought absurd to say the *he is in heaven*, while he still dwells on earth. If it be replied that this is true in regard to his Divine nature, the mode of expression means something else, namely, that while he was man, he was *in heaven* . . . [and therefore] that what properly belongs to one nature is applied to another, [so] we ought not seek any other solution" (Calvin, *Commentary on the Gospel According to John*, trans. William Pringle, in *CNTC* 17 (Grand Rapids: Baker, 2003), 1:121.

[60] David Alan Black, "The Text of John 3:13," *GTJ* 6 (1985): 49-66. See, also, the very important article by Larry Overstreet, "John 3:13 and the Omnipresence of Jesus Christ," *JBTM* Vol. 2 No. 2 (Fall 2004): 135-153 for more evidence of the text's authenticity and significance in establishing this very truth of omnipresence.

[61] William Hendriksen, *New Testament Commentary: Exposition of the Gospel According to John* (Grand Rapids: Baker, 1953), 1:129 n.70.

participle in the present tense. The most obvious meaning is to take it at face value. Jesus is the Son of Man who has come down from heaven, yet in a way that allows him still to be in heaven. Again, this is only possible if Jesus Christ the Son of God has a presence beyond the confines of his earthly body. As such it suggests that Christ is omnipresent. In John 1:18, this notion is again supported as the Word who has become flesh (John 1:14) is said to be "in the bosom of the Father." In addition to Hendriksen, who cited this reference (John 1:18) to give evidence of this truth, so Murray Harris is in agreement that the text can be interpreted this way.[62] Leon Morris agrees. He says of John 1:18: "It is possible that we should punctuate with a comma after 'begotten,' thus giving three titles of Christ: Only begotten, God, he who is in the bosom of the Father."[63] Morris continues:

> This final expression brings out the closeness of the Father and the Son. It also carries overtones of affection . . . . The copula "is" expresses a continuing union. The only begotten is continually in the bosom of the Father. When the Word became flesh his cosmic activities did not remain in abeyance until the end of his earthly life. There are mysteries here that we cannot plumb, but we must surely hold that the incarnation meant the adding of something to what the Word was doing, rather than the cessation of most of his activities.[64]

In John 4:46-54, John records the account of the "second sign Jesus did when he had come out of Judea into Galilee" (4:54). In this familiar story, the man is desperate for Jesus' bodily presence to be beside his dying son, so as to be made well.[65] Jesus does not go with the man but merely tells the man that his son will be delivered. "Go your way; your son lives," utters Jesus. The man believes the testimony of the Lord then returns to his home to find that the fever left the boy completely at the same time that Jesus pronounced the cure. Obviously space is not a barrier to the Son of God. This account may be taken to illustrate the divine power of Christ. This must be conceded, but it also sheds

---

[62] See Harris, *Jesus as God*, 94-96 for three interpretive options. In concluding this section of his study on John 1:18, he discusses the significance of the verse in its entirety on the Gospel of John. He says, "In the whole of John's Gospel, verse 18 has a twofold function. It links the Prologue and the remainder of the Gospel by highlighting the dual themes of the Father as directly and fully known to the Son and the Son as the unique Exegete of the Father . . . . In the second place . . . verse 18 forms one of two "bookends" that support and give shape to the whole Gospel, for 1:1 and 1:18 (at the beginning and the end of the Prologue) and 20:28 (at the end of the Gospel) all use θεος of Jesus, whether he be thought of as the eternally preexistent Logos (1:1), *the incarnate Son (1:18)* [emphasis added], or the risen Christ (20:28). The evangelist thereby indicates that the acknowledgment of the messiahship of Jesus (20:31) necessarily involves belief in his deity" (Harris, *Jesus as God*, 103). What is significant is that Harris says that John 1:18 speaks of the incarnate Christ. Yet this same person is in the bosom of the Father, while exegeting the Father on earth. This can only be true if Jesus is present beyond the confines of his material body.

[63] Morris, *The Gospel According to John*, 101.

[64] Morris, *The Gospel According to John*, 101.

[65] See Calvin, *Commentary on the Gospel According to John*, 1:179.

light on the ground for Jesus' ability to exercise that power in a remote place from his bodily presence.⁶⁶

Another passage from John's gospel also gives insight to the possibility of the presence of Christ beyond the physical body. In John 5:19-20, again utilizing the concept of "seeing" as in the incident with Nathanael, John employs another term yet keeps the connotation of observing. This time Jesus states that he does only what he sees his Father doing. The Greek, once more uses a present tense, which is significant. In verse 19, Jesus says: οὐ δύναται ὁ Υἱὸς ποιεῖν ἀφ' ἑαυτοῦ οὐδὲ ἐὰν μή τι βλέπῃ τὸν Πατέρα ποιοῦντα (the Son can do nothing of himself, but what he sees the Father do). What is important in this section is that the works, for which the Jews want to kill Christ, which he performed earlier in the chapter, are the platform for Jesus' argument that he *now* sees the Father doing, and so he does the same also. The relationship that is required for Jesus to see, and to be shown (v. 20) things by the Father necessitate something beyond Jesus' observation with human eyes. A spiritual proximity alone, which transcends the limitations of Christ's body permit the Son of God in his unbroken fellowship with the Father to observe and imitate the godly works. Jesus, in addition to standing before men in his physical body, inhabits the spiritual sphere of God's immediate presence where he can plainly "see" the Father. This yet again points in the direction of Jesus Christ's omnipresence.

One last look at John's gospel will show again how it is necessary for Jesus the Son of God to be a person who transcends the limits of his body, if we are to make sense of statements about him. In John 10:38, Jesus challenges those he addresses that if he is truly performing his Father's works, then they should believe on him on account of the works he is performing. To this challenge Jesus adds that "the Father is in Me, and I in Him" (John 10:38). A similar expression is found in John 14:20. "At that day," Jesus says, "you will know that I am in My Father, and you in Me, and I in you" (John 14:20). What is significant in this text is that although Jesus speaks of a future day of the disciples knowing, what it is they will know in the future, was nonetheless true at the time he speaks to them. For Jesus to be "in the Father and in them," requires Jesus to transcend his own body. He was in them, even while speaking to them. This surely refers to the presence of God in all believers. Yet in the immediate context, Jesus also declares a coming day, when because of a special love the Father will exhibit to certain individuals who have greatly loved Jesus, both the Father and Jesus himself will manifest themselves to those disciples that have loved Christ, and moreover will indwell them as a habitation (John 14:23).⁶⁷

---

⁶⁶ This is evident in Doriani's observations on another of Jesus' miracles. He says: "The next miracle in Matthew is similar [to the healing of a leper]. A centurion comes pleading for his suffering servant. Jesus says simply, 'I will go and heal him.' There is a discussion of Jesus' agency, but it only shows that Jesus can heal at a distance, hinting at the divine attribute of omnipresence ([Matt] 8:5-13)," (Daniel Doriani, "The Deity of Christ in the Synoptic Gospels," *JETS* 37 [1994], 343).

⁶⁷ Carson mentions two ways of dealing with this passage. "Presumably," he notes, "this manifestation of the Father and the Son in the life of believer is *through the Spirit* [emphasis added], although the text does not explicitly say so. Other New Testament

Even if this is to occur after the resurrection, which is almost certainly the case, the presence of Jesus, along with the Father's presence, necessarily requires that Jesus in some way transcends his body so he can spiritually indwell the believers who love him.

D.1.2. The Gospel of Matthew

We have already noted Matthew 18:20 in our discussion thus far.[68] It remains to see another familiar text from Matthew which again, supports our thesis. In the words known as "The Great Commission," Jesus gives the disciples a task to reach the world for the cause of Christ. This is a twofold ministry, with a singular goal. As those who spent time with Jesus learning from him, the believers were now to "disciple the nations." This discipleship program is the singular focus and it is brought about by "baptizing," and "teaching."[69] The first matter of baptism, is Matthew's shorthand (in this text) for Mark's equivalent to preach the Gospel (Mark 16:16). The initial work is to get people to believe so as to receive eternal life. Once people have believed, the second matter of teaching the converts continues the discipleship program proper. In addition to giving this task to his church, Jesus gave them a very encouraging promise. Christ said that "I am with you always, even to the end of the age" (Matthew 28:20).[70] Of course, this is the resurrected Lord that made such a promise, yet this should not make a difference. Christ is preparing to ascend physically to the Father, so it cannot be that he will be bodily with his disciples. The presence that Christ promises is not the presence of the Holy Spirit, though that would be true also after the "coming" of the Holy Spirit on the day of Pentecost. It is Jesus' presence of himself that will accompany the believers as they continue his work. "Here then," states France, "the Jesus who through his physical birth became 'God with us' continues to fulfill that role even after his earthly presence is withdrawn."[71] This is only comprehensible given Christ's

---

passages testify to the dwelling of the Son in the Christian (*e.g.* Eph. 3:17); this is the only place where the Father and the Son are linked in this task. Those who think that the Father and Son are present in the believer *only through* the Holy Spirit see the indwelling in this verse as indistinguishable from the gift of the Spirit. Others join with Augustine in thinking that this text coupled with vv. 25-26 argues for the indwelling of the Triune God in the believer (*In Johan. Tract.* lxxvi. 4)" (Carson, *The Gospel According to John*, 504).

[68] On this text [Matt 18:20], Hagner states, "This presence of Jesus should not be understood as a metaphor (as in the case of Paul's statement in 1 Cor 5:4) but is the literal presence of the resurrected Christ, in keeping with the promise to be articulated in 28:20 (cf. 1:23b). The community founded by Jesus (16:18) is assured that he will be present in that community until the close of the age" (Donald A. Hagner, *Matthew 14-28* [Dallas: Word, 1995], 533).

[69] For a different understanding of the relationship of the key terms in the commission, see D.A. Carson, *Matthew* (Grand Rapids: Zondervan, 1984), 597.

[70] Carson states, "The period between the commission and the consummation is of indefinite length; but whatever its duration, it is the time of the church's mission and of preliminary enjoyment of her Lord's presence" (Carson, *Matthew*, 599).

[71] R.T. France, *Matthew: Evangelist and Teacher* (Downers Grove, IL: InterVarsity, 1989), 312. This is a most helpful book, which includes "Matthew's Portrait of Jesus"

presence beyond the body. As God, Jesus is omnipresent by virtue of the divine nature. Only this truth, can explain this text.

D.1.3. Romans

In Romans 8:10, the Apostle Paul states that "if Christ is in you, the body is dead because of sin, but the Spirit is life because of righteousness."[72] In the broader context, Paul is contrasting the carnal mind of death, which cannot obey the will of God, with the mind of a spiritually attuned person. In fact, Paul's argument hinges on the truth that the readers are "in the Spirit," as he declares, "if indeed the Spirit of God dwells in you" (Rom 8:9a). Both the indwelling of the Holy Spirit and the believer's "walk" in the Spirit are characteristics true of those who please God. Paul adds the categoric warning as follows in the next part of the verse: "Now if anyone does not have the Spirit of Christ, he is not His" (Rom 8:9b). This reference to the "Spirit of Christ" is probably not referring to the immaterial property of the person of the Son of God–his spiritual entity or human soul, but rather as is earlier mentioned in the passage, a reference to the Holy Spirit, the third person of the Trinity. Immediately following this clear warning, Paul inserts the verse cited at the beginning of our discussion, namely Romans 8:10. In Greek it reads thus: "εἰ δὲ Χριστὸς ἐν ὑμῖν τὸ μὲν σῶμα νεκρὸν διὰ ἁμαρτίαν τὸ δὲ πνεῦμα ζωὴ διὰ δικαιοσύνην." We are particularly concerned with the phrase: "Christ in you." Douglas Moo states matters well. "Paul now speaks of "Christ" being in the Roman Christians," declares Moo, "whereas in v. 9 it was "the Spirit of God" who was said to be dwelling in believers."[73] Moo continues his discussion saying:

(279-317) as the last chapter is titled.

[72] "One of the most important texts concerning the presence of Christ and particularly his bodily presence in the believer is Romans 8:9-11. Here we have a concentration of 'in' language. Paul has already described the believer as ἐν Χριστῷ (8:1). In this passage, they are not ἐν σαρκὶ but ἐν πνεύματι. However, it is the language of Christ and the Spirit being 'in' the believer that is perhaps most interesting." (see Peter Orr, *Christ Present and Absent: A Study in Pauline Christology*. Ph.D. thesis, [Durham, UK: University of Durham, 2011], 157). I am thrilled to see a scholar of the NT take on this theme. The presence and absence of Christ is an intriguing topic, indeed. Orr speaks of the interdependence but non-identity of Christ and the Spirit. This is helpful and is a corrective to those writers that suggest that Christ is present *only* by the Holy Spirit. Though Orr clearly recognizes that the Holy Spirit does indwell the believer, he also posits Christ's absence, as He is in heaven at the right hand of God, but this local presence in heaven does not exhaust his presence, which, can also be said to indwell the individual believer in addition to the presence of the Holy Spirit.

[73] Douglas Moo, *The Epistle to the Romans* (Grand Rapids: Eerdmans, 1996), 491. Murray says, "'And if Christ is in you'—this variation of terms shows that the indwelling of the Spirit of God, having the Spirit of Christ, and Christ in us are all to the same effect. This does not mean, however, that there is any blurring of the distinction between Christ and the Holy Spirit. Neither does it eliminate the distinctive modes of indwelling or the distinctive operations of the respective persons of the Godhead. But it does underline the intimacy of the relationship that exists between Christ and the Holy Spirit in that union by which the believer becomes the habitation of both." (see John Murray, *The Epistle to the Romans* [Grand Rapids: Eerdmans, 1968], I.288-89).

What this means is not that Christ and the Spirit are equated or interchangeable, but that Christ and the Spirit are so closely related in communicating to believers the benefits of salvation that Paul can move from one to the other almost unconsciously. Again, it is clear that the believer who by faith has come to be joined with Christ (see Rom. 6:1-11) has not *only Christ* [emphasis added] but also the Spirit resident within. The indwelling Spirit and the indwelling Christ are distinguishable but inseparable. Moreover, the quick and unstudied movement from "Spirit of God" (v. 9a) to "Spirit of Christ" (v. 9b) to "Christ" (v. 10a) to "Spirit" (vv. 10b-11) reveals the "practical trinitarianism" that already characterizes the NT.[74]

As Thomas Schreiner notes, surely with an eye to the impending theological controversies to arise within the church, "Texts like these [Rom 8:9-10] provided the raw materials from which the church later hammered out the doctrine of the Trinity."[75]

Christ indeed dwells within believers. Commentating on this text in Paul, Haldane asserts: "if He [Christ, specifically] be *in us*, then the consequences here stated follow. Jesus Christ, in regard to His Divine nature, is everywhere present. . ."[76] This passage from Paul, therefore is further evidence that the divine nature of Christ allows him to be present beyond the confines of his locally restricted bodily presence in heaven, this time indwelling Christians.[77]

D.1.4. Galatians

In Galatians 2:20, Paul again asserts the truth that Jesus indwells believers. The famous line from this text: "Christ lives in me," is parallel to Romans 8:10. It is possible to read this passage in a strictly metaphorical way. Rather than Jesus literally dwelling in the writer, what is being said is more along the lines of "When I am obedient it is like God is living through me." This approach has strength, as the spiritualized identification with Christ's death (which is not literally true of any Christian) immediately precedes this affirmation that now, as a result of this amazing benefit of Christ's death, the individual "no longer lives" (again this is a spiritual notion), but that Christ lives in or through the person so identified with Christ.[78] If this type of reading is sustained, then this

---

[74] Moo, *Romans*, 491. Also, so argues Thomas R. Schreiner, *Romans* (Grand Rapids: Baker, 1998), 413-14.

[75] Schreiner, *Romans*, 414.

[76] Robert Haldane, *Romans* (Carlisle, PA: Banner of Truth, 1996 [1874, 9th ed.]), 341.

[77] By focusing on a related theme of the believer being "in Christ," Witherington notes the significance for this in establishing the truth of omnipresence. He states: "one of the most prevalent phrases throughout the Pauline *corpus* is ἐν Χριστῳ ("in Christ"). As Moule has pointed out, though some of this usage means no more than one is a Christian, there are numerous examples where it is actually being used to say something about the Christian's condition or religious location, and only about an *omnipresent being* [emphasis supplied] can one suggest that in some sense *that* being is the place where and the person in whom believers dwell" (Ben Witherington III, *The Many Faces of the Christ: The Christologies of the New Testament and Beyond* [New York: Crossroad, 1998], 110).

[78] Longenecker speaks of a "Christian mysticism" in regard to this text (Richard N.

text does not support the claim for Jesus' omnipresence. But is that the right reading of this passage? There is nothing in the text that demands such a reading. In fact the phrase "but Christ lives in me" makes perfect sense if taken literally. Paul is concerned to show the manifold effects of the sacrificial ministry that Jesus undertook in both his death *and* resurrection. Admittedly, Paul does not mention the resurrection per se, but the notion that as a believer, he has experienced a crucifixion with Christ, yet now has a "life to live in the flesh" certainly pushes the theme (if not the word) of resurrection to the fore of Paul's discussion. Just as Paul has a life to live in the flesh, so Christ continues to live, yet not merely for or through himself, but can now as resurrected Lord after dying for his own, indwell them literally and live through them as they yield to his presence and guidance. This can only be true, if literal, given the omnipresence of Christ.[79]

D.1.5. Ephesians

A study of Paul's prayers is a very rewarding experience. In Eph 3:14-20 there is an example of one of those prayers. Paul has spiritual matters as the driving force of his petitions for the brethren in Ephesus. One of the requests Paul voices to the Father (v. 14) is "that Christ may dwell in your hearts through faith" (3:17). In context this is seen as a parallel to the "strengthening of the inner man" by the Holy Spirit (v. 16). Despite the similarity of this language with current popular pietistic notions of how to become a Christian today, namely by "receiving Christ in the heart," Paul is not addressing evangelistic needs in this prayer. "The verb," states Lincoln, "indicates that the focus of the prayer request is not on an initial reception of Christ but on believers' experience of his constant presence."[80]

Longenecker, *Galatians* [Dallas: Word, 1990], 92-93). Still Longenecker affirms a "reality of personal communion between Christians and God," that can be characterized as both being in Christ, and as having the indwelling Spirit of God or the indwelling Christ reside in believers. This appears to treat the passage as both mystical and literal.

[79] Machen warns against reading Paul as a mystic, but affirms his presence in Christians by stating: the Christian life "involves a new life, and that new life, in its quality as well as in its source, is the life of Christ. Look at Christians, says, Paul, and you see so many manifestations of Christ." J. Gresham Machen, *Notes on Galatians*, ed. John H. Skilton (Birmingham, AL: Solid Ground, 2006), 160.

[80] Andrew T. Lincoln, *Ephesians* (Dallas, TX: Word, 1990), 206. Lincoln sees the connection between the Spirit and Christ as equivalent. He says, "Believers do not experience Christ except as Spirit and do not experience the Spirit except as Christ. The implication, as far as this prayer is concerned, is that the greater experience of the Spirit's power will mean the *character of Christ* [emphasis added] increasingly becoming the hallmark of believers' lives" (206). This seems to make a case for a "spiritualized" reading of Jesus Christ's presence. This is confirmed by noting how Lincoln addresses the meaning of the notion of *Christ in the heart*. "What is its significance" asks Lincoln, "in the writer's prayer for his readers? Its force is that the *character of Christ* [emphasis added], the pattern of the Christ-event, should increasingly dominate and shape the whole orientation of their lives" (207). That this is a valid application of the passage is not in question. That this is the *meaning* of the words: "that Christ may dwell in your hearts" is debatable. Lincoln himself appears to refer to this more so as a literal residence (quoted in the body of our text). Also, Lincoln speaks of "Christ dwelling in the

This is a carefully phrased prayer by the apostle, and its sense is derived from the particular wording. The desire for Christ's indwelling is not that of the permanent salvific entrance of Jesus Christ into a person's life at the time of conversion, but a more dynamic and continual presence that is conditioned on abiding faith. "The progressive character of Christ's indwelling," asserts Wood, "is apparent from the intransitive use of the verb κατοικῆσαι in the present continuous tense. It is as the Christian keeps on trusting ("through faith") that Christ continues to indwell."[81] This is reminiscent of our discussion of God's various kinds of "presence." Here Paul speaks of a "presence" of Christ which is similar to God's moral presence with believers. The dynamic character, however, speaks of a level of degrees of this presence. The abiding Christ in person, mediates all the fullness of God (Ephesians 3:19b) to those who unswervingly believe. This can only be true if Jesus Christ can be present beyond the limited bodily presence. This passage in Paul, although a prayer, shows his belief in the omnipresence of Jesus Christ.

D.1.6. Colossians

One of the most important passages for establishing the identity of Jesus Christ is found in Colossians 1:15-21. Here, Paul asserts in the strongest language, Jesus' unqualified status as God. I believe that the traditional doctrine of the two natures finds biblical support in this passage.[82] Christ is spoken of in exalted terms. He is the "Firstborn over all creation" (1:15b). This speaks of his rank over the created order.[83] In as much as he is exalted over the universe, Jesus is

---

heart" as a "reality for them" (207). The ambiguity in this section stems from Lincoln's close alignment of the Holy Spirit and Christ without allowing a distinction (as Douglas Moo did in his discussion of Rom 8:10). This forces Lincoln to speak of Christ's *character* as the defining element of the Spirit's influence in the lives of Christians. George Stoeckhardt is surely correct as he notes of this verse, "Not only the graces and virtues of Christ dwell in the Christians, but *Christ Himself* [emphasis added], the exalted God-Man, dwells personally and truly in the hearts of believers, even as Paul testifies Gal. 2:20: 'Christ lives in me.' That is the blessed, wonderful *unio mystica*. He in us and we in Him" (George Stoeckhardt, *Ephesians*, trans. Martin S. Sommer [St. Louis, MO: Concordia, 1952], 169).

[81] A. Skevington Wood, *Ephesians* (Grand Rapids: Zondervan, 1978), 51.

[82] The language of Paul unites both natures in the single person as he says of Jesus that "He is the image of the invisible God, the Firstborn over all creation." The first part of this designation has to do with Jesus' human nature: as man Jesus is the *imago dei par excellance*. On this specific point, see Charles Lee Feinberg, "The Image of God," *BSac* 129 [1972]: 236-47, esp. 244-47. His deity is affirmed in the latter expression, as "Firstborn over creation," which denotes his rank over the created order as Creator.

[83] Bartels, speaking of the Greek term πρωτοτοκος, says, "As a title for the mediator of creation, it is used in Col. 1:15, as is demonstrated by parallel sayings in v. 16, 'in him all things were created . . . all things were created through him and for him,' and v. 17, 'He is before all things, and in him all things hold together.' Both supporters and opponents of the suggestion that πρωτοτοκοας in Col. 1 echoes Hel[lenistic] mythical ideas agree that the statement is a confession of the supreme rank of the pre-existent Christ as the mediator in the creation of all things" (Colin Brown, ed., *The New International Dictionary of New Testament Theology* [Grand Rapids: Zondervan, 1986], s.v. "πρωτοτοκος," by K.H. Bartels). Also see the helpful article S. Herbert Bess, "The Term

God. This is confirmed as Paul continues in the next verse to show Christ as Creator: "For by Him all things were created that are in heaven and that are on earth. . . . All things were created through Him and for Him" (1:16). This language is similar to John's gospel, which is another classic passage linking Christ's status as God with his role of Creator (cf. John 1:1-3).

It is a particular expression that Paul uses in Colossians 1:17, that emerges in this context as a support for our thesis. In Greek it reads: και αυτος εστι προ παντων και τα παντα εν αυτω συνεστηκε. It is this latter part of the verse which is significant. All of the created order is held together *in* or *by* Christ.[84] "Not only is the universe created in him and by him," posits Lohse, "but it is also established permanently in him alone."[85] What is highlighted by Paul here is the transcendence of Christ. He is the principle of cohesion for the entire cosmos. This sustaining work can only be undertaken directly by Christ, given he is absolutely beyond the created realm–including his own physical body. It is no wonder that patristic writers, who commented on the incarnation of Christ, also maintained that Jesus continued to rule the world as its governing and guiding principle. The Logos was made flesh, but in such a way that he still fills all creation, and transcends it, so that in Christ "all things hold together." This lends further support to the doctrinal affirmation for Jesus' omnipresence. For without this attribute, a merely localized Jesus Christ could not accomplish such a role reserved for deity alone.

Another passage in Colossians must be addressed. In 1:24-29, Paul discusses his own specific role in the ongoing drama of God's covenant program as it involves bringing the light to the Gentiles. Paul speaks of the "mystery which has been hidden from the ages . . . but has now been revealed to His saints" (1:26). Next Paul explains that "God willed to make known what are the riches of the glory of this mystery among the Gentiles" (1:27a). Here, specifically, Paul adds the content of this mystery in no uncertain terms; it is: "Christ in you, the hope of Glory" (1:27b). Paul speaks of the Gentile portion of the Church as recipients of this newly-revealed knowledge. The Gentiles as a corporate entity have Christ in them. This is no doubt a great assurance as Paul is using the Jewish title of Messiah at this point. What had been (incorrectly) thought by Jews, that Messiah was exclusively for them, Paul counters by stressing the presence of the Christ within Gentiles as co-blessed along with believing Jews. There is a mixed covenant community.

Of course, the passage may be applied at the individual level, so as to encourage the particular Christian within the congregation, yet Paul is speaking of the Gentiles as a corporate entity. "Christ in you" requires, yet again, the possibility of Jesus Christ exceeding the confines of his local heavenly presence, so

---

'Son of God' in Light of Old Testament Idiom," *GJ* 6 (1965): 17-24.

[84] Murray J. Harris says: "As in v. 16d, τα παντα refers to 'the universe' . . . 'the sum of things.' As in v. 16a, εν αυτω is locat. ('in Him') rather than instr. ('by Him')" (Murray J. Harris, *Colossians and Philemon* [Grand Rapids: Eerdmans, 1991], 47). Harris also says, "What Christ has created he maintains in permanent order, stability, and productivity. He is the source of unity (sun-, together) and cohesiveness or solidarity (συνιστημι, cohere) of the whole universe" (Harris, *Colossians*, 47).

[85] Lohse, *Colossians and Philemon*, 52.

as to be "in" the Gentiles. As O'Brien claims, "Christ . . . was 'in them' not simply 'among them, . . . the verb ἐστιν points to Christ's indwelling them as Gentile believers."[86] This suggests that omnipresence is a non-negotiable attribute of Jesus, so that God may bring about the blessings associated with the Old Testament covenants that were forward looking to include the Gentiles in days ahead.

D.1.7. Hebrews

In chapter 1 of this book, the author presents a high Christology,[87] which is similar to that found in Paul and John.[88] Jesus Christ is spoken of as the "Son" by whom God has spoken to the church in these latter days (Heb 1:1-2). Moreover, this Son has been appointed as the heir of the coming age. Clearly, in Hebrews in these introductory verses, Jesus' role as communicating God's will for humanity supersedes eminently any and all previous revelations.[89] There is a sort of tension involved in unraveling the nature of the person described as the Son. Murray Harris refers to this as a "divine-human paradox."[90] This is so because both natures of the Son, the divine and the human nature, are spoken of by the author of this epistle. It is as a man that Christ is the heir. Yet, this same one is described in grandiose terms in Hebrews 1:3, and in 1:8-9, which reveal the Son to be God. We will examine the latter reference first, and then conclude this section by analyzing verse 3, as it offers further evidence for Jesus Christ's omnipresence. In these verses (1:8-9), we find elements for both a high Christology and also an element of distinction between persons in the Godhead, which is helpful for theology proper. What is the nature of the expression: "But about the Son, [He, God the Father, says]: 'Your throne, O God, is forever and

---

[86] Peter T. O'Brien, *Colossians, Philemon* (Dallas: Word, 1982), 87.

[87] Harris has captured this very well, for the entire book, in his survey of the epistle. "That he [the author of Hebrews] believes in the full deity of Jesus," states Harris, "is clear: Jesus is described as the perfect representation of God's glory and nature (1:3); he not only existed before he appeared on earth (10:5), before Melchizedek (7:3), before human history began (1:2), or before the universe was created (1:10), but he also existed and exists eternally (7:16; 9:14; 13:8); like his Father he may be called 'Lord;' he is creator (1:10), sustainer (1:3), and heir (1:2) of the universe, that is, everything in time and space (τοὺς αἰῶνας, 1:2); he is 'Son' (υἱός) and 'the Son of God' (ὁ υἱὸς τοῦ θεοῦ), the timeless ὤν of 1:3 pointing to a natural, not adoptive, sonship; he is worshiped by angels (1:6) and is the object of human faith (12:2); he is sovereign over the world to come (2:5); and passages referring to Yahweh in the OT are applied to him" (Harris, *Jesus as God*, 225).

[88] Helpful for assessing the Christology of this epistle is Mark Saucy, "Exaltation Christology in Hebrews: What Kind of Reign?," *TrinJ* 14 (1993): 42-63; and Daniel J. Ebert IV, "The Chiastic Structure of the Prologue To Hebrews," *TrinJ* 13 (1992): 163-79, esp. 170-79.

[89] "The consummation of the revelatory process, the definitive revelation," notes Morris, "took place when he who was not one of 'the goodly company of the prophets' but the very Son of God came" (Leon Morris, *Hebrews* [Grand Rapids: Zondervan, 1981], 13). Also see Donald Guthrie, *Hebrews* (Grand Rapids: Eerdmans, 1983; reprint, 1993), 62-63.

[90] Harris, *Jesus as God*, 225.

ever, and the scepter of Your kingdom is a scepter of Justice. You have loved righteousness and hated lawlessness; that is why God, your God, has anointed You, rather than Your companions, with the oil of joy" (HCSB)? This is a word of comparison. The writer expresses the superiority of the Son to the angels, and by extension to all the fathers who received God's revelation in times past. The words are quoted from Psalm 44:6-7 (LXX), (45:6-7 [Masoretic text]). In the Old Testament, the words addressing the Jewish King were certainly spoken of in a typological fashion. "The appellation ὁ θεός that was figurative and hyperbolic when applied to a mortal king," states Harris, "was applied to the immortal Son in a literal and true sense."[91] Harris adds this important observation: "Jesus is not merely superior to the angels. Equally with the Father he shares in the divine nature, ὁ θεός v. 8) while remaining distinct from him (ὁ θεος σου, v. 9)."[92] There is an "essential" unity between Father and Son, as well as a "functional" subordination of the Son to the Father. The unity is because Christ is truly God, the subordination because he is also truly man. As Tsoukalas affirms: "The writer of Hebrews applies the Psalm's confession to Jesus, the Son of God, and thus testifies to the incarnate deity of the Son of God."[93]

In the formative verses (1:1-3) of this epistle, we have an amazing description of the nature of the Son, "through whom also He [the Father] made the world" (1:2b, NASB). The author continues: "And He [the Son] is the radiance of His [the Father's] glory and the exact representation of His [the Father's] nature, and upholds all things by the word of His [the Son's] power" (1:3a-b, NASB). These terms, employed by the writer, have generated much discussion. Jesus is said to be ὃς ὤν ἀπαυγασμα τῆς δοξης και χαρακτηρ τῆς ὑποστασεως αὐτου. First it should be noted that "the relative ὃς finds its antecedent in υἱω."[94] This passage definitively describes the Son. Second, the expression: ἀπαυγασμα τῆς δοξης is correctly translated by the NASB as "the radiance [active sense] of His glory."[95] As Morris notes, "we see the glory of God in Jesus, and we see it as it really is."[96] It is important not to confuse the "radiance" or effulgence with the glory. Dods's note is helpful. "The ὑποστασις," suggests Dods, "is the na-

---

[91] Harris, *Jesus as God*, 227. See, also, Paul Ellingworth, *Commentary on Hebrews* (Grand Rapids: Eerdmans, 1993), 122-25. "This [1:8] and the following quotation (vv. 10-12)," notes Ellingworth, "are used to show that the Son is addressed in scripture both as God and Lord . . . . V.8a expresses briefly the eternity of the Son, a theme developed in vv. 10-12. The point of v. 8b, for the author of Hebrews, seems to be that the Son exercises royal power, whereas the angels are mere λειτουργοι, (v. 7)" (122).

[92] Harris, *Jesus as God*, 227.

[93] Steven Tsoukalas, *Knowing Christ in the Challenge of Heresy: A Christology of the Cults a Christology of the Bible* (Lanham, MD: University Press of America, 1999), 131.

[94] Marcus Dods, *The Epistle to the Hebrews* (reprint, Grand Rapids: Eerdmans, 1990), 250. Dods notes of this section: "The two clauses, ὤν . . . φερων τε, are closely bound together and seem intended to convey the impression that during Christ's redemptive activity on earth there was no kenosis, but that the Divine attributes lent efficacy to His whole work" (250).

[95] See Colin Brown, ed., *NIDNTT*, s.v. "ἀπαυγασμα," by Ralph P. Martin, who notes the definitive character of Christ's revelation of God.

[96] Morris, *Hebrews*, 14.

ture, the δοξα its quality, [and] the απαυγασμα its manifestation."[97] Based on this insight, one does well to note the specific biblical meaning of the term *hypostasis*. The word "ὑποστασεως [is] rendered 'person' in [the] A[uthorised] V[ersion]; [and] 'substance,' the strict etymological equivalent, in [the] R[evised V[ersion]]," states Dods.[98] "To the English ear, perhaps," Dods posits, "'nature' or 'essence' better conveys the meaning. It has not the strict meaning it afterwards acquired in Christian theology, but denotes all that from which the glory springs and with which it is identical."[99] So Christ is said to be the *character* of God's nature or essence. In the NIV, the translation: "the exact representation of his being," well captures the notion of χαρακτηρ τῆς ὑποστασεως αὐτοῦ. The word χαρακτηρ is a *hapax legomenon* in the New Testament.[100] Gess states:

> The context of Heb[rews] 1 makes it clear that the writer's purpose was to stress the glory of the Son who had entered history and the uniqueness of the revelation of God in the unique One.... The Son who controls the beginning and the end (v. 2) stands in unique relationship (a) to God whose effulgence (απαυγασμα) and stamp (χαρακτηρ) he is; (b) to the universe which he upholds; and (c) to the church he has purified from sins.[101]

Our observations on Hebrews will now conclude by noting the "sustaining" nature of Christ's work as expressed by this author. Christ is the Creator. He also "carries the creation along," so to speak. The Greek term "φερων," notes Morris, "has a meaning like 'carrying along'.... The concept is dynamic, not static."[102] Tsoukalas also suggests that the creation is actively sustained by Jesus.[103] Excellent comments on the meaning of this idea are found in Marcus Dods. "The present [tense of] φερων," declares Dods, "seems necessarily to involve that during the whole of His earthly career, this function of upholding nature [the universe] was being discharged."[104] Again, this type of assertion makes little sense if the work it describes is not undertaken by an omnipotent and omnipresent Jesus. What is significant is that in reality, what the author of Hebrews actually asserts is anachronistic in that it is the Son who has spoken, even in the Incarnation, who is at the same time the Creator and sustainer of all. The incarnate Jesus, according to this letter, must be omnipresent for such a task.

D.1.8. Revelation

One final passage will be cited to sustain the claim of the central thesis concerning Jesus' omnipresence. In John's vision of the resurrected and glorious

---

[97] Dods, *Epistle to the Hebrews*, 251.
[98] Dods, *Epistle to the Hebrews*, 251.
[99] Dods, *Epistle to the Hebrews*, 251. Also, see Brown, ed., *NIDNTT*, s.v., "ὑποστασις," by Günther Harder.
[100] See Brown, ed., *NIDNTT*, s.v., "χαρακτῆρ," by Johannes Gess.
[101] "χαρακτῆρ," by Johannes Gess.
[102] Morris, *Hebrews*, 14.
[103] Tsoukalas, *Knowing Christ*, 131.
[104] Dods, *Epistle to the Hebrews*, 252.

Chapter 7: Biblical and Theological Evidence for Jesus Christ's Omnipresence

Christ, there is a marked emphasis on Jesus as sovereign and almighty. Indeed, it is this vision of Christ, and the total Christology of the Apocalypse that lends credence to the "Christos Pantocrator" theme explicated in the early centuries of the church age.[105] In John's vision, he notices the Jesus is "in the middle of the lampstands [as] one like a Son of man" (Rev 1:13) and "holding in his right hand seven stars" (Rev 1:16). These seven golden lampstands (Rev 1:12) are explained to be the seven churches to whom Jesus Christ sends his message through John (Rev 1:19-20). The number seven is a figurative number and entails the concept of totality, so the message of Christ to these seven local congregations is a word to the entire church for the entire church age.[106] What is significant for our purposes, is to notice that as the first message unfolds, that Jesus is described as "the One who walks among the seven golden lampstands [churches]" (Rev 2:1). Christ is seen as present among *all* the churches. This is not to be thought of as Jesus physically taking a stroll through the local assemblies. On the contrary, Christ, despite his localized presence in heaven (Rev 4-5) is still present among his own. In his comments on Revelation 2:1 Ladd states, "The words also indicate the constant vigilance and *watchful presence* [emphasis supplied] of Christ not only over Ephesus but over all the churches."[107] This is possible, as stated before, only if Jesus Christ is omnipresent.[108]

D.2. Theological Evidence for Jesus Christ's Omnipresence

In order to establish the thesis of Jesus Christ's omnipresence even in the incarnate state one must begin by asserting the true deity of Jesus Christ. For Christ to be understood as fully God, he must share all the divine attributes. Of course, it is not necessary to rehearse the oft-cited and well-known arguments for Jesus' deity in their totality, merely what is helpful for our main point.[109]

---

[105] See Theodore Stylianopoulos, "A Christological Reflection," in *Jesus Christ – The Life of the World: An Orthodox Contribution to the Vancouver Theme*, ed. Ion Bria (Geneva: World Council of Churches, 1982), 29-55.

[106] This is based on a "historical reading" of the text. See Robert L. Thomas, "Excursus 1: The Chronological Interpretation of Revelation 2-3," in *Revelation 1-7: An Exegetical Commentary* (Chicago: Moody, 1992), 505-15.

[107] George Eldon Ladd, *A Commentary on the Revelation of John* (Grand Rapids: Eerdmans, 1972; reprint, 1993), 38. Similarly, Boxall claims, "the presence of Christ with his people may be experienced either as salvation or as judgement." See Ian Boxall, *The Revelation of Saint John* (Peabody, MA: Hendrickson, 2006), 48.

[108] Fuller also sees the significance of Rev 2-3 for this issue. See George C. Fuller, "The Life of Jesus After the Ascension (Luke 24:50-53; Acts 1:9-11)," *WTJ* 56 (1994): 391-98, esp. 397.

[109] For classic evangelical treatments of Christ's deity see G.C. Berkouwer, *Studies in Dogmatics: The Person of Christ*, trans. John Vriend (Grand Rapids: Eerdmans, 1955), 155-92; Robert L. Reymond, *A New Systematic Theology of the Christian Faith* (Nashville: Thomas Nelson, 1998), 205-316; and Benjamin B. Warfield, *The Lord of Glory: A Classic Defense of the Deity of Jesus Christ* (Vestavia Hils, AL: Solid Ground, 2003).

D.2.1. Jesus as God: Divine Attributes

One of the main arguments for Jesus' deity is the fact that he possesses or shares in divine attributes.[110] This approach is standard fare in evangelical theology.[111] For example, Grudem's treatment of the deity of Christ contains a section which shows Jesus "Possessed Attributes of Deity." Interestingly enough, in this discussion, Grudem says something specifically about omnipresence. "The divine attribute of *omnipresence* is not directly affirmed to be true of Jesus during his earthly ministry."[112] "However," Grudem claims, "while looking forward to the time that the church would be established, Jesus could say, 'Where two or three are gathered in my name, *there am I* in the midst of them' (Matt. 18:20)."[113] In a similar argument, Reymond says the same thing quoting the same texts as Grudem but adds this insight: "Not only was Jesus invoking the language of the Immanuel title but he was also claiming that he is himself personally always with his own, not just in the power and presence of his Holy Spirit but present himself as the omnipresent savior."[114]

If Jesus' deity is dependent on him sharing equally in all divine attributes, then Jesus must be omnipresent. Otherwise to cast doubt on his omnipresence is to jeopardize his true deity. Of course, some form of kenosis may allow one to argue that omnipresence, along with other relative attributes, is not exercised, yet most evangelicals affirm the possession of these as otherwise Jesus must be less than God. Hence Murray Harris follows suit and argues for Jesus deity, among other ways, by stating: "Divine Status [is] claimed by or accorded to Jesus, [and that Jesus is the] Possessor of Divine attributes (John 1:4; 10:30; 21:17; Eph. 4:10; Col. 1:19; 2:9)."[115] He specifically argues that "Christ shares the divine nature (Phil. 2:6) and attributes (Eph. 4:10; Col. 1:19; 2:9)."[116] By

---

[110] In their excellent work, Bowman & Komoszewski affirm Jesus' deity throughout the book utilizing the acronym, H.A.N.D.S. To prove Jesus is God they show that Jesus shares in the *H*onors, *A*ttributes, *N*ames, *D*eeds, and *S*eat of God. This book in my opinion settles the question in a superlative manner. See Robert M. Bowman & J. Ed. Komoszewski, *Putting Jesus in His Place: The Case for the Deity of Christ* (Grand Rapids: Kregel, 2007). They discuss the divine attributes on pages 73-123. That Jesus has the attribute of omnipresence is ably presented on pages 115-18.

[111] See J. Oliver Buswell, *A Systematic Theology of the Christian Religion* (Grand Rapids: Zondervan, 1962), 2:69; John F. Walvoord, *Jesus Christ Our Lord* (Chicago: Moody, 1969), 22-32; Paul Enns, *The Moody Handbook of Theology* (Chicago: Moody, 1989), 224-27; Charles C. Ryrie, *Basic Theology* (Wheaton, IL: Victor, 1986), 247-49; and Robert L. Reymond, *Jesus Divine Messiah: The New and Old Testament Witness* (Fearn: Christian Focus, 2003), 271-74.

[112] Grudem, *Systematic Theology*, 548.

[113] Grudem, *Systematic Theology*, 548.

[114] Robert L. Reymond, *A New Systematic Theology of the Christian Faith* (Nashville: Thomas Nelson, 1998), 234. This is a corrective insight to suggestions, like James White's noted earlier, that Jesus is present [only] "by the Holy Spirit."

[115] Murray J. Harris, *Jesus as God: The New Testament Use of* Theos *in Reference to Jesus* (Grand Rapids: Baker, 1992), 316.

[116] Harris, *Jesus as God*, 168.

Chapter 7: Biblical and Theological Evidence for Jesus Christ's Omnipresence

referencing Ephesians 4:10, Harris is specifically affirming Jesus' omnipresence.[117]

As a comparison is made with the attributes of deity ascribed to God the Father in the Bible, some interesting truths come to the fore concerning the person of God the Son incarnate. These attributes include the so-called relative attributes, as indicated above.[118] Moreover, as the Father is eternal (Ps 90), so is Christ (John 1:1-2; Rev 1:8, 17). God is immutable (Ps 102:12-28; Mal 3:6), and the same is said to be true of Jesus (Heb 13:8). God is Holy (Exod 15:11-13; Ps 99; Rev 15:4), and Jesus is too (Luke 1:35; 4:34; Acts 2:27; 3:14). These attributes show Christ to be God.

There are references in the Bible that speak of Jesus as God. For example, Titus 2:13 is a familiar text that refers to Jesus as "our great God and savior."[119] Also Romans 9:5 declares that "from them [the forefathers], by physical descent, came the Messiah, who is God over all, blessed forever."[120] In 2 Peter 1:1 the writer declares that the Christians had obtained a faith "through the righteousness of our God and Savior Jesus Christ." These particular texts prompted Macleod to say of them, that they are "explicit assertions of deity."[121]

---

[117] Harris makes this point more specifically in his more accessible work. See Murray J. Harris, *3 Crucial Questions about Jesus: Did Jesus Exist? Did Jesus Rise from the Dead? Is Jesus God?* (Grand Rapids: Baker, 1994), 67.

[118] Christ exhibits omniscience in passages that show his superhuman knowledge. See Mark 2:8, where the knowledge is immediate and not mediated; and John 2:25, again where it specifically states that Christ did not need anyone to testify about the condition of man, as he intrinsically knew what is in man. Furthermore, as Walvoord declares, "In keeping with His omniscience He [Jesus] is declared to have the wisdom of God (I Cor. 1:30)" (Walvoord, *Jesus Christ Our Lord*, 29). Walvoord also cites Acts 1:24; John 6:64; John 13:1, 11; 18:4; and 19:28 in support of Jesus' all encompassing knowledge. For a summary of Christ as omnipotent, Walvoord's words suffice admirably: "The evidence for the omnipotence of Christ is as decisive as proof for other attributes. Sometimes it takes the form of physical power, but more often it refers to authority over creation. Christ has power to forgive sins (Matt. 9:6), all power in heaven and in earth (Matt. 28:18), power over nature (Luke 8:25), power over His own Life (John 10:18), power to give eternal life to others (John 17:2), power to heal physically, as witnessed by His many miracles, as well as power to cast out demons (Mark 1:29-34), and power to transform the body (Phil. 3:21)" (29).

[119] After his thorough study of this text, Harris states, "It seems highly probable that in Titus 2:13 Jesus Christ is called 'our great God and Savior' " (Harris, *Jesus as God*, 185). Also, see Reymond, *Jesus Divine Messiah*, 471-73.

[120] Harris favors the reading of Romans 9:5 as speaking of Christ as God. See Harris, *Jesus as God*, 170-71, for his summary conclusions. Also helpful on this text is Bruce M. Metzger, "The Punctuation of Rom. 9:5," in *Christ and Spirit in the New Testament: Studies in Honour of C.F.D. Moule*, ed. Barnabas Lindars and Stephen S. Smalley (Cambridge: Cambridge University Press, 1973), 95-112. For an alternate reading which maintains that the doxology is speaking of Israel's God [the Father], as a clause standing independently, see James D.G. Dunn, *Romans 9-16* (Dallas: Word, 1988), 528-29.

[121] Donald Macleod, *The Person of Christ* (Downers Grove, IL: InterVarsity, 1998), 248.

The Omnipresence of Jesus Christ

In today's climate of liberal scholarship, academic theology no doubt threatens the faith of many believing Christians, particularly as it relates to the deity of Christ.[122] B.B. Warfield's words from another generation have remained true to our own day. "One of the most portentous symptoms of the decay of vital sympathy with historical Christianity which is observable in present-day academic circles," claims Warfield, "is the widespread tendency in recent Christological discussion to revolt from the doctrine of the Two Natures in the Person of Christ."[123]

Evangelicals, however, rightly insist that the biblical testimony categorically affirms the genuine deity of Jesus because he shares in the divine attributes. "There is unusual significance to most of the divine attributes," notes Walvoord, "Their individual character is such that if it be proved that Christ possessed certain divine attributes it necessarily follows that he possessed *all* divine attributes (emphasis added)."[124] Walvoord lists several designations of the preincarnate Jesus.[125] In the Old Testament Christ is said to be: *Jehovah* (Zech 12:10, cf. Rev 1:7; Jer 23:5-6, cf. 1 Cor 1:30; Isa 6:5, cf. John 12:41); *Elohim* (Isa 40:3, cf. Luke 3:4; Isa 9:6-7, cf. Rom 15:6; Eph 1:3; 5:5, 20; and 2 Pet 1:1); and *Logos* (Gen 1:3 [concept]; Ps 33:6 [LXX], cf. John 1:1-3, 14). Moreover, Jesus is predominantly spoken of in the New Testament as the Son. This idea also goes back to the Old Testament. In Proverbs, the wise Agur asked about the name of God and the name of God's Son (Prov 30:4). In Daniel's prophecy, the famous vision of the heavenly Son of Man (Dan 7:13) is most likely the background for Jesus Christ's favorite self-designation. This Danielic figure receives the kingdom, and therefore is the recipient of world-wide wor-

---

[122] I realize how subtle this may be. It dawned on me as I read Marcus J. Borg's chapter on "Jesus and God" in Marcus J. Borg and N.T. Wright, *The Meaning of Jesus: Two Visions* (San Francisco: HarperCollins, 1999), 145-56. Borg, although he denies that Jesus spoke of himself using the exalted "I am" statements of John's gospel, nonetheless is willing to use terminology as "incarnation," "Son of God," "Jesus is the image of God," "the embodiment and incarnation of God," etc., but sees these designations as culturally conditioned and not literally true. According to Borg, these are all metaphorical ways of expressing Jesus as a man in like kind to all other men, save that his openness to God was greater. Even the great creeds are accepted by Borg as he notes: "I can say the creed without misgivings." However, he adds, "I do not see it as a set of literally true doctrinal statements to which I am supposed to give my intellectual assent" (155). This begs the question of what the drafters themselves meant by the language they employed. To his credit, Borg does make a significant claim in this chapter that is refreshing, in my opinion, given Borg's status as a mainline scholar. He believes that the exalted language found in our present New Testament is not merely the result of the post-Easter faith of the disciples but "the high estimate of him expressed by these metaphors [as cited above] also flows out what his followers experienced in the pre-Easter Jesus" (148). Nonetheless, this is not finally, an acceptable "picture" of Jesus Christ as presented by Borg.

[123] Benjamin Breckinridge Warfield, *The Person and Work of Christ* (Phillipsburg, NJ: P & R, 1950), 211.

[124] John F. Walvoord, "Series in Christology–Part 2: The Preincarnate Son of God," *BSac* 104 (1944): 155-56.

[125] Walvoord, "Series in Christology–Part 2," 158-68.

Chapter 7: Biblical and Theological Evidence for Jesus Christ's Omnipresence

ship. This is fulfilled in Christ as we see the adoration given to the Redeemer in Revelation 4-5. It is safe to assert that Jesus Christ is God manifest in the flesh, and that in the flesh, he manifests all the divine attributes (Col 2:9).

D.2.2. Jesus as God: Two Natures

That Jesus Christ is God is a basic axiom of any evangelical Christology. As stated at the outset of this work, the real issue with regards to Jesus Christ is the way of conceiving the incarnation in terms of "how." Historically, the church spent much time and energy in the midst of fierce theological debate to finally arrive at a doctrinal statement that carefully interprets the biblical witness. According to Gerald Bray, the Chalcedonian definition of faith is really an interpretation of John 1:14.[126] The definition of Chalcedon did not receive absolute universal recognition, but it did satisfy a large portion of the church, and it has, as a statement of faith about the incarnation, stood the test of time. The truth that emerges then from the teaching of the New Testament is that Jesus Christ is one person in two natures.[127]

A most helpful treatment of these issues is provided by Bray.[128] Most significant is the understanding of what Christians were attempting during the formative eras of Christian thinking about how Jesus could be thought of as God. "Christianity acted as a transforming agent on the philosophical vocabulary," notes Bray, "altering the context in which words were employed and thereby giving them new meanings."[129] This is imperative to highlight so as to ward off suggestions that the "pure" teaching of the New Testament was "Hellenized" by the later Fathers of the church.[130] Bray shows that the terms: "being" and "nature" originally had conceptual distinctions. "Being = what a thing is; Na-

---

[126] See Gerald Bray, *Steps of Understanding: Key Events in Jesus' Life* (Fearn: Christian Focus, 1998), 27.

[127] A most extensive treatment of Christology by Medieval theologians is found in the very challenging book by Richard Cross, *The Metaphysics of the Incarnation: Thomas Aquinas to Duns Scotus* (Oxford: Oxford University Press, 2002). Also, see Eleanor Stump, "Aquinas' Metaphysics of the Incarnation," in *The Incarnation*, 197-218. These works have bolstered my contention that Christology is the most important doctrine to deal with, as well as shown me that it is the doctrine most likely to be misrepresented, even by those who profess love for Jesus Christ.

[128] Gerald Bray, *Creeds, Councils and Christ: Did the Early Christians Misrepresent Jesus?* (Fearn: Christian Focus, 1997), 144-71.

[129] Bray, *Creeds, Councils and Christ*, 145.

[130] It is probably more correct to speak of a "Christianization of pagan philosophy" rather than a "Paganizing (Philosophizing) of Christian teaching." Given the absolute duality inherent in the contemporary intellectual climate, the framers of Nicaea and Chalcedon would never had affirmed that a "Purely Spiritual" entity such as the "One," or God, could ever become Incarnate, had they been "won over," so to speak, by Hellenistic presuppositions about the nature of reality, including God. The Gnostic threat to Christianity was evidently a valiant attempt to maintain the absolute distinction of matter and spirit, so as not to implicate deity in any contact with material of any sort. Gnosticism, and not Classical Orthodoxy, was the real ideology, in all its forms, which truly succumbed to the lure of refined philosophy, and thereby became in its theological assertions deviant from biblical Christianity.

ture = what a thing is *like*," says Bray.[131] But by the time the theologians were discussing the Trinity and incarnation, these terms became virtually synonymous. "Christians who have asked this question [relation of 'person' to 'nature'] have always felt it necessary to distinguish *person* from *nature* in God," Bray claims. Yet, an important observation must be made. Bray continues,

> Moreover, God is not one person, but three. Each person possesses in himself an objective reality which puts him on par with the One Being of God. This belief became the most important issue in fourth and fifth century theological debates, and during the course of them the subtleties which had distinguished *nature* from *being* practically disappeared. To say the three persons shared one being meant the same thing as saying they had one nature.[132]

"The technical terms used by the Councils of the Church in her definitions," notes Ferrier, "provide theologians with a universal language that is sufficiently clear and precise to help them avoid equivocation in interpreting the truths taught by Scripture and Tradition."[133] A look at some of these terms and their use in the doctrine of the hypostatic union is essential to a correct understanding of the incarnation, and hence the fact that Jesus is one person in two natures. A look at "nature" and "person" will help further the discussion. Following this a look at the concept of the unity of person, and the mode or manner of union will round off this section.

Chalcedon clearly distinguished between "person" and "nature" in its definition. What does "person" mean? In today's world, which basically affirms an evolutionary perspective of reality, "person" has significant psychological overtones and means more than was intended by the framers of Christian dogmatic confession. The issue was squarely addressed in our own day in 1998 at a European Society for the Study of Science and Theology (ESSAT) meeting held in Durham, UK.[134] Although the book, which grew out of this conference, is

---

[131] Bray, *Creeds, Councils and Christ*, 146.

[132] Bray, *Creeds, Councils and Christ*, 146.

[133] Francis Ferrier, *What is the Incarnation?* trans. Edward Sillem (New York: Hawthorn, 1962), 24:77.

[134] The result of this conference was the following volume: Niels Henrik Gregersen, Willem B. Drees, and Ulf Görman, eds., *The Human Person in Science and Theology* (Grand Rapids: Eerdmans, 2000). A basic concern in this text is to chart a mediating course between extremes of physicalist reductionism and on the other hand computational functionalism. In attempting this goal the broad direction is that of establishing a bio-cultural paradigm which respects the individualist tradition yet grants the significant contributions of the relational understanding of personhood. Also helpful are Reinhold Niebuhr, *The Nature and Destiny of Man: A Christian Interpretation* (New York: Charles Scribners Sons, 1941); Leslie Stevenson, *Seven Theories of Human Nature* (New York: Oxford University Press, 1987 [1974]); William H. Baker, *In the Image of God: A Biblical View of Humanity* (Chicago: Moody, 1991); Patrick Grant, *Spiritual Discourse and the Meaning of Persons* (New York: St. Martin's, 1994); Kevin J. Corcoran, *Rethinking Human Nature: A Christian Materialist Alternative to the Soul* (Grand Rapids: Baker Academic, 2006); Joseph Torchia, *Exploring Personhood: An Introduction to the Philosophy of Human Nature* (Lanham, MD: Rowman & Littlefield, 2007); and J.P. Moreland, *The Recalcitrant Imago Dei: Human Persons and the Failure of*

stimulating reading, there is a bias as "[a]ll authors grant a general naturalist perspective."[135] Hence even the theologians who contribute in this particular volume are assuming much that will not satisfy evangelicals. Yet a healthy warning is issued forth in the introduction of this book in the following words: "the very attempt to derive a theological understanding of the *human* person from the doctrine of the Trinity," notes Gregersen, "appears to go far beyond the intention of the Nicene Creed."[136] We must still strive, however, to understand what was meant in the creeds concerning Jesus Christ.

Rowan Williams has provided an extremely helpful article on the question of person.[137] Citing Anthony Hanson's disapproval of "orthodox" Christology which in Hanson's view, does not accept the human personality of Jesus, Williams tackles this matter admirably. Of course, Hanson is reacting to the anhypostatic and enhypostatic notions of the incarnation, in which the person of the Son of God assumes an inpersonal human nature.[138] At this point Williams perceptively counters the very challenge of Hanson, by indicating a serious assumption embedded in this reaction to orthodox Christology. "Now one curious point in all this," remarks Williams, "is the assumption that *hypostatsis* [person] means (or includes in its meaning) 'personality', the assumption, that is, that it is a psychological category."[139] Williams adds that historically this is not so. Surprisingly, even Hanson agrees that it is not so, "and yet," says Williams, "the argument proceeds by taking it for granted that it *is* so."[140] Here emerges, according to Williams, the dire need of definition. After surveying some historical discussion, especially John of Damascus, Williams concludes that "we are dealing with an ontological concept, *not* an exclusively anthropological one."[141] Next, Williams cites a careful distinction made by Thomas Aquinas "between the idea that the Word 'assumes' a man, and the idea that the Word, by assuming human nature, as it were, 'constitutes' a man (*terminus assumptionis*, 'the end product of the act of taking–on')."[142] Hence Williams

---

Naturalism (London: SCM, 2009).

[135] Ibid., 8.

[136] Ibid., 12.

[137] See Rowan Williams, excellent discussion in "'Person' and 'Personality' in Christology," *Drev* 94 (1976): 253-60. Also see Anthony Tyrrell Hanson, *Grace and Truth: A Study in the Doctrine of the Incarnation* (London: SPCK, 1975). It is this text that Williams engages.

[138] This, again, is a common assault on classic Christology. Much misunderstanding abounds on this matter. "Following a long tradition in the church," Donald Bloesch asserts, "I affirm both the *anhypostasia* (impersonal humanity) and *enhypostasia* (personality in God). Jesus has no independent human personality: he has his personality in God. These terms as originally used do not mean that Christ's human nature lacks personality (as we understand it today). Instead, it has no independent existence or being. . . . Jesus is not autonomous or self-existent. God is the acting subject in Jesus" (*Jesus*, 56-57). This is a correct insight. I, along with theologians such as Bloesch, affirm the human nature of Jesus.

[139] Williams, "'Person' and 'Personality' in Christology," 254.

[140] Williams, "'Person' and 'Personality' in Christology," 254.

[141] Williams, "'Person' and 'Personality' in Christology," 256.

[142] Williams, "'Person' and 'Personality' in Christology," 258.

may add: "The *esse*, the actuality, or effective reality, or principle of activity, or act of being, of Jesus of Nazareth is never other than the *esse* of God."[143] This is clearly what Chalcedon set out in its definition. Not the denial of Christ as a man, but the affirmative claim that he is so much more. Both natures are preserved in the union in the singularity, which as Williams claims is the "unitary form of continuity, the ultimate ground of continuous identity"[144] that is the Son of God the second person of the Trinity. This is why Jesus could claim a direct continuation of subjective existence both before the world was created in loving relation with the Father and the present reality of his speaking directly to his first century listeners (cf. John 17:5).

"Person" cannot be what many moderns assume it is when discussing the historic doctrines of incarnation and Trinitarianism.[145] The claim of classic Christology that the *person of the Word* assumes a human nature as opposed to being united to a fully human person, is necessary to maintain the singularity of the person of Jesus Christ. Furthermore, it safeguards against the idea that the humanity of Jesus was pre-existent. Jesus' human nature is a created human nature that is subject to all the limitations of contingent reality, yet was free from the sinful nature associated with every other human person.[146] The humanity as Berkouwer asserts, "never existed in abstraction from the divine."[147] Yet the unity of person in both natures is fundamental to the Chalcedonian Creed which repeatedly asserts it is the *self-same* Christ which is being spoken of in the creedal affirmations. Now a brief look at nature will follow. So the personal in Jesus Christ is the Person of the Trinity referred to as the Son, an ontological being from all eternity.

"Nature" or *ousia* (essence) as finally expressed in the Trinitarian debates, is also a term needing some explanation. The doctrine of the Trinity was finally "settled," so to speak, by expressing that God is one in nature; three in persons. Because there is but one God, the Triune conception necessitates that the three persons in the Godhead must be equally possessors of the basic nature of God. So the three persons share the essential "whatness" of God, without identifying each other with the "whoness" of personal distinction. The nature of God is that which defines God as God.

---

[143] Williams, "'Person' and 'Personality' in Christology," 258.

[144] Williams, "'Person' and 'Personality' in Christology," 257.

[145] For a historical survey of the use of person in philosophy and Christianity, see Georgios F.E. Chatzipantelis. *Από το Προσωπείο και το 'Ατομο στο Πρόσωπο" Οι Πρωτοεργάτες Ενός Δημιουργικού Θεολογικού Διαλόγου περί Προσώπου και τα Μείζονα Κείμενα Τους* (Thessaloniki: Mediamarbles, 2011). For a host of various approaches to the human constitution, including physicalism, idealism, and dualism, see the wonderful book, Peter Van Inwagen & Dean Zimmerman, eds. *Persons: Human and Divine*. New York: Oxford, 2007.

[146] On Christ's humanity see the well-presented study by Marilyn McCord Adams, *What Sort of Human Nature? Medieval Philosophy and the Systematics of Christology* (Milwaukee: Marquette University Press, 1999).

[147] G.C. Berkouwer, *Studies in Dogmatics: The Person of Christ*, trans. John Vriend (Grand Rapids: Eerdmans, 1955), 293.

Chapter 7: Biblical and Theological Evidence for Jesus Christ's Omnipresence

The essence of God therefore is deity.[148] One must beware that it is not deduced to mean that the essence of God may be abstracted from consideration of the persons, and as such deny that any of the persons manifests the essence completely. This must be resisted. Each of the persons manifests the entire essence of deity.[149] "In his own being," asserts Bray, "God remains wholly other – completely different from his creation, whatever analogies might be drawn between it and him."[150] So when one speaks of the incarnation discussing the person Jesus Christ, one must affirm with Weinandy, "The wholly other divine Son of God truly becomes an authentic man without losing his wholly otherness as God."[151]

On the manner of the union within incarnational theology, it is best to recall our discussion of *enhypostatic* Christology. A helpful proposal, based on historical study, has been presented by Brian Daley on this very important matter.[152] Daley is one of the foremost authorities on Leontius of Byzantium. As Daley cites Leontius, one grasps the desire to remain faithful to Chalcedon. "What is under discussion," says Leontius, is not simply a matter of phrasing, but the modality of the whole mystery revealed in Christ: a mode of union, namely, that has come into being in a substantial, and not simply a relational, way, so that the Word is, within a complete humanity, what "the inner person", in the Apostle's words, in each of us-co-existing, and contributing after the union to the definition of the whole person.[153] "The chief issue in Christology during that embattled century after Chalcedon," Daley immediately explains, "is for Leontius not the nature of the God who has appeared in Christ, nor the natural constitution of the human person . . . but the manner in which those utterly distinct realities, joined in the one we confess to be the Son of God, work together to form a single, concrete, contingent, historical individual."[154] Methodologically, Leontius began with the result, that is, the person of Christ, rather than speculating on abstract divinity and humanity and how to bring them together. No doubt, there is something paradoxical in the person of Christ, and this Leontius, and Daley readily acknowledge. Yet the use of a familiar analogy found in the soul-body union that constitutes a human being, is utilized by Leontius, which thus "allows its [the incarnation's] different levels of being to remain in

---

[148] See Richard A. Muller, *Dictionary of Latin and Greek Theological Terms: Drawn Principally from Protestant Scholastic Theology* (Grand Rapids: Baker, 1985), 105-06.

[149] See the helpful discussion in Gerald Bray, *The Doctrine of God* (Downers Grove, IL: InterVarsity, 1993), 197-202.

[150] Bray, *The Doctrine of God*, 58.

[151] Thomas G. Weinandy, *Does God Suffer?* (Notre Dame, IN: University of Notre Dame Press, 2000), 199. This quote appears in Weinandy's chapter entitled: "The Incarnation–The Impassible Suffers." This chapter is a veritable treasure chest of incarnational theology.

[152] See Brian E. Daley, "Nature and the 'Mode of Union': Late Patristic Models for the Personal Unity of Christ," in *The Incarnation: An Interdisciplinary Symposium on the Incarnation of the Son of God*, ed. Stephen T. Davis, Daniel Kendall, and Gerald O' Collins (Oxford: Oxford University Press, 2002), 164-96.

[153] Daley, "Nature and the 'Mode of Union,'" 166.

[154] Daley, "Nature and the 'Mode of Union,'" 166-67.

tact and operative in themselves."[155] Despite the possibility that a general understanding of this analogy may be detrimental to sound Christology rather than a defense of it, we will hear from Leontius. He adds elements to this way of thinking from Aristotelian metaphysics to secure how this union is an ontological union not merely relational. In this as Daley explains, "it is 'union, not nature' that serves as the foundation of the subject's inner identity."[156]

In conclusion, the teaching of Chalcedon may be expressed in such a way that there is unity at the level of person; it is the Son of God who is incarnate as Jesus Christ, and there is distinction with regards to the natures; as God Jesus shares the deity or fundamental essence of Godhead, and Jesus is fully man without being merely man. "The doctrine of the Two Natures," states Warfield, "supplies, in a word, the only possible solution to the enigmas of the life-manifestation of the historical Jesus."[157] It is the mystery of this hypostatic union in which Jesus Christ is one person in two natures that necessitates that as God, Christ is essentially omnipresent by virtue of the divine nature.

D.2.3. Jesus as God: Two Wills

Because Jesus Christ was seen as one person in two natures, theologians also debated the question of more than one will in Christ. As it was thought, will was a function of nature, then Christ must have two wills since he is a two-natured person.[158] In scripture there was some evidence of this. A classic passage utilized in support of the two wills in Christ is Jesus' prayer in Gethsemane. In Matthew 26:39 Jesus agonizingly states: "not as I will, but as You will." As the God–Man, Christ in two natures, can act and speak out of either nature and what is said or done may still be predicated of the person. There is still one subject at the center of any activity. So one need not infer a split personality or

---

[155] Daley, "Nature and the 'Mode of Union,'" 168. Thomas Weinandy offers a serious critique of the use of this familiar analogy to illustrate the incarnation. "While the Cappadocians defended the full divinity and the full humanity of Christ," states Weinandy, "they nonetheless conceived the union after the manner of the soul-body and so spoke, ambiguously (and in the end, in the light of Chalcedon, wrongly) of the Incarnation as a 'mixing' or 'mingling' . . . of the divine and the human natures. Here, as with Tertullian, they seem to be employing a Stoic understanding. Moreover, it is within a Christological setting that Gregory of Nazianzus first employed within Christian theology the Neoplatonic term used to explain the relationship between the soul and the body – [perichoresis]. This 'mixing' and 'coinherence' jeopardizes the integrity of the natures. Moreover, the attributes of each new nature now 'coinhere' with one another. This results in a dubious conception the human nature's deification, one that boarders on Docetism. According to Gregory of Nyssa the humanity is like a drop of vinegar in the sea of divinity" (Weinandy, *Does God Suffer?* 185).

[156] Daley, "Nature and the 'Mode of Union,'" 170.

[157] Warfield, *Person and Work of Christ*, 262.

[158] Famous in challenging this is Bernard Lonergan. Yet one must ponder the question regarding Jesus status as both man and God, as Feinberg asks: "If Christ has a fully human and a fully divine nature, he must be everything God and man are. But how could there be a divine mind or a human mind without each having the capacity to will?" (Feinberg, "The Incarnation of Jesus Christ," 241). Particularly helpful on this question is Gerald O'Collins, *Christology: A Biblical, Historical and Systematic Study of Jesus* (New York: Oxford University Press, 1995), 224-49.

internal conflict that is *permanent*, yet one senses here a genuine human fear of what lay before Jesus in drinking the cup of God's wrath. According to Luke 22:43, Jesus is strengthened by angelic presence, and as a result Christ's human will, was ultimately subject to the Father (Matt 26:42), and the divine will, which Jesus as God no doubt also willed, was finally fulfilled.[159] Another passage also lends weight to the notion of more than one will in Christ. In John 6:38, Christ says of himself: "I have come down from heaven, not to do My own will, but the will of Him who sent Me" (NASB). This text certainly underscores the unity of purpose between the Father and the Son. Christ affirms the determination he has to readily undertake all his Father's bidding. But if, as the incarnate Son of God, he does not possess an additional will of his own in distinction to the divine will he shares with his Father, then his argument, that he does indeed do his Father's will as *opposed to his own*, is empty and meaningless.[160]

Those opposed to the idea of two wills in Christ are driven by the desire to uphold the integrity of Jesus' genuine humanity.[161] However, it is no more incoherent to affirm two wills as it is to affirm two natures in Christ. Indeed, it appears that an inconsistency emerges if one tries to hold to a Christ in two natures with only one will. It must result in Jesus possessing a merely human will, as is evidenced by the real struggle cited in the anguish at Gethsemane, for clearly Christ is not expressing a sole divine will that he undergo and not undergo the divine wrath, at the same time. This would through confusion into the mind of God. Indeed, this would be a genuine contradiction, and as such an insurmountable problem for evangelicals. Historically, the position of those seeking to establish a *monothelite* doctrine, according to Bloesch, was the unfortunate result "that the human nature was no longer capable of its own distinctive natural acts. Jesus had only one will – the divine."[162] In this way the problem of conflict is swept aside. On the other hand, "The sixth Ecumenical Council," notes Erickson, "ruled clearly in favor of the Dyothelite position."[163] Erickson adds: "The bishops were concerned to preserve the full humanity of Jesus. As a complete human being, he could not have lacked anything that per-

---

[159] As Gerald O'Collins says: "Mainstream Christians when interpreting this passage [Mark 14:36, 'not what I want, but what You want'] or its equivalents in the other Gospels, normally commented: 'Not what I want as man, but what you and I as God will.' Since Christ through his human will desired not to die, we might speak of a non-sinful 'discord' or tension between his human will and the divine will he shared with the Father" (Gerald O'Collins, *Incarnation* [New York: Continuum, 2002], 85).

[160] Jesus uses a similar expression in John 5:30: "I can do nothing on My own initiative. As I hear, I judge; and My judgment is just, because I do not seek My own will, but the will of Him who sent Me."

[161] See Gerald Hawthorne, *The Presence and the Power* (Dallas: Word, 1991), 212-14. Walvoord opts for one will in Christ. He does this by focusing on the will not as desire, but as "resulting moral decision" (Walvoord, *Jesus Christ our Lord*, 119-20).

[162] Donald Bloesch, *Jesus Christ: Savior and Lord* (Downers Grove, IL: InterVarsity, 1997), 59.

[163] Millard J. Erickson, *The Word Became Flesh: A Contemporary Incarnational Christology* (Grand Rapids: Baker, 1991), 75.

tains to a human being, including human actions and a human will."[164] Without wishing to re-enter this historical debate, it is here contended that the only reasonable explanation, given the assumption of one will in Christ, would be the result that Jesus has only a *human* will. But from the historical setting, as Erickson points out: "Christ's full humanity, then, required two natural wills."[165] Ironically, this is denied by those wishing to emphasize Jesus' full humanity, especially modern advocates of a kenotic type Christology that relish the idea of Christ possessing one will.[166] The obvious question then is how does one explain that Jesus is God's agent expressing God's saving plan, in short manifesting the *divine will* for the world? In affirming only one will for Christ raises more problems that it purports to solve. Furthermore, in challenging the idea of two wills, it also raises the possibility that two natures should also be given up. This path seems to be headed in the wrong direction. Along with the church council of A.D. 680, I affirm two wills in the incarnate Christ.

D.2.4. Jesus as God: Two Minds

Theologian John Walvoord, who argued for a single-will understanding of Christ's person, nonetheless affirms a two-minds Christology. "There was no point in the life of Christ," asserts Walvoord, "when He suddenly became aware of the fact that He was God."[167] He continues the discussion with the following claim:

> His divine self-consciousness was as fully operative when He was a babe in Bethlehem as it was in His most mature experience. There is evidence, however, that the human nature developed and with it a human self-consciousness came into play. In view of the varied forms of manifestation of the divine and human natures, it seems possible to conclude that He had both a divine and a human self-consciousness, that these were never in conflict, and that Christ sometimes

---

[164] Erickson, *The Word Became Flesh*, 75.

[165] Erickson, *The Word Became Flesh*, 75.

[166] See Hawthorne, *The Presence and the Power*, 214. Hawthorne's Christology is driven by desire to present Jesus in every way as human as we are. It would be strange indeed if despite all his efforts the sole will in Christ turned out to be a divine will. In conversation with a fellow student on this matter some time ago concerning more than one will in Christ, an answer was given praising Hawthorne's achievements, and my friend asked the question, "when Christ prayed to the Father in Gethsemane, if He had a divine will, in union with the Father's then his prayer admits the foolishness of "not my will, but *mine* be done" does it not?" I cite this example of how it must be the human will that Christ possesses if a modern day monothelitism is affirmed. Of course the simple answer is: Yes, in a sense that is correct; but Christ had a human and a divine will, which makes sense of the remainder of scriptural witness to the two-natured Christ, God manifest in the flesh.

[167] Walvoord, *Jesus Christ our Lord*, 118. I think there is a slight problem with Walvoord's presentation of the one will, but it plays no defining role in the end as Walvoord affirms two minds. As indicated already he is probably asserting the truth that despite Christ having, or being in, two natures he is still one willer as subject.

Chapter 7: Biblical and Theological Evidence for Jesus Christ's Omnipresence

thought, spoke and acted from the divine self consciousness and at other times from the human.[168]

Thomas Morris, in various works, has also advocated a view which defends that Jesus has two minds.[169] In this way of explaining the incarnation, Christ has two minds that function in an asymmetrical accessing fashion. The divine mind contains the human mind but is not contained by it. There is no straightforward symmetric reciprocal accessing of the divine and human minds. The data in the human mind is obvious to the omniscient divine mind, while the knowledge in the divine mind is not immediately comprehended by the human mind. There is merit to this proposal which no doubt builds on the early patristic notion of more than one will in Christ. It best explains how Christ is one person in two natures, than does any kenotic or sub-kenotic rival explanation. A two minds approach allows that contrasting descriptions of Christ's knowledge in the Bible can both be true, because it permits full force to both types of data found in the New Testament. The strength of Morris's approach is that it diffuses all claims that the incarnation is incoherent. Morris shows it is possible to be perfectly rational in advocating the central and classic concepts of the incarnation by use of important, but over-looked, distinctions.

One need not be in concert with Morris's position wholesale.[170] There are a few elements of his discussion that one may seriously question. The possibility of multiple incarnations must be resisted. There is a uniqueness and finality to the person of Christ. There is, therefore, no possibility that Jesus will have a rival. Also, there is certainly something to be gained in keeping the claim that

---

[168] Walvoord, *Jesus Christ our Lord*, 118-19.

[169] See Thomas V. Morris, "The Metaphysics of God Incarnate," 110-27, esp.,122-27, in *Trinity, Incarnation, and Atonement: Philosophical and Theological Essays*, ed. Ronald J. Feenstra & Cornelius Plantinga, Jr. (Notre Dame, IN: University of Notre Dame Press, 1989); idem, *Anselmian Explorations: Essays in Philosophical Theology* (Notre Dame, IN: University of Notre Dame Press, 1987), 213-41; and idem, *The Logic of God Incarnate* (Ithaca: Cornell University Press, 1986; reprint Eugene, OR: Wipf and Stock, 2001). For a recent defense, and improvement on Morris' model, see John Feinberg, "The Incarnation of Jesus Christ" in *In Defense of Miracles: A Comprehensive Case for God's Action in History*, ed. Douglas Geivett & Gary R. Habermas (Downers Grove, IL: InterVarsity, 1997), 226-46. For a critique of Morris's "two-minds" model, see John Hick, *The Metaphor of God Incarnate: Christology in a Pluralistic Age* (Louisville: Westminster John Knox, 1993), 47-60. In my estimate, Hick's criticisms are not compelling. His *a priori* commitment to a mere historical man in Jesus Christ will never provide the "religious" satisfaction he requires so as to affirm Christ as truly God the Son in an incarnational Christology. Moreover, his conviction that Johannine statements equating Jesus' oneness with the Father are no more than religious opinions of the later church and not really words which Jesus uttered, safely eliminate the biblical testimony, and therefore show Hick's proposal as seriously wanting, in light of an evangelical insistence on the accuracy and integrity of the Bible's presentation of Jesus.

[170] O'Collins shares the dual nature approach but does not succumb to Morris's perceived weaknesses. See Gerald O'Collins, *Christology*, 224-47.

in the incarnate Christ, propositions with regard to Jesus Christ's properties are "reduplicative;" which Morris is willing to give up.[171]

How one explains this concept of two minds is significant. Williams, who was fully cognizant of the Patristic emphasis of two natures in Christ, and the fear that some had that this two-natured Christology denied "personality" to the man Jesus, nonetheless grants that the Chalcedon definition, in addition to the divine nature and mind of the incarnate Lord, "does allow a human mind to Christ – a fact commonly ignored or distorted by critics of Chalcedon."[172] So as Christ has two wills because he is a two-natured person, so he has two minds. This is necessary for explaining the presence of both strands of material in the New Testament concerning the knowledge of Christ. In some sense, Jesus as a man develops and gains knowledge, as do all other human beings (Luke 2:52). On the other hand, categoric claims are made in the Bible concerning Jesus' knowledge of all things (John 16:29; 21:17 cf. Col 2:3). Only a two-minds approach, coupled with the reduplicative propositions that as man, Christ gains knowledge, and as God he knows all things, makes sense of all types of data in the scriptural witness to the person of Jesus Christ.

At this point it is helpful to recall our presentation of Anthony Lane's and Ronald Leigh's positions on the incarnation.[173] One of the emerging themes that characterize their work is the methodology of starting Christology from below. By doing this the doctrine of the pre-existence of the Son of God is neglected in their proposals.[174] Coupled with this methodology of "Christology

---

[171] See Morris, *The Logic of God Incarnate*, 46-55.

[172] Williams, "'Person' and 'Personality' in Christology," 256.

[173] See A.N.S. Lane, "Christology Beyond Chalcedon," in *Christ the Lord: Studies in Christology Presented to Donald Guthrie*, ed. Harold H. Rowdon (Leicester: Inter Varsity, 1982), 257-81; and Ronald W. Leigh, "Jesus: the One-natured God-man," *CSR* 11, no. 2 (1982): 124-37.

[174] The discounting of the doctrine of pre-existence in *formulating* a Christology is suspect. Lane in particular asserts that the Trinity should not shape our Christology. In contrast to this attitude, it is better to assume the stance of Reginald Fuller on pre-existence. Fuller defends the legitimacy and necessity of pre-existence in the face of radical criticism, which is much more severe than Lane's protestations. See Reginald Fuller, *Christ and Christianity*, comp. and ed. with an introduction by Robert Kahl (Valley Forge, PA: Trinity Press International, 1994), 153-60. Indeed, the New Testament affirms the pre-existence of Christ. If it does not, or if it is neglected, as in the case of Lane and Leigh, then to explain that Jesus is God will have to be explained in some kind of adoptionistic framework. This is inescapable given the assumptions that pre-existence has no influence on our Christology. Passages that affirm pre-existence, beyond those mentioned in the dissertation already, include Heb 1:5-14; 7:3, cf. 2:9; 10:5-7; 1 Cor 15:47; Col 1:15-18; Gal 4:4; and Rom 8:3. These verses along with Dan 7:13; and Mic 5:2; show us that preexistence is an important biblical theme. No doubt, this is troubling for those who seek to discount our Lord's deity. John Knox said, "Belief in the pre-existence of Jesus is incom-patible with a belief in his genuine normal humanity . . . We can have the humanity without the pre-existence and we can have the pre-existence without the humanity. There is absolutely no way of having both" (quoted in Macleod, *The Person of Christ*, 64). See Macleod's able refutation (65-70), where among other arguments, he appeals to the enhypostatic concept to maintain continuity between the

Chapter 7: Biblical and Theological Evidence for Jesus Christ's Omnipresence

from below," is the kenotic condition of limitation that the Son of God partakes of in becoming man. As such, so the familiar argument goes, Christ did not have omniscience. Although we will treat Philippians 2 in the next chapter, a provisional discussion on the question of omniscience is necessary.

Leigh rejects any notion of an antinomy.[175] He applies this to deny specifically Jesus' omniscience.[176] Lane also speaks of limitations[177] and applies this particularly to Christ's knowledge.[178] In support of this claim, Lane cites Luke 2:52 and Mark 13:32. From the Marcan text, Lane deduces that Jesus himself, denied his omniscience, and from the Lukan text, Lane asserts that affirming "the omniscience of the historical Jesus has no biblical basis and indeed runs counter to the clear teaching of the Gospels."[179]

What is evident in these proposals is that the humanity of Jesus is utilized as a sort of filter for understanding the divine nature. Only that which, per Lane and Leigh, may be rationally harmonious with Jesus' evident humanity may be reasonably spoken of in terms of his deity. Methodologically, they are consistent. But are they correct? I believe that a problem surfaces as one accounts for *all* the data. What Lane and Leigh attempt is to take one strand of teaching (Jesus acquisition of knowledge) and use it as primary for explaining statements that appear to counter the assertion. For example, Leigh and Lane claim that the New Testament clearly teaches that Jesus is not omniscient. What they must do, however, is to eliminate such passages that do *prima facie* speak of Jesus knowing all things or possessing all knowledge (John 16:30; 21:17; and Col 2:3). In John 16:30, the disciples affirm that Jesus knows all things.[180] Hawley and Comfort express matters well. "Now they [the disciples] were con-

---

Logos and Jesus, in whom the Word was made flesh. Orthodox Christology must have both pre-existence and assumed humanity. This can be had properly only with a method that employs "Christology from above." Lane and Leigh should take note of the high price they are paying to engage the person of Christ as they do.

[175] Leigh, "Jesus," 130.
[176] Leigh, "Jesus," 130., n. 23.
[177] Lane, "Christology beyond Chalcedon," 270.
[178] Lane, "Christology beyond Chalcedon," 271.
[179] Lane, "Christology beyond Chalcedon," 271.
[180] D.A. Carson, comes to a different conclusion based on the disciples' statement. Carson says, "They happily confess that Jesus knows all things – which is probably not so much an affirmation of Jesus' omniscience as of his utter mastery of all he has to tell them about God and his ways" (Carson, *The Gospel According to John* [Grand Rapids: Eerdmans, 1991], 548). Carson adds that "the final sentence, *This makes us believe that you came from God*, though formally embracing a true conclusion, betrays just how feeble a foundation supports the immature faith they have so far attained" (548). In contrast, Morris's comment must be heeded. "It is probably significant," notes Morris, "that they do not say that they understand fully and all that Jesus is saying. Instead they say that they know that he knows all things. They have full confidence in him. Jesus had answered has answered the question in their heart (it had not been spoken, v. 19), and they ascribe to him power to do this always (cf. 2:25). This in turn gives them assurance of his divine origin. Their confession is certainly an inadequate one, but we should not overlook the fact that they bring their words to a close with an expression of trust" (Leon Morris, *The Gospel According to John* [Grand Rapids: Eerdmans, 1995], 631).

vinced that Jesus' impressive knowledge about future events," they state, "marked him unquestionably as the Son of God come from God. To say that Jesus knew "all things" was tantamount to saying that he was omniscient and, therefore, divine."[181] Commenting on John 21:17, Carson, who did not sense that John 16:30 speaks of Christ's omniscience, has something different to say of this text. "When Peter is grieved (v. 17)," notes Carson, "it is not because Jesus changed verbs, but because the same question is being asked for the third time. . . . There is no trace of self-righteousness in Peter's response. He can only appeal to the fact that the Lord *knows everything* [emphasis supplied], and therefore knows Peter's heart."[182]

In Colossians, Paul asserts that in Christ are all the treasures of wisdom and knowledge. In context Paul is discussing the need to focus on Christ as the source of knowledge of things divine, yet a categoric statement is made by Paul when he mentions the person of Christ. In him "the treasures are "hidden" (ἀποκρυφοι)" notes O'Brien, "not in the sense that they are "kept concealed . . ."" but that they exist (εἰσιν) being "deposited" or "stored up" in Christ."[183] These texts add insight to the knowledge that Jesus is described as having. This knowledge as Lohse says, is described by "the modifier, "all" (παντες), [which] bans all exceptions."[184] This can only mean in Jesus we find an omniscient being. As already noted in this book, Leigh went to such lengths as to challenge the inspiration of Peter's avowal that Jesus "knows all things."[185] Leigh even claims that the passage in Colossians 2:3 which states that "in whom [Jesus] are hidden all the treasures of wisdom and knowledge" really speaks of the "believer's fullness of wisdom and knowledge in Christ, rather than an indication

---

[181] Philip W. Comfort and Wendell C. Hawley, *Opening the Gospel of John* (Wheaton, IL: Tyndale, 1994), 264.

[182] Carson, *Gospel According to John*, 678. Similarly, Beasley-Murray asserts, "The pain or grief of Peter was not due to Jesus' framing his question with the use of Peter's own word . . . but is explained by Jesus' act when for the third time he put the same question to him, as though to ask whether there was any substance in his avowal of love, any ground for accepting its reality . . . . [Peter] could only appeal to the Lord's *totality of knowledge* (emphasis added), which included his knowledge of Peter's heart; he [Jesus] more than all people could tell that he was speaking the truth" (George R. Beasley-Murray, *John* [Waco, TX: Word, 1987], 405).

[183] Peter T. O'Brien, *Colossians, Philemon* (Dallas: Word, 1982), 95.

[184] Eduard Lohse, *Colossians and Philemon*, trans. William R. Poehlmann and Robert J. Karris, ed. Helmut Koester (Philadelphia: Fortress, 1971), 82.

[185] See Leigh, "Jesus," 130 n. 23. This is a valiant attempt by Leigh to discount some direct testimony which renders his argument null and void. The section dealing with Peter's words that Jesus knows everything, is presented by Leigh, in such a way as to cast doubt on the truthfulness of the assertion. If indeed Peter has not got the facts straight at this time, one would have to conclude that this is either a clear misconception on his part concerning the person of Christ, or he is plainly lying about the said knowledge he has of Jesus' omniscience. The context suggests that Peter is in fact truthful at this point rather than lying as he did when he denied knowing Christ. Moreover there is no disavowal by Jesus to correct this evidently incorrect Christology in Peter's mind, if indeed it was mistaken. In contrast to Leigh, I believe both Peter, and Jesus affirmed Christ's omniscience in this text.

Chapter 7: Biblical and Theological Evidence for Jesus Christ's Omnipresence

of Christ's omniscience."[186] One must question the use of these texts to further this claim. The suggestion that part of the scripture is not inspired is unacceptable. Furthermore, in the Colossians 2 passage, verse three categorically affirms Jesus' omniscience as the ground for the acquisition of the believer's fullness of the knowledge of God's mystery in Christ. The believer's limited, but full, knowledge is spoken by Paul in verse two, not verse three. It is Christ's knowledge of all things which is the ground for him sharing with the believers that are *in Christ*. This kind of mishandling of these biblical statements is unacceptable for establishing doctrine, in that one set of truths is used to jettison the other set of equally binding truths. Rather, a method and concept that allows both is preferable.[187] This is to be found in a model of a two-natured Christ, who exhibits two minds.

How, then does one counter this claim concerning Jesus' lack of omniscience, especially as it appears that Mark 13:32 leans in that direction? It might be suspected that I would turn the tables on Leigh and Lane and in my own formulations of Christology utilize the *clear* teaching on Christ's omniscience to eliminate or re-define those passages that speak of Christ's ignorance or gaining of knowledge. This is how some of the Fathers of the church addressed Mark 13:32, for example.[188] It is possible to adopt a reading of Mark's text that

---

[186] See Leigh, "Jesus," 130 n. 23. It is granted that in context, the need to find in Christ the knowledge that Paul sees as essential to Christian growth, is a matter of importance. But when Paul speaks of the person of Christ, he exalts the incarnate Lord by stressing the absolute nature of his knowledge.

[187] Leigh has been challenged by Edwin Wallhout, "Chalcedon: Still Valid," *Christian Scholar's Review* 13 (1983): 48-53. In this same issue, Leigh has a "Response," 54-60. From the exchange of these essays, is clear that Leigh focuses the key issue by posing the question: "what characteristics are essential to deity?" (57). In his one-natured model, Leigh denies what he perceives to be the error implicit in the Chalcedonian formula, namely, "the attempt to combine contradictory characteristics such as omniscience and limited knowledge" (57). Therefore, in Leigh's estimate, the problem is only in the "faulty models . . . which theologians have forced on the Bible" (58). One may wonder if the clear biblical teaching that God cannot die (1 Tim 6:16) be harmonized with the death of Jesus (1 Cor 15:1-3), which is central to the gospel, or is this another imposition of the Bible? The Bible categorically asserts that God cannot die, that Jesus is God, and that Jesus died. To explain this obvious dilemma is what Chalcedon was all about. Leigh is negating the true biblical portrayal of Jesus as fully God (without any so-called non-essential attributes) and as fully man. To reduce God as being able to exist as a non-omniscient being is tantamount to suggesting that imperishability is not an essential attribute of deity. Leigh's position, although attractive in what it proposes positively, is suspect in what it denies, namely a fully divine God, and consequently a truly divine Jesus. *All* attributes are essential to deity. They are what make God, God! For another refutation of Leigh, see Thomas V. Morris, "The Natures of God Incarnate," *CSR* 14 (1984): 35-44 (with a "Reply by Ronald Leigh," 44-45).

[188] How is Mark 13:32 compatible with Jesus' omniscience? It is possible that Jesus is using the moment in his discussion of eschatology as a didactic tool underscoring the need for the Christian disciples to continue their task without getting bogged down in the details of the end. This would mean that the significance of Christ's statement was not purely a word concerning his knowledge but a word emphasizing their need for con-

The Omnipresence of Jesus Christ

denies what appears there at first sight. This would, however, indict one to the same charges I am leveling at Lane and Leigh. An alternate explanation must be sought.

It is best to conclude, with Lane and Leigh, that Mark 13:32 does speak of Jesus' limited knowledge. This way the surface reading of the text is affirmed. However, what I contest is that these types of verses are the *only* kind of language in the New Testament concerning Jesus' knowledge. Clearly, I do not believe that they are. Then the problem becomes a little different. How can one and the same person be both limited in knowledge and omniscient at the same time? This is the real crux of the matter, and it now becomes squarely a theological issue. Rather than using one set of truths to eliminate or re-define the other (as Lane and Leigh clearly attempt), we must hold to both strands of teaching. Catholic theologian Gerald O'Collins has grasped the need for this. "With respect to his divinity Christ is omniscient," notes O'Collins, "but with respect to his humanity he is limited in knowledge."[189] This should be the preferred approach for those who truly believe in Jesus Christ as one person in two natures (of course this rules out Leigh). Another Catholic scholar exclaimed a similar understanding, which alone does justice to the complete biblical picture of Christ. William Most puts it thus:

> Our commentators seem to have forgotten that there are two ways of writing about Jesus in the New Testament: (1) to note things associated with His divinity, (2) to note things associated with His humanity. Since He had both a true humanity and a true divinity, both forms of speech were proper. . . . Accordingly Mk

---

tinued ignorance. This approach was a common way of maintaining the absolute omniscience of Christ in the early church. See Christopher A. Hall, *Mark* (Downers Grove, IL: InterVarsity, 1998), 190-96. Hall cites, as an example, Augustine, who claimed, "Jesus was 'ignorant' in this sense, so to speak, among his disciples, of that which they were not yet able to know from him" (93). This is very similar to the incident with Jesus on the road to Emmaus with the two disciples. It appears in the text that Jesus does actually deceive the pair by claiming that he was to go on farther in his journey. In Luke 24:28, the word is προσεποιησατο (to pretend) in the Greek. If Jesus really knew the time of his return (as surely He must as God) then the purpose was, as in the case on the road to Emmaus, for a moment, to benefit his disciples by not disclosing the fact that he knew, in order for them to progress via ordinary means, without tempting them to ascertain this specific supernatural knowledge. Similarly, when the disciples asked Jesus in Acts 1:6 concerning the time of instituting the visible kingdom, Christ directed them to an immediate task of evangelizing, leaving the timing of God's plan with the Father. For an overview of Patristic solutions to this "omniscience" question, see Raymond Moloney, "Approaches to Christ's Knowledge in the Patristic Era," in *Studies in Patristic Christology*, ed. Thomas Finan and Vincent Twomey (Dublin: Four Courts, 1998), 37-66; and Lionel Wickham, "The Ignorance of Christ: A Problem for Ancient Theology," in *Christian Faith and Philosophy in Late Antiquity*, ed. Lionel R. Wickham and Caroline P. Bammel (Leiden: Brill, 1993), 213-26.

[189] Gerald O'Collins, *Christology: A Biblical, Historical, and Systematic Study of Jesus* (Oxford: Oxford University Press, 1995), 234.

Chapter 7: Biblical and Theological Evidence for Jesus Christ's Omnipresence

13:32 would mean: As far as human means of knowledge are concerned, I do not have that information.[190]

A two-minds view concerning Jesus Christ is biblically warranted by the various strands of information concerning the person of Jesus. Lane is particularly mistaken with his approach, which is ironic, seeing that he, unlike Leigh, affirms the two nature doctrine. Lane is inconsistent in his explanation. His method forces him to emphasize excessively the limitations of Christ as if they are the only truths revealed about Jesus in the Bible. Lane's betrayal of the Chalcedonian definition's insistence that both natures retain their respective properties after the union is the major problem in his proposal, as evidenced by his denial of omniscience in the Lord. Surely this is not the case. By claiming that Christ's knowledge and miracles can be mirrored in other biblical characters, Lane appears to implicitly reduce the incarnation to a degree Christology. The truth is to be found in allowing full force to both strands of data found in Scripture. Dennis Johnson's warning is apropos. He cautions,

> attempts to resolve the question of the inner experience of Christ either by minimizing the reality of his human change or by calling into question the New Testament claims regarding his divine constancy of life tend to jeaopardize [sic] not merely some fourth - or fifth- century theological formulations but the christological perspective, and consequently the soteriological presupposition, of the New Testament itself.[191]

In conclusion, it is theologically necessary to argue for two minds and two wills in Christ so as to make a compelling synthetic case of all the material available. As a two-natured person, Christ has two wills. Now we will turn to the claim that Jesus as the unique God-Man, also has two modes of presence.

---

[190] William G. Most, *The Consciousness of Christ* (Front Royal, VA: Christendom, 1980), 66. Most continues his discussion and quotes Pope Gregory the Great, who said of Mark 13:32, "[Jesus] knew the day and hour of judgment *in* the nature of humanity, but yet not *from* the nature of humanity" (66). Evangelical theologian Wayne Grudem is in line with these Catholic scholars. "The distinction of two wills and two centers of consciousness," posits Grudem, "helps us understand how Jesus could learn things and yet know all things. On the one hand, with respect to his human nature, he had limited knowledge (Mark 13:32; Luke 2:52). On the other hand, Jesus clearly knew all things (John 2:25; 16:30; 21:17). Now this is only understandable if Jesus learned things and had limited knowledge with respect to his human nature but was always omniscient with respect to his divine nature, and therefore he was able at any time to 'call to mind' whatever information would be needed for his ministry. In this way we can understand Jesus' statement concerning the time of his return: 'But of that day or that hour no one knows, not even the angels in heaven, nor the Son, but only the Father' (Mark 13:32). The ignorance of the time of his return was true of Jesus' human nature and human consciousness only, for in his divine nature he was certainly omniscient and certainly knew when he would return to the earth" (Grudem, *Systematic Theology*, 561).

[191] Dennis Edward Johnson, "Immutability and Incarnation: An Historical and Theological Study of the Concepts of Christ's Divine Unchangeability and His Human Development" (Ph.D. diss., Fuller Theological Seminary, 1984), 539.

D.2.5. Jesus as God: Two Modes of Presence

As we have already examined the early church and also have taken a careful look at Calvin's approach, it has become certain from the biblical witness that these theological affirmations about Christ's omnipresence are sound. Indeed, as a corollary to Jesus's Two-Natures, it is best to accept him as an individual who is unique possessing two-wills and two minds. It is due to his unique personal constitution that also requires two modes of presence. He is locally present as a human/divine person because of his humanity, and he is everywhere present as a divine/human person because of his deity. So Christ has two presences.

D.2.5.1. Introduction

The very expression "Jesus as God" assumes the contention that in the historical person of Jesus of Nazareth, there is revealed something beyond his humanity. It is essential to understand that Christ's "Godness" is affirmed in addition to his "humanness." As God, Jesus is omnipresent because of the divine nature. As throughout this book I have attempted to show certain truths about the person of Christ from church history, theology and biblical interpretation, those truths are now summarily applied in affirming a dual notion of Christ's presence.

D.2.5.2 Divine Essence

The underlying assumption is that the Man Jesus reveals God to us, and therefore this divinity that is revealed exceeds his humanity. So Wells is right when he says, "The central constituent in the God-man is therefore God for the same reason that the central constituent in the creation is the Creator."[192] Then Wells, speaking of Israelitess who encountered Christ in the first century, adds, "Monotheistic Jews in the New Testament knew that in Jesus they had come face to face with the one God."[193] We can only assert that in Jesus one encounters God if he has a divine nature. And now, since the ascension, he is with us as Emmanuel, because of that very divine essence, which he shares in as a member of the Trinity.

No doubt, as a man Jesus lived in a historically conditioned existence. Given the widespread acceptance of the truth of Jesus' manhood as genuine humanity (Heb 2:14-17; 4:14-15; and 5:7-8), the real matter is to show how Jesus was true God in addition to being man.[194] After all, Jesus wept, he slept, he got hungry, thirsty, and tired. He had to travel on foot. He was a real man that had a

---

[192] Wells, *The Person of Christ*, 178.

[193] Wells, *The Person of Christ*, 179.

[194] I realize that some are concerned with remnants of a docetic strain in contemporary Christianity, and this is due to an overwhelming influence of a sustained emphasis on the deity of Christ. However, when one looks at the academic world of theology a marked resistance to Jesus as God is certainly the norm. Only evangelicals have maintained a consistent avowal that in Jesus of Nazareth one finds in an ontological sense Yahweh, Israel's God. I seek only to keep this emphasis. However, I wholeheartedly affirm the genuine humanity of Christ. I am grateful that another recent volume was published to defend Jesus' divinity. See Christopher W. Morgan and Robert A. Peterson, eds. *The Deity of Christ* (Wheaton, IL: Crossway, 2011).

real body that bled when it was beaten, and Jesus finally died on what is now known as "Good Friday," probably in A.D. 33. As a genuine humanity was assumed by the Son of God, Christ was limited in his bodily presence. He could be only in one place at a time. He was born in Bethlehem, and so in terms of his body, he was not also in Jerusalem at the time of his birth. There is nothing in this that denies that Jesus as God remains omnipresent. In his extremely well-written and helpful article on John 3:13 Overstreet claims that this passage fundamentally asserts Christ's omnipresence.[195] As this verse and the additional biblical data shown above testify, both aspects of Christ's presence must be affirmed. There are two modes of presence that reflect the two-natured person's different properties tied to his status as God incarnate.

As no metaphysical alteration occurs to the divine nature when the person of the Word takes a human nature into his personal subsistence, God undergoes no mutation in the incarnation. Certainly a [meta]physical addition is expressly implied by the incarnation per se. Christ can be locally present and restrictedly so by virtue of the human nature limited to his body, and also be present beyond the confines of the body, omnipresent in fact, by virtue of the divine nature. It is the divine essence in Jesus that makes him an omnipresent being.

D.2.5.3 Person

Because of the doctrine of the hypostatic union, the union of natures in Christ is personal. Moreover, he remains one person. It is the person, God the Son incarnated as Jesus. In addition to this, by utilizing the *communicatio idiomatum* doctrine, one may state that it is indeed Jesus that is omnipresent. It is the *person*, who is omnipresent because divine, despite genuine humanity; and, it is the *person* who is encountered in the bodily presence of Jesus Christ because human, despite genuine deity. As with Jesus' knowledge, so with his presence; the one truth about Jesus as man cannot be used to eliminate the other truth about Jesus as God, but both must be affirmed. Because of his human nature and the human body, Christ is present in heaven and thereby absent from the earth. However, because this same Christ Jesus is God in the divine nature, he is also all-over present; indeed, he is omnipresent.

E. Conclusion

The biblical evidence cited undergirds the reality of Jesus Christ transcending his local bodily presence which is in heaven, awaiting his bodily return to the earth in the second coming. Also, as we looked at John's gospel in particular, omnipresence was seen to be true of Jesus during his earthly sojourn before his death, resurrection, and ascension. The doctrine of the deity of Christ is no mere speculative matter. It is essential to grasping the identity of Jesus Christ, which in turn permits one to see the nature and importance of his work, as well as to comprehend his continuing function as the Mediator.

The most significant observation that one must make in regard to omnipresence is that the traditional distinction between possession and use of this specific omni-attribute may not be sustained without violating the nature of what it is to be present. Omnipresence as presented both biblically and theologically

---

[195] Larry Overstreet, "John 3:13 and The Omnipresence of Jesus Christ," *JBTM* Vol. 2 No. 2 (Fall 2004): 135-153.

hence solves the kenosis question. It shows that a kenotic Christology cannot do justice to the constitution of Christ's person. Kenotic Christology does harm where evangelicals can least afford it–in relation to the deity of Christ. That Jesus Christ is God incarnate means he is a two-natured person. As the unique Son of God, Jesus as one person in two natures has and exercises two wills, two minds, and two modes of presence. What remains in this study before our conclusion is presented, is to focus on the passage used by several theologians and exegetes to argue for a kenotic type of Christology, namely Philippians 2:5-8. To this *pericope* we now turn.

CHAPTER 8

AN EXEGETICAL AND THEOLOGICAL LOOK AT PHILIPPIANS 2:5-8

A. Introduction

It is evidently clear that many evangelical Christologies that deny omnipresence do so because of a commitment to a kenotic or sub-kenotic theology of the incarnation. This kenotic type of Christology has claimed the biblical justification of Philippians 2:5-8. In this chapter this passage will be examined and an interpretation will be offered that discounts any type of kenotic theology.[1] Several works will be noted for their importance in dealing with this hotly debated text. Before presenting the exposition we affirm, other approaches will be mentioned that illustrate the "traditional" interpretation of the text.

B. The Passage

One runs the risk of severing a passage out of its context, and possibly miss its intended meaning by isolating it as must be done for our purposes. Having said this, however, it is imperative to state clearly that it is a possible rendering of the meaning of the passage that will finally be presented. To do this will involve interaction with several commentators and theologians who have reflected on this scripture. Before the formal analysis begins, the text will be laid out in two translations. The Greek text will be analyzed subsequently, particularly those expressions that have fostered a kenotic Christology.

B.1. Philippians 2:5-8

New Revised Standard Version:

5. Let the same mind be in you that was in Christ Jesus,
6. who, though he was in the form of God,
   did not regard equality with God as something
   to be exploited,
7. but emptied himself,
   taking the form of a slave,
   being born in human likeness.

---

[1] Even if my reading of the passage is not heeded, and a more traditionalist reading is maintained that asserts that this text describes the act of the incarnation rather than as presupposing the incarnation, I would advocate that a non-kenotic approach may still be in-tact. Dennis Johnson in his dissertation, "Immutability and Incarnation," evidences just such an approach. And more recently, my dissertation supervisor, Stephen J. Wellum, does this admirably. See, "The Deity of Christ in the Apostolic Witness," in Morgan and Peterson, eds. *The Deity of Christ*, 121-27.

And being found in human form,
8. he humbled himself
and became obedient to the point of death–
even death on a cross.

Holman Christian Standard Bible:
5. Make your own attitude that of Christ Jesus,
6. who, existing in the form of God,
did not consider equality with God
As something to be used for His own advantage.
7. Instead He emptied Himself
by assuming the form of a slave
taking on the likeness of men.
And when He had come as a man in His external form
8. He humbled Himself by becoming obedient to the point of
death–even to death on a cross.

This passage forms a unit which is usually linked together as 2:5-11 or 2:6-11. We are chiefly concerned with the first part of the passage and therefore our own investigation will focus from verses 5 through 8.[2] The majority in the scholarly community believes this passage to be a pre-Pauline hymn. And furthermore, it is assumed that Paul has used and slightly emended the hymn for his own purposes.[3] A rare and challenging exception is Gordon Fee.[4] Widespread attention has focused on the pre-Pauline setting, and therefore naturally speculation abounds. "Much of the exegetical confusion," notes Silva, "in fact, may be blamed on the tendency to overemphasize the pre-Pauline setting of our

---

[2] Hurtado starts his analysis with vv. 9-11, and subsequently he looks at the "circumstance" for the exaltation with a treatment of vv. 6-8. (Larry W. Hurtado, *How on Earth Did Jesus Become God? Historical Questions about Earliest Devotion to Jesus.* [Grand Rapids: Eerdmans, 2005], 89-95).

[3] The abundance of literature on this passage is remarkable. Certain key works must be mentioned. Probably the most important study is Ralph P. Martin, *A Hymn of Christ: Philippians 2:5-11 in Recent Interpretation and in the Setting of Early Christian Worship* (Downers Grove, IL: InterVarsity, 1997 [1967]). See, also, Ralph P. Martin and Brian J. Dodd, eds., *Where Christology Began: Essays on Philippians 2* (Louisville: Westminster John Knox, 1998). More recently the important linguistic study has been issued in Daniel J. Fabricatore, *Form of God, Form of a Servant: An Examination of the Greek Noun μορφη in Philippians 2:6-7* (Lanham, MD: University Press of America, 2010). Fabricatore has presented an able case for retaining the traditional understanding of the passage and equating kenosis with taking on humanity. His proposal, however, is consonant with the conclusion I have reached *about* the incarnation. "The μορφη of God, which denotes the visible appearance of God, a manifestation which is the very δοξα of God, was *veiled* for almost all of our Lord's earthly life and ministry" (214). Of the many commentaries that abound on Paul's Philippian letter, F.W. Beare, *The Epistle to the Philippians* (Peabody, MA: Hendrickson, 1987 [1959]) contains a well-written brief appendix by Eugene Fairweather on "Kenosis" (159-74).

[4] See Gordon D. Fee, *Paul's Letter to the Philippians* (Grand Rapids: Eerdmans, 1995), 39-46.

passage, and thus to wrest it from the only context in which it has come down to us."⁵ One would do well to heed the warning.

B.2. The Traditional Framework

What has become virtually axiomatic in studies of Philippians 2:5-11, is a "descent- ascent" framework.⁶ What this means is that the so-called hymn is rehearsing the chronological descent, of the pre-existing Son of God in the incarnation as he becomes man, then after explaining the work of Christ culminating in a shameful death, Jesus experiences an ascent to a Lordly status, which, ends the passage. Furthermore, it is argued that this functions in the epistle as an exhortation to humility on the part of the Christian community at Philippi so as to emulate the attitude that was in the mind of Christ.⁷ For example, note Moule's comments on this framework. "Of course there is no denying that the 'pattern' of Phil. II. 5-11 as a whole," asserts Moule, "is the pattern of descent followed by ascent, humiliation followed by exaltation: it is, as it were, a V-pattern – from heaven to the depths and up again."⁸

---

⁵ Moisés Silva, *Philippians* (Grand Rapids: Baker, 1992), 105.

⁶ Although exegetically this is supportable in the passage by explaining the participial phrases after the expression "emptied himself," to show *means*, i.e., "'by' taking the form of a servant," and "'by' taking on human likeness," it is by no means the only way to express the connection.

⁷ Martin claims, "Of more permanent influence [than the kenotic theory] has been the approach to the Pauline *pericope* in the interest of finding here the ethical example of Christ" (Martin, *A Hymn of Christ*, 68). Martin surveys some of the most important studies yet concludes that this tradition has remained stronger in Anglo-speaking theologians and commentators, and has certainly declined on the continent, especially Germany. This approach does have strong contextual support, but certain assumptions are in place, as Martin notes. The most significant matter for the ethical interpretation is to establish the correct reading of verse 5. "We may accept the reading φρονεῖτε in the first part of the sentence," argues Martin, "as the better attested reading: 'Having this mind in you (or, among you)'. The second half of the sentence reads only ὃ καὶ ἐν Χριστῷ where it is necessary to add a verb *ad sensum*" (70). Martin explains that there are two ways to do this. First, as in the AV or KJV tradition, what is supplied is "ἐφρονήθη or ἦν to produce the translation: 'which was (the mind which was) in Christ Jesus'" (70). Second, Martin notes a way made famous by Adolf Diessmann that many have followed. This view will "supply φρονεῖτε (or φρονεῖν δεῖ) to give a parallelism with the first part of the sentence. This sense is then: 'Have this mind among yourselves (i.e. in your church-life) which you have as those who are in Christ Jesus'" (70.). Silva adopts this type of exhortation. Also see Martin's further discussion on the "ethical interpretation" in his appendix (84-88).

⁸ See C.F.D. Moule, "The Manhood of Jesus in the New Testament," in *Crisis in Christology: Essays in Quest of Resolution*, ed. William R. Farmer (Livonia, MI: Dove Booksellers, 1995), 49. Moule also adds others' speculations on the structure, with the comment: "as some aver, [Jesus is exalted] up to an even higher status than before – which would require a pattern more like a square-root symbol!" (49). Granting the legitimacy of the traditional framework, Moule nonetheless qualifies it by adding a pertinent observation: "But that, I believe," Moule stresses, "need not prevent our seeing, at the same time, a straight line pattern in it, by which height is *equated* with depth, humilia-

B.3. Traditional Interpretation

Given the assumed pattern as indicated above that most interpreters have, we will examine some of the various interpretations of the text.[9] We will look at the "ethical" interpretation, and the "incarnational" interpretation.

B.3.1. Ethical interpretation

Already mentioned is this widespread notion of the sense of the passage. The ethical interpretation has been defended by several writers. "It is striking," observes Hengel, "that the hymn occurs not in a context of dogmatic argument, but within ethical exhortations from the apostle."[10] Even Silva, who gives up the reading often associated with this emphasis, allows the force of this aspect in the text.[11] By keeping the context clear, this approach links the exhortation of thinking like Christ to the need to be humble (as evidenced by Christ) as an expression of putting others first (2:3-4). "The demonstrative τοῦτο ("this" [of verse 5]) points back to verses 1-4," says MacLeod. He adds: "It is followed by the present imperative φρονεῖτε, of which it is the object ('think'). In short, they were to have among themselves the frame of mind, disposition, or mindset that he had just described." Finally, MacLeod concludes, highlighting the ethical emphasis, "They could develop this attitude by following Jesus' example."[12] Many have echoed this insight. "Paul introduces the great example of Christ Jesus," O'Brien states similarly, "for such a way of life, that is, of humility, in his exhortation. The Philippians are to have among themselves the same disposition and manner of life as Christ Jesus in his freely willed renunciation of the heavenly power and glory that he possessed before the incarnation."[13] As O'Brien has mentioned the incarnation, it is significant to turn to this kind of interpretation of this passage.

---

tion is *identified* with exaltation. Indeed, the very paradox of the truth lies in the fact that what, in ordinary human estimation, is a V-pattern of descent followed by ascent is, in the eyes of God, a straight line of equation: the two diagrams, therefore, positively need to be there together, if the paradox is to be expressed" (49).

[9] For a very helpful survey, see Peter O' Brien, *The Epistle to the Philippians* (Grand Rapids: Eerdmans, 1991), 253-71.

[10] Martin Hengel, "Christological Titles in Early Christianity," in *The Messiah: Developments in Earliest Judaism and Christianity. The First Symposium on Judaism and Christian Origins*, ed. James H. Charlesworth (Minneapolis: Fortress, 1992), 441.

[11] Silva asserts, "We conclude . . . that εν Χριστω Ιησου in Phil. 2:5 is a reference to the Philippians' relationship to Christ and that the verse is best understood thus: "Be so disposed toward one another as is proper for those who are united in Christ Jesus" (Silva, *Philippians*, 109). Silva adds, "Does this conclusion lead us to abandon the ethical interpretation of vv. 6-11? By no means!" (109). Barth offers a similar reading of this verse, Karl Barth *Epistle to the Philippians* Trans. James W. Leitch (Louisville: Westminster John Knox, 2002), 59.

[12] See David J. MacLeod, "Imitating the Incarnation of Christ: An Exposition of Philippians 2:5-8," *Bsac* 158 (2001): 310-11. As his title indicates, MacLeod assumes the V-pattern in this text.

[13] O'Brien, *Epistle to the Philippians*, 254.

B.3.2. Incarnational interpretation.

This is not to be thought of as an alternate interpretation from the previously mentioned ethical approach, but as an adequate grounding for it. Although I resist the view that suggests that the context for explaining this passage is how Christ becomes incarnate, I do believe the ethical approach needs to be sustained so as to understand Paul's exhortation to the Philippian Christians. I believe that the context alone warrants such a reading, and the exhortation takes Christ as an example to be emulated in his attitude of service to others, even at the greatest of all costs. "Paul does not think it is ridiculous idealism to appeal to the example of Christ as a moral pattern for believers" notes Witherington, "Rather, he believes that by God's Spirit and Grace, believers too can be obedient even unto death."[14]

As we have discussed in some depth both, the history and theology, as well as category differences for kenotic thinking in the book already, it will remain to use the word "kenotic" as a catch-all designation in this chapter. Specific nuances of particular writers will be noted in the discussion. Here we begin with a broad look at the incarnational scenario which is part and parcel of the traditional framework.

B.3.3. Literary Structure.

Since the time of Lohmeyer's monumental work on this passage, many commentators have sought out the literary structure of the so-called hymn. Lohmeyer's contribution, *Kyrios Jesus* was released in 1928. For an informative analysis of his thesis one should consult Colin Brown's masterful essay.[15] Looking at the entire pericope, Lohmeyer developed a structure of six stanzas each consisting of three lines. Although Lohmeyer used the term *strophe*, its original German meaning could connote "stanza," "verse," or "strophe," it is, therefore, advisable to follow Brown and explain that "stanza" is used for each of the six three lined sections, and "strophe" to be used for the two broader passages each containing three stanzas.

Lohmeyer's rendering is as follows:

(1) [The one] existing in the form of God
considered it not plunder to be like God,

(2) but sacrificed himself,
having taken the form of a slave, having become an image of humanity;

(3) and [though] being found "as Son of Man"
he humbled himself, having become obedient unto death [death on a cross].

(4) And therefore God exalted him highly
and bestowed on him the name above every name,

---

[14] Ben Witherington III, *Friendship and Finances in Philippi: The Letter of Paul to the Philippians* (Valley Forge: PA: Trinity, 1994), 67.

[15] See Colin Brown, "Ernst Lohmeyer's *Kyrios Jesus*," in Ralph P. Martin and Brian J. Dodd, eds., *Where Christology Began*, 6-42. This is a fine analysis of Lohmeyer's work.

(5) that at the name of Jesus
every knee should bow in heaven, earth, and the underworld,
(6) and every tongue acclaim:
"Jesus Christ is Lord" to the glory of God, the Father.[16]

One is immediately struck by some differences here from the English translations cited earlier. Nonetheless, this is a fair presentation and approach to the text. "Content corresponds to structure," asserts Brown. He develops the meaning of the arrangement thus:

> The first three stanzas are characterized by the framing of the verb by two participles, except that the first has an infinitive verb as a noun ("to be equal with God") instead of a participle. In the last three stanzas nouns take the place of participles. The wording is unique, and does not correspond to Paul's customary style. The first stanza (v.6) refers to the remote object before the immediate one. In the second stanza (v.7) the participles are juxtaposed asyndectically without conjunctions in the second and third lines. The fifth stanza (v.10) separates the genetives in the Greek ("in heaven and on earth and under the earth") from the nouns to which they belong. The sixth stanza (v.11) interrupts the connection between the first and third lines with the cry: "Jesus Christ is Lord."[17]

Although Lohmeyer's rendering of the passage permits one to discount the traditional framework, as will be done shortly, Brown discerns the assumption of the V-pattern in this presentation. "The emphatic "And therefore" (v.9) which governs the last three stanzas," declares Brown, "introduces a new turn. The first three stanzas depict *Christ's way from heaven to earth* [emphasis added] and death, and the last three his exaltation."[18]

B.3.4. Theological Insights

What have interpreters done with this text? One thing for sure is that it is assumed that Paul is describing the pre-existent Christ (or more correctly Son of God) as existing in the form of God and then becoming incarnate described by the familiar "He emptied himself." J.B. Lightfoot, may serve as the classic illustration for this approach. His summary paraphrase/interpretation is as follows:

> Reflect in your own minds the mind of Christ Jesus. Be humble, as He also was humble. Though existing before the worlds in the Eternal Godhead, yet did not cling with avidity to the prerogatives of His divine majesty, did not ambitiously display His equality with God; but divested Himself of the glories of heaven, and took upon Him the nature of a servant, assuming the likeness of men. Nor was this all. Having thus appeared among men in the fashion of a man, He humbled Him-

---

[16] Brown, "Ernst Lohmeyer's *Kyrios*," 8-9.
[17] Brown, "Ernst Lohmeyer's *Kyrios*," 9.
[18] Brown, "Ernst Lohmeyer's *Kyrios*," 9.

self yet more, and carried out His obedience even to dying. Nor did He die by a common death: He was crucified, as the lowest malefactor is crucified.[19]

As Martin begins his exegesis proper of the text (v. 6a), the title of his chapter is "The Pre-existent Being."[20] Paul's expression "who, existing in the form of God," has itself been well studied.[21]

Cullmann in his classic study of New Testament Christology has an ingenious approach. In agreement with most interpreters that the "who" of verse six is Jesus Christ, he elaborates that this is a Heavenly Man who is pre-existent.[22] This is not necessitated by the text, and the supporting evidence that Cullmann cites is not compelling. True, Paul speaks of the Man from heaven in 1 Corinthians 15, but this could be a reference to the future coming of Christ.[23] Cullmann's "Heavenly Man" thesis must be abandoned.

Käsemann develops at great length the concept of a Hellenistic, pre-Christian Gnostic influence on the writer who penned this material.[24] As such he has been very vocal in discounting the "ethical approach." In its place he advocates a "kerygmatic" understanding that links verse 5 with verse 11 and shows the real concern to be Christ's Lordship over creation, and not an ethical appeal based on Christ's example.

Another way of deciding how to best conceive of the passage is the Adam – Christ parallel. Most famous in this regard is C.H. Talbert.[25] His is an extreme

---

[19] J.B. Lightfoot, *St. Paul's Epistle to the Philippians: A Revised Text with Introduction, Notes and Dissertations* (Peabody, MA: Hendrickson, 1995), 110.

[20] Martin, *Hymn of Christ*, 99.

[21] See O'Brien, *Epistle to the Philippians*, 205-11. "The expression does not refer simply to external appearance," claims O'Brien, "but pictures the preexistent Christ as clothed in the garments of divine majesty and splendour" (211).

[22] See Oscar Cullmann, *The Christology of the New Testament*, trans. Shirley C. Guthrie and Charles A.M. Hall (Philadelphia: Westminster, 1963), 174-81. O'Brien notes, "The notion of a preexistent humanity is foreign to the entire NT, and not only to Paul" (O'Brien, *Epistle to the Philippians*, 267).

[23] See C.K. Barrett, *The First Epistle to the Corinthians* (Peabody, MA: Hendrickson, 1968), 375-78.

[24] Ernst Käsemann, "A Critical Analysis of Philippians 2:5-11," trans. Alice F. Carse, *Journal for Theology and Church* 5 (1968): 45-87.

[25] Charles H. Talbert, "The Problem of Pre-Existence in Philippians 2:6-11," *JBL* 86 (1967): 141-53. This article makes a good case for its conclusion regarding the need to modify the traditional framework. I am less happy with Talbert's designation of "Mythical," for the view that speaks of Jesus as pre-existing. This is almost degrading of those who adhere to the traditional understanding of Christ's pre-existence based on this scripture. One may well adhere to the pre-existence of Christ as I do, with an affirmation that the text of Phil 2:5-8, rather than delineating the incarnation, presupposes it. More cogent are Talbert's observations with regard to the background of the Servant Songs. He asserts the influence of Isaiah as informing the description of Jesus (152-53). A revival of sorts of this "Adam Christology" view is now found in James D.G. Dunn, *Christology in the Making: A New Testament Inquiry into the Origin of the Doctrine of the Incarnation* (Grand Rapids: Eerdmans, 1989 [1980]), 98-128. Here, Dunn goes to great lengths to deny that the hymn contains any reference to a pre-existing Christ.

case of the view that assumes a correct understanding of structure necessarily leads to a correct view of meaning.[26] What is most significant in Talbert's approach is his resistance to the traditional framework. While one may have some reservations about his way of handling the text, it is best to agree with Talbert that the traditional framework needs to be modified. He states that Joachim Jeremias's approach to structure is a needed alternative to Lohmeyer.[27] He spends most of his article explaining the parallelisms inherent in the text. Finally, he concludes that a four 'strophe' approach is more accurate than Lohmeyer's six stanza outline, and Jeremias's three strophe approach, and that sections one and two of the hymn address the same historical scenario, namely Jesus' earthly ministry. As Christ's earthly career is discussed in the second section, so Talbert argues, it is the earthly life of Jesus that appears in the first.

Yet, another approach to the passage, which is similar to Talbert's, but draws on a different tradition, is that of J. Murphy-O'Connor.[28] He utilizes the Wisdom tradition, and focuses on Jesus as man. God elevates Christ because of his obedience, unlike the disobedience of Adam.

What then is the "form of God"? Again, the approaches are varied. It must refer to some manner of possessing deity. The expression ἐν μορφῇ Θεοῦ ("form of God," v. 6a) must be conceptually identical with Christ being ἴσα Θεῷ ("equal with God," v. 6b).[29] Lightfoot has set the standard. Anyone looking at this question needs to begin with Lightfoot's studies on "form of God."[30] Many have challenged his work but Hawthorne is a more recent defender of his view.[31] As Christ was said to "exist" in this form of God coupled with the nature of Godhead implicit in the term, it is not surprising that the "incarnational interpretation" has received such widespread acclaim. It appears straightforward enough. This view, however, which affirms Christ's position as God in the pre-existent state, as this classic approach based on the V-pattern insists, must deal with the next matter of explaining what the concept of "robbery" or "a thing to be grasped" is precisely. This is no easy task. This strange phrase οὐχ ἁρπαγμὸν ἡγήσατο το ειναι ισα Θεω "He . . . did not regard equality with

---

[26] See Robert Strimple's perceptive critique in "Philippians 2:5-11 in Recent Studies: Some Exegetical Conclusions," *WTJ* 41 (1979), 251-52.

[27] On Jeremias's approach, see Joachim Jeremias, "Zu Phil. ii.7: Ἑαυτον Ἐκενωσεν," *NovT* 6 (1963): 182-88; and Martin, *Hymn of Christ*, 32-35.

[28] Jerome Murphy-O' Connor, "Christological Anthropology," *RB* (January 1976): 25-50. Cullmann, *Christology of the New Testament*, 177-80, also highly favors this approach. Also, see the brief piece by Andrew J. Bandstra,"'Adam' and 'The Servant' in Philippians 2:5ff.," *CTJ* (1966): 213-16.

[29] Fee asserts: "This, then, is what it means for Christ to be "in the 'form' of God": it means "to be equal with God," not in the sense that the two phrases are identical, but both point to the same reality" (Fee, *Paul's Philippians*, 207). A most thorough study is found in Fabricatore, *Form of God*, 135-202.

[30] Lightfoot, *Epistle to the Philippians*, 127-37.

[31] Gerald F. Hawthorne, *Philippians* (Dallas: Word, 1983), 82.

Chapter 8: An Exegetical and Theological Look at Philippians 2:5-8

God a thing to be grasped" (NASB [updated ed.]), has caused a lot of difficulty for interpreters. A thorough study has been undertaken by N.T. Wright.[32]

Silva, within the traditional framework, explains this section thus, "the apparent meaning of these striking lines is that the divine and pre-existent Christ did not regard the advantage of His deity as grounds to avoid the incarnation."[33] Moule gives an interesting interpretation. "I agree with those who interpret *harpagmos* not, concretely, as 'something worth snatching,'" says Moule, "but abstractly, as 'the act of snatching' (i.e., virtually 'acquisitiveness'), and who render the phrase. . . in some such way as: 'Jesus did not reckon that equality with God meant snatching: on the contrary, he emptied himself.'"[34] I must, however, agree with Bruce who says, "There is no question of Christ's trying to snatch or seize equality with God: that was already his because he was *in very nature God*"[35] This much seems certain as Christ was equal to God. Bruce continues, "Neither is there any question of his trying to retain it by force."[36] This also appears sound as the text does not yield this sense. "The point is rather," adds Bruce, "that he did not treat his equality with God as an excuse for self-assertion or self-aggrandizement."[37]

The traditional approach sees verse 2:7 as an explanation of the incarnation.[38] The familiar words "He emptied himself" are believed to be a description of the act of incarnation. Theologians who have utilized some form of kenotic understanding have generally appealed to this very passage. The commentary literature certainly supports this trend, even when it does not enter the forum of discussing Christology proper.[39] Silva, gives a general warning. By

---

[32] See N.T. Wright, "ἁρπαγμός and the Meaning of Philippians 2:5-11," *Journal of Theological Studies* 37 (1986): 321-52. This essay presents a helpful chart outlining several scholarly contributions on this passage (342-43). This article, with some additional material, is reproduced in N.T. Wright, *The Climax of the Covenant: Christ and the Law in Pauline Theology* (Minneapolis: Fortress, 1993), 56-98 in a chapter entitled "Jesus Christ is Lord: Philippians 2.5-11."

[33] Silva, *Philippians*, 113. See also Martin, *A Hymn of Christ*, 134-53, for interpretive options.

[34] Moule, "The Manhood of Jesus," 48-49. See, also, Silva, *Philippians*, 117, who nicely lays out the interpretive options on this difficult scripture.

[35] F.F. Bruce, *Philippians* (Peabody, MA: Hendrickson, 1995 [1983]), 69.

[36] Bruce, *Philippians*, 69.

[37] Bruce, *Philippians*, 69.

[38] See John Eadie, *A Commentary on the Greek Text of Paul's Letter to the Philippians* (Birmingham, AL: Solid Ground, 2005 [1885]), 109-19; Fabricatore, *Form of God*, 160-66; Marvin R. Vincent, *The Epistles to the Philippians and to Philemon* (Edinburgh: T and T Clark, 1979), 57-63, and an excursus, 78-90.

[39] Beyond studies already mentioned, the following also take verse 7, "He emptied Himself," as a reference to the incarnation in one way or another. See A.B. Bruce, *The Humiliation of Christ: In Its Physical, Ethical, and Official Aspects* (Grand Rapids: Eerdmans, 1955), 15-23; Archibald Thomas Robertson, *Word Pictures in the New Testament*, vol. 4, *The Epistles of Paul* (Grand Rapids: Baker, n.d.), 444-45; Millard Ross Cherry, "The Christology of Philippians 2:5-11" (Th.D. diss., Southern Baptist Theological Seminary, 1956), 136-219; Daniel T. Knapp, "The Self-Humiliation of Jesus Christ

equating the verbs in vv. 7 and 8, he suggests that "the central thought of the whole Christ-hymn is embodied in the two main verbs, εκένωσεν and εταπείνωσεν, which illuminate each other. It is specious to drive a sharp wedge between these verbs."[40] However, there is a difference in meaning.

New Testament scholars are often cautious about making definitive theological statements, especially on a passage such as this that has generated so much divergence of opinion. Nevertheless, only a theological reading of Scripture does it justice as God's word designed to speak beyond its original setting. Despite its obvious original occasional provenance, which prompted the writing in the first place, the Bible as it now stands speaks still in a theological voice to us today. On this very text, one of the greatest exegetes from a past generation provides a "theological" exposition on the text. "*Emptied himself (εαυτον εκένωσεν)* [is a] First aorist active indicative of κενοω, [to] empty," declares A.T. Robertson. He continues, "Of what did Christ empty himself? Not of his divine nature. That was impossible. He continued to be the Son of God."[41] Nothing is objectionable in content here; but moreover, nothing is wrong with Robertson's *method* either. He is using a theological axiom to control the sense of the text. No doubt, he would claim to find the justification for such a move within the text itself or from other texts. Be that as it may, it is the only way to do biblical theology, and subsequently systematic theological exposition of the Bible. If Robertson the biblical scholar may be excused for this, so might the theologians who have attempted a theological reading in interpreting this text. To a theological exposition we now turn.

B.4. Alternate Framework

Some suggestions have been made in our presentation to this point for a need to abandon the traditional framework.[42] This needs some explanation. It is not in

---

and Christ-like Living: A Study of Philippians 2:6-11," *EvJ* 15 (1997): 80-96; Robert E. Wilson, "He Emptied Himself," *JETS* 19 (1976): 279-81; and Chrestos Patitsas, "*Kenosis* According to Saint Paul," *GOTR* 27 (1982): 67-82.

[40] Silva, *Philippians*, 119. Silva favorably quotes Marvin Vincent, saying eauton ekenwsen "is used as a 'graphic expression of the completeness of his self-renunciation. It includes all the details of humiliation which follow, *and is defined by these*. Further definition belongs to speculative theology.' " But also in speaking about this very expression of Christ emptying Himself and its context in the hymn, Silva posits, "We may want to deny that the passage speaks primarily to ontological issues regarding the nature of the Trinity, but it would appear futile to deny that Phil. 2:5-7 has some strong implications for these issues" (125).

[41] Robertson, *Word Pictures*, 4:444.

[42] Steven Tsoukalas is helpful in addressing the theological problems that surface if the traditional V-pattern framework is not abandoned. He notes (1) First the notion that Christ does not consider equality with God as robbery, either amounts to Christ not possessing equality with God or that having it he abandons it in the incarnation; (2) if Christ truly exists as God before the incarnation, then what of his subsequent exaltation? It appears to necessitate that Christ is elevated to a status higher than equality with God, which appears absurd or his exaltation has no meaning for him; and (3) kenosis cannot be avoided without "semantic gymnastics" (Steven Tsoukalas, *Knowing Christ in the Challenge of Heresy: A Christology of the Cults, A Christology of the Bible* [Lanham,

Chapter 8: An Exegetical and Theological Look at Philippians 2:5-8

question that the New Testament employs the descent – ascent pattern for explaining the coming of Christ. John's gospel abounds with this type of language. Paul, himself makes much of pre-existence in his letters: Romans 8:3; 2 Corinthians 8:9; Galatians 4:4; Colossians 1:15-21; 1 Timothy 3:16, just to cite a few references. Therefore, the previous statements, as well as the present interpretation must be judged in the clear affirmation of Jesus Christ's preexistence as God the Son. As I proceed in explaining Philippians 2:5-8, this must be kept fully in mind. What needs modification is the widely held belief that the Philippians 2:5-8 passage itself, actually teaches the descent as occurring in the expression "He emptied himself." One may question whether contextually this is the case. David Wells senses the uneasiness that sits with kenotic affirmations that mesh well with this framework, and his words are refreshing, yet he still concedes that the kenosis is for the purpose of incarnation. He puts the matter this way. "Kenotic theories misplaced the element of humiliation. Undoubtedly they were correct to emphasize the costliness of the incarnation for the one who surrendered his riches for our poverty."[43] Wells adds, "It is possible, however, to make too much of this . . . . If the emphasis of Philippians 2:5-11 is to be sustained, the element of humiliation is to be associated, *not with Christ's incarnation, but with his atonement.*"[44] In speaking of the specific phrase, "emptied Himself," Vincent says the words are "[n]ot used or intended here in a metaphysical sense to define the limitations of Christ's incarnate state, but as a strong and graphic expression of the completeness of his self-renunciation."[45] These observations are helpful and they lead in the direction of abandoning the incarnational interpretation, to replace it with a view of the passage that *assumes the already incarnate status of Jesus Christ.*

Let us examine once again the subject of the verb. In verse six it merely states "who." The "who" is none other than Christ Jesus clearly spoken of by Paul in verse five. This designation "Christ Jesus" is mostly reserved by Paul to describe the *already incarnate* Son of God.[46] Admittedly, on one or two instances, Paul may refer to "Christ" and attach a pre-existent referent to it (1 Tim 1:15).[47] But here in Philippians this pre-existence concept is not essential to make good sense of the passage.[48] Therefore, one may assume an already

---

MD: University Press of America, 1999], 99-101). In this helpful work, Tsoukalas acknowledges his dependence on Robert Reymond's analysis of the Philippians text. My approach draws on Reymond as well.

[43] David F. Wells, *The Person of Christ: A Biblical and Historical Analysis of the Incarnation* (Alliance, OH: Bible Scholar, 1992), 139 [emphasis added].

[44] Wells, *The Person of Christ*, 139.

[45] Marvin Vincent, *Philippians and Philemon*, 59.

[46] See Robert L. Reymond, *A New Systematic Theology of the Christian Faith* (Nashville: Thomas Nelson, 1998), 253, who makes this point.

[47] Reymond, *A New Systematic Theology*, 262.

[48] See George Howard, "Phil 2:6-11 and the Human Christ," *CBQ* 40 (1978): 377, for a similar assessment.

incarnate Christ, as described in verse five, as the subject of this Christological passage.[49]

B.5. Alternative Interpretation

Obviously much hinges on how one sees the framework. The traditional view sought its justification from grammatical considerations. For example, as already noted, the participles in verses 7 and 8, were said to modify the main verb.[50] The main verb in verse 7 is εκένωσεν (emptied). On the traditional reckoning the means of the emptying is "by taking the form of a servant." These aorist participles, however, may legitimately be translated as "having taken the form of a servant," and "having become in the likeness of men," which is how it is rendered in Lohmeyer's structure cited earlier. H. Wheeler Robinson helpfully explains the aorist forms as "aorists of antecedent action."[51]

Here is a preliminary rendering of the passage:

> 5. Have this mind in you, which also *was* in Christ Jesus (already incarnate),
> 6. Who, Being in the form of God
>   did *not* consider his equality(possessed) with God (the Father)
>   a thing to be grasped/seized/exploited (used for self aggrandizement/for his own advantage),[52]
> 7. But he poured himself out (living for others ending in death [the true kenosis]),
>   Having (already) taken the form of a slave
>   and having (already) become in the likeness of men
> 8. and being (already) found in appearance as a man
>   he humbled himself
>   becoming obedient unto death–even death on a cross.

Along with New Testament scholar Gordon Fee, I believe that the way Paul wrote or dictated this piece needs no "original setting" to make sense of it. I do

---

[49] Fee, *Paul's Philippians*, 197, says of our text, "Here is the closest thing to Christology that one finds in Paul."

[50] See Fee, *Paul's Philippians*, 195-96, as an example.

[51] See H. Wheeler Robinson, *The Cross of the Servant* (London: SCM, 1924), 104n.23. Also, see my brief discussion in Charles Brand, Charles Draper, & Archie England, eds., *Holman Illustrated Bible Dictionary* (Nashville: Holman, 2003), s.v. "Kenosis" by Doros Zachariades.

[52] The philological work of Hoover is thought by many to be definitive for explaining the meaning of this problematic expression. See Roy W. Hoover, "The Harpagmos Enigma: A Philological Solution," *HTR* 61 (1971): 95-119. Hoover concludes that *harpagmos* means "something to use for one's own advantage" (Hoover, "Harpagmos Enigma," 118). He is followed by N.T. Wright, "ἁρπαγμος and the Meaning of Philippians 2:5-11," 321; 344-52; Dennis Johnson, "Immutability and Incarnation: An Historical and Theological Study of the Concepts of Christ's Divine Unchangeability and His Human Development" (Ph.D. diss., Fuller Theological Seminary, 1984), 388-89; and Silva, *Philippians*, 116-18, for example.

not take it to be a hymn.⁵³ In this, I side with Fee against the majority.⁵⁴ Yet, I disagree with Fee, who still sees this passage in light of the "traditional framework." Given our presentation, from a somewhat different perspective, let us proceed to fill out the exposition.

Paul is often reflecting on Old Testament scripture as he writes New Testament letters. For example, in Romans Paul draws on Old Testament scriptures to develop his argument about the gospel of Christ. This appears also to be the case in this passage of Philippians concerning the Christ of the gospel. Richard Bauckham has written a helpful volume, which draws this out superbly.⁵⁵ When one examines the full passage and notices the Old Testament language in 2:10-11, it becomes evident that Paul is reflecting on Isaiah. It is in the great prophet that words about "tongues confessing and knees bowing" originate, as one can see in Isaiah 45:23. Moreover in Isaiah 52:13 the prophet predicted that the servant of Yahweh would be exalted after he would deal prudently and sprinkle many (confirmed in Masoretic text). In 53:12 Isaiah reports that the Servant would "pour out his soul unto death." This is very likely the idea driving Paul's "He emptied himself;" they are conceptually identical.⁵⁶ The humility involved

---

⁵³ Fee lists four lines of evidence to sustain this: (1) the word *hymnos* is usually used with songs or poems specifically offering praise to a divinity or esteemed person listing the reasons for this; (2) there is no analogy forthcoming that matches the Philippians text to show it as hymnodic; (3) despite the poetic structure of vv. 6-8, the following verses have a combination of a syntax, including a *hina* and *oti* clause, which as Fee states: "is not the stuff of hymns but of argumentation;" and (4) If the structure of verses 9-11 appeared elsewhere in the letter, no one would have imagined it to be from a hymn. See Fee, *Paul's Philippians*, 193 n. 4.

⁵⁴ See Fee, *Paul's Philippians*, 40-42, for some helpful comments on this matter of the passage's alleged hymnodic background.

⁵⁵ Richard Bauckham, *God Crucified: Monotheism and Christology in the New Testament* (Grand Rapids: Eerdmans, 1998), 51-53; 56-61. There is much to praise in this work. I find helpful the connection made with the servant songs of Isaiah. Also, Bauckham sees more to the phrase "He emptied Himself" than most. Although he still acknowledges the V-pattern of the "traditional framework," his comments are refreshing: "The pouring out or emptying is the self-renunciation in service and obedience, which begins with incarnation and leads inexorably to death. Paul then glosses the word 'death' (from Isaiah) with the phrase 'even death on a cross' to indicate that the form of death was this appropriately shameful end to the self-humiliation already described in Isaiah 53" (60).

⁵⁶ Dennis Johnson also shares this view, even though he maintains the V-pattern for the passage as a whole. "Although," notes Johnson, "objections have been raised against interpreting ἑαυτὸν ἐκένωσεν as an allusion to the death of the *Ebed Yahweh*, these are not unanswerable. On balance, the evidence seems to support this understanding of v. 7a" (Dennis Edward Johnson, "Immutability and Incarnation," 397). Also see W. Warren, "On ἑαυτὸν ἐκένωσεν," *JTS* 12 (1911): 461-63; and Robert B. Strimple, "Philippians 2:5-11 in Recent Studies: Some Exegetical Conclusions," *WTJ* 41 (1979): 247-68, esp. 265-68.

in this description is overwhelming, so Paul also claims that Christ humbled himself.[57]

Specific examples of Christ not using his equality as God to selfishly serve himself are forthcoming in the gospel narratives. The *locus classicus* for such a stance by Jesus is undoubtedly John 13.[58] A particularly amazing example is the temptation scene in Luke 4:3, where the devil said to him: "If you are the Son of God, command this stone to become bread." After 40 days of constant temptation (v. 2), he is hungry. As a true man, Jesus needed food for his yet unglorified human body. The temptation was real as the hunger was real. The parallel to Philippians is very probable.[59] As God's Son, Jesus is God's equal; as Creator, Jesus Christ can turn water into wine, and presumably stone into bread. Yet in taking the road less-traveled, in humility, he undergoes hunger and forfeits the use of the power he had to promote his own well-being.[60] In a manner re-

---

[57] Tsoukalas, *Knowing Christ*, 101-104, also offers an interpretation of this passage that is commensurate with the above exposition.

[58] Evangelical commentators, Philip Comfort & Wendell Hawley make this observation concerning the supper scenario in John 13-17: "They [Jesus and His disciples] enjoyed a dinner together, which very likely was the Passover meal. Jesus washed the disciples' feet as a sign of servanthood and an example of humility for the disciples to emulate. . . . The opening scene of this chapter (13:1-16) is symbolic of Jesus' coming from God to serve humanity and his subsequent return to God. This symbolism is verbalized in Philippians 2:5-11." See Philip W. Comfort & Wendell C. Hawley, *Opening the Gospel of John: A Fresh Resource for Teaching and Preaching the Fourth Gospel* (Wheaton, IL: Tyndale, 1994,) 209. They add four telling parallels from John 13 with Philippians 2, *Opening the Gospel of John*, 210.

[59] Moule says: "Jesus began his public career in this very humble way, by accepting baptism at the hands of John [the Baptizer] . . . . instantly, on the heels of it, follows a prolonged testing by 'the Opposition'. . . .Matthew and Luke go into more detail about this testing, and show that it is a direct challenge to Jesus to doubt or misuse his position as Son of God. The whole gospel story can be seen as a picture of Jesus working out this sonship day by day in terms of eager obedience to plan of God–an obedience which, in the end, leads to death" (C.F.D. Moule, *The Gospel According to Mark* [Cambridge: Cambridge University Press, 1965], 11).

[60] It is in light of these observations that the challenge to the church at Philippi makes sense, not in imitating God the Son who became incarnate, but imitating the already incarnate God-Man, who's genuinely true humanity, nonetheless thought of others and forfeited his rights. For a helpful analysis on the "hymn" see Dennis Bratcher, "The Poured-Out Life: The Kenosis Hymn in Context, 1-7" Accessed 7/6/2007 http://www.crivoice.org/kenosis.html; Internet. Bratcher uses the threefold grid: "privilege-servanthood-exaltation." There is no need to posit an incarnational context, but it is compatible with an already incarnate Christ moving *horizontally* from privilege to servanthood and ultimately *vertically* to exaltation. Bratcher sees Paul as an example of how this may be worked out in an individual Christian's life, like Christ. He says, "Paul deliberately uses himself and his circumstances to illustrate the proper exercise of the role of servant exemplified by Christ. Paul repeatedly uses the word *phronein* (to set one's mind on, to have an attitude) to refer to the mind-set of humility and selflessness to which he originally called the Philippians and which the Kenosis Hymn illustrates (2:5; cf. 2:2; 1:7). He also uses it to refer to his own attitude of selfless commitment, which he

flecting a Servant's heart, Jesus obeyed his Father in this instant, and in every other instant, even unto the death on a cross. He poured out his life for others even unto death–he gave his life as a ransom for many. This is the true meaning of the Philippians text. No kenosis but the cross.

C. Kenotic Theologians

It is time to re-visit a couple of theologians we met a while back in previous chapters of the book. Millard Erickson and Gerald Hawthorne are two evangelicals that have adopted a kenotic type of Christology. I will not rehearse all their arguments at this point, but I want to mention Erickson's rational for denying omnipresence to Jesus. In addition, a brief review of Ronald Feenstra's proposal will highlight a particular problem evident in many kenotic–type approaches to the incarnation.

C.1. Millard Erickson

"Rather than suggest that God gave up certain attributes of divinity as well as certain attributes of humanity in becoming incarnate," Erickson posits, "I prefer to emphasize that what he did in the incarnation was to add something to each nature, namely, the attributes of the other nature."[61] Commenting on our passage from Philippians, Erickson states, "Thus, I would interpret the participle λαβων ("taking") in Philippians 2:7 as an instrumental participle, so that it should be rendered, "He emptied himself *by taking* the form of a servant (emphasis added)."[62] In another place Erickson continues his reasoning. "May not the incarnation be a matter of divine self-limitation, freely chosen and appropriate to deity?" asks Erickson.[63] To bolster this approach, Erickson speaks of promises made by God, and he also mentions the Creation, which according to Erickson places limitation on God.[64] "The incarnation can be thought of along those lines," Erickson argues. "While giving up the divine nature would be a surrender of deity," he adds, "and even giving up certain of its attributes might well be, a voluntary decision to restrict the independent exercise of some attrib-

---

invites them to share (3:15). He uses the same word to highlight the wrong mind-set, that of selfish preoccupation with earthly values (3:19), and to commend their own concrete expression of the proper concern for others (4:10). It is this willingness to lay aside all rights of personal privilege, to submit in the spirit of servanthood to the needs and concerns of others, that is the heart of this letter. From Paul's side we see it as one who is a faithful servant following the Servant-Christ. From the Philippians' side it is as those who are obligated to exhibit that servanthood as followers of Christ. To show Christ as a servant, then, is to illustrate what being 'in Christ' entails" ("Poured-Out Life," 4).

[61] Millard J. Erickson, *The Word Became Flesh: A Contemporary Incarnational Christology* (Grand Rapids: Baker, 1991), 555.

[62] Erickson, *The Word Became Flesh*, 555.

[63] Erickson, *The Word Became Flesh*, 549.

[64] Erickson, *The Word Became Flesh*, 549. I find it interesting that Erickson argues this way. No doubt there is a point to his rationale. However, the Bible mentions creation not to speak of any limitation on God, but on the contrary to uphold the greatness of God. This appears to be God's own use of the creation as *God's own* work in his response to Job (Job 38-41; also see Isa 40:18-30).

utes is not necessarily a forfeiture of deity."[65] Erickson is crystal clear in terms of his belief in limitations for Jesus Christ. He says, "Omnipresence is the attribute where the necessity of limitation involved in the incarnation is clearest." Erickson adds, "As God, Jesus had the capability of being everywhere."[66] To this, he includes the following poignant observation. Notes Erickson,

> Yet, for the period of his earthly incarnation, he limited himself to the restrictions in location which having a physical human body entailed. He had possessed the capability of active omnipresence: being pure spirit, he was not limited to any particular place and time. But as part of the decision to become incarnate, he also decided not to exercise that capability, or to make it latent, for a period of time.[67]

I believe this manner of speaking concerning the specific attribute of omnipresence, as in Erickson's proposal, is not tenable. It appears that with the use of expressions such as "What we are saying is that his basic powers were not lost, but only the ability to exercise them," and "Jesus did not give up the qualities of God, but gave up the privilege of exercising them,"[68] is a valiant attempt to make a distinction between "'nature' and 'conditions'" as Erickson claims, yet it cannot work with omnipresence. The simple fact is that omnipresence by definition is more than the ability to be everywhere; it is that one who is omnipresent *is* everywhere by necessity. A distinction that may be used with omnipotence cannot be utilized with teaching about Christ's presence in relation to the created order.[69] It must be conceded that Erickson's examples illustrate the possibility of how omnipotence may be temporarily given up in the sense of use, but they do not aid his argument for omnipresence. In Erickson's exposition what is really being said is counter to his basic framework of distinguishing the possession of attributes with their use. For example, in saying that Christ is "no longer pure spirit," Erickson evidently means that a divine contraction has taken place for the second person of the Trinity in the incarnation. Therefore, it is not the case that "*Who* he was" has not changed but merely what he does. The "Who" has undergone a metaphysical alteration in Erickson's proposal not merely a metaphysical addition. What is evident in this entire approach is that Erickson attempts to use the truth of Christ's humanity to become the filter for explaining the deity. Brown makes this point concerning the kenotic theology. "E.L. Mascall," notes Brown, "has described kenoticism as a kind of inverted monophysitism: 'Whereas the monophysitism of the Eutychians absorbed the human nature into the divine, that of the kenoticists ab-

---

[65] Erickson, *The Word Became Flesh*, 549.
[66] Erickson, *The Word Became Flesh*, 561.
[67] Erickson, *The Word Became Flesh*, 561.
[68] Erickson, *The Word Became Flesh*, 550.
[69] It is possible to envision an omnipresent God becoming not omnipresent, not by any change in the being of God, but by the extinction of the created order. This would render God the only being, and as such there would be "nowhere" for him to be present. That the Bible portrays God as determined to save his creation and not in any way ready to dispense with it, it is safe to say that he will always be omnipresent in regards to it as a created entity.

sorbs the divine nature into the human.'"[70] One is, therefore, forced to reconsider the biblical witness to the divine nature and somehow make it compatible with a truly human person.[71] It is this starting point of Erickson's endeavor which places him in his self-defined characterization of advocating a kenotic type of Christology. As such, it can legitimately be said that Erickson's understanding of Christ does not do full justice to the deity of Jesus despite his claims. The rationale that God freely entered this state of affairs does not suffice to maintain the full deity of Jesus as it includes God [the Son] in becoming less than who he is prior to the incarnation. Erickson has attempted to argue for a view of the incarnation as a kenosis by addition, but as his statements have made explicitly clear, there is an inherent inability for Christ to be omnipresent during his earthly ministry. Erickson explains his view in the following way:

> He [God the Son] made a voluntary decision to limit the exercise of his omnipresence for a certain period of time. This is not to imply that he could have overridden the decision at any moment. He had willed that from approximately 4 B. C. to A. D. 29 he would not have the free use of his omnipresence. It was that he was pretending that he could not use it; *he really could not* [emphasis added].[72]

This language is clear in its expression of limitation. Recall the statement quoted earlier, which follows immediately upon this kenotic explanation, "What we are saying is that his basic powers were not lost, but *only the ability to exercise them*" (emphasis added). Erickson next says the same thing regarding omniscience, and then continues with an illustration of a softball game where parents were placed under a rule to bat left-handed so as to make the game fair for the children. The application to the incarnation is vivid in the subsequent explanation. "Now one's ability as a right-handed batter was not diminished," posits Erickson, "but it could not be exercised because of the requirement to bat from the left-handed-batters [sic] box. Although one was *still able to bat right-handed* (emphasis supplied), one was not allowed to in that particular game."[73] In his discussion, Erickson has claimed that in the incarnation Christ could not exercise omnipresence because his ability to do so was freely rescinded, yet at the same time based on this interesting illustration from the world of sports,

---

[70] Colin Brown, *Jesus in European Protestant Thought 1778-1860* (Durham, NC: Labyrinth, 1985), 254.

[71] This is the case in Hawthorne's position as well. He claims: "The particular view of the Person of Christ . . . . which seems most in harmony with the whole teaching of the New Testament is the view that, in becoming a human being, the Son of God willed to renounce the exercise of his divine powers, attributes, prerogatives, so that he might live fully within those limitations which inhere in being truly human" (Gerald F. Hawthorne, *The Presence and the Power: The Significance of the Holy Spirit in the Life of Jesus* [Dallas: Word, 1991], 208). Roger Helland, "The Hypostatic Union: How Did Jesus Function?" *EvQ* 65 (1993): 311-27, is another attempt to pursue this approach. Helland relies on Hawthorne in this article. Helland's [and Hawthorne's] approach is ably refuted by David Parker, "Jesus Christ: Man of Faith, or Saving Son of God?" *EvQ* 67 (1995): 245-64.

[72] Erickson, *The Word Became Flesh*, 549.

[73] Erickson, *The Word Became Flesh*, 550.

that Christ was able to exercise omnipresence. There is a confusion that emerges in that Erickson cannot betray his evangelical insistence that Jesus of Nazareth is God, but also that this must also be a limited God somehow, if we are to make sense and affirm the full humanity of this very same Jesus.

Erickson has heightened the problem, so to speak, rather than providing a satisfactory explanation. With an abundantly clear difference in meaning between omniscience and omnipresence it seems to follow that any talk of Jesus merely possessing omnipresence but not exercising it (voluntarily or otherwise) is nothing more than verbal sleight of hand. The very definition of the term omnipresence, if words mean anything, requires that Jesus not only possess, but also exercise or use it, which is conceptually necessitated by the definition.

Kenotic approaches to the incarnation have an additional problem that is insurmountable. By equating the kenosis with the incarnation, it is clear that the desire is to safeguard the true and full humanity of Jesus Christ.[74] What this view leads to, however, is to a position that must either abandon the true and full humanity of Jesus after the ascension, where the relative attributes are now once again not only possessed but exercised, or one must continue the kenotic emphasis and insist that Jesus Christ the Son of God, as long as he remains the God-Man, will never again exercise the relative attributes.

C.2. Ronald Feenstra

Of all the writers I have read, only Ronald Feenstra attempted to diffuse this obvious problem concerning the question of whether Jesus Christ now again possesses and exercises all the relative attributes of deity since the ascension.[75] He does so with an ingenious distinction between kenosis and incarnation. Christ underwent incarnation by taking on humanity, and he also emptied himself so as to share our lot, that is share in our limitations.[76] By carefully distinguishing these notions, Feenstra attempts to deal with the problem of Christ's continuing humanity now, and by implication forever. The widespread criticism of Kenotic Christology is only legitimate according to Feenstra, when directed against forms of the theory that do not make this distinction. Indeed, Feenstra admits the weightiness of the challenge as it is this very objection that has led to his novel theory. In short, Feenstra's approach discussing Jesus' sharing of our human limitations, asserts: "He joins us in these experiences, not simply because he is incarnate, but by virtue of his kenotic self-emptying for the purpose of sharing our condition."[77] "Christ's kenosis," adds Feenstra, "can therefore be seen as a temporary sharing of our condition in this life, while his Incarnation is viewed as his becoming human, with the Incarnation continuing after the kenosis ceases."[78] Problems with Feenstra's position include the high

---

[74] See Hawthorne, *Presence and the Power*, 212.

[75] See Ronald J. Feenstra, "Reconsidering Kenotic Christology," in *Trinity, Incarnation, and Atonement: Philosophical and Theologicals Essays*, ed. Ronald J. Feenstra and Cornelius Plantinga, Jr. (Notre Dame, IN: University of Notre Dame Press, 1989), 128-52.

[76] Feenstra, "Reconsidering Kenotic Christology," 148.

[77] Feenstra, "Reconsidering Kenotic Christology," 149.

[78] Feenstra, "Reconsidering Kenotic Christology," 149.

price he is willing to pay for the earthly sojourn of Jesus. In this model we have a fully blown kenotic model. Even if the distinction is maintained as Feenstra suggests, the limitations of the kenotic (and incarnate) Christ, while on the earth, are real as the attributes are really given up, not by virtue of the incarnation per se, according to Feenstra, but nonetheless as embraced by Christ in the conceptually distinct kenosis. However, contrary to his assertions this is not the portrait of Christ that emerges from reading the gospels and taking into account all the data.[79] Moreover, the position advocated by Feenstra asserts that in the exalted state Christ retains his incarnate status, but the kenosis is reversed. This means that Jesus *now* is in possession of and fully exercises the so-called relative attributes. If Christ can be human without being kenotically emptied, he can undergo the work of redemption as God the Son; if he cannot undergo the work of redemption unless kenotically emptied, then it is a mere man who dies on the cross. Better is the view we are advocating, which affirms that both limitation is seen in New Testament passages, and that relative attributes are nonetheless possessed and exercised by Jesus of Nazareth. Therefore, Feenstra is right about the possibility of incarnation without kenosis; this is precisely my view. He is wrong, however, in finally preferring a kenotically emptied Christ.

D. Conclusion

I chose to focus on the doctrine of omnipresence because it fascinates me that Jesus is with me, even though he is in heaven. I believe that in examining the incarnation with a kenotic Christology is a consistent methodologically sound procedure as undertaken by many evangelicals. I also believe, however, that the desire to keep a distinction between possession and use falters upon this very doctrine of omnipresence. So the suggested course of action is to abandon a kenotically informed Christology for a robust declaration that Christ has and exercises all divine attributes for they are in their sum the essence of deity. Kenosis is countered by omnipresence, and therefore this attribute suggests the model of kenotic Christology is suspect.

---

[79] See C.F.D. Moule, *The Origin of Christology* (Cambridge: Cambridge University Press, 1977), 156-58. "A more satisfactory approach [for understanding Jesus]," notes Moule, "is to rely on the total impression gained, cumulatively, by putting side to side the various portraits that are presented by the traditions of Jesus in his various activities: teaching, healing, disputing, training his disciples, and so forth" (156). On this overall "picture" of Christ, one is well served by Geerhardus Vos, *The Self-Disclosure of Jesus: The Modern Debate about the Messianic Consciousness* (George H. Doran, 1924; Phillipsburg, NJ: P & R, 2002); H.E.W. Turner, *Jesus Master and Lord: A Study in the Historical Truth of the Gospels* (London: Mowbray, 1954); and, more recently, Darrell L. Bock, *Jesus According to Scripture: Restoring the Portrait from the Gospels* (Grand Rapids: Baker, 2002). Also, see Daniel Doriani, "The Deity of Christ in the Synoptic Gospels," *JETS* 37 (1994): 333-50; Philip B. Payne, "Jesus' Implicit Claim to Deity in His Parables," *TrinJ* 2 (1981): 3-23; and for the Gospel of John's perspective, see Marianne Meye Thompson, *The Incarnate Word: Perspectives on Jesus in the Fourth Gospel* (Peabody, MA: Hendrickson, 1988); and Robert H. Gundry, *Jesus the Word According to John the Sectarian: A Paleofundamentalist Manifesto for Contemporary Evangelicalsim, Especially Its Elites in North America* (Grand Rapids: Eerdmans, 2002).

Rather than a theology of *kenosis*, the New Testament presents a Christological theology of *krypsis* (hiding or concealing).[80] The divine glory of the eternal Word was not rescinded or given up in any way. Rather it was concealed by the assumption of human nature. In John's gospel this is expressed as follows: "The Word became flesh and took up residence among us. We observed his glory, the glory as the only Son from the Father, full of grace and truth" (John 1:14, Holman Christian Standard Bible). On occasion the glory shone through, so to speak, and became manifest to those with whom Jesus ministered. A clear manifestation of this glory was seen by three disciples on the mount of transfiguration (Matt 17:1-9). Yet, it was seen also as Jesus performed miracles that only God could directly accomplish as Jesus did on several instances. For example, after performing his first sign (miracle) in Cana of Galilee, Jesus "displayed His glory, and His disciples believed in Him" (John 2:11, Holman Christian Standard Bible). I agree with Josef Seifert, who claims that the one underlying compelling reason for our faith in Jesus Christ as God's Son, although faith is a gift of God, is the uninventable glory of God manifest in Jesus. "With all the miracles and words of Christ," notes Seifert, "it is most of all His very being and His life which manifest God to us."[81] To this he adds: "His passion and crucifixion and the words which He spoke from the cross, although the passion first scandalized even His Apostles, reveal in a hidden form behind all humiliation this unspeakable divine glory which no man could ever have invented or made up."[82]

Philippians 2:5-8 does not teach the kind of kenotic Christology advocated by some evangelicals.[83] In fact, it does not address the kenotic issue at all in the way theologians are fond of discussing this matter. Rather, the text is a magnificent piece of theology about Christ's vocation as the Servant of Yahweh, who as Lord God himself, lays down his life for his sheep. As Ryrie asserts, despite his avowal of the traditional framework, he nonetheless catches the correct focus of the passage. "The central passage on the *kenosis*, Philippians 2:5-11,"

---

[80] See Crisp, *Divinity and Humanity*, 147-53, for a nicely presented argument for theological krypsis. Berkouwer in a similar manner speaks of "Christ Incognito." He says, "One can provisionally describe the idea under discussion by that the humanity of Christ does not as such *reveal*, but rather *conceals*, God" (*The Person of Christ*, 333).

[81] Josef Seifert, "The Uninventable Glory of God as the Deepest Reason for Our Faith in Jesus Christ," in *Theos, Anthropos, Christos: A Compendium of Modern Philosophical Theology*, ed. Roy Abraham Varghese (New York: Peter Lang, 2000), 452.

[82] Seifert, "The Uninventable Glory," 452.

[83] After examining the matter quite thoroughly, Hall claims, "No place remains for the assertion that our Lord ceased to be omnipotent, omnipresent and omniscient, as touching His Godhead, during His earthly life, except upon the Arian and Socinian ground that He was not God. This is not to base our ideas upon metaphysical considerations, but to take what is revealed concerning the nature of God in Holy Scripture as eternal truth." See Francis J. Hall, *The Kenotic Theory: Considered with Particular Reference to its Anglican Forms and Arguments* (New York: Longmans, Green, 1898), 137. See also E.H. Gifford, *The Incarnation: A Study of Philippians II:5-11* (London: Hodder and Stoughton, 1897). Gifford also rejects the kenotic view, but in agreement with Hall sees the text as referring to the incarnation.

Chapter 8: An Exegetical and Theological Look at Philippians 2:5-8

Ryrie claims, "begins with an exhortation to humility of mind, following the example of Christ who left glory to suffer on the cross."[84] He also adds:

> He [Jesus] did not give up Deity or the use of attributes; He added humanity. It seems to me that even evangelicals blunt the point of the passage by missing its principal emphasis. . . and focusing on trying to delineate what limitations Christ experienced in His earthly state. To be sure, the God-*Man* experienced limitations; but equally sure the *God*-Man evidenced the prerogatives of Deity. Therefore, conservatives suggest that the *kenosis* means the veiling of Christ's preincarnate glory, which is true only in a relative sense.[85]

---

[84] Charles C. Ryrie, *Basic Theology* (Wheaton, IL: Victor, 1986), 260.
[85] Ryrie, *Basic Theology*, 260.

CHAPTER 9

CONCLUSION

The thesis concerning Jesus Christ as God manifest in the flesh as one person in two natures, thereby remaining omnipresent, despite the reality of human limitations inherent in incarnate state, has been presented on several fronts. We have shown its denial or rejection, as well as its neglect in selected evangelical Christologies. In contrast to many popular kenotic views of the incarnation, it is argued, from a survey of the early church, and from looking at John Calvin's Christology, that omnipresence is a non-negotiable attribute of deity, that Jesus must possess [and use] if he is truly God. This question of omnipresence is an issue which requires attention as it goes to the heart of how we conceive the incarnation. By selecting omnipresence as the attribute of investigation, it is helpful in order to show that the traditional ways of dealing with the so-called relative attributes of deity in relation to the incarnate Christ are incorrect. Omniscience, omnipotence, and omnipresence are eliminated by postulating a distinction between possession and use. However, simply stated, presence is not something one has, but is something one is. Jesus, as the God-Man *is* omnipresent. To talk of Christ possessing but not using omnipresence is tantamount to my saying: "I have a person, but I do not use my person," rather than correctly stating "I am a person." This concession must be granted because of the nature of the concept of a person's presence. I believe that this attribute has caused greater difficulty for those who attempt an explanation of the incarnate Christ by utilizing the aforementioned distinction between possession and use of the attributes. Omnipresence has been subsumed under omniscience in order to safely eliminate it, and therefore not having to deal with the full force of its denial. On the other hand, denying omniscience to Jesus causes other problems for those who claim that Jesus had or possessed omniscience but merely did not use it. As Ronald Feenstra has pointed out, this cannot work for a sub-kenotic model. One is either forced to embrace a fully kenotic model (as Feenstra himself does) or one is to reject kenoticism altogether as is proposed in this book. If Christ has omniscience, then the proposition that Christ knows that he has all knowledge is necessarily included in the knowledge he has. With this given, then to speak as if Christ could live out his life without knowing of his omniscience violates that affirmation that he has all knowledge in his possession. Of course, one may make this kind of distinction with omniscience, yet it cannot work as a "solution" to the understanding of the person of Christ incarnate. In other words, if one utilizes this approach, one must live with necessary inherent tensions that preclude a coherent Christology.

One can make this distinction with omnipotence and it is possible to work.[1] Although I grant this possibility in theory, I do not believe that is what occurred

---

[1] It is argued in theory, that God, even with omnipotence, has certain limitations. The

in the incarnation, as that would appear to ignore certain passages that show Jesus performing miracles that require God's power, and would also violate the Chalcedonian confession of faith that the natures are united in one person in such a manner that each nature retains its respective properties.

Is a kenotic or sub-kenotic Christology justified by New Testament data or is there another way to account for the texts that seemingly bespeak of say ignorance, weakness, and locality? The New Testament has not provided a systematic Christology that addresses some of the questions we ordinarily pose to such an undertaking. To grasp what the total message about Christ in reality is according to the Bible one must synthesize much material. In the various attempts to do this very necessary task, several competing theories and explanations have emerged. My main contention in challenging the kenotic approaches to the incarnate Christ is that they appear to do less justice to the teaching concerning Christ's status as God than is in reality found in the New Testament. Moreover, I believe that evangelicals, who themselves are committed to Jesus' deity implicitly undermine that very conviction with their proposals in affirming a kenotic type of Christology. What is required to do justice to all strands of data found in the New Testament is a final "portrait" of Christ who is said to be both human and divine, and moreover, fully human and fully divine. Both Hebrews 2:17 and Colossians 2:9 must be included in a biblically faithful Christology. Dawe has is right in the following statement:

> There are two contrasting convictions in all Christian belief about Jesus Christ. On the one hand, the Christian is concerned with the person of Jesus Christ. He is known personally and spoken of in intimate terms of human relationship. On the other hand, Christian faith speaks of this same Jesus Christ in great, overarching terms. He is the eternal Word of God, the first-born of all creation and the sustainer of the universe (John 1:1; Col. 1:15; Heb. 1:3). He is God's agent of creation and will be the consummation of the universe. No matter how far human imagination goes in picturing the outer reaches of space, no matter how far into the future imagination stretches toward a world of moon stations and space travel, we will never outrun the presence of Jesus Christ.[2]

From the early church era, the best exponent of the type of Christology advocated in this book is Athanasius of Alexandria. He advocated that the Bible presents us with a "double account of the Savior." In this, Athanasius is affirming both types of material that show Jesus to be on the one hand a limited locally restricted man, and on the other hand, that Jesus is the all knowing, all pow-

---

traditional arguments about square circles and married bachelors have often been invoked as "things" God cannot do. Moreover, God is seen as being unable to create free human beings that necessarily do good and only good by compulsion as that would destroy freedom. In a related argument, which has become quite popular, God's omnipotence is said to include the ability to curtail this power, otherwise he would not be all-powerful. For this approach, see C. Stephen Evans, "The Self-Emptying of Love: Some Thoughts on Kenotic Christology," in *The Incarnation: An Interdisciplinary Symposium on the Incarnation of the Son of God*, ed. Stephen T. Davis, Daniel Kendall, and Gerald O'Collins (Oxford: Oxford University Press, 2002), 254, 260-63.

[2] Donald G. Dawe, *Jesus: Lord for All Times* (Atlanta: John Knox, 1975), 106.

erful and omnipresent God.³ This is imperative to make sense of and to include all elements for the final portrait. In the Reformation era, John Calvin has a similar commitment. In the contemporary milieu this picture has been erased and another has been posited in its place. The kenotic Christology propagated by many today would not be claimed by Athanasius, the Chalcedonian Fathers, or Calvin. I take my stand along with these exponents of a Christology which I believe is the most satisfying and faithful to the New Testament.

Having surveyed the early church era and traced the key Christological developments, what one finds is a perceptive weaving of both strands of truth concerning Jesus which are uncovered in the primary sources. The great achievement of Chalcedon in A.D. 451 was a marvel of concise, precise, and lucid theological reasoning that has stood the test of time. Chalcedon must continue to serve as ὅρος (the boundary marker) which we dare not cross. It is a basic axiom of pious evangelical faith that Jesus is *one person* in *two natures*.

We still need an answer to the "mechanics" issue. Just how is it that Jesus, or more precisely, the Word, became flesh? The insights provided by Leontius of Byzantium (or Jerusalem), and John of Damascus⁴ concerning the inpersonal human nature shows us precisely how. God did not select a "fully blown" man and somehow sent his Son to come and indwell that person, rather it was God the Son, who is the person both before and after the incarnation, who is central as the subject of predication. Now as a human nature is adopted in addition to the Son's divine nature, a new entity emerges: Jesus Christ of Nazareth, who is God over all. No alteration occurred to the person of the Son, but an addition was had in the personal union. Now, because Christ is *in* two natures, the scripture gives us hints as to the kind of person he is with strange sounding statements about him: "The Lord of Glory is crucified," "The Son of Man is in Heaven," and "God redeems the Church with his blood." All these are true, yet only possible because of the incarnation in the manner outlined above. Therefore, contrary to some moderns who are willing to give up "reduplicative statements" about Jesus Christ, the only way to make "sense" of the person is to embrace the view which appears to be nonsense–namely that in Jesus Christ one encounters both man and God. It is in the reduplicative tradition, which claims that Christ *qua* man is local, limited in power, and ignorant; and, Christ *qua* God is omnipresent, omnipotent, and omniscient, that one finds the only satisfactory handling of all biblical materials. Jesus does not reveal God to us by his humanity alone, for he is not merely human. We cannot therefore assume that it is a type of God potency in Jesus that points us to God. We must unashamedly affirm that the man from Nazareth is also God manifested in the flesh, but not confined by the flesh. In a theology of *krypsis*, it is possible to say that Jesus as God-Man not only made clear, on occasion that he is God, but

---

³ Henry P. Liddon is an able exponent of this approach as similarly found in Athanasius. See H.P. Liddon, *The Divinity of our Lord and Saviour Jesus Christ* (New York: Scribner, Welford, 1868), 440-500, esp. 453-79.

⁴ Though we reject the Damascene's contention for perichoresis in the person of the Son; this best serves that particular Trinitarian doctrine that sees the interpenetration of the persons within the Godhead.

that in many, if not most, instances, because of the reality of the humanity, he also concealed his true identity.

Calvin's use of the *communicatio idiomatum* is a worthy model. What one believes and confesses about Jesus of Nazareth is a basic matter, and goes to the heart of Jesus' own question concerning his identity. We must think rightly of Jesus Christ. With this "tool" of the "exchange of properties," as advocated by Calvin, we may correctly posit that the *Man* Jesus is omnipresent. We cannot, however, claim that the humanity of Jesus is omnipresent or that the body of Jesus is omnipresent. Focusing on the person, and not on the abstract natures in our Christological predication, serves to keep our statements from being problematic or even heretical. Of course, this has much to do with how we conceive the incarnation.

A non-kenotic model which was widely sampled both in the early Church era and in John Calvin's Christology is the approach which we follow. This is in contrast to the prevailing current evangelical ways of understanding Jesus Christ. As David Steinmetz argued for the "superiority of pre-critical exegesis,"[5] so I am advocating the superiority of pre-modern theologizing about the person of Christ. Most notably, the work of John Calvin needs to be sought out as a model.

The most important conclusions to be drawn from the research conducted are the following. First, only a non-kenotic Christology does justice to passages of scripture that clearly indicate Jesus is fully God. A kenotic reading of Philippians 2:5-8 is consistent with much that is presented in the Bible, but is counter to Paul's unequivocal declaration that in Jesus one finds the "fullness of deity in bodily form" (Col 2:9).[6] A kenotically conceived incarnation that denies omnipresence to Jesus, does not sit well with such clear passages that show Jesus as present with his own, and in whom, the whole cosmos finds its coherence. Also, as outlined in both patristic sources and in Calvin's view, this omnipresent Christ does not become so after the ascension of Christ, but is wholly true of Jesus even before his body is resurrected to ascend. During his so-called earthly sojourn, Jesus is nonetheless Lord God almighty filling heaven and earth. Only a non-kenotic approach appears to grasp both types of New Testament teaching concerning the person of the incarnate Son.

Second, it follows that kenotic views of the incarnation cannot explain how Jesus can have and exercise omnipresence now, *and* still be genuinely human, given the presuppositions of this approach which equates kenosis with incarnation. Either kenosis or genuine humanity must be given up after the ascension

---

[5] David C. Steinmetz, "The Superiority of Precritical Exegesis," in *A Guide to Contemporary Hermeneutics: Major Trends in Biblical Interpretation*, ed. Donald K. McKim (Grand Rapids: Eerdmans, 1986), 65-77.

[6] See Robert L. Reymond, *Jesus Divine Messiah: The New and Old Testament Witness* (Fearn: Mentor, 2003), 438-40. "Precisely how it is that this totality of the very essence of deity 'permanently dwells is in him [Jesus] Paul specifies by the Greek adverb σωματικῶς ... [which] means 'bodily,' that is 'in bodily form, indicating that the manner in which the permanent abode of the full plentitude of deity in Jesus is to be understood in incarnational terms. In short, Paul intends to say that in Jesus we have to do with the very 'embodiment' or incarnation of deity, or as he says elsewhere, Christ is God 'manifest in the flesh' (1 Tim 3:16)" (439).

in this model. If one appeals to the fact that Jesus' body is now glorified, it does not suffice to explain how he can be omnipresent, for even though indeed he is glorified, his body is still localized. To be a real human being, according to kenotic approaches, necessitates the self divesting of independent use of the relative attributes in the first place so an incarnation can be achieved. If now the central tenets of such a view can be given up, as they must, for Jesus says to his disciples, "I am with you always," then this begs the question of why the kenosis was necessary in the first place. The approach adopted in this book does not exhibit this problem.

Third, and this is perhaps the most important of all, by focusing attention on omnipresence, and finding that the distinction maintained in kenotic models cannot work with omnipresence, this truth about Christ's person leads to an alternative understanding of how *all* the relative attributes must be thought of in relation to the incarnate Christ. Omnipresence must not be thought of as being possessed but simply not used. This betrays the very definition of the term. One may posit that omniscience and omnipotence, attributes that might indeed uphold the said distinction between possession and use, may in fact also be *both* possessed and used by Jesus. Hence, a view that claims Jesus is omnipresent becomes key in settling the kenosis question. To put it another way, it is not necessary to say that because it is conceivable to posit a distinction between Jesus' possession of omnipotence, and his exercise of it, that indeed that is what occurs in the incarnation. As all evangelicals insist on the possession of the omni-attributes, it is a small step to argue that he actually utilizes them also. And it is a necessary step when one takes into consideration the type of works Jesus undertakes. He is spoken of as creating new mature wine from the jars full of water (John 2:1-11). He heals blindness, lameness, and raises the dead (John 9:1-41; John 5:1-15; and 11:1-44; cf. Matt 15:29-31; and Mark 1:29-34). He categorically declares to do the very works his Father is doing (John 5:19-23), so to posit that Jesus does not use omnipotence is to say that God the Father does not as well. Moreover, Christ walks on water, multiplies a few fish and loaves into enough food to feed several thousands of people, and controls the movement of fish so his disciples can catch an unprecedented load during the waking hours of a bright morning (John 6:16-21; Matt 14:22-33; 14:13-21; Mark 6:30-44; Luke 9:10-17; John 6:1-15; Luke 5:1-11). He calms the storm on the authority of his word alone (Mark 4:35-41), and he sends demons fleeing, again with a mere word (Matt 8:23-34; Mark 9:14-27). These are not descriptions of a mere man, but neither are they descriptions of a God-Man who does not use the divine attribute of omnipotence.

The heart of the issue appears to be the burning question: "Can Christ be truly human without being merely human?" Evangelicals have agreed that Jesus is man and that Jesus is God, yet many have not dealt with this question directly. Erickson, and Lane, for example have failed to convince me that the authors of the Chalcedonian definition of faith missed the truth in arguing that Jesus was and is both a limited human being and at the same time fully God upholding the universe as the omnipotent and omnipresent creator. It is within the framework of this very question that the doctrine of Jesus' omnipresence becomes key in disclosing the true nature of a person's Christology. As said already, and it bears repeating as we come to a close, to deny that Christ is omnipresent after the incarnation is to deny his presence with his own (Matt. 18:20; 28:20; John 14:23; and Rev. 2:1); his presence with God, while on earth (John 1:18; 3:13; and 5:19-20), and his upholding the universe (Col.1:17). On the question of the "truly human/merely human" issue in relation to the incarnate Son of God, one must pay special heed to Thompson's words. "For Jesus to be truly human must he be exactly and only like all other humans?" asks Thompson. To which she immediately replies:

> The answer of the fourth evangelist to that question is *no*. He does accept Jesus' humanity; but he also confesses that he who was known as the 'son of Joseph' is also the Son of God, that he who became flesh is the Word of God, that he who performed signs is the light of the world and bread from heaven, and that the one who died on the cross is the resurrection and the life (emphasis supplied).[7]

Given the entirety of the material concerning Jesus Christ, it is much harder to argue that he does not exercise the relative attributes, especially when one sees that omnipresence cannot be explained with the traditional distinctions without, either compromising the basic meaning of omnipresence, or adhering to contradictory statements concerning the ability to exercise the relative attributes. The only other feasible alternative for those who insist on this way of expressing their understanding of Jesus Christ, is to embrace a *fully kenotic* view that claims unequivocally that Jesus gives up the divine attributes in the incarnation. This approach is at least consistent, though, in my opinion, blatantly unbiblical. Therefore, a non-kenotic Christology is the preferred option.

---

[7]Marianne Meye Thompson, *The Incarnate Word: Perspectives on Jesus in the Fourth Gospel* (Peabody, MA: Hendrickson, 1988), 128.

BIBLIOGRAPHY

Books

Adams, Marilyn McCord. *Christ and the Horrors: The Coherence of Christology.* New York: Cambridge, 2006.

Aldwinckle, Russell F. *More Than a Man: A Study in Christology.* Grand Rapids: Eerdmans, 1976.

Allison, C. FitzSimons. *The Cruelty of Heresy: An Affirmation of Christian Orthodoxy.* Harrisburg, PA: Morehouse Publishing, 1994.

Altaner, Berthold. *Patrology.* Translated by Hilda C. Graff. Edinburgh: Nelson, 1958.

Anatolios, Khaled. *Athanasius: The Coherence of His Thought.* New York: Routledge, 1998.

—. *Athanasius.* The Early Church Fathers, Edited by Carol Harrison. New York: Routledge, 2004.

—. *Retrieving Nicaea: The Development and Meaning of Trinitarian Doctrine.* Grand Rapids: Baker, 2011.

Anderson, Norman. *The Mystery of the Incarnation.* Downers Grove, IL: InterVarsity Press, 1978.

Arabatzis, Christos Ath. *Patristic Hermeneutics: $4^{th} - 14^{th}$ Centuries.* Translated and Edited by George Dion Dragas. Patristic Monograph, Vol. 1. Columbia, MO: Magnarva Editions, 2013 [2012].

Arnold, Duane W.-H. *The Early Episcopal Career of Athanasius of Alexandria.* Christianity and Judaism in Antiquity, Edited by Charles Kannengiesser. Notre Dame: University of Notre Dame Press, 1991.

Armstrong, Donald, ed. *Who Do You Say That I Am? Christology and the Church.* Grand Rapids: Eerdmans, 1999.

Astley, Jeff, David Brown, and Ann Loades, eds. *Christology: Key Readings in Christian Thought.* Louisville: Westminster/John Knox, 2009.

Ayers, Lewis. *Nicaea and its Legacy: An Approach to Fourth-Century Trinitarian Theology.* New York: Oxford, 2004.

Baillie, D.M. *God was in Christ: The Historical Jesus and the Message of Christ Woven into the Doctrines of Incarnation and Atonement.* New York: Charles Scribner's Sons, 1948.

Balla, Peter. *Challenges to New Testament Theology.* Tübingen: Mohr Siebeck, 1997. Reprint, Peabody, MA: Hendrickson Publishers, 1998.

Ban, Joseph D., ed. *The Christological Foundation for Contemporary Theological Education.* Macon, GA: Mercer University Press, 1988.

Barr, William R., ed. *Constructive Christian Theology in the Worldwide Church.* Grand Rapids: Eerdmans, 1997.

Barth, Karl. *Church Dogmatics I.I. The Doctrine of the Word of God.* 2nd. ed.

Translated by Geoffrey W. Bromiley. Edited by G. W. Bromiley and T. F. Torrance. Edinburgh: T and T Clark, 1975.
—. *Church Dogmatics: A Selection with Introduction*. Edited by Helmut Gollwitzer. Louisville: Westminster/John Knox, 1994.
Bauckham, Richard. *God Crucified: Monotheism and Christology in the New Testament*. Grand Rapids: Eerdmans, 1998.
Beasley-Murray, George R. *John*. Word Biblical Commentary, vol. 36. Waco, TX: Word Books, 1987.
Beeley, Christopher A. *The Unity of Christ: Continuity and Conflict in Patristic Tradition*. New Haven, CT: Yale University Press, 2012.
Behr, John. *The Way to Nicaea: Formation of Christian Theology, Volume 1*. Crestwood, NY: St. Vladimir's Seminary Press, 2001.
Berkhof, Hendrikus. *Two Hundred Years of Theology: A Report of a Personal Journey*. Grand Rapids: Eerdmans, 1989.
Berkouwer, G. C. *Studies in Dogmatics: The Person of Christ*. Translated by John Vriend. Grand Rapids: Eerdmans, 1955.
Bethune-Baker, James. *An Introduction to the History of Christian Doctrine to the Time of the Council of Chalcedon*. London: Methuen and Co., 1903.
Bird, Michael F. *Jesus is the Christ: The Messianic Testimony of the Gospels*. Downers Grove, IL: InterVarsity, 2012.
Blanchard, John. *Meet the Real Jesus*. Auburn, MA: Evangelical Press, 1989.
Bloesch, Donald G. *Jesus Christ: Savior and Lord*. Vol. 4 of *Christian Foundations*. Downers Grove, IL: InterVarsity, 1997.
Bock, Darrell L. *Jesus According to Scripture: Restoring the Portrait from the Gospels*. Grand Rapids: Baker, 2002.
—. (and Daniel B. Wallace). *Dethroning Jesus: Exposing Popular Culture's Quest to Unseat the Biblical Christ*. Nashville: Thomas Nelson, 2007.
Bonhoeffer, Dietrich. *Christ the Center*. Translated by Edwin H. Robertson. San Francisco: Harper Collins Publishers, 1978.
Borg, Marcus. *Jesus, a New Vision: Spirit, Culture, and the Life of Discipleship*. New York: HarperCollins, 1987.
—. *Jesus in Contemporary Scholarship*. Valley Forge, PA: Trinity, 1994.
Borg, Marcus, and N.T. Wright. *The Meaning of Jesus: Two Visions*. San Francisco: Harper, 1999.
Borland, James A. *Christ in the Old Testament*. Fearn, Great Britain: Mentor, 1999.
Bowie, Walter Russell. *Jesus and the Trinity*. Nashville: Abingdon, 1960.
Bowman Jr., Robert M. & J. E.D Komoszewski. *Putting Jesus in His Place: The Case for the Deity of Christ*. Grand Rapids: Kregel, 2007.
Boyd, Gregory A. *Cynic Sage or Son of God: Recovering the Real Jesus in an Age of Revisionist Replies*. Wheaton, IL: BridgePoint, 1995.
Bray, Gerald. *Biblical Interpretation: Past and Present*. Downers Grove, IL: InterVarsity, 1996.
—. *Creeds, Councils, and Christ: Did Early Christians Misrepresent Jesus?* Fearn, Great Britain: Mentor, 1997.
—. *The Doctrine of God*. Contours of Christian Theology., ed. Gerald Bray.

Downers Grove, Il: InterVarsity, 1993.
—. *Steps of Understanding: Key Events in Jesus' Life*. Fearn, Great Britain: Mentor 1998.
Brown, Colin. *Jesus in European Protestant Thought 1778-1860*. Durham, NC: Labyrinth, 1985.
Brown, Harold O.J. *Heresies: Heresy and Orthodoxy in the History of the Church*. Reprint, Peabody, MA: Hendrickson Publishers, 1998.
Bruce, Alexander B. *The Humiliation of Christ: In Its Physical, Ethical, and Official Aspects*. 4th. ed. Grand Rapids: Eerdmans, 1955.
Bruce, F.F. *The Gospel and Epistles of John*. Grand Rapids: Eerdmans. Reprint, 2001.
Brunner, Emil. *The Christian Doctrine of God*. Dogmatics, vol. 1. Translated by Olive Wyon. Philadelphia: Westminster, 1950.
Byrne, James M., ed. *The Christian Understanding of God Today: Theological Colloquium on the Occasion of the 400th Anniversary of the Foundation of Trinity College, Dublin*. Studies in Theology. Dublin: The Columba Press, 1993.
Calvin, John. *Institutes of the Christian Religion*. Edited by John T. McNeill. Translated by Ford Lewis Battles. Library of Christian Classics, vols 20-21. Philadelphia, PA: Westminster, 1960.
Capes, David B., April D. DeConick, Helen K. Bond, & Troy Miller, eds. *Israels's God and Rebecca's Children: Christology and Community in Early Judaism and Christianity. Essays in Honor of Larry W. Hurtado and Alan F. Segal.* Waco, TX: Baylor University Press, 2007.
Carey, George. *God Incarnate: Meeting the Contemporary Challenges to a Classic Christian Doctrine.* Downers Grove, IL: InterVarsity, 1978.
Carroll, Robert. *Jeremiah: A Commentary*. Old Testament Library. Philadelphia: Westminster, 1986.
Carson, D.A. *The Gospel According to John*. The Pillar New Testament Commentary. Grand Rapids: Eerdmans, 1991.
—. *Jesus the Son of God: A Christological Title Often Overlooked, Sometimes Misunderstood, and Currently Disputed.* Wheaton, IL: Crossway, 2012.
Cassian, John (Saint). *On the Incarnation of the Lord Against Nestorius.* New Ed. Translated with Notes by Edgar C.S. Gibson. Ex Fontibus Co., 2012.
Cave, Sydney. *The Doctrine of the Person of Christ*. Duckworth's Theology Series. London: Duckworth, 1925.
Cerfaux, Lucien. *Christ in the Theology of St. Paul*. Translated by Geoffrey Webb and Adrian Walker. New York: Herder and Herder, 1959.
Charlesworth, James H., ed. *The Messiah: Developments in Earliest Judaism and Christianity.* The First Princeton Symposium on Judaism and Christian Origins. Minneapolis: Fortress, 1992.
Charnock, Stephen. *The Existence and Attributes of God*. Grand Rapids: Baker Book House, 1996.
Chemnitz, Martin. *The Two Natures in Christ*. Translated by J.A.O. Preus. St. Louis, MO: Concordia Publishing House, 1971.
Chesnut, Glenn F. *Images of Christ: An Introduction to Christology*. San

Francisco: Harper and Row, 1984.
Chung, Sung Wook., ed. *Christ the One and Only: A Global Affirmation of the Uniqueness of Jesus Christ.* Grand Rapids: Baker, 2005.
—., ed. *John Calvin and Evangelical Theology: Legacy and Prospect.* Louisville: Westminster/John Knox, 2009.
Clark, Gordon H. *The Incarnation.* Jefferson, MD: The Trinity Foundation, 1988.
Clifford, Anne M. and Anthony J. Godzieba, eds. *Christology: Memory, Inquiry, Practice.* Annual Publication of the College Theology Society 2002, Volume 48. Maryknoll, NY: Orbis Books, 2003.
Comfort, Philip W., and Wendell C. Hawley. *Opening the Gospel of John.* Wheaton, IL: Tyndale Publishers, 1994.
Copan, Paul, ed. *Will the Real Jesus Please Stand Up? A Debate between William Lane Craig and John Dominic Crossan: Moderated by William F. Buckley, Jr.* Grand Rapids: Baker Books, 1998.
Cottret, Bernard. *Calvin: A Biography.* Translated by M. Wallace McDonald. Grand Rapids: Eerdmans, 2000.
Creed, John Martin. *The Divinity of Jesus Christ.* Cambridge: Cambridge University Press, 1938.
Creel, Richard E. *Divine Impassibility: An Essay in Philosophical Theology.* Cambridge: Cambridge University Press, 1986.
Crisp, Oliver D. *Divinity and Humanity.* Current Issues in Theology, Edited by Iain Torrance. New York: Cambridge, 2007.
—. *God Incarnate: Explorations in Christology.* London: T and T Clark, 2009.
Crisp, Oliver D. and Fred Sanders, eds. *Christology Ancient and Modern: Explorations in Constructive Dogmatics.* Grand Rapids: Zondervan, 2013.
Cross, Richard. *The Metaphysics of the Incarnation: Thomas Aquinas to Duns Scotus.* Oxford: Oxford, 2002.
Crossan, John Dominic. *The Historical Jesus: The Life of a Mediterranean Jewish Peasant.* San Francisco: Harper, 1991.
Crouzel, Henri. *Origen.* Translated by A. S. Worrall. Edinburgh: T and T Clark, 1989.
Cullmann, Oscar. *The Christology of the New Testament.* Rev. ed. Translated by Shirley C. Guthrie and Charles A.M. Hall. Philadelphia: Westminster, 1963.
Dalferth, Ingolf U. *Becoming Present: An Inquiry into the Christian Sense of the Presence of God.* Leuven: Peeters, 2006.
Davenport, S.F. *Immanence and Incarnation.* London: Cambridge, 1925.
Davies, Norman. *Europe: A History.* Oxford: Oxford, 1996.
Davis, Leo Donald. *The First Seven Ecumenical Councils (325-787): Their History and Theology.* Collegeville, MN: Liturgical, 1983.
Davis, Stephen T., ed. *Encountering Jesus: A Debate on Christology.* Atlanta: John Knox, 1988.
Davis, Stephen T., Daniel Kendall, and Gerald O'Collins, eds. *The Incarnation: An Interdisciplinary Symposium on the Incarnation of the Son of God.* Oxford: Oxford, 2002.

Davis, Thomas J. *This is My Body: The Presence of Christ in Reformation Thought.* Grand Rapids: Baker, 2008.
Dawe, Donald G. *The Form of a Servant: A Historical Analysis of the Kenotic Motif.* Philadelphia: The Westminster Press, 1963.
—. *Jesus: Lord of All Times.* Atlanta: John Knox, 1975.
Dawson, Gerrit Scott. *Jesus Ascended: The Meaning of Christ's Continuing Incarnation.* Phillipsburg, NJ: P & R Publishing, 2004.
De Jonge, Marinus. *Jesus: Inspiring and Disturbing Presence.* Translated by John E. Steely. Nashville: Abingdon, 1974 [1971].
—. *God's Final Envoy: Early Christology and Jesus' Own View of His Mission.* Grand Rapids: Eerdmans, 1998.
DeVries, Dawn. *Jesus Christ in the Preaching of Calvin and Schleiermacher.* Columbia Series in Reformed Theology. Louisville: Westminster/John Knox, 1996.
Di Berardino, Angelo., ed. *Encyclopedia of the Early Church,* Vol. 1. Translated by Adrian Walford. New York: Oxford, 1992.
Dods, Marcus. *The Incarnation of the Eternal Word.* 2d. ed. London: Seeley, Burnside, and Seeley, 1849.
Dorner, Isaak August. *Divine Immutability: A Critical Reconsideration.* Translated by Robert R. Williams and Claude Welch. Fortress Texts in Modern Theology. Minneapolis: Fortress, 1994.
Dragas, George Dion. *Athanasiana: Essays on the Theology of Saint Athanasius.* London, 1980.
—. *Saint Athanasius of Alexandria: Original Research and New Perspectives.* Patristic Theological Library, Edited by George Dion Dragas. Rollinsford, NH: Orthodox Research Institute, 2005.
Driscoll, Mark & Gerry Breshears. *Vintage Jesus: Timeless Answers to Timely Questions.* Wheaton, IL: Crossway, 2007.
Dunn, James D.G. *Christology in the Making: A New Testament Inquiry into the Origins of the Doctrine of the Incarnation.* 2nd ed. Grand Rapids: Eerdmans, 1989.
Eckardt, A. Roy. *Reclaiming the Jesus of History: Christology Today.* Minneapolis: Fortress, 1992.
Eddy, Paul Rhodes and Gregory A. Boyd. *The Jesus Legend: A Case for the Historical Reliability of the Synoptic Jesus Tradition.* Grand Rapids: Baker, 2007.
Ellis, E. Earl. *Christ and the Future in New Testament History.* Leiden: E.J. Brill, 2001.
Enns, Paul. *The Moody Handbook of Theology.* Chicago: Moody, 1989.
Erickson, Millard J. *The Word Became Flesh: A Contemporary Incarnational Christology.* Grand Rapids: Baker, 1991.
Evans, C. Stephen. *The Historical Christ and the Jesus of Faith: The Incarnational Narrative as History.* Oxford: Oxford, 1996.
Evans. Craig. *Fabricating Jesus: How Modern Scholars Distort the Gospels.* Downers Grove, IL: InterVarsity, 2006.
Evans, David Beecher. *Leontius of Byzantium: An Origenist Christology.*

Washington, DC: Dumbarton Oaks Center for Byzantine Studies, 1970.
Fairbairn, Donald. *Grace and Christology in the Early Church.* Oxford Early Christian Studies, Edited by Gillian Clark and Andrew Louth. New York: Oxford, 2003.
Farmer, William R., ed. *Crisis in Christology: Essays in Quest of Resolution.* Vol. 3 of *Great Modern Debates.* Edited by Roy Abraham Varghese. Livonia, MI: Dove Booksellers, 1995.
Farrow, Douglas. *Ascension and Ecclesia: On the Significance of the Ascension for Ecclesiology and Christian Cosmology.* Grand Rapids: Eerdmans, 1999.
Fee, Gordon D. *Paul's Letter to the Philippians.* The New International Commentary on the New Testament. Grand Rapids: Eerdmans, 1995.
—. *Pauline Christology: An Exegetical-Theological Study.* Peabody, MA: Hendrickson, 2007.
Feenstra, Ronald J., and Cornelius Plantinga, Jr., eds. *Trinity, Incarnation, and Atonement: Philosophical and Theological Essays.* Library of Religious Philosophy, vol. 1. Notre Dame, IN: University of Notre Dame Press, 1989.
Feinberg, John S. *No One Like Him: The Doctrine of God,* Foundations of Evangelical Theology. Wheaton, IL: Crossway, 2001.
Ferrier, Francis. *What is the Incarnation?* Translated by Edward Sillem. New York: Hawthorn Books, 1962.
Finan, Thomas, and Vincent Twomey, eds. *Studies in Patristic Christology.* Dublin: Four Courts, 1998.
Florovsky, Georges. *The Byzantine Fathers of the Fifth Century.* Translated by Raymond Miller, Anne-Marie Döllinger-Labriolle, and Helmut Wilhelm Schmiedel. Vol. 8 of *The Collected Works of Georges Florovsky.* Edited by Richard S. Haugh. Vaduz, Liechtenstein: Büchervertriebsanstalt, 1987.
—. *The Byzantine Fathers of the Sixth to Eighth Centuries.* Translated by Raymond Miller, Anne-Marie Döllinger-Labriolle, and Helmut Wilhelm Schmiedel. Vol. 8 of *The Collected Works of Georges Florovsky.* Edited by Richard S. Haugh. Vaduz, Liechtenstein: Büchervertriebsanstalt, 1987.
—. *The Eastern Fathers of the Fourth Century.* Translated by Catherine Edmunds. Vol. 7 of *The Collected Works of Georges Florovsky.* Edited by Richard S. Haugh. Vaduz, Liechtenstein: Büchervertriebsanstalt, 1987.
Frame, John M. *The Doctrine of God.* A Theology of Lordship. Phillipsburg, NJ: Presbyterian and Reformed, 2002.
—. *No Other God: A Response to Open Theism.* Phillipsburg, NJ: Presbyterian and Reformed, 2001.
France, R.T. *The Gospel of Mark.* New International Greek Testament Commentary. Grand Rapids: Eerdmans, 2002.
—. *Matthew: Evangelist and Teacher.* Downers Grove, IL: InterVarsity, 1989.
Frei, Hans W. *The Identity of Jesus Christ: The Hermeneutical Bases for Dogmatic Theology.* Philadelphia: Fortress, 1975.
Fries, Paul, and Tiran Nersoyan, eds. *Christ in East and West.* Macon, GA: Mercer University Press, 1987.
Fuller, Reginald H. *Christ and Christianity: Studies in the Formation of Christology.* Compiled and edited, with an introduction, by Robert Kahl.

Valley Forge, PA: Trinity Press International, 1984.
Fulton, John. *The Chalcedonian Decree: Historical Christianity, Misrepresented by Modern Theology, Confirmed by Modern Science, and Untouched by Modern Criticism.* New York: Thomas Whittaker, 1892.
Galot, Jean. *Who is Christ? A Theology of Incarnation.* Translated by M. Angeline Bouchard. Chicago: Franciscan Herald, 1981.
Gavrilyuk, Paul L. *The Suffering of the Impassible God: The Dialectics of Patristic Thought.* Oxford Early Christian Studies, eds. Gillian Clark and Andrew Louth. New York: Oxford, 2004.
Geisler, Norman, and H. Wayne House, with Max Herrera. *The Battle for God: Responding to the Challenge of Neotheism.* Grand Rapids: Kregel, 2001.
George, Timothy. *Theology of the Reformers.* Nashville: Broadman Press, 1988.
Gerrish, B.A. *Grace and Gratitude: The Eucharistic Theology of John Calvin.* Minneapolis: Fortress, 1993.
Gifford, E.H. *The Incarnation: A Study of Philippians II. 5-11.* London: Hodder & Stoughton, 1897.
Gore, Charles. *The Incarnation of the Son of God.* Bampton Lectures, 1891. London: John Murray, 1892.
—. *Dissertations on Subjects Connected With the Incarnation.* London: John Murray, 1907.
Gottlieb, Anthony. *The Dream of Reason: A History of Philosophy from the Greeks to the Renaissance.* New York: W.W. Norton and Company, 2000.
Goulder, Michael, ed. *Incarnation and Myth: The Debate Continued.* London: SCM Press Ltd., 1979.
Grabowski, Stanislaus J. *The All-Present God: A Study in St. Augustine.* London: B. Herder Book Co., 1954.
Grant, Robert M. *Irenaeus of Lyons.* The Early Church Fathers. Edited by Carol Harrison. New York: Routledge, 1997.
—. *Jesus after the Gospels: The Christ of the Second Century.* Louisville: Westminster/John Knox Press, 1990.
Green, Michael, ed. *The Truth of God Incarnate.* London: Hodder and Stoughton, 1977.
Gregersen, Niels Henrik., Willem B. Drees, and Ulf Görman, eds. *The Human Person in Science and Theology.* Issues in Science and Theology, ed. Niels Henrik Gregersen. Grand Rapids: Eerdmans, 2000.
Grenz, Stanley J. *A Primer on Postmodernism.* Grand Rapids: Eerdmans, 1996.
—. (and Roger E. Olson). *20th Century Theology: God and the World in a Transitional Age.* Downers Grove, IL: InterVarsity, 1992.
Griffin, David. *A Process Christology.* Philadelphia: Westminster, 1973.
Grillmeier, Aloys. *Christ in Christian Tradition.* Vol. 1, *From the Apostolic Age to Chalcedon (451).* 2nd ed. Translated by John Bowden. Atlanta: John Knox Press, 1975.
—. *Christ in Christian Tradition.* Vol. 2, pt. 1, *From Chalcedon to Justinian I.* 2nd rev. ed. Translated by Pauline Allen and John Cawte. Atlanta: John Knox Press, 1975.

Grillmeier, Aloys, and Theresia Hainthaler. *Christ in Christian Tradition.* Vol. 2, pt. 2, *From the Council of Chalcedon (451) to Gregory the Great (590-604).* Translated by Pauline Allen and John Cawte. Louisville: Westminster/John Knox Press, 1995.

—. *Christ in Christian Tradition.* Vol. 2, pt. 4, *From the Council of Chalcedon (451) to Gregory the Great (590-604).* Translated by O.C. Dean. Louisville: Westminster/John Knox Press, 1996.

Grindheim, Sigurd. *Christology in the Synoptic Gospels: God or God's Servant?* London: T & T Clark, 2011.

Gromacki, Robert. *The Virgin Birth: A Biblical Study of the Deity of Jesus Christ.* Rev. ed. Grand Rapids: Kregel Pubishers, 2002.

Grudem, Wayne. *Systematic Theology: An Introduction to Biblical Doctrine.* Grand Rapids: Zondervan / Leicester, England: InterVarsity Press, 1994.

Gunn, James. *Christ the Fulness of the Godhead: A Study in New Testament Christology.* Neptune, NJ: Loizeaux Brothers, 1982.

Gunton, Colin E. *Christ and Creation.* Grand Rapids: Eerdmans, 1992.

—. *Yesterday and Today: A Study in Continuities in Christology.* London: Darton, Longman, and Todd Ltd., 1983.

Hagner, Donald A. *Matthew 14-28.* Word Biblical Commentary, vol. 33b. Dallas: Word, 1995.

Hall, Francis J. *The Kenotic Theory: Considered with Particular Reference to Its Anglican Forms and Arguments.* London: Longmans, Green & Co., 1898.

Hall, Stuart G. *Doctrine and Practice in the Early Church.* Grand Rapids: Eerdmans, 1992.

Hallman, Joseph M. *The Descent of God: Divine Suffering in History and Theology.* Minneapolis: Fortress, 1991.

Hanson, Anthony Tyrell. *Grace and Truth: A Study in the Doctrine of the Incarnation.* London: SPCK, 1975.

Hanson, R.P.C. *The Search for the Christian Doctrine of God: The Arian Controversy 318-381.* Edinburgh: T and T Clark, 1988.

Hardy, Edward Rochie, ed. *Christology of the Later Fathers.* Library of Christian Classics, vol. 3. Philadelphia: The Westminster Press, 1954.

Harris, Murray J. *Exegetical Guide to the Greek New Testament: Colossians and Philemon.* Grand Rapids: Eerdmans, 1991.

—. *Jesus as God: The New Testament Use of* Theos *in Reference to Jesus.* Grand Rapids: Baker Book House, 1992.

—. *3 Crucial Questions About Jesus.* Grand Rapids: Baker, 1994.

Harrison, Everett F. & Charles F. Pfeiffer, eds. *The Wycliffe Bible Commentary.* Chicago: Moody, 1962.

Hasel, Gerhard. *New Testament Theology: Basic Issues in the Current Debate.* Grand Rapids: Eerdmans, 1978. Reprint, 1993.

Hawthorne, Gerald F. *Philippians.* Word Biblical Commentary, vol. 43. Dallas: Word Publishing, 1983.

—. *The Presence and the Power: The Significance of the Holy Spirit in the Life and Ministry of Jesus.* Dallas: Word Publishing, 1991.

Hebblethwaite, Brian. *The Incarnation: Collected Essays in Christology.*

Cambridge: Cambridge, 1987.
Helm, Paul. *Eternal God: A Study of God without Time*. Oxford: Oxford, 1988.
—. *John Calvin's Ideas.* New York: Oxford, 2004.
—. *Calvin: A Guide for the Perplexed.* London: T & T Clark, 2008.
Hendriksen, William. *New Testament Commentary: Exposition of the Gospel According to John*. 2 vols. Grand Rapids: Baker Book House, 1953, 1954.
Hengel, Martin. *Studies in Early Christology*. Edinburgh: T and T Clark, 1995.
Henry, Carl F.H. *The Identity of Jesus of Nazareth*. Nashville: Broadman, 1992.
Heron, Alasdair, I. C. *A Century of Protestant Theology*. Philadelphia: Westminster, 1980.
Hick, John. *The Metaphor of God Incarnate: Christology in a Pluralistic Age.* Louisville: Westminster/John Knox Press, 1993.
—. ed. *The Myth of God Incarnate*. Reprint ed. London: SCM Press, 1993 [1977].
Higgins, A.J.B. *The Son of Man in the Teaching of Jesus.* Society for New Testamemt Studies Monograph Series, Edited by R. McL. Wilson. London: Cambridge, 2005 [1980].
Hodge, A.A. *Evangelical Theology: Lectures on Doctrine*. Carlisle, PA: The Banner of Truth Trust, 1976. Reprint, 1990 [1890].
Hodgson, Peter C. *Jesus – Word and Presence: An Essay in Christology.* Minneapolis: Fortress, 2007 [1971].
Holmes, Stephen R., and Murray A. Rae, eds. *The Person of Christ.* London: T and T Clark, 2005.
Hoogland, Marvin P. *Calvin's Perspective on the Exaltation of Christ: In Comparison with the Post-Reformation Doctrine of the Two States*. Kampen: J.H. Kok, 1966.
Horton, Michael S. *Lord and Servant: A Covenant Christology.* Louisville: Westminster/John Knox, 2005.
Huffman, Douglas S., and Eric L. Johnson, eds. *God under Fire: Modern Scholarship Reinvents God*. Grand Rapids: Zondervan, 2002.
Hughes, Frederick Stephen. *Where is Christ? A Question for Christians.* Boston: Houghton Mifflin Co., 1919.
Hurst, L.D., and N.T. Wright, eds., *The Glory of Christ in the New Testament: Studies in Christology in Memory of George Bradford Caird*. Oxford: Clarendon Press, 1987.
Hurtado, Larry W. *Lord Jesus Christ: Devotion to Jesus in Earliest Christianity.* Grand Rapids: Eerdmans, 2003.
Hussey, J.M. *The Orthodox Church in the Byzantine Empire*. Oxford History of the Christian Church. Oxford: Clarendon Press, 1986.
Inbody, Tyron L. *The Many Faces of Christology*. Nashville: Abingdon, 2002.
Jahn, Curtis A. *We Believe in Jesus Christ: Essays in Christology*. Milwaukee: Northwestern Publishing House, 1999.
Jansen, John Frederick. *Calvin's Doctrine of the Work of Christ*. London: James Clarke and Company, Ltd., 1956.
Jensen, David H. *In the Company of Others: A Dialogical Christology.* Cleveland, OH: Pilgrim Press, 2001.

Jewett, Robert, ed. *Christology and Exegesis: New Approaches*. Decatur, GA: Scholars, 1985.
John of Damascus. *Exposition of the Orthodox Faith*. Translated by S.D.F. Salmond. Early Church Fathers: Nicene and Post Nicene Series 2, vol. 9. Peabody, MA: Hendrickson Publishers, 1995.
Johnson, Luke Timothy. *The Real Jesus: The Misguided Quest for the Historical Jesus and the Truth of the Traditional Gospels*. San Francisco: Harper Collins, 1996.
Jones, Paul H. *Christ's Eucharistic Presence: A History of the Doctrine*. American University Studies Series 7. Theology and Religion, vol. 157. New York: Peter Lang Publishing, Inc., 1994.
Käfer, Anne. *Inkarnation und Schöpfung*. Theologische Bibliothek Töpelmann Band 151, Herausgegeben von O. Bayer, W. Härle, & F. Nüssel. Berlin: Walter de Gruyter, 2010.
Kärkkäinen, Velli-Matti. *Christology: A Global Introduction. An Ecumenical, International, and Contextual Perspective*. Grand Rapids: Baker, 2003.
Kaye, John. *Some Account of the Council of Nicaea in Connexion with the Life of Athanasius*. London: Francis & John Rivington, 1853.
Keating, James F. and Thomas Joseph White, eds. *Divine Impassibility and the Mystery of Human Suffering*. Grand Rapids: Eerdmans, 2009.
Keil, C.F. and F. Delitzsch. *Commentary on the Old Testament*. Vol. 8, *Jeremiah and Lamentations*. Peabody, MA: Hendrickson Publishers, 1989.
Kelly, J.N.D. *Early Christian Doctrines*. Rev. ed. San Francisco: Harper Collins Publishers, 1978.
—. *Early Christian Creeds*. 3rd ed. New York: Longham, 1999.
Kidner, Derek. *Psalms 73-150: A Commentary on Books III-V of the Pslams*. London: InterVarsity, 1975.
Kim, Seyoon. *The Son of Man as the Son of God*. Grand Rapids: Eerdmans, 1985 [1983].
Knox, John. *The Humanity and Divinity of Christ: A Study of Pattern in Christology*. London: Cambridge, 1967.
Komoszewski, J. ED., M. James Sawyer, and Daniel B. Wallace. *Reinventing Jesus: How Contemporary Skeptics Miss the Real Jesus and Mislead Popular Culture*. Grand Rapids: Kregel, 2006.
Kuschel, Karl-Josef. *Born before All Time? The Dispute over Christ's Origin*. Translated by John Bowden. New York: Crossroad, 1992.
Ladd, George Eldon. *A Commentary on the Revelation of John*. Grand Rapids: Eerdmans, 1972. Reprint, 1993.
LaDue, William J. *Jesus Among the Theologians: Contemporary Interpretations of Christ*. Harrisburg, PA: Trinity Press International, 2001.
Lane, Anthony N. S. *John Calvin: Student of the Church Fathers*. Grand Rapids: Baker Book House, 1999.
Lawton, John Stewart. *Conflict in Christology: A Study of British and American Christology, From 1889-1914*. London: SPCK, 1947.
Lee, Bernard J. *Jesus and the Metaphors of God: The Christs of the New Testament*. New York: Paulist Press, 1993.

Letham, Robert. *The Work of Christ*. Contours of Christian Theology, ed. Gerald Bray. Downers Grove, Il: InterVarsity Press, 1993.

Lewis, Gordon R., and Bruce A. Demarest. *Integrative Theology: Historical, Biblical, Systematic, Apologetic, Practical.* 3 vols. in 1. Grand Rapids: Zondervan, 1996.

L'Hullier, Peter. *The Church of the Ancient Councils: The Disciplinary Work of the First Four Ecumenical Councils.* Crestwood, NJ: Saint Vladimir's Seminary Press, 1996.

Liddon, Henry Parry. *The Divinity of Our Lord and Saviour Jesus Christ: Eight Lectures Preached before the University of Oxford in the Year 1866.* 2nd ed. New York: Scribner, Welford, and Co., 1868.

Lienhard, Marc. *Luther: Witness to Jesus Christ: Stages and Themes of the Reformer's Christology.* Translated by Edwin H. Robertson. Minneapolis: Augsburg Publishing House, 1982.

Lightfoot, J.B. *St Paul's Epistle to the Philippians: A Revised Test with Introduction, Notes, and Dissertations.* Peabody, MA: Hendrickson Publishers, 1995.

Lincoln, Andrew T. *Ephesians*. Word Biblical Commentary, vol. 42. Dallas: Word, 1990.

—. (and Angus Paddison), eds. *Christology and Scripture: Interdisciplinary Perspectives.* London: T & T Clark, 2008.

Little, V.A. Spence. *The Christology of the Apologists.* New York: Charles Scibners Sons, 1935.

Loader, William. *The Christology of the Fourth Gospel: Structure and Issues.* 2nd rev. ed. Frankfurt am Main, Germany: Peter Lang, 1992.

Loeschen, John R. *The Divine Community: Trinity, Church, and Ethics in Reformation Theologies.* Kirksville, MO: Sixteenth Century Journal Publishers, 1981.

Lohse, Eduard. *Colossians and Philemon.* Translated by William R. Poehlmann and Robert J. Karris. Edited by Helmut Koester. Philadelphia: Fortress, 1971.

Longenecker, Richard N. *Galatians*. Word Biblical Commentary, vol. 41. Dallas: Word, 1990.

Luce, A.A. *Monophysitism Past and Present: A Study in Christology.* London: SPCK, 1920.

Luttenberger, Gerard H. *An Introduction to Christology in the Gospels and the Early Church.* Mystic, CT: Twenty-Third Publications, 1998.

Machen, J. Gresham. *The Virgin Birth of Christ.* New York: Harper and Row, 1930.

MacKenzie, Ian M. *The Dynamism of Space: A Theological Study into the Nature of Space.* Norwich: The Canterbury Press, 1995.

Mackintosh, H.R. *The Doctrine of the Person of Jesus Christ.* International Theological Library. New York: Charles Scribner's Sons, 1912.

Macleod, Donald. *The Person of Christ.* Contours of Christian Theology, ed. Gerald Bray. Downers Grove, IL: InterVarsity Press, 1998.

Macquarrie, John. *Christology Revisited.* Harrisburg, PA: Trinity Press

International, 1998.
—. *Jesus Christ in Modern Thought*. London: SCM Press; Philadelphia: Trinity Press International, 1990.
Marmadoro, Anna, and Jonathan Hill, eds. *The Metaphysics of the Incarnation*. New York: Oxford, 2011.
Marsh, Clive. *Christ in Focus: Radical Christocentrism in Christian Theology*. London: SCM, 2005.
Marshall, I. Howard. *I Believe in the Historical Jesus*. Rev. ed. Iowa Falls, IA: World Bible Publishers, 2002.
—. *The Origins of New Testament Christology*. Updated ed. Downers Grove, IL: InterVarsity, 1990.
Martens, Elmer A. *God's Design: A Focus on Old Testament Theology*. Grand Rapids: Baker Book House, 1981.
Martens, Peter W. *In the Shadow of the Incarnation: Essays on Jesus Christ in the Early Church in Honor of Brian E. Daley, S.J.* Notre Dame: University of Notre Dame Press, 2008.
Martin, Ralph P. *A Hymn of Christ: Philippians 2:5-11 in Recent Interpretation and in the Setting of Early Christian Worship*. Downers Grove, IL: InterVarsity Press, 1997.
—. (and Brian J. Dodd), eds. *Where Christology Began: Essays on Philippians 2*. Louisville: Westminster/John Knox Press, 1998.
Matera, Frank J. *New Testament Christology*. Louisville: Westminster/John Knox Press, 1999.
Matzoukas, Nikos, ed. *Ιωάννου Δαμασκηνοῦ Ἔκδοσις Ἀκριβὴς τῆς Ὀρθοδόξου Πίστεως*. Thessaloniki: University of Thessaloniki, 1998.
Maximus the Confessor, *On the Cosmic Mystery of Jesus Christ*. Translated by Paul M. Blowers & Robert Louis Wilken. Popular Patristics Series, 25, ed. John Behr. Crestwood, NY: St. Vladimir's Seminary Press, 2003.
McCready, Douglas. *He Came Down From Heaven: The Preexistence of Christ and the Christian Faith*. Downers Grove, IL: InterVarsity, 2005.
McGinnis Andrew M. *The Son of God Beyond the Flesh: A Historical and Theological Study of the* extra Calvinisticum. T&T Clark Studies in Systematic Theology Vol. 29, Ed. John Webster, Ian A. McFarland, and Ivor Davidson. Bloomsbury: T & T Clark, 2014.
McGrath, Alister E. *The Making of Modern German Christology 1750-1990*. Grand Rapids: Zondervan, 1994 [1987].
McGrath, James F. *John's Apologetic Christology*. Society for New Testament Studies Monograph Series. Cambridge: Cambridge University Press, 2001.
McGukin, John A. *St. Cyril of Alexandria: The Christological Controversy: Its History, Theology and Texts*. Supplements to Vigiliae Christianae, vol. 23. Leiden: E.J. Brill, 1994.
McIntyre, John. *The Shape of Christology: Studies in the Doctrine of the Person of Christ*. Edinburgh: T and T Clark, 1997.
McKinion, Steven A. *Words, Imagery, and the Mystery of Christ: A Reconstruction of Cyril of Alexandria's Christology*. Supplements to

Vigiliae Christianae, vol. 55. Leiden: Brill, 2000.
McKinney, Richard W.A., ed. *Creation Christ and Culture: Studies in Honour of T.F. Torrance*. Edinburgh: T and T Clark, 1976.
McKnight, Scot. *The Story of the Christ*. Grand Rapids: Baker, 2006.
Meijering, E.P. *God Being History: Studies in Patristic Philosophy*. Amsterdam: North-Holland Publishing Company, 1975.
Meyendorff, John. *Christ in Eastern Christian Thought*. Washington, DC: Corpus Books, 1969.
Mins, Denis. *Irenaeus*. Washington, DC: Georgetown University Press, 1994.
Moloney, Raymond. *The Knowledge of Christ*. Problems in Theology. New York: Continuum, 1999.
Moltmann, Jürgen. *Jesus Christ for Today's World*. Translated by Margaret Kohl. Minneapolis: Fortress Press, 1994.
—. *The Trinity and the Kingdom of God: The Doctrine of God*. Translated by Margaret Kohl. San Francisco: Harper and Row, 1981.
—. *The Way of Jesus Christ: Christology in Messianic Dimensions*. Translated by Margaret Kohl. Minneapolis: Fortress Press, 1993.
Molnar, Paul D. *Incarnation and Resurrection: Toward a Contemporary Understanding*. Grand Rapids: Eerdmans, 2007.
Moo, Douglas. *The Epistle to the Romans*. New International Commentary on the New Testament. Edited by Gordon D. Fee. Grand Rapids: Eerdmans, 1996.
Morey, Robert. *The Trinity: Evidence and Issues*. Grand Rapids: World Publishing, 1996.
Morris, Leon. *The Gospel According to John*. Rev. ed. New International Commentary on the New Testament. Grand Rapids: Eerdmans, 1995.
Morris, Thomas V. *Anselmian Explorations: Essays in Philosophical Theology*. Notre Dame, IN: University of Notre Dame Press, 1987.
—. *The Logic of God Incarnate*. Ithaca and London: Cornell University Press, 1986. Reprint, Eugene, OR: Wipf and Stock Publishers, 2001.
Most, William G. *The Consciousness of Christ*. Front Royal, VA: Christendom Press, 1980.
Moule, C.F.D. *The Origin of Christology*. Cambridge: Cambridge University Press, 1977.
Muller, Richard A. *Christ and the Decree: Christology and Predestination in Reformed Theology from Calvin to Perkins*. Studies in Historical Theology 2. Durham, NC: The Labyrinth Press, 1986.
Need, Stephen W. *Truly Divine and Truly Human: The Story of Christ and the Seven Ecumenical Councils*. Peabody, MA: Hendrickson, 2008.
Neill, Stephen, and Tom Wright. *The Interpretation of the New Testament 1861-1986*. 2nd ed. Oxford: Oxford, 1960. Reprint, 1988.
Neville, Robert C. *God the Creator: On the Transcendence and Presence of God*. Chicago: University of Chicago Press, 1968.
Niesel, Wilhelm. *The Theology of Calvin*. Translated by Harold Knight. Philadelphia: Westminster, 1956.
Norris, Richard A., ed. *The Christological Controversy*. Sources of Early

Christian Thought. Philadelphia: Fortress Press, 1980.
O'Brien, Peter T. *Colossians, Philemon*. Word Biblical Commentary. Dallas: Word, 1982.
—. *The Epistle to the Phillippians*. The New International Greek Testament Commentary. Grand Rapids: Eerdmans, 1991.
O'Collins, Gerald. *Christology: A Biblical, Historical, and Systematic Study of Jesus*. Oxford: Oxford, 1995.
—. *Incarnation*. New York: Continuum, 2002.
O'Grady, John F. *Models of Jesus Revisited.* New York: Paulist, 1994.
Oakes, Edward T. *Infinity Dwindled to Infancy: A Catholic and Evangelical Christology.* Grand Rapids: Eerdmans, 2011.
Oden, Thomas C. *After Modernity . . . What?* Grand Rapids: Eerdmans, 1990.
Oliphint, K. Scott. *God With Us: Divine Condescension and the Attributes of God.* Wheaton, IL: Crossway, 2012.
Olyott, Stuart. *Jesus is Both God and Man: What the Bible Teaches about the Person of Christ.* Auburn, MA: Evangelical Press, 2000 [1984].
O'Neill, J.C. *Who Did Jesus Think He Was?* Leiden; New York: E.J. Brill, 1995.
Ottley, Robert L. *The Doctrine of the Incarnation.* London: Methuen and Co., 1946 [1896].
Pannenberg, Wolfhart. *Jesus – God and Man.* Translated by Lewis L. Wilkins and Duane A. Priebe. Philadelphia: Westminster, 1977 [1968].
Papadopoulos, Stylianos G. *ΑΘΑΝΑΣΙΟΣ Ο ΜΕΓΑΣ ΚΑΙ Η ΘΕΟΛΟΓΙΑ ΤΗΣ ΟΙΚΟΥΜΕΝΙΚΗΣ ΣΥΝΟΔΟΥ.* Athens, 1975.
Parker, T.H.L. *Calvin: An Introduction to His Thought*. Louisville: Westminster/John Knox Press, 1995.
Pelikan, Jaroslav. *The Christian Tradition: A History of the Development of Doctrine*. Vol. 1, *The Emergence of the Catholic Tradition (100-600)*. Chicago: The University of Chicago Press, 1971.
—. *The Christian Tradition: A History of the Development of Doctrine.* Vol. 2, *The Spirit of Eastern Christendom (600-1700)*. Chicago: The University of Chicago Press, 1974.
—. *The Christian Tradition: A History of the Development of Doctrine.* Vol. 4, *Reformation of Church and Dogma (1300-1700)*. Chicago: The University of Chicago Press, 1984.
Peterson, David, ed. *The Word Became Flesh: Evangelicals and the Incarnation.* Carlisle, UK: Paternoster Press, 2003.
Peterson, Robert A. Sr., *Calvin and the Atonement*. Phillipsburg, NJ: Presbyterian and Reformed Publishing Company, 1983. Reprint, Fearn, Great Britain: Mentor, 1999.
Petterson, Alvyn. *Athanasius.* Harrisburg, PA: Morehouse Publishing, 1995.
Placher, William C. *A History of Christian Theology: An Introduction.* Philadelphia: Westminster, 1983.
Pohle, Joseph. *Christology-A Dogmatic Treatise on the Incarnation*. Adapted and edited by Arthur Preuss. St. Louis: B. Herder Book Co., 1952.

Prestige, G.L. *Fathers and Heretics: Six Studies in Dogmatic Faith with Prologue and Epilogue being the Bampton Lectures for 1940*. London: SPCK, 1948.

—. *God in Patristic Thought*. London: Society for Promoting Christian Knowledge, 1952.

Principe, Walter Henry. *William of Auxerre's Theology of Hypostatic Union*. Toronto: Pontifical Institute of Mediavel Studies, 1963.

Quinn, Philip L. & Charles Taliafero., eds. *A Companion to Philosophy of Religion*. Malden, MA: Blackwell. 1999 [1997].

Raitt, Jill. *The Colloquy of Montbéliard: Religion and Politics in the Sixteenth Century*. New York; Oxford: Oxford, 1993.

Ramm, Bernard L. *An Evangelical Christology: Ecumenic and Historic*. Nashville: Thomas Nelson Publishers, 1985.

—. *The Evangelical Heritage: A Study in Historical Theology*. Grand Rapids: Baker, 1973, Reprint 2000.

Rea, Michael., ed. *Oxford Readings in Philosophical Theology Volume 1: Trinity, Incarnation, Atonement*. Oxford: Oxford, 2009.

Reinhartz, Adele. *Jesus of Hollywood*. New York: Oxford, 2007.

Relton, Herbert M. *A Study in Christology: The Problem of the Relation of the Two Natures in the Person of Christ*. London: Society for Promoting Christian Knowledge, 1917.

Reymond, Robert L. *Jesus Divine Messiah: The New and Old Testament Witness*. Fearn, Scotland: Christian Focus Publications, 2003.

—. *A New Systematic Theology of the Christian Faith*. 2d ed. Nashville: Thomas Nelson Publishers, 1998.

Richardson, Cyril C., ed. *Early Christian Fathers*. Translated and Ed. Eugene R. Fairweather, Edward Rochie Hardy, and Massey Hamilton Shepherd. Library of Christian Classics, vol. 1. Philadelphia: Westminster, 1953.

Riches, John K. *A Century of New Testament Study*. Valley Forge, PA: Trinity Press International, 1993.

Robertson, Jon M. *Christ as Mediator: A Study in the Theologies of Eusebius of Caesarea, Marcellus of Ancyra, and Athanasius of Alexandria*. Oxford Theological Monographs. New York: Oxford, 2007.

Rohls, Jan. *Reformed Confessions: Theology from Zurich to Barmen*. Translated by John Hoffmeyer. Louisville: Westminster/John Knox Press, 1998.

Rosemond, K. *La Christologie de saint Jean Damascene*. Ettal: Buch Kuntsverlag, 1959.

Ross, Hugh. *Beyond the Cosmos: The Extra-Dimensionality of God. What Recent Discoveries in Astronomy and Physics Reveal about the Nature of God*. Colorado Springs: NavPress Publishing Group, 1996.

Rowdon, Harold H., ed. *Christ the Lord: Studies in Christology Presented to Donald Guthrie*. Downers Grove, IL: InterVarsity Press, 1982.

Rowe, J. Nigel. *Origen's Doctrine of Subordination: A Study in Origen's Christology*. European University Studies Series 23, vol. 272. Berne: Peter Lang, 1987.

Runia, Klaas. *The Present-Day Christological Debate*. Issues in Contemporary Theology, Edited by I. Howard Marshall. Downers Grove, IL: InterVarsity, 1984.

Rusch, William G., ed. and trans. *The Trinitarian Controversy*. Sources of Early Christian Thought. Philadelphia: Fortress, 1980.

Ryrie, Charles C. *Basic Theology*. Wheaton, IL: Victor Books, 1986.

Sadler, M.F. *Emmanuel: The Incarnation of the Son of God. The Foundation of Immutable Truth*. rev. ed. London: George Bell and Sons, 1879.

Sampson, Philip, Vinay Samuel, and Chris Sugden, eds. *Faith and Modernity*. Oxford: Regnum Books International, 1994.

Sanders, Fred and Klaus Issler, eds. *Jesus in Trinitarian Perspective: An Introductory Christology*. Nashville: Broadman and Holman, 2007.

Sanday, William. *Christology and Personality: Containing, I. Christologies Ancient and Modern, II. Personality in Christ and in Ourselves*. New York: Oxford, 1811.

Saward, John, ed. *The Scandal of the Incarnation: Irenaeus against Heresies*. Selected and introduced by Hans Urs von Balthasar. San Francisco: Ignatius, 1990.

Schaff, Philip. *The Creeds of Christendom: With a History and Critical Notes*. 3 vols. Reprint, Grand Rapids: Baker Book House, 1998.

Schleiermacher, Friedrich, D.E. *The Christian Faith*. Translated by H.R. Mackintosh and J.S. Stewart. Edinburgh: T and T Clark, 1989.

Schuele, Andreas, and Günther Thomas, eds. *Who is Jesus Christ for Us Today? Pathways to Contemporary Christology*. Louisville: Westminster/John Knox, 2009.

Schwarz, Hans. *Christology*. Grand Rapids: Eerdmans, 1998.

Sell, Alan P.F. *Theology in Turmoil: The Roots, Course and Significance of the Conservative–Liberal Debate in Modern Theology*. Grand Rapids: Baker Book House, 1986.

Sellers, R. V. *Two Ancient Christologies: A Study in the Christological Thought of the Schools of Alexandria and Antioch in the Early History of Christian Doctrine*. London: SPCK, 1940.

Shelley, Bruce L. *Church History in Plain Language*. Nashville: Thomas Nelson Publishers, 1995.

Shuster, Marguerite, and Richard Muller, eds. *Perspectives on Christology: Essays in Honor of Paul K. Jewett*. Grand Rapids: Zondervan, 1991.

Schults, F. LeRon, and Brent Walters, eds. *Christology and Ethics*. Grand Rapids: Eerdmans, 2010.

Silva, Moisés. *Philippians*. Baker Exegetical Commentary on the New Testament. Grand Rapids: Baker Book House, 1992.

Skarsaune, Oskar. *Incarnation: Myth or Fact?* Translated by Trygve R. Skarsten. St. Louis: Concordia Publishing House, 1991.

Smith, James, K.A. *Speech and Theology: Language and Logic of Incarnation*. Radical Orthodoxy Series, ed. John Milbank, Catherine Pickstock, and Graham Ward. New York: Routledge, 2002.

Spence, Alan. *Christology: A Guide for the Perplexed*. London: T&T Clark,

2008.

Stein, Robert H. *Jesus the Messiah: A Survey of the Life of Christ*. Downers Grove, IL: InterVarsity, 1996.

Stevens, Maryanne, ed. *Reconstructing the Christ Symbol: Essays in Feminist Christology*. New York: Paulist Press, 1993.

Stevenson, J., ed. *Creeds, Councils and Controversies: Documents Illustrating the History of the Church, AD 337-461.* New ed. Revised by W. H. C. Frend. London: SPCK, 1989.

Stoeckhardt, George. *Ephesians*. Translated by Martin S. Sommer. Concordia Classic Commentary Series. St. Louis: Concordia Publishing House, 1952.

Stott, John. *The Incomparable Christ*. Downers Grove, IL: InterVarsity, 2001.

Stott, John, ed. *Obeying Christ in a Changing World*. Vol. 1, *The Lord Christ*. Glasgow: Fountain Books, 1977.

Strobel, Lee. *The Case for the Real Jesus: A Journalist Investigates Current Attacks on the Identity of Christ.* Grand Rapids: Zondervan, 2007.

Studer, Basil. *Trinity and Incarnation: The Faith of the Early Church*. Translated by Matthias Westerhoff. Edited by Andrew Louth. Collegeville, MN: Liturgical, 1993.

Sturch, Richard. *The Word and the Christ: An Essay in Analytical Christology*. New York: Oxford, 2003 [1991].

Swinburne, Richard. *Was Jesus God?* New York: Oxford, 2008.

Talbert, Charles H. *The Development of Christology During the First Hundred Years: And Other essays on Early Christian Christology.* Supplements to Novum Testamentum, eds. M.M. Mitchell & D.P. Moessner. Leiden: Brill, 2011.

Tanner, Kathryn. *Jesus, Humanity and the Trinity: A Brief Systematic Theology.* Minneapolis: Fortress, 2001.

—. *Christ the Key*. Current Issues in Theology, ed. Iain Torrance. New York: Cambridge, 2009.

Taylor, Vincent. *The Person of Christ in New Testament Teaching*. London: Macmillan and Co. Limited., 1958.

Tenney, Merrill C. *John*. In vol. 9 of *The Expositor's Bible Commentary*. Edited by Frank E. Gaebelein, 3-203. Grand Rapids: Zondervan.

Thompson, J.A. *The Book of Jeremiah*. The New International Commentary on the Old Testament. Grand Rapids: Eerdmans, 1980.

Thornhill, John. *Modernity: Christianity's Estranged Child.* Grand Rapids: Eerdmans, 2000.

Thornton, Lionel Spencer. *The Incarnate Lord: An Essay Concerning the Doctrine of the Incarnation in its Relation to Organic Conceptions.* London: Longmans, Green and Co., 1928.

Torrance, Iain R. *Christology After Chalcedon: Severus of Antioch and Sergius the Monophysite.* Eugene, OR: Wipf and Stock, 1998 [1988].

Torrance, Thomas F. *Theology in Reconciliation: Essays Towards Evangelical and Catholic Unity in East and West.* Grand Rapids: Eerdmans, 1975.

—. *The Christian Doctrine of God: One Being Three Persons*. Edinburgh: T and T Clark, 1996.

—. *Divine Meaning: Studies in Patristic Hermeneutics*. Edinburgh: T and T Clark, 1995.
—. *Trinitarian Perspectives: Toward Doctrinal Agreement*. Edinburgh: T and T Clark, 1994.
—. *Space, Time and Incarnation*. Edinburgh: T and T Clark, 1997 [1969].
—. ed. *The Incarnation: Ecumenical Studies in the Nicene–Constantinopolitan Creed*. Edinburgh: Handsel, 1981.
Tozer, A.W. *The Knowledge of the Holy*. New York: HarperCollins, 1962.
Tsoukalas, Steven. *Knowing Christ in the Challenge of Heresy: A Christology of the Cults, A Christology of the Bible*. New York: University Press of America, 1999.
Turner, H.E.W. *Jesus Master and Lord: A Study in the Historical Truth of the Gospels*. 2nd ed. London: A.R. Mowbray and Co. Limited, 1954.
—. *The Pattern of Christian Truth*. London: A.R. Mowbray and Co. Limited, 1954.
Van Den Brom, Luco J. *Divine Presence in the World: A Critical Analysis of the Notion of Divine Omnipresence*. Studies in Philosophical Theology, vol. 5. Edited by H.J. Adriaanese and Vincent Brümmer. Kampen: Kok Pharos Publishing House, 1993.
VanGemeren, Willem A. *Psalms*. In vol. 8 of *The Expositor's Bible Commentary*. Edited by Frank E. Gaebelein, 3-880. Grand Rapids: Zondervan, 1991.
Vanhoozer, Kevin J., ed. *The Trinity in a Pluralistic Age: Theological Essays on Culture and Religion*. Grand Rapids: Eerdmans, 1997.
van Driel, Edwin Chr. *Incarnation Anyway: Arguments for Supralapsarian Christology*. Academy Series, American Academy of Religion, Edited by Kimberly Rae Connor. New York: Oxford, 2008.
van Ruler, Arnold A. *Calvinist Trinitarianism and Theocentric Politics: Essays toward a Public Theology*. Toronto Studies in Theology, vol. 38. Translated by John Bolt. Lewiston, NY: The Edwin Mellen Press, 1989.
Varghese, Roy Abraham., ed. *Theos, Anthropos, Christos: A Compendium of Modern Philosophical Theology*. American University Studies. Series 7. Theology and Religion, vol. 208. New York: Peter Lang Publishing, Inc., 2000.
Vonier, Anscar. *The Personality of Christ*. Christological Trilogy, Book 1., Asuumption Press, 2013 [1915].
Vos, Geerhardus. *The Self-Disclosure of Jesus: The Modern Debate about the Messianic Consciousness*. George H. Doran, 1926. Reprint, Phillipsburg, NJ: Presbyterian and Reformed Publishing Company, 2002.
Wainwright, Geoffrey., ed. *Keeping the Faith: Essays to Mark the Centenary of Lux Mundi*. Philadelphia: Fortress, 1988.
Walvoord, John. *Jesus Christ our Lord*. Chicago, IL: Moody Press, 1969.
Warfield, Benjamin B. *Calvin and Augustine*. Philadelphia: Presbyterian and Reformed Publishing Company, 1974.
—. *Christology and Criticism*. New York: Oxford University Press, 1929.
—. *The Person and Work of Christ*. Philadelphia, PA: Presbyterian and

Reformed Publishing Company, 1950.

Weinandy, Thomas G. *Does God Change? The Word's Becoming in the Incarnation.* Studies in Historical Theology Volume 4. Still River, MA: St. Bede's Publications, 1985.

—. *Does God Suffer?* Notre Dame, IN: University of Notre Dame Press, 2000.

—. *In the Likeness of Sinful Flesh: An Essay on the Humanity of Christ.* Edinburgh: T and T Clark, 1993.

—. *Athanasius: A Theological Introduction.* Great Theologians Series, Edited by John Webster, Trevor Hart, and Douglas B. Farrow. Burlington, VT: Ashgate, 2007.

—. (and Daniel A. Keating), eds. *The Theology of St. Cyril of Alexandria: A Critical Appreciation.* London: T & T Clark, 2003.

Welch, Claude. *God and Incarnation in Mid-Nineteenth Century German Theology: G. Thomasius, I.A. Dorner, A.E. Biedermann.* Translated and edited by Claude Welch. A Library of Protestant Thought. New York: Oxford University Press, 1965.

Wells, David F. *The Person of Christ: A Biblical and Historical Analysis of the Incarnation.* Alliance, OH: Bible Scholar Press, 1984.

Wendel, François. *Calvin: Origins and Development of His Religious Thought.* Translated by Philip Mairet. Preses Universitaires de France: 1950. Reprint, Grand Rapids: Baker, 1997.

Wesche, Kenneth Paul. *On the Person of Christ: The Christology of Emperor Justinian.* Edited and Introduced by Kenneth Paul Wesche. Crestwood, NY: St. Vladimir's Seminary Press, 1991.

Weston, Frank. *The One Christ: An Enquiry into the Manner of the Incarnation.* London: Forgotten Books, 2012 [1914].

White, James R. *The Forgotten Trinity: Recovering the Heart of Christian Belief.* Minneapolis: Bethany House Publishers, 1998.

White, Stephen K., ed. *Life-World and Politics: Between Modernity and Postmodernity. Essays in Honor of Fred R. Dallmayr.* Notre Dame, IN: University of Notre Dame Press1989.

Widdicombe, Peter. *The Fatherhood of God From Origen to Athanasius.* Revised Ed. Oxford Theological Monographs. New York: Oxford, 2000 [1994].

Wilkins, Michael J., and J.P. Moreland, eds. *Jesus under Fire: Modern Scholarship Reinvents the Historical Jesus.* Grand Rapids: Zondervan Publishers, 1995.

Williams, David T. *Have This Mind: Following the Example of Christ.* Lincoln, NE: iUniverse, 2007.

—. Kenosis *of God: The Self-Limitation of God: Father, Son and Holy Spirit.* Bloomington, IN: iUniverse, 2009.

Willis, E. David. *Calvin's Catholic Christology: The Function of the So-Called Extra Calvinisticum in Calvin's Theology.* Leiden, The Netherlands: E.J. Brill, 1966.

Wingren, Gustaf. *Man and the Incarnation: A Study in the Biblical Theology of Irenaeus.* Translated by Ross Mackenzie. Philadelphia: Muhlenberg, 1959.

Witherington, Ben, III. *The Jesus Quest: The Third Search for the Jew of Nazareth*. 2nd ed. Downers Grove, IL: InterVarsity, 1997.
—. *The Many Faces of the Christ: The Christologies of the New Testament and Beyond*. New York: Crossroad Publishing Company, 1998.
Wood, A. Skevington. *Ephesians*. In vol. 11 of *The Expositor's Bible Commentary*. Edited by Frank E. Gaebelein, 3-92. Grand Rapids: Zondervan, 1978.
Wright, Chris. *The Uniqueness of Jesus.* Thinking Clearly, Edited By Clive Calver. London: Monarch Books, 2001 [1997].
Wright, N.T. *The Climax of the Covenant: Christ and the Law in Pauline Theology.* Minneapolis: Fortress, 1993 [1991].
Wyatt, Peter. *Jesus Christ and Creation in the Theology of John Calvin.* Princeton Theological Monograph Series 42, ed. Dikran Y. Hadidian. Allison Park, PA: Pickwick Publications, 1996.
Wyrwa, Dietmar., ed. *Die Weltlichkeit des Glaubens in der Alten Kirche: Festschrift für Ulrich Wickert zum siebzigsten Geburtstag.* Beihefte zur Zeitschrift für die neutestamentliche Wissenschaft: Und die Kunde der älteren Kirche, Band 85, ed. Erich Gräßer. Berlin: Walter de Gruyter, 1997.
Young, Brad H. *Jesus the Jewish Theologian*. Peabody, MA: Hendrickson Publishers, 1995.
Young, Frances M., with Andrew Teal. *From Nicaea to Chalcedon: A Guide to the Literature and its Background.* 2d. ed. Grand Rapids: Baker, 2010 [1983].
Young, Frances. *God's Presence: A Contemporary Recapitulation of Early Christianity.* Current Issues in Theology, Edited by Iain Torrance. New York: Cambridge, 2013.
Zahl, Paul F.M. *A Short Systematic Theology.* Grand Rapids: Eerdmans, 2000.
Zizioulas, John D. *Being as Communion: Studies in Personhood and the Church*. Crestwood, NY: St. Vladimir's Press, 1993.
Zuck, Roy B., ed. *Vital Christology Issues: Examining Contemporary and Classic Concerns*. Grand Rapids: Kregel, 1997.

Articles

Abernathy, David. "Jesus is the Eternal Son of God." *St. Francis Magazine* 6:2 (April, 2010): 327-94.
Adeney, Walter F. "The Transcendental Element in the Consciousness of Christ." *American Journal of Theology* 3 (1899): 99-107.
Anatolios, Khaled. "'The Body as Instrument': A Reevaluation of Athanasius' Logos-Sarx Christology." *Coptic Church Review* 18 (1997): 78-84.
Armstrong, A.H. "The Plotinian Doctrine of NOUS in Patristic Thought." *Vigiliae Christianae* 8 no. 4 (1954): 234-38.
Backus, Irena. "John of Damascus, De Fida Orthodoxa: Translations by Burgundio (1153/54), Grosseteste (1235/40 and Lefèvre d'Etaples (1507)." *Journal of the Warburg and Courtauld Institutes* 49 (1986):211-17.
Bandstra, Andrew J. "'Adam' and 'The Servant' in Philippians 2:5 ff." *Calvin*

Theological Journal (1966): 213-16.

Barclift, Philip L. "The Shifting Tones of Pope Leo the Great's Christological Vocabulary." *Church History* 66 no. 2 (1997): 221-39.

Barnard, L.W. "Origen's Christology and Eschatology." *Anglican Theological Review* (1964): 314-19.

Bates, Gordon. "The Typology of Adam and Christ in John Calvin." *The Hartford Quarterly* 5 (1965): 42-81.

Bayne, Tim. "The Inclusion Model of the Incarnation: Problems and Prospects." *Religious Studies* 37 (2001): 125-41.

Black, David Alan. "The Text of John 3:13." *Grace Theological Journal* 6 (1985): 49-66.

—. "The Discourse Structure of Philippians: A Study in Textlinguistics." *Novum Testamentum* 37 (1995): 16-49.

Blaising, Craig A. "Chalcedon and Christology: A 1530th Anniversary," in *The Bib-Sac Reader*, ed. John F. Walvoord and Roy B. Zuck. Chicago: Moody Press, (1983): 93-104.

Blaser, Klauspeter. "Calvins Lehre von den drei Ämtern Christi." *Theologische Studiën* 105 (1970): 3-52.

Boersma, Hans. "Alexandrian or Antiochene? A Dilemma in Barth's Christology." *Westminster Theological Journal* 52 (1990): 264-80.

Braaten, Carl E. "Modern Interpretations of Nestorius." *Church History* 32 no. 3 (1963): 251-67.

Bray, Gerald L. "The Double Procession of the Holy Spirit in Evangelical Theology: Do We Still Need it?" *Journal of the Evangelical Theological Society* (1998): 415-26.

—. "The *Filioque* Clause in History and Theology." *Tyndale Bulletin* 34 (1983): 93-144.

—."Recent Trends in Christology," in *Constructive Christian Theology in the Worldwide Church*, ed. William R. Barr. Grand Rapids: Eerdmans, (1997): 291-301.

Breck, John. "Reflections on the 'Problem' of Chalcedonian Christology." *St. Vladimir's Theological Quarterly* 33 (1989): 147-57.

Bucur, Bogdan G. "Foreordained From All Eternity: The Mystery of the Incarnation According to Some Early Christian and Byzantine Writers." *Dumbarton Oaks Papers* 62 (2008): 199-215.

Carson, Ronald A. "The Motifs of 'Kenosis' and 'Imitatio' in the Work of Dietrich Bonhoeffer, With an Excursus on the 'Communicatio Idiomatum.'" *Journal of the American Academy of Religion* 43 (1975): 542-553.

Chia, Roland. "*ΜΙΑ ΟΥΣΙΑ ΤΡΙΕΣ ΥΠΟΣΤΑΣΕΙΣ*: St. Athanasius and the Doctrine of the Trinity." *Jian Dao* 9 (1990): 27-48.

Craig, William Lane. "Hugh Ross's Extra-Dimensional Deity: A review Article." *Journal of the Evangelical Theological Society* 42 (1999): 293-304.

Cross, Richard. "Individual Natures in the Christology of Leontius of Byzantium." *Journal of Early Christian Studies* 10 (2002): 245-65.

—. "Perichoresis, Deification, and Christological Predication in John of Damascus." *Mediaeval Studies* 62 (2000): 69-124.

Daley, Brian. "Origenism of Leontius of Byzantium." *Journal of Theological Studies* 27 (1976): 333-69.

den Bok, M. Bac, A.J. Beck, & K. Bom. "More than Just an Individual: Scotus's Concept of Person from the Christological Context of Lectura III 1." *Franciscan Studies* 66 (2008): 169-96.

Doriani, Daniel. "The Deity of Christ in the Synoptic Gospels." *Journal of the Evangelical Theological Society* 37 (1994): 333-50.

Dragas, George Dion. "The Anti-Apollinarist Christology of St. Gregory of Nyssa: A First Analysis." *The Greek Orthodox Theological Review* 42 no. 3-4 (1997): 299-314.

Du Toit, A.B. "The Incarnate Word-A Study of John 1:14." *Neotestamentica* 2 (1968): 9-21.

Dyck, Grace M. "Omnipresence and Incorporeality." *Religious Studies* 13 (1977): 85-91.

Erickson, Millard J. "Evangelical Christology and Soteriology Today." *Interpretation* 49 (1995): 255-66.

—."God and Change." *Southern Baptist Journal of Theology* 1 (1997): 38-51.

Feinberg, John S. "The Incarnation of Jesus Christ," in *In Defense of Miracles: A Comprehensive Case for God's Action in History*, ed. R. Douglas Geivett and Gary R. Habermas. Downers Grove, IL: InterVarsity Press, 1997.

Fennema, David A. "John 1:18 'God the Only Son.'" *New Testament Studies* 31 (1985): 24-35.

Ferrara, Dennis M. "'Hypostatized in the Logos:' Leontius of Byzantium, Leontius of Jerusalem and the Unfinished Business of the Council of Chalcedon." *Louvain Studies* 22 (1997): 311-27.

Forrest, Peter. "The Incarnation: A Philosophical Case for Kenosis." *Religious Studies* 36 (2000): 127-40.

Freddoso, Alfred J. "Logic, Ontology and Ockham's Christology." Accessed March 2006. Available from: http://www.nd.edu/~afreddos/papers/looc.htm; Internet.

—. "Human Nature, Potency and the Incarnation." Accessed March 2006. Available from: http://www.nd.edu/~afreddos/papers/humnat.htm; Internet.

Gawrisch, Wilbert R. "On Christology, Brenz and the Question of Ubiquity." In *No Other Gospel: Essays in Commemoration of the 400th Anniversary of the Formula of Concord 1580-1980*, ed. Arnold J. Koelpin. Milwaukee: Northwestern Publishing House, 1980.

Gibbs, John G. "The Relation Between Creation and Redemption According to Phil. II.5-11." *Novum Testamentum* 12 (1970): 270-83.

Gockel, Matthias. "A Dubious Christological Formula? Leontius of Byzantium and the Anhypostastos - Enhypostasis Theory." *Journal of Theological Studies* 51 (2000): 515-32.

Gray, Patrick. "Through the Tunnel with Leontius of Jerusalem: The Sixth-

Century Transformation of Theology." *Byzantina Australiensia* 10 (1996): 187-96.

Haji, Ishtiyaque. "God and Omnispatiality." *International Journal for Philosophy of Religion* 25 (1989): 99-108.

Hanson, R.P.C. "The Arian Doctrine of the Incarnation." *Arianism: Historical and Theological Reassessments.* Papers from the Ninth International Conference on Patristic Studies. September 5-10, 1983, Oxford England. Edited by Robert C. Gregg. Philadelphia: The Philadelphia Patristic Foundation Limited, 1985.

Havrilak, Gregory. "Chalcedon and Orthodox Christology Today." *St. Vladimir's Theological Quarterly* 33 (1989): 127-45.

Helland, Roger. "The Hypostatic Union: How Did Jesus Function?" *Evangelical Quarterly* 65 (1993): 311-27.

Heron, Alasdair. "'Logos, Image, Son': Some Models and Paradigms in Early Christology," in *Creation, Christ, and Culture: Studies in Honour of T.F. Torrance*, ed. Richard W.A. McKinney. Edinburgh: T & T Clark, (1976): 43-61.

—. "*Communicatio Idiomatum* and *Deificatio* of Human Nature: A Reformed Perspective." *Greek Orthodox Theological Review* 43 (1998): 367-76.

Hoover, Roy W. "The Harpagmos Enigma: A Philological Solution." *Harvard Theological Review* 64 (1971): 95-119.

House, Dennis K. "The Relation of Tertullian's Christology to Pagan Philosophy." *Dionysius* 12 (1988): 29-36.

Howard, George. "Phil. 2:6-11 and the Human Christ." *Catholic Biblical Quarterly* 40 (1978): 368-87.

Hunter, William B. "Milton on the Incarnation: Some More Heresies." *Journal of the History of Ideas* 21 (1960): 349-69.

Jeremias, Joachim. "Zu Phil. ii.7: 'Ἑαυτὸν Ἐκένωσεν.'" *Novum Testamentum* 6 (1963): 182-88.

Kannengiesser, Charles. "Athanasius of Alexandria and the Foundation of Traditional Christology." *Theological Studies* 34 (1973): 103-13.

Karakoli, Constantine. "Η ΟΙΚΟΥΜΕΝΙΚΗ ΣΥΝΟΔΟΣ ΤΗΣ ΝΙΚΑΙΑΣ ΚΑΤΑ ΤΟΝ ΜΕΓΑΝ ΑΘΑΝΑΣΙΟΝ" in Σπουδαστήριον Ιστορικής Θεολογίας Πανπιστήμιον Θεσσαλόνικης Χαριστήριον εἰς τον καθηγητήν Παναγιώτην Κ Χρήστου, ed. George Mantzarides. Thessaloniki: University of Thessaloniki, 1967.

Käsemann, Ernst. "A Critical Analysis of Philippians 2:5-11." Translated by Alice F. Carse. *Journal for Theology and Church* 5 (1968): 45-87.

Kelly, C.J. "The God of Classical Theism and the Doctrine of Incarnation." *International Journal for Philosophy of Religion* 35 (1994): 1-20.

Knapp, Daniel T. "The Self-Humiliation of Jesus Christ and Christ-Like Living: A Study of Philippians 2:6-11." *Evangelical Journal* 15 (1997): 80-96.

Kratz, Wolfgang. "Christus – Gott und Mensch: Einige Fragen an Calvins Christologie." *Evangelische Theologie* 19 (1959): 209-19.

Krausmüller, Dirk. "Making Sense of the Formula of Chalcedon: The Cappadocians and Aristotle in Leontius of Byzantium's *Contra Nestorianos et Eutychianos*." *Vigiliae Christianae* 65 (2011): 484-513.

Kvanvig, Jonathan. "The Incarnation and the Knowability Paradox." *Synthese* 173 (March 2010): 89-105.

La Croix, Richard. "Aquinas on God's Omnipresence and Timelessness." *Philosophy and Phenomenological Research* 42 (1982): 391-99.

Lane, Anthony. "Christology Beyond Chalcedon." In *Christ the Lord: Studies in Christology Presented to Donald Guthrie*, ed. Harold H. Rowdon. Leicester: InterVarsity, 1982.

Lang, U.M. "Anhypostatos-Enhypostatos: Church Fathers, Protestant Orthodoxy, and Karl Barth." *Journal of Theological Studies* 49 (1998): 630-57.

Lieb, Michael. "Milton and the Kenotic Christology: Its Literary Bearing." *English Literary History* 37 (1970): 342-60.

Leigh, Ronald W. "Jesus: The One-Natured God-Man." *Christian Scholar's Review* 11 (1982):124-37.

—."A Reply to Edwin Walhout." *Christian Scholar's Review* 13 (1983): 54-60.

Levine, Baruch. "On the Presence of God in Biblical Religion." In *Religion in Antiquity: Essays in Memory of Erwin Ramsdell Goodenough*, ed. Jacob Neusner. Studies in the History of Religions, vol. 14. Leiden: Brill, 1968.

Link, Christian. "Die Entscheidung der Christologie Calvins und ihre theologische Bedeutung: Das sogenannte Extra-Calvinisticum." *Evangelische Theologie* 47 (1987): 97-119.

—. "Incarnation and Creation: Interpreting the World through the Doctrine of the Trinity." Translated by Christoph Stenschke. *Greek Orthodox Theological Review* 43 (1998): 327-38.

Lore, Andrew. Solving a Paradox Against Concrete-Composite Christology: A Modified Hylomorphic Proposal." *Religious Studies* 47, No. 4 (2011): 493-502.

Lynch, John Joseph. "Leontius of Byzantium: A Cyrillian Christology." *Theological Studies* 36 (1975): 455-71.

MacKinnon, D.M. "Prolegomena to Christology." *Journal of Theological Studies* 33 (1982): 146-60.

MacLeod, David J. "Imitating the Incarnation of Christ: An Exposition of Philippians 2:5-8." *Bibliotheca Sacra* 158 (2001): 308-30.

Marshall, John S. "The Christology of Chalcedon." *Anglican Theological Review* (1960): 117-25.

McCormack, Bruce. "For Us and Our Salvation: Incarnation and Atonement in the Reformed Tradition." *Greek Orthodox Theological Review* 43 (1998): 281-316.

Morris, Thomas V. "The Natures of God Incarnate." [With a response by Ronald Leigh.] *Christian Scholar's Review* 14 (1984): 35-45.

Moutafakis, Nicholas J. "Christology and its Philosophical Complexities in the thought of Leontius of Byzantium." *History of Philosophy Quarterly* 10 (1993): 99-119.

Muller, Richard A. "Directions in the Study of Barth's Christology." *Westminster Theological Journal* 48 (1986): 120-34.

—."Incarnation, Immutability, and the Case for Classical Theism." *Westminster Theological Journal* 45 (1983): 23-36.

Need, Stephen W. "Language, Metaphor, and Chalcedon: A Case of Theological Double Vision." *Harvard Theological Review* 88 no. 2 (1995): 237-55.

Nesteruk, Alexei V. "The Universe Transcended: God's 'Presence in Absence' in Science and Theology." *European Journal of Science and Theology* 1 (2005): 7-19.

Norris, Richard, Jr. "Chalcedon Revisited: A Historical and Theological Reflection." In *New Perspectives on Historical Theology: Essays in Memory of John Meyendorff*, ed. Bradley Nassif. Grand Rapids: Eerdmans, 1996.

O'Connor, J.M. "Christological Anthropology in Phil., II, 6-11." *Revue Biblique* 83 (1976): 25-50.

O'Neill J.C. "Hoover on Harpagmos Reviewed: With a Modest Proposal Concerning Philippians 2:6." *Harvard Theological Review* 81 (1988): 445-49.

Osborne, Thomas. "Faith, Philosophy, and the Nominalist Background to Luther's Defense of the Real Presence." *Journal of the History of Ideas* 63 no. 1 (2002): 63-82.

Overstreet, R. Larry. "John 3:13 and the Omnipresence of Jesus Christ." *Journal for Baptist Theology and Ministry* 2 (2004): 135-153.

Padgett, Alan G. "Testing Models of the Incarnation: From Revelation to Historical Science." *Journal of Christian Theological Research* 6 (2001) [journal on-line]. Accessed May 2003. Available from http://apu.edu/~CTRF/jctr.html; Internet.

Parker, David. "Jesus Christ: Man of Faith or Saving Son of God?" *Evangelical Quarterly* 67 (1995): 245-64.

Parvis, Sara. "Christology in the Early Arian Controversy: The Exegetical War," in Andrew T. Lincoln & Angus Paddison, eds. *Christology and Scripture: Interdisciplinary Perspectives.* Library of New Testament Studies, 348, ed. Mark Goodacre. London: T & T Clark, 2007.

Patitsas, Chrestos. "*Kenosis* According to Saint Paul." *The Greek Orthodox Theological Review* 27 (1982): 67-82.

Peters, David G. "The 'Extra Calvinisticum' and Calvin's Eucharistic Theology." Unpublished paper, Wisconsin Lutheran Seminary Library, nd.

Picirilli, Robert E. "He Emptied Himself." *Biblical Viewpoint* 3 (1969): 23-30.

Pollard, T Evan. "Exit the Alexandrian Christ: Some Reflections on Contemporary Christology in the Light of New Testament Studies." *Colloquium* 13 (1980): 16-23.

Poon, Wilson. "'You Must Name Him Jesus:' Being Named as Kenosis." *Theology* 103 (2000): 433-36.

Raitt, Jill. "The Person of the Mediator: Calvin's Christology and Beza's

Fidelity." *Occasional Papers of the American Society for Reformation Research* 1 (1977): 53-80.
Ramelli, Ilaria L. E. "Origen's Anti-Subordinationism and its Heritage in the Nicene and Cappadocian Line." *Vigiliae Christianae* 65 (2011): 21-49.
Raschko, Michael B. "Aquinas's Theology of the Incarnation in Light of Lombard's Subsistence Theory." *The Thomist* 65 (2001): 409-39.
Rees, Silas. "Leontius of Byzantium and His Defence of the Council of Chalcedon." *Harvard Theological Review* 24 no. 2 (1931): 111-19.
Reist, Irwin W. "The Christology of Irenaeus." *Journal of the Evangelical Theological Society* 13 (1970): 241-51.
Richardson, Cyril. "Trinity and Enhypostasia." *Canadian Journal of Theology* 5 (1959): 73-78.
Salas, Jr., Victor. "Thomas Aquinas on Christ's *Esse*: A Metaphysics of the Incarnation." *The Thomist* 70 (2006): 577-603.
Scalise, Brian T. "Perichoresis in Gregory Nazianzen and Maximus the Confessor." *Eleutheria* 2 no. 1 (2012): 58-76.
Schwöbel, Christoph. "The Triune God of Grace: The Doctrine of the Trinity in the Theology of the Reformers." In *The Christian Understanding of God Today: Theological Colloquium on the Occasion of the 400th Anniversary of the Foundation of Trinity College*, Dublin, ed. James M. Byrne. Dublin: Columba, 1993.
Senor, Thomas D. "The Compositional Account of the Incarnation." *Faith and Philosophy* 24 (2007): 52-71.
Shults, F. Leroy. "A Dubious Christological Formula: From Leontius to Karl Barth." *Theological Studies* 57 (1996): 431-47.
Simpson, Theo. "More Questions About Christology." *Journal of Theology for Southern Africa* 34 (1981): 49-57.
Stead, G. Christopher. "The Scriptures and the Soul of Christ in Athanasius." *Vigiliae Christianae* 36 (1982): 233-50.
Stogianou, Vasilliou P. "*Η Χριστολογία των Επιστολών Ιγνατίου του και Θεοφόρού*" in *Σπουδαστήριον Ιστορικής Θεολογίας" Πανεπιστήμιον Θεσσαλονίκης Συμπόσιον εις τον Καθηγητήν Παναγιώτην Κ Χρήστου*, ed. George Mantzarides. Thessaloniki: University of Thessaloniki, 1967.
Strimple, Robert. "Philippians 2:5-11 in Recent Studies: Some Exegetical Conclusions." *Westminster Theological Journal* 41 (1979): 247-68.
Sturch, Richard. "Inclusion and Incarnation: A Response to Bayne." *Religious Studies* 39 (2003): 103-06.
Talbert, Charles H. "The Problem of Pre-Existence in Philippians 2:6-11." *Journal of Biblical Literature* 86 (1967): 141-53.
Theodorou, Andrea. "*Στοιχεία Επιδράσεως της Ελληνικής Σκέψεως επί της Αιρέσεως του Αρειανισμού.*" *Patristic and Byzantine Review* 8 (1989): 201-25.
Torrance, Thomas F. "The Doctrine of the Holy Trinity According to St. Athanasius." *Anglican Theological Review* 71 (1989): 395-405.
Tylenda, Joseph N. "Christ the Mediator: Calvin versus Stancaro [with

translation of Calvin's First Treatise against Stancaro]." *Calvin Theological Journal* 8 (1973):5-16.

——. The Controversy on Christ the Mediator: Calvin's Second Reply to Stancaro." *Calvin Theological Journal* 8 (1973): 131-57.

van Den Brom, L.J. "God's Omnipresent Agency." *Religious Studies* 20 (1984): 637-55.

Voyles, Richard J. "The Fear of Death and a False Humanity as the Human Dilemma: The Argument of Influence in Athanasius' Christology." *Patristic and Byzantine Review* 8 (1989): 135-44.

Walhout, Edwin. "Chalcedon: Still Valid." *Christian Scholar's Review* 13 (1983): 48-53.

Ware, Bruce A. "An Evangelical Reformulation of the Doctrine of the Immutability of God." *Journal of the Evangelical Theological Society* 29 (1986): 431-46.

Warren, W. "On *ΕΑΥΤΟΝ ΕΚΕΝΩΣΕΝ*, Phil. II 7. *Journal of Theological Studies* 12 (1911): 461-63.

Wesche, Kenneth Paul. "The Christology of Leontius of Jerusalem: Monophysite or Chalcedonian?" *St. Vladimir's Theological Quarterly* 31 no. 1 (1987): 65-95.

Wickham, L.R. "Soul and Body: Christ's Omnipresence (De Tridui Spatio p. 29o, 18-294, 13)." In *The Easter Sermons of Gregory of Nyssa: Translation and Commentary. Proceedings of the Fourth International Colloquium on Gregory of Nyssa Cambridge, England: 11-15 September, 1978*. Patristic Monograph Series no. 9, ed. Andreas Spira and Christoph Klock. Cambridge, MA: The Philadelphia Patristic Foundation, Ltd., 1981.

Widdicombe, Peter. "Athanasius and the Making of the Doctrine of the Trinity." *Pro Ecclesia* 6 (1997): 456-78.

Wilken, Robert L. "Tradition, Exegesis, and the Christological Controversies." *Church History* 34 (1965): 123-45.

Williams, George Huntston "Christology and Church-State Relations in the Fourth Century." *Church History* 20, no. 3 (1951): 3-33.

——. "Christology and Church-State Relations in the Fourth Century (Concluded)." *Church History* 20, no. 4 (1951): 3-26.

Williams, Rowan. "'Person' and 'Personality" in Christology." *Downside Review* 94 (1976): 253-60.

Wilson, Robert E. "He Emptied Himself." *Journal of the Evangelical Theological Society* 19 (1976): 279-81.

Winslow, Donald F. "Christology and Exegesis in the Cappadocians." *Church History* 40 no. 4 (1971): 389-96.

Wright, N.T. "*ἁρπαγμός* and the Meaning of Philippians 2:5-11." *Journal of Theological Studies* 37 (1986): 321-52.

Yarnold, Edward J. " 'Videmus Duplicem Statum': The Visibility of the Two Natures of Christ in Tertullian's *Adversus Praxean."* Studia Patristica.* Leuven: Peeters, 1989.

Yeago, David S. "The New Testament and the Nicene Dogma: A Contribution to Theological Exegesis." *Pro Ecclesia* 3 (1994): 152-64.
Zachman, Randall C. "Jesus Christ as the Image of God in Calvin's Theology." *Calvin Theological Journal* 25 (1990): 45-62.

Theses and Dissertations

Ahern, Patrick Francis. "A Study of the Omnipresence and Immensity of God." Master's thesis, Loyola University, 1951.
Blount, Douglas Keith. "An Essay on Divine Presence." Ph.D. diss., University of Notre Dame, 1997.
Butler, Michael E. *Hypostatic Union and Monotheletism: The Dyothelite Christology of St. Maximus the Confessor.* Ph.D. diss. New York: Fordham University, 1993.
Callender, Elizabeth Jarrell. "A Theology of Spatiality: The Divine Perfection of Omnipresence in the Theology of Karl Barth." Ph.D. thesis, University of Otago, 2011.
Cherry, Millard Ross. "The Christology of Philippians 2:5-11." Th.D. diss., The Southern Baptist Theological Seminary, 1956.
Clayton, Allen L. "The Orthodox Recovery of a Heretical Proof Text: Athanasius of Alexandria's Interpretation of Proverbs 8:22-30 in Conflict with the Arians." Ph.D. diss., Southern Methodist University, 1988.
Daley, Brian. "Leontius of Byzantium: A Critical Edition of His Works with Prolegomena." Ph.D. diss., Oxford University, 1978.
Daley, Chauncey R. "Christology of Athanasius of Alexandria." Ph.D. diss., Southern Baptist Theological Seminary, 1954.
Edmonson, Stephen Bud. "Christ the Mediator: Calvin's Eclectic Christology." Ph.D. diss., Yale University, 1999.
Fickett, Harold J., Jr. "A Comparative Study of the Christology of Origen and Calvin Based on the *Peri Archon* and the Institutes of the Christian Religion." Th.D. diss., Eastern Baptist Theological Seminary, 1949.
Fracea, Ilea. "*Ο ΛΕΟΝΤΙΟΣ ΒΥΖΑΝΤΙΟΣ: Βίος και Συγγράματα.*" Ph.D. diss., University of Athens, 1984.
Fuerst, Adrian. "The Omnipresence of God in Selected Writings Bertween 1220-1270." DST thesis, The Catholic University of America, 1951.
Johnson, Dennis Edward. "Immutability and Incarnation: An Historical and Theological Study of the Concepts of Christ's Divine Unchangeability and His Human Development." Ph.D. diss., Fuller Theological Seminary, 1984.
Kennedy, Kevin Dixon. "Union with Christ as Key to John Calvin's Understanding of the Extent of the Atonement." Ph.D. diss., The Southern Baptist Theological Seminary, 1999.
Lynch, John Joseph. "Prosopon and the Dogma of the Trinity: A Study of the Background of Conciliar Use of the Word in the Writings of Cyril of Alexandria and Leontius of Byzantium." Ph.D. diss., Fordham University, 1973.

Orr, Peter. *Christ Present and Absent: A Study in Pauline Christology.* Ph.D. thesis, University of Durham, 2011.

Prest, Loring A. "The Disposition of the Divine Attributes of Omniscience, Omnipresence and Omnipotence in the Incarnate Christ." Th.M. thesis, Grace Theological Seminary, 1984.

Schultz, Thomas. "The Doctrine of the Person of Christ with an Emphasis upon the Hypostatic Union." Th.D. diss., Dallas Theological Seminary, 1962.

Stonebraker, Eleanor. "Heroes and Beggars: A Lutheran Takes a Look at the Extra Calvinisticum, Inside and Out." M.T.S. thesis, Trinity Lutheran Seminary, 1991.

Twombly, Charles Craig. "Perichoresis and Personhood in the Thought of John of Damascus." Ph.D. diss., Emory University, 1992.

Wolfe, David A. "The Omnipresence of God." Th.M. thesis, Grace Theological Seminary, 1981.

Zachariades, Theodore. "The Omnipresence of Jesus Christ: A Neglected Aspect of Evangelical Christology." Ph.D. diss., The Southern Baptist Theological Seminary, 2004.

Author Index

Abanes, Richard,   4
Adams, Marilyn M.,   166
Ahern, Patrick F.,   136
Allison, Gregg R.,   19
Anastos, Milton V.,   87
Anatolios, Khaled,   71, 74, 75, 76, 77, 78
Armstrong, Donald,   31
Ayres, Lewis,   61, 68, 71

Baillie, D.M.,   3, 39, 54
Bainton, Roland,   127
Baker, William H.,   164
Balla, Peter,   29
Bandstra, Andrew J.,   188
Barnard, L.W.,   69, 70
Barrett, C.K.,   187
Bartels, K.H.,   154
Barth, Karl,   184
Bauckham, Richard,   4, 52, 193
Bavinck, Herman,   11
Beare, F.W.,   182
Beasley-Murray, George R.,   174
Behr, John,   61
Benjamin, Walter,   4
Berkhof, Hendrikus,   24, 27
Berkhof, Louis,   58
Berkouwer, G.C.,   3, 21, 40, 54, 159, 166, 200
Berthold, George C.,   100
Bess, S. Herbert,   154
Bethune-Baker, James,   61, 85
Bird, Michael F.,   4, 19
Black, David A.,   30, 32, 147
Blaising, Craig A.,   75, 91
Blanchard, John,   22
Blaser, Klauspeter,   106
Blocher, Henri,   7, 54
Bloesch, Donald G.,   22, 26, 165, 169
Blount, Douglas K.,   136, 137, 138

Bock, Darrell L.,   4, 13, 30, 199
Boettner, Lorraine,   58
Bonner, Gerald,   81
Booij, Th.,   133
Borg, Marcus J.,   161
Bowman Jr., Robert M.,   6, 22, 160
Borg, Marcus, J.,   4, 28
Bowie, Walter R.,   6
Braaten, Carl E.,   85
Bratcher, Dennis,   194
Bray, Gerald,   6, 7, 8, 9, 12, 25, 33, 69, 114, 163, 164, 167
Bright, William,   92
Broad, C.D.,   24
Bromiley, Geoffrey W.,   106
Brown, Colin,   25, 185, 186, 197
Brown, Dan,   3
Brown, David,   37
Brown, Harold O.J.,   24, 92
Brown, Peter,   81
Bruce, A.B.,   36, 38, 106, 189
Bruce, F.F.,   146, 189
Brunner, Emil,   132
Boxall, Ian,   159
Boyd, Gregory A.,   4
Burridge, Richard,   5
Buswell, Oliver,   13, 58, 160
Byrne, James M.,   8, 24

Callender, Elizabeth J.,   136, 137
Cameron, Michael,   83
Cameron, Nigel M. de S.,   31
Carey, George,   34
Carnell, E.J.,   58
Carroll, Robert P.,   134
Carson, D.A.,   149, 150, 173, 174
Castelo, Daniel,   9
Cave, Sydney,   3
Chadwick, Henry,   81, 82, 83
Chafer, Lewis S.,   58

Chapman, John, 95
Charlesworth, James H., 4, 21
Charnock, Stephen, 135, 138
Charry, Ellen T., 75
Chatzipantelis, Georgios F.E., 166
Cherry, Millard R., 189
Chestnut, Glenn F., 61
Chia, Roland, 73
Chung, Sun Wook, 20
Clark, Gordon H., 6, 22
Clark, Mary T., 62, 81, 82
Clark, Stephen, 4
Clayton, Allen, L., 72, 77
Clayton, Paul B., 81
Coakley, Sarah, 92
Colish, Marcia L., 23
Comfort, Philip W., 173, 194
Copan, Paul, 28
Corcoran, Kevin J., 164
Cottret, Bernard, 112
Cragg, Gerald R., 25
Craig, William Lane, 4, 137
Cranfield, C.E.B., 32
Creed, John M., 19, 39
Creel, Richard E., 9
Crisp, Oliver, 13, 19, 20, 80, 200
Cross, Richard, 98, 101, 163
Crossan, John D., 4
Crouzel, Henri, 69, 70
Cullmann, Oscar, 52, 187, 188

Daley, Brian E., 96, 167, 168
Daley, Chauncery R., 76
Davies, Norman, 22, 23
Davis, Leo, D., 71, 92, 93, 94
Davis, Stephen T., 3, 20
David, Thomas J., 115
Dawe, Donald G., 37, 38, 203
Delitzsch, F., 134
Demacopoulos, George E., 81
Demarest, Bruce A., 45
DeVries, Dawn, 116, 129
Dods, Marcus, 157, 158

Dockery, David S., 30
Doriani, Daniel, 149, 199
Dorner, Issak A., 10, 36, 106
Dorner, J.A., 25, 26, 27
Dowey, Edward A., 128
Dragas, George, 75, 76, 104
Drickamer, J.M., 14
Drijvers, Hans J.W., 81
Dunn, James D.G., 32, 161, 187
Dünzl, Franz, 71
Dyck, Grace C., 132

Eadie, John, 189
Ebert IV, Daniel J., 156
Eckhardt, A. Roy, 5
Edmundson, Stephen B., 106, 112, 128
Ehrman, Bart D., 19
Ellingworth, Paul, 157
Ellis, Brannon, 114
Ellis, E. Earl, 30
Enns, Paul, 44, 160
Erickson, Millard J., 2, 6, 7, 9, 11, 15, 16, 22, 25, 33, 45-46, 47, 133, 169, 170, 195, 196, 197
Ernest, James D., 77
Evans, Craig A., 4, 19, 21
Evans, David B., 97
Evans, C. Stephen, 33, 37, 43-44, 203

Fabricatore, Daniel J., 182, 189
Fairburn, Donald, 71, 86
Fairweather, Eugene R., 6, 9, 182
Farmer, William R., 31, 32
Farnell, F. David, 30
Farrow, Douglas, 111
Fee, Gordon, D., 20, 182, 188, 192, 193
Feenstra, Ronald J., 40-43, 198
Ferrier, Francis, 164
Feinberg, John, S., 6, 8, 15, 138, 139, 154, 168, 171

Author Index

Fickett, Harold J., 68, 71
Fiddes, Paul S., 10
Fitzgerald, Allan D., 6, 81
Florovsky, Georges, 71, 80, 85, 86, 87, 88, 89, 92, 101, 102
Forrester, D.W., 38
Forsyth, P.T., 39
Foxgrover, David, 106
Fracea, Ilie, 96
Frame, John M., 8, 133, 138
France, R.T., 150
Frei, Hans W., 2
Fries, Paul, 50
Fuesrt, Adrian, 135
Fuller, George C., 159
Fuller, Reginald H., 29, 30, 172

Galot, Jean, 3, 13, 143
Garlow, James, L., 4
Gathercole, Simon J., 4, 19
Gawrish, Wilbert R., 108
Gay, Peter, 22
Geisler, Norman L., 9, 11
Gelpi, Donald, J., 51
George, Timothy, 113, 123
Gerrish, Brian A., 115
Gess, W.F., 38, 158
Gifford, E.H., 200
Giles, Kevin, 6, 7
Gottlieb, Anthony, 1
Grant, Patrick, 164
Gravrilyk, Paul, 9, 85
Green, Michael, 3
Gockel, Matthias, 96
Gould, Graham, 5
Goulder, Michael, 3
Grabowski, Stanislaus J., 84, 138
Grant, Herbert, 63, 64
Green, Michael, 34
Greene, Colin, J., 20
Greene, Oliver, J.D., 25
Greer, Rowan A., 81
Gregersen, Niels H., 164

Grenz, Stanley J., 23, 28, 29
Grillmeier, Aloys, 61, 66, 68, 69, 75, 80, 82, 85, 86, 87, 88, 89, 90, 91, 92, 93, 94, 95, 96, 99
Grudem, Wayne, 7, 9, 13, 140, 176
Gruenler, Royce G., 9
Gundry, Robert H., 199
Gunton, Colin E., 14, 15, 40
Guthrie, Donald, 53, 156

Hagner, Donald A., 150
Haire, J.L.M., 39, 95
Haldane, Robert, 152
Hall, Christopher A., 77, 80, 85, 87, 88, 92, 175
Hall, Francis J., 200
Hanegraaff, Hank, 4
Hanson, Anthony T., 165
Hanson, R.P.C., 71, 73, 74, 75, 76
Harder, Günther, 158
Hardy, Edward R., 88, 89, 96, 100
Harris, Murray J., 13, 61, 148, 155, 156, 157, 160, 161
Harrison, Carol, 81
Hart, David B., 9
Hart, Trevor, 116
Hartshorne, Charles, 9
Hasel, Gerhart, 29
Hawley, Wendell C., 173
Hawthorne, Gerald F., 5, 17, 44, 47-48, 169, 170, 188, 197, 198
Hay, Camillus, 81
Hayes, Michael A., 21
Hebblethwaite, Brian, 8, 34
Helland, Roger, 197
Helm, Paul, 11, 107, 136
Hendrickson, William, 147
Hengel, Martin, 184
Henry, Carl F.H., 2, 50
Herrick, Gregory J., 30
Heron, Alasdair, 16, 24

Hick, John, 3, 34, 35, 171
Highfield, Ron, 11
Hill, Jonathan, 15, 19
Hodge, Charles, 58
Hodgson, Peter C., 20, 29
Holdaway, David, 21
Holmes, Stephen R., 19, 117, 125
Hoogland, Marvin P., 36, 108
Hoover, Roy W., 192
Horton, Michael S., 22
House, Dennis K., 68
House, H. Wayne, 9, 11, 39, 44
House, Paul R., 135
Howard, George, 191
Hurtado, Larry W., 182

Inbody, Tyron L., 20

Jacobsen, Douglas, 22
Jahn, Curtis A., 31, 109, 127
James, William, 1
Janke, James R., 31, 127
Jansen, John F., 106
Jensen, David H., 20
Jeremias, Joachim, 188
Johnson, Dennis E., 10, 36, 177, 181, 192, 193
Johnson, Elizabeth A., 3
Johnson, Luke T., 4
Johnson, Paul, 23
Jones, Paul H., 115, 117
Jones, Peter, 4
Jowers, Dennis W., 7.

Kaiser, Christopher, B., 1
Kannengiesser, Charles, 74, 75, 76
Karakoli, Constantine, 71
Kärkkäinen, Matti, 20
Käsemann, Ernst, 187
Kay, James F., 29
Kaye, John, 74
Keating, Daniel A., 86

Keil, C.F., 134
Kelly, J.N.D., 65, 67, 68, 69, 75, 80, 89, 90, 91, 92
Kelly, Robert A., 108
Kelsey, Catherine L., 28
Kendall, Daniel, 3
Kennedy, Kevin D., 106
Kim, Seyoon, 4
King, Robert H., 29
Knapp, Daniel T., 189
Komoszewski, J. Ed., 4, 22, 160
Kratz, Wolfgang, 106

Ladd, George E., 159
LaDue, William J., 15
LaHaye, Tim, 19
Lancel, Serge, 6, 81
Lane, A.N.S., 35, 51-57, 60, 91, 112, 172, 173
Lang, U.M., 95-96, 99
Lawrence III, Melvin E., 81
Lawton, John Stewart, 3
Lee, Patrick, 12
Leftow, Brian, 136
Leigh, Ronald W., 35, 51, 57-60, 91, 172, 173, 174, 175
Levine, Baruch A., 135
Lewis, Gordon R., 45
L'Hullier, Peter, 92, 93
Liddon, Henry P., 31, 204
Lienhard, Joseph T., 72, 119
Lightfoot, J.B., 187, 188
Lightner, Robert P., 44
Lincoln, Andrew T., 153
Link, Christian, 1, 106
Linnemann, Eta, 30, 32
Lister, Rob, 9
Little, Paul, 58
Little, V.A. Spence, 64
Lobkowicz, Nikolaus, 26
Lohse, Eduard, 155, 174
Long, D. Stephen, 9
Longenecker, Richard N., 152
Loofs, Friedrich, 85, 86, 96, 98

Author Index

Loubinos, John L., 37
Louth, Andrew, 100
Lynch, John J., 97, 99

Machen, J. Gresham, 31, 153
Macintosh, H.R., 3, 25, 26, 27, 36, 39, 106
Mack, Burton L., 4
Macleod, Donald J., 13, 22, 44, 161, 172, 184
Macquarrie, John, 21, 26, 27, 33, 36, 38, 40, 91
Madden, Nicholas, 70
Maier, Paul L., 4
Malaty, Tadrosy, 50
Maloney, Raymond, 176
Mantzarides, George, 72
Margerie, Bertrand de, 15
Marmadoro, Anna, 15, 19
Marrou, Henri, 81
Marsh, Clive, 20
Marshall, I. Howard, 20, 25, 30, 54
Marshall, John S., 91
Martens, Elmer A., 141
Martensen, H.L., 54
Martin, Ralph P., 157, 182, 183, 187, 189
Maschke, Timothy, 51
Matera, Frank J., 20, 21
McCall, Thomas H., 7
McClymond, Michael J., 19
McCormack, Bruce L., 15, 111
McDonnel, K., 121
McDurmon, Joel, 19, 22
McEnhill, Peter, 39
McGinnis, Andrew, 109
McGrath, Alister E., 31
McGuikin, J.A., 85, 86
McIntyre, John, 3, 15, 40, 50, 91, 96
McKim, Donald K., 25, 109
McKinnion, Steven A., 86
McKnight, Scot, 21

McLelland, Joseph, 109, 119
Meagher, Robert, 6
Meijboom, Hajo U., 32
Metzger, Bruce M., 161
Meyerndorff, J., 101, 103
Miles, Todd L., 20
Mitchell, H.G., 134
Moberley, R.C., 54
Molnar, Paul, 7, 20
Moltmann, Jügen, 4, 8, 10
Moo, Douglas, 151
Moreland, J.P., 4, 164
Morey, Robert, 6
Morgan, Christopher W., 20, 178
Morgan, Robert, 30
Morris, Leon, 148, 156
Morris, Thomas V., 15, 35, 170, 171
Most, William G., 29, 176
Moule, C.F.D., 183, 189, 194, 199
Moutafakis, Nicholas J., 98
Muller, Herbert J., 23
Muller, Richard A., 12, 106, 110, 111, 166
Murphy-O'Connor, Jerome, 188
Murray, John, 151

Nagel, Norman E., 109
Nash, Ronald, H., 9
Need, Stephen, W., 61, 71, 91
Neill, Stephen, 29
Nersoyan, Tiran, 50
Niebuhr, Reinhold, 164
Niesel, Wilhelm, 108, 113, 116
Norris Jr., Richard A., 65, 74, 77, 78, 80, 81, 86, 87, 92, 94

Oakes, Edward T., 19, 20, 24
Oakes, Robert, 138
Oberman, Heiko A., 107, 123, 124

O'Brien, Peter T., 156, 174, 184, 187
O'Collins, Gerald, 3, 8, 13, 14, 19, 40, 168, 169, 171, 176
O'Connor, John B., 101
Oden, Thomas C., 30, 33
O'Grady, John F., 15
Oliphant, K. Scott, 8
Olson, Roger E., 28
Olyott, Stuart, 19
O'Neill, J.C., 30
Orchard, John B., 32
Orr, Peter, 151
Osborne, Catherine, 73
Osborne, Eric, 66
Osborne, Grant, 32
Ottley, Robert, 3
Overstreet, Larry, 178

Packer, J.I., 58
Pannenberg, Wolfhart, 3
Papanikolaou, Aristotle, 81
Parker, David, 197
Parker, T.H.L., 128
Patitsas, Chrestos, 190
Patterson, L., 81
Payne, Philip B., 199
Pelikan, Jaroslav, 101, 106
Peterson, Alvyn, 72, 73, 76, 77, 78
Peterson, David, 20
Peterson, Robert A., 20, 108, 128, 178
Picirilli, Robert E., 44
Pinnock, Clark, 8, 33
Piper, John, 7
Placher, William C., 23
Pokorny, Petr, 21
Porter, Stanley, E., 21
Prest, Loring A., 46-47, 132
Prestige, G.L., 80, 85
Privette, Jeffrey S., 33
Purdy, Vernon, 21

Quasten, Johannes, 61, 63, 65, 68, 73, 76, 78, 80, 85, 88

Rae, Murray A., 19
Raitt, Jill, 16, 48, 111
Ramelli, Ilaria L.E., 68
Ramm, Bernard, L., 3, 22, 37
Reid, Michael, 31
Reist, Irwin, W., 64
Relton, Herbert M., 96
Reymond, Robert L., 5, 13, 22, 30, 159, 160, 161, 191, 205
Richard, Lucien, 37
Richardson, Cyril C., 62
Richardson, Kurt A., 113, 114
Riches, John K., 29
Rieger, Jeorg, 19
Robertson, Archibald T., 74, 189, 190
Robertson, Edwin H., 109
Robertson, Jon M., 75
Robinson, John A.T., 32
Rogers, Jack, 112
Rohls, Jan, 110
Romanides, John S., 81
Rosemond, K., 101
Ross, Hugh, 137
Rowe, Arthur, 19
Rowe, J. Nigel, 68, 69
Runia, Klaas, 34
Rusch, William G., 80
Russell, Norman, 87
Ryrie, Charles C., 132, 160, 201

Sampson, Philip, 22
Samuel, Vinay, 22
Sanders, Fred, 19
Sanders, John, 8
Sarot, Marcel, 10
Saucy, Mark, 156
Sawyer, M. James, 4
Scipioni, L.I., 87
Schaff, Philip, 92, 93, 94, 110
Schlink, Edmund, 51

Author Index

Schmidt, Frederick, 22
Schrag, Calvin O., 22
Schreiner, Susan E., 128
Schreiner, Thomas R., 152
Schuele, Andreas, 19
Schultz, F. LeRon, 20, 96
Schwarz, Hans, 19
Schwöbel, Christoph, 114, 127
Sell, Alan P.F., 27
Sellers, R.V., 68, 80
Shelley, Bruce L., 23
Sheppard, G.T., 25
Siefert Josef, 200
Siggins, Ian D.K., 109
Silva, Moisés, 183, 184, 189, 190, 192
Skarsaune, Oscar, 50
Skevington Wood, A., 154
Spence, Alan, 20, 22
Spitz, Lewis W., 23
Stalker, James, 20
Stead, Christopher, 76
Stein, Robert H., 31
Steinmetz, David C., 205
Stephenson, J., 1
Stoeckhardt, George, 154
Stogianou, Vasilliou P., 62
Stonebraker, Eleanor, 110, 126, 127
Stott, John, 13, 19
Strimple, Robert, 188, 193
Strobel, Lee, 19
Strong, Augustus H., 44
Studer, Basil, 71, 82, 91, 94, 103, 104
Stump, Eleanor, 163
Stylianopoulos, Theodore, 159
Sugden, Chris, 22
Swinburne, Richard, 20

Talbert, Charles H., 187
Taylor, Vincent, 36, 39
Temple, William, 39
Tenney, Merrill C., 146

TeSelle, Eugene, 81, 82, 84
Thiessen, Henry C., 32
Thomas, Günther, 19
Thomas, Moly, 37
Thomas, Robert L., 30, 32, 159
Thomasius, Gottfried, 17, 38
Thompson, J.A., 134
Thompson, Marianne M., 199, 207
Thornhill, John, 23
Thornton, Lionel Spencer, 3
Tombs, David, 21
Toon, Peter, 31
Torchia, Joseph, 164
Torrance, Alan J., 6, 10
Torrance, Thomas F., 7, 13, 32, 62, 73, 74, 75, 79, 80, 112, 113
Tozer, A.W., 135
Tsoukalas, Steven, 157, 158, 190, 193
Turner, H.E.W., 199
Twombly, Charles, 75, 100, 101, 103
Tylenda, Joseph N., 112, 119, 120, 121, 122

van Bruggen, Jakob, 13
van Buren, Paul, 106
van Den Brom, Luco J., 136
van Driel, Edwin C., 20
VanGemeren, Willem A., 133
van Inwagen, Peter, 1
van Loon, Hans, 87
Vincent, Marvin R., 189, 190, 191
von Rad, Gerhard, 141
Vos, Geerhardus, 29, 199
Voyles, Richard J., 74, 75

Wagner, Walter H., 62
Wallace, Daniel B., 4
Wallace, Ronald S., 116, 128
Wallhout, Edwin, 175
Walters, Brent, 20

Walvoord, John F., 17, 44, 144, 146, 160, 161, 162, 170
Ware, Bruce A., 7, 8, 11
Warfield, Benjamin B., 2, 31, 114, 115, 159, 162, 168
Webster, Douglas D., 3
Weinandy, Thomas G., 9, 10, 14, 26, 62, 75, 86, 167
Wellum, Stephen J., 181
Wells, David, 6, 13, 21, 22, 34, 36, 40, 178, 191
Wendel, François, 114, 119, 124, 125
Wendland, Paul O., 31, 127
Wenham, John, 32
Wessell, Susan, 87
West, Rebecca, 6
Wheeler Robinson, H., 192
White, James R., 145
Whitehead, Alfred North, 3
Wickham, Lionel R., 104, 176
Widdicombe, Peter, 73, 75
Wilken, Robert, 73, 85, 86
Wilkins, Michael J., 4
Williams, Rowan, 51, 72, 165, 166, 171

Willis, E. David, 107, 111, 123, 125, 127, 128
Wills, Gary, 6
Willis-Watkins, David, 109
Wilson, Robert E., 190
Wingren, Gustaf, 62, 63, 64
Witherington III, Ben, 4, 5, 20, 152, 185
Wolfe, David A., 138
Wright, Christopher, 20
Wright, N.T., 4, 28, 29, 31, 162, 189, 192
Wyatt, Peter, 116, 117, 124, 126

Yarnold, Edward J., 65, 66
Yerkes, James, 26
Young, Frances M., 76

Zachariades, Theodore, 11, 192
Zacharias, Ravi, 146
Zachman, Randall C., 129
Zathureczky, Kornel, 4
Zigmund, Helen A., 116

Scripture Index

Genesis
1:3   162
19:24   6, 127n.81

Exodus
15:11-13   161
25-27   141
33:14   141

Deuteronomy
6:4   6
26:15   142
32:39   6

1 Samuel
4   141

2 Samuel
7:13   141

1 Kings
5-6   141
8:12   141
8:27   135n.19

2 Chronicles
3-7   141

Psalms
11:4   143
14:2   143
33:6   162
44:3   64
44:6-7   157
44:8   157
44:9   157
45:6-7   6
46:1   140
73:25   143
90   161
99   161
102:12-28   161

115   142
115:3   143
115:15   143
139   131-133
139:1-6   132
139:7   131-132
139:7-12   132, 133
140:13   140

Job
11:7-9   135n.19
38-41   195n.64

Proverbs
8   72, 72n.62, 72n.64
30:4   162

Ecclesiastes
12:12   21

Isaiah
6:5   162
9:6   64
9:6-7   162
40:3   162
40:18-30   195n.64
44:6   6
44:8   6
45:1-7   142
45:5-6   6
45:23   193
48:12-16   6
52:13   193
53   193n.55
53:2-3   64
53:12   193
61:1   6
63:8-10   6
66:1   135n.19

Jeremiah
23   133-135

23:5-6   134, 162
23:16   134
23:23-24   133
23:24   134
23:39   134
25:1-14   141

Ezekiel
10   141

Daniel
4:28-35   142
5:1-31   142
7:13   162, 172n.144

Micah
5:2   172n.144

Zechariah
12:10   162

Malachi
3:6   161

Matthew
3:13-17   6
3:17   143
6:9   143
8:23-34   206
9:6   161n.118
12:6   143n.50
12:28   16n.44
14:13-21   206
14:22-33   206
15:29-31   206
16:13   3-4
16:15   3
16:18   150n.68
17:1-9   200
17:5   143, 144
18:20   150, 150n.68, 160, 207
24:36   59
26:11   117
26:24   144n.52

26:42   168
28:18   161n.118
28:18-20   135n.19
28:19   6
28:20   117, 150, 150n.68, 207

Mark
1:29-34   161n.118, 206
6:30-44   206
2:8   59, 161n.118
4:35-41   206
8:31   147n.58
9:14-27   206
13:32   53, 59, 173, 175, 175n.188, 176, 176n.190
14:36   169n.159
16:16   150

Luke
1:35   6, 161
2:40   119
2:52   53, 120, 172, 173, 176n.190
3:4   162
4:3   194
4:34   161
5:1-11   206
8:25   161n.118
9:10-17   206
11:13   143
22:43   168
24:7   147n.58
24:28   175n.188

John
1:1   148n.62, 203
1:1-2   161
1:1-3   155, 162
1:1-18   6, 14n.39
1:3   70
1:4   160
1:14   13, 70, 103n.194, 120, 148, 162, 163, 200

Scripture Index

1:18   55n.32, 59, 147, 148, 148n.62, 207
1:26   71
1:27   14n.39, 71
1:29   120-121
1:30   14n.39
1:48-49   145
1:51   143n.50
2:1-11   206
2:11   200
2:19-20   146
2:19-21   146
2:22   146
2:24-25   59
2:25   161n.118, 173n.180, 176n.190
3:13   14n.39, 90, 121, 147, 178, 207
3:16   1n.2
3:16-17   14n.39
3:31   14n.39
3:34   14n.39
4:24   138
4:34   14n.39
4:46   148
4:54   148
5:1-15   206
5:19   149
5:19-20   149, 207
5:19-23   206
5:20   149
5:23   144
5:30   169n.119
5:37   14n.39
6:1-15   206
6:16-21   206
6:32   143
6:33   14n.39
6:38   14n.39, 169
6:41-42   14n.39
6:51   14n.39
6:64   161n.118
7:28-29   14n.39
7:39   6

8:23   14n.39
8:26   14n.39
8:42   14n.39
8:58   14n.39, 103n.194, 120
9:1-41   206
9:39   14n.39
10:17-18   146, 147n.58
10:18   161n.118
10:30   160
10:36   14n.39
10:38   149
11:1-44   206
12:41   162
12:44-50   14n.39
13   194
13-17   194n.58
13:1   161n.118
13:1-16   194n.58
13:11   161n.118
14:7-9   59
14:20   149
14:23   144, 149, 207
16:17   173
16:19   173n.180
16:28   14n.39, 115n.34
16:29   172
16:30   173, 176n.190
17:2   161n.118
17:3   144
17:5   14n.39, 166
17:8   14n.39
17:24   14n.39
18:4   161n.118
19:28   161n.118
20:19-33   6
20:28   148n.62
20:31   148n.62
21:17   59, 160, 172, 173, 176n.190

Acts
1:24   161n.118
2:27   161
2:32   147n.57

2:33   6
3:14   161
7:44-50   135n.19
10:41   147n.58
12:22-31   135n.19
17:28   84, 139
17:31   147n.58
20:28   121, 122, 122n.65

Romans
6:1-11   152
6:4   147n.57
6:9   152
6:10   152
6:10-11   152
8:3   172n.144, 191
8:9   151
8:9-10   152
8:9-11   151n.72
8:10   151, 152, 154n.80
8:15-17   6
9:5   161, 169n.159
13:13-14   82n.107

1 Corinthians
1:30   161n.118, 162
2:8   90, 121, 122
5:4   150n.68
8:6   6
15   187
15:1-3   175n.187
15:6   162
15:47   172n.144

2 Corinthians
8:9   191
8:15-17   6

Galatians
2:20   152
4:4   1n.2, 143, 172n.144, 191

Ephesians
1:3   162

3:14   153
3:14-20   153
3:16   153
3:17   150n.67, 153
3:19   154
4:6   6
4:10   160
5:2   162
5:5   162

Philippians
1:7   194n.60
2   48, 172
2:2   194, 194n.60
2:3-4   184
2:5   183n.7, 184, 184n.11, 187, 194n.60
2:5-7   190n.40
2:5-8   43n.26, 145, 179, 181-201, 187n.25
2:5-11   37n.6, 39, 182, 191, 200
2:6   1n.2, 160, 186, 187, 188
2:6-8   182n.2, 193n.53
2:6-9   48
2:6-11   182
2:7   39, 48, 186, 189, 189n.39, 190, 192, 195
2:8   190, 192
2:9   186
2:9-11   182n.2, 193n.53
2:10   186
2:10-11   193
2:11   186, 187
3:15   195n.60
3:19   195n.60
3:21   161n.118
4:10   195n.60

Colossians
1   154n.83
1:15   154, 154n.83, 203
1:15-18   172n.144
1:15-21   154, 191
1:16   154n.83, 155, 155n.84

Scripture Index

1:17   154n.83, 155, 207
1:19   160
1:24-29   155
1:26   155
1:27   155
2   174
2:3   59, 172, 173, 174
2:9   1n.2, 160, 162, 203

1 Thessalonians
4:14   147n.58

1 Timothy
1:15   191
2:5   6
3:16   1n.2, 191, 205n.6
6:16   147, 175n.187

Titus
2:13   161, 161n.119

Hebrews
1   156, 158
1:1-2   156
1:1-4   143
1:2   1n.2, 156n.87
1:3   117, 156, 156n.87, 203
1:5-14   172n.144
1:6   156n.87
1:8   6
1:8-9   156
1:10   156n.87
2:5   156n.87
2:9   172n.144
2:14-17   178
2:17   203
4:14-15   178

5:7-8   178
7:3   156n.87, 172n.144
7:16   156n.87
9:14   156n.87
10:5   156n.87
10:5-7   172n.144
12:2   156n.87
13:8   156n.87, 161
13:20   147n.57

1 Peter
1:2   6
1:21   147n.57

2 Peter
1:1   161, 162

1 John
1:1   121, 122
3:16   121
5:12   144

Revelation
1:4-5   6
1:5-2:1   141
1:7   162
1:8   161
1:12   159
1:13   159
1:16   159
1:17   161
1:19-20   159
2:1   159, 207
4-5   162
4:5   159
15:4   161
20:11-14   140

Subject Index

Adam, 187-188
adoption(ism), 7, 7n.14, 8, 124
Alexandrian Christology, 76
allegory, 62, 62n.6
Ambrose, 82
Andreae, Jacob, 16n.45, 48n.60
angels, 67, 143, 146, 157, 168
Anselm, 2n.4, 6
antinomy, 58-59
Antiochene Christology, 76
Apollinarianism, 51, 80n.101
Aquinas, Thomas, 109n.11, 123n.67, 138, 139, 165
Arian crisis, 72-80, 85-86
Arianism, 72n.61, 112n.23, 112
Aristotelian metaphysics, 98
Athanasian Creed, the, 7
Athanasius, 71, 71-80, 86n.135, 104, 129, 203, 204
Augustine, 2n.4, 6, 9, 81-85, 82n.107, 104, 107n.3, 115n.34, 116, 117, 139, 150n.67, 175n.188

baptism, 150
Barth, Karl, 136, 137
Berkeley, George, 23
Beza, Theodore, 16n.45, 48n.60
Biel, Gabriel, 129
Bultmann, Rudolph, 25n.25, 29

Calvin, John, 16, 17, 22, 109-130, 177, 202, 204, 205
Cappadocians, the, 104n.196, 167n.155
Chalcedon, 17, 30, 35, 40-41, 50-58, 52n.9, 65, 80, 81, 91-95, 91n.150, 91n.152, 99, 103, 104, 131, 163, 164, 165, 167-168, 171, 175n.188, 204
Chalcedonian Fathers, 204

Christ, 63, 137; *ascension of,* 70, 110, 110n.15, 15, 183, 191, 198; *baptism of,* 194n.59; *centrality of,* 126; *Creator,* 155, 158, 178, 194, 203; *death of,* 2, 70n.55, 90, 147, 152, 153, 193n.55, 195, 200, 207; *deity (divine) of,* 5, 15n.44, 16, 17, 33, 39n.14, 41n.42, 46, 47, 57, 60, 66, 70, 76, 78, 99, 104, 111, 113, 115, 118, 120, 152, 154, 155, 157, 159-179, 173, 176, 177-179, 188, 189, 197, 198, 201, 202, 203, 205n.6; *descent of,* 14n.39, 26, 38, 90, 108, 109, 129, 183n.8, 191; *Emmanuel,* 178; *eternal generation of,* 72, 72n.64, 114; eternality of, 72, 83, 114n.34, 125, 161; *exaltation of,* 183, 194n.60; *finality of,* 171; *glory of,* 69, 78, 104, 184, 200, 201; *grace of,* 117, 155; *holy,* 161; *humanity of,* 52-53, 85-88, 90, 99, 101-103, 104; *humiliation of,* 36, 38n.9, 46, 183n.8, 190n.40, 191, 193-194, 193n.55, 194n.60, 200; *hypostatic union,* 2, 2n.5, 93, 93n.160, 95, 164, 179; *identity of,* 50, 154, 205; *immanence of,* 88, 111; *impassible,* 103n..196; *immutable,* 117, 119, 129, 161; *knowledge,* 15n.44, 16n.46, 59, 202; *life,* 2; *Logos,* 56, 63, 69-70, 72n.64, 76-77, 79, 80, 80n.100, 86, 101, 110n.15, 155, 162; *Lord,* 183, 186, 187, 205; *Mediator,* 79, 83, 110, 121, 121n.64; *Messiah,* 155, 161; *miracles of,* 15n.44, 56, 65, 130n.91, 146, 177, 200, 203,

Subject Index

206, 207; *mystery of*, 14, 175; *nature of*, 78; *obedience of*, 188, 194n.59; *omnipotence*, 15n.44, 42, 46, 48, 53, 56, 60, 148, 158, 196, 202, 204, 206; *omnipresence*, 2, 15, 16, 28, 41, 45, 46, 48, 58, 60, 64, 67n.34, 70, 79-80, 83, 84, 88, 90, 94, 104, 106, 107, 115, 129, 131, 144, 145-179, 195, 196, 197-198, 199, 202, 204, 205, 206; *omniscience*, 15n.44, 41, 43, 46, 48, 53-54, 56, 58, 59, 60, 161n.118, 173, 197-198, 202, 204, 206; *one nature*, 59; *person of*, 2, 7, 13n.39, 16, 26n.26, 46, 49n.60, 57-58, 78, 93n.160, 99, 101, 104, 108, 110n.15, 129, 131, 151, 163, 166, 167, 171, 179, 203; *power of*, 184; *pre-existence of*, 172n.174, 183, 184, 186, 187n.25, 191; *presence of*, 177-179, 203; *properties (attributes) of*, 14n.41, 16, 35, 38, 39n.14, 41, 41n.23, 44, 46, 47, 48n.59, 57-58, 93, 94, 98n.176, 118, 120-121, 157n.94, 160, 171, 206; *providence of*, 116; *resurrection of*, 146, 149, 153, 207; *Savior*, 76, 161, 203; *self-consciousness*, 170; *soul of*, 76, 151; *suffering of*, 86, 90; *transcendence*, 79, 80, 88, 111, 126, 149, 155; *two minds*, 170-177; *two natures*, 16, 28, 34-35, 40, 41, 57, 65, 68, 69, 88n.137, 94n.164, 96n.168, 103n.194, 107, 110, 111, 117, 122n.65, 125, 125n.76, 154, 156, 162, 163, 166, 168, 171, 176, 179, 204; *two wills*, 168-170; *ubiquity of*, 109, 122; *unique*, 171; *unity of*, 87, 94, 99, 102, 119, 120, 129, 166; *wisdom of*, 173-174; *Word*, 63, 64, 66, 66n.31, 70-71, 72n.84, 77-80, 78, 79, 83, 84, 86, 89, 90, 93-95, 97n.173, 99-100, 102, 103, 110n.188, 103n.196, 109, 114n.30, 120, 122, 129n.88, 148, 167, 203, 204, 207; work, 2, 13n.39

Christology, 1, 2, 5, 6, 13, 19, 26-27, 28, 30, 50, 52n.9, 62, 68, 104, 156, 159, 163, 166, 172, 177, 202, 203
Christos Pantocrator, 159
communicatio idiomatum, 14, 16, 16n.45, 48n.60, 70n.55, 79, 90, 109, 118-123, 179, 205
conversion, 154
covenant, 141-142, 154
created order, 9, 11
creeds, 13n.38, 162n.122, 165
Cyril of Alexandra, 109n.11, 124

deity, 145
Descartes, René, 23
Diessmann, Adolf, 183n.7
docetism, 52, 53, 54, 89n.142, 124

enhypostatic Christology, 2n.5, 14, 54, 54n.27, 96n.168, 98-99, 100n.184, 165
Enlightenment, the, 22, 22n.11, 23, 24, 33, 35
eternal life, 73, 144, 150
Evagrius Ponticus, 97
Eutyches, 88-91, 124
Eutychianism, 51, 131
extra Calvinisticum, 60, 107-112, 107n.3, 109n.11, 110n.15, 111n.18, 129n.88, 147

faith, 5, 14n.40, 33, 69, 91n.150, 126, 152, 153, 154, 161, 200, 203
fall, the, 63

Gnostics, 62, 163n.130
God, *constancy*, 12; *Creator*, 10, 12, 62, 108, 116, 135n.18; *eternal*, 161; *faithful*, 11; *freedom*, 45; *fullness of*, 154; *glory of*, 157-158, 182n.3; *gracious*, 9, 185; *heavenly Father*, 143; *hiddenness of*, 134n.15; *holy*, 10, 143, 161; *immanence*, 55n.32; *immutable*, 9, 10, 11n.30, 12, 52, 55, 66n.31, 67, 161; *impassible*, 9n.23, 11, 12, 52, 55; *incorporeality of*, 132n.5; *involvement of*, 10, 11; *knowledge*, 133-135; *knowledge of*, 126-129; *Lord*, 133, 135; *majesty*, 108, 116-118, 142; *monarchia*, 67-68, 67n.35; *mutable*, 9; *omnipresence*, 131-133, 132n.5, 132n.6, 135-145, 138n.29, 196n.69; *omniscience*, 132; *otherness of*, 10; *presence* (essential, 138-140; moral, 140-142, 154; heavenly, 142-143; Christological, 143-145); *relationality*, 9; *Savior*, 10; *simplicity*, 10; *spatiality*, 136-137; *Spirit*, 11, 138; *subordinationism*, 115; *timeless*, 136; *transcendent*, 11, 12, 55n.32, 64, 66-67, 66n.31, 74, 108, 110, 132, 134, 134n.15, 140; *ubiquity*, 135; *unity*, 74; *wrath*, 168, 169; *cosmos, and the*, 155
Great Commission, the, 150
Gregory of Nazianzus, 168n.155

Gregory of Nyssa, 104n.200, 168n.155

Hegel, Georg W.F., 26
hellenization, 51-52, 187
Hilary of Poitiers, 113
Holy Spirit, 16n.44, 47, 63, 65, 116, 124, 127, 132n.5, 137, 141, 143, 144, 149n.67, 150, 151, 151n.72, 151n.73, 152, 153, 153n.80, 160, 185
Hume, David, 23

imago Dei, 59, 154
Incarnation, the, 1, 1n.2, 2, 3, 7, 8, 15, 17, 26, 41, 42-43, 38, 38n.9, 45, 51, 56, 59, 62, 63, 70, 72n.64, 73, 76, 80, 83-101, 93n.159, 96n.169, 101n.188, 107, 110n.15, 117, 118, 125, 126, 137, 143, 144, 144n.51, 145, 158, 163, 167, 171, 177, 179, 181n.1, 182n.3, 183, 187n.25, 189, 191, 195, 197, 202, 203
Irenaeus, 62-64

John of Damascus, 16, 18, 22, 96, 100-104, 131, 165, 204

Kahler, Martin, 25n.25
Kant, Immanuel, 22, 23, 24, 26-27
kenosis, 10, 16, 36-49, 56, 70, 110n.15, 118, 145, 160, 170, 171, 172, 179, 185, 189, 190n.40, 191, 196-197, 198-199, 200, 201, 202
kingdom, the, 157, 162
krypsis, 200, 204

Leontius of Byzantium, 16, 61, 95-100, 95n.168, 101, 103, 131, 167

Subject Index

Locke, John, 23
Lombard, Peter, 123n.67
Lord's Supper (Eucharist), 16, 104, 110, 110n.15, 111n.18, 112, 115, 119, 123
Luther, Martin, 117, 118, 119, 122, 126, 126n.76, 127, 127n.81

Marcellus of Ancyra, 72n.64
Mariology, 85
Melanchthon, Philip, 126
Mentzer, Balthazar, 107
metaphor, 34
modernity, 23
Monergism, 95
Monophysitism, 59n.52, 89, 89n.141, 95n.167, 98, 196
Monothelitism, 95
'myth', 33-34

Nestorianism, 51, 102, 123-126, 131
Nestorius of Constantinople, 85-86, 126n.77
Nicene Creed, the, 74, 165
Nicene theology, 71-80

Origen, 68-71, 72, 79
orthodoxy, 91-92, 105, 163, 165
Owen, John, 126n.76

pantheism, 10
paradox, 53, 167
Pentecost, 150
perichoresis, 80n.98, 145, 204n.4
Pope, Alexander, 23

prayer(s), 153-154
preaching (teaching), 129, 150

recapitulation, 62-63, 63n.7
regula fidei, 68, 69
Renaissance, the, 23
revelation, 12, 24, 26, 31n.55, 47, 116, 127, 143-144, 145, 156, 157, 158

salvation, 63, 63n.7, 73, 105, 113, 128-129
Schleiermacher, Frederich D.E., 26, 27-28
scopos of Scripture, 78
soul(s), 69-70, 97n.173
subordination(ism), 7, 7n.13
suffering, 11, 52, 63

theism, 10
theology, 1n.2, 3, 8-13
theophany, 141
theotokos, 85-86
Tertullian, 64-71, 104
Thumm, Theodore, 107
Trinity, the, 1n.2, 6-8, 55, 55n.32, 56, 68, 112-116, 113n.29, 137, 152, 163, 165, 166, 178
typology, 62n.6

Ursinus, Zacharias, 109n.11

Word, the, 6
worship, 11-12, 140-141, 162
Wrede, William, 29

www.ingramcontent.com/pod-product-compliance
Lightning Source LLC
Chambersburg PA
CBHW050435240426

43661CB00055B/2395